SMASHING HITLER'S GUNS

OSPREY
PUBLISHING

SMASHING HITLER'S GUNS

THE RANGERS AT POINTE-DU-HOC
D-DAY, 1944

STEVEN J. ZALOGA

OSPREY PUBLISHING
Bloomsbury Publishing Plc
Kemp House, Chawley Park, Cumnor Hill, Oxford OX2 9PH, UK
29 Earlsfort Terrace, Dublin 2, Ireland
1385 Broadway, 5th Floor, New York, NY 10018, USA
E-mail: info@ospreypublishing.com
www.ospreypublishing.com

OSPREY is a trademark of Osprey Publishing Ltd

First published in Great Britain in 2022

22 23 24 25 26   10 9 8 7 6 5 4 3 2 1

Uncredited photos are from official US government sources including the National Archives and Records Administration, Library of Congress, The Ordnance Museum at Aberdeen Proving Ground and the US Army Heritage and Education Center.

Maps by www.bounford.com
Index by Zoe Ross

Typeset by Deanta Global Publishing Services, Chennai, India
Printed and bound in Great Britain by CPI (Group) UK Ltd, Croydon CR0 4YY

Osprey Publishing supports the Woodland Trust, the UK's leading woodland conservation charity.

To find out more about our authors and books visit www.ospreypublishing.com. Here you will find extracts, author interviews, details of forthcoming events and the option to sign up for our newsletter.

Contents

List of Illustrations

8 One of the 155mm GPF guns in its kettle gun pit on Pointe-du-Hoc in August 1943. The gun is mounted on a standard Rheinmetall-Borsig Drehsockel mount to facilitate traverse of the gun. The guns were subsequently fitted with a camouflage umbrella overhead.

9 The 155mm GPF guns used a Drehsockel (swivel socket) mounting in the kettle gun pits as seen on the right. To conserve space in the enclosed casemates, the guns were supposed to be re-mounted on the more compact schwere Drehbettung 32. To. These were in short supply and never reached Pointe-du-Hoc before D-Day. As a result, none of the 155mm guns was deployed in the completed casemates. (Author)

10 The US Army was very familiar with the 155mm GPF gun deployed at Pointe-du-Hoc, since the American Expeditionary Force had been equipped with the same weapon in 1917–1918. It continued to serve in the US Army for coastal defense in World War II. This example was preserved for many years at the Ordnance Museum at Aberdeen Proving Ground, Maryland. It was displayed in transport mode as seen here. (Author)

11 The Regelbau H636a command post bunker on Pointe-du-Hoc in August 1943 as construction was nearing completion. The shed in front of it housed the battery's optical rangefinder until the new bunker was completed.

12 The Regelbau H636a command post bunker at Pointe-du-Hoc after its capture by the Rangers. The forward observation cupola had an applique of rough concrete and stone added over the basic concrete shell for camouflage.

13 Kettle gun pit No. 6 is the least damaged example at Pointe-du-Hoc. The area around the gun pedestal had been filled with earth over the years. (Author)

14 Bauwerk 468 is one of two surviving Regelbau 694 gun casemates at Pointe-du-Hoc. It was heavily damaged by bombing and naval gun fire. The small concrete structure to the right is the remains of the personnel shelter of kettle gun pit No. 5 that had been located immediately in front of it. (Author)

15 The western Regelbau H502 Doppelgruppenstand personnel bunker, located between gun pits No. 4 and No. 5. This bunker had accommodations for twenty troops in two rooms. It has a defensive Tobruk machine gun pit on the roof to the left. The Ranger memorial can be seen off in the distance in the upper right. (Author)

16 Life in an Atlantic Wall strongpoint was cramped, damp, and dank. This is the interior of a restored Regelbau 502 Gruppenstand bunker at Stützpunkt Lohengrin near Vlissingen. This small room would have accommodated ten soldiers and their equipment. (Author)

17 The only element of the Pointe-du-Hoc strongpoint to remain in German hands through June 8 was the western Regelbau L409A Flak bunker. The two surviving Regelbau 694 gun casemates can be seen near the skyline toward the right. (Author)

18 A view of the back side of the Regelbau H636 command post bunker with the Ranger memorial on top. This structure has been significantly rebuilt over the years for safety reasons. For example, the observation post on the top of the bunker has been plated over. (Author)

19 The Rangers undertook extensive cliff-scaling exercises along the English coast using a variety of toggle ropes and lightweight ladders. This is an exercise at Hive Beach, Burton Bradstock, Dorset in the spring of 1944.

33 The destroyer USS *Thompson* seen off the coast of Normandy on D-Day while being refueled by the battleship USS *Arkansas*. *Thompson* began its D-Day actions shelling German strongpoints on Pointe-et-Raz-de-la-Percée. It was involved later in the morning against targets in the Vierville draw, and relieved the USS *Satterlee* off Pointe-du-Hoc in the early evening.

34 The 1st Platoon of Charlie Company, 2nd Rangers in LCA-418 in Weymouth harbor on June 1, 1944 prior to their boarding the HMS *Prince Charles*. The Ranger Force B commander, Capt Ralph Goranson, can be seen in the far lower left smiling at the cameraman. In the back row, left to right, are T5 Paul B. Byzon (WIA), Sgt Walter Geldon (KIA), S/Sgt Harry Wilder (WIA), Sgt Julius Belcher and S/Sgt Oliver E. Reed (WIA). In the near row, the soldier next to Goranson with his head turned is his radioman, Sgt Donald Scribner, to his left (face obscured) 1 Sgt Henry S. Golas (KIA), followed by Sgt Joseph Angyal.

35 Much of the fighting by Goranson's Ranger Force C took place around the "Folie Gambier," nestled in the cliff face to the west of the Vierville draw. This image was taken before the war, and the stone house was heavily damaged by naval gunfire on D-Day. The ruins were torn down in the 1990s and few traces remain.

36 This overhead view of the Vierville draw area was taken in 1947.

37 Goranson's Force B was assigned to eliminate the German strongpoint at Pointe-et-Raz-de-la-Percée. The WN 74 strongpoint included two 76.5mm FK17(t) along the edge of the cliff in timber revetments. This one survived the repeated naval shelling on D-Day.

38 Goranson's Force B spent much of D-Day trying to overcome the numerous trench defenses and bunkers of the WN 73 defense nest. On top of the hill are the remnants of the Gambier stone barn used as a barracks by the 11./GR.726. Below it is a section of the trench system including two concrete shelters. The trench section in the foreground was filled in by American engineer troops in mid-June to make it easier to walk up the hill.

39 The D-Day bombardment of Pointe-du-Hoc dislodged a large chunk of the cliff, creating a heap of rocky soil beneath. This facilitated the Ranger scaling effort in this sector. Rudder set up his command post immediately above this location.

40 During the 75th anniversary of D-Day, troops of the 75th Ranger Regiment scaled the cliffs of Pointe-du-Hoc as part of the commemoration ceremonies. The climb took place in the same part of the cliff used by the Rangers on D-Day. This provides a very clear example of the height of the cliffs as well as their topography. Rope nets were used for safety reasons rather than toggle ropes as used on D-Day. The Ranger memorial on top of the command post bunker can be seen in the upper right. (US Air Force photo by Master Sgt. Andy M. Kin, Regional Media Center AFN Europe. DoD)

41 A good impression of the height of the Pointe-du-Hoc cliffs can be seen in this photo during the 2019 75th anniversary commemoration by the 75th Ranger Regiment. This provides some idea of the German soldier's perspective on D-Day. (US Army photo by Photo by Sgt. Henry Villarama, US Army Europe. DoD)

42 Col. J. Earl Rudder at the Ranger Force A command post on Pointe-du-Hoc. He is still wearing the standard gear for assault infantry on D-Day including the assault vest and the waterproof gas mask bag on his chest. Behind him is Eikner's EE-84 signal lamp, the essential tool for contacting the Navy warships off shore on D-Day.

43 On D-Day, the critical link between Army units and Navy warships was the Shore Fire Control Party like this one near Les Dunes de Varreville on June 10,

of Fox Company. A medic from the 116th Infantry, 29th Division can be seen to the right with the divisional insignia on his shoulder above the medic's brassard.

54 Rudder's command post on Pointe-du-Hoc was established in a crater on the edge of the cliff near the eastern Flak bunker. The walls of the bunker are visible at the extreme left. This photo was taken on D+2 after the arrival of the relief column. Several German prisoners can be seen under escort above the crater, being led down to the beach for transfer to ships offshore.

55 The fields east of Pointe-du-Hoc were converted into Emergency Landing Strip (ELS) A-1 starting on June 7 by the 834th Engineer Aviation Battalion even before the strongpoint was secured. It was eventually enlarged and improved as Advanced Landing Ground (ALG) A-1 later in June to provide air support during the Normandy campaign. Pointe-du-Hoc can be seen in the upper left of the image.

56 One of the Schneider 155mm howitzers of 9.Batterie, Artillerie-Regiment-1716 in WN 83 at Maisy-Les Perruques was knocked off its concrete pad by the preliminary Allied bombardment. The howitzer was flipped over in the process and lost one of its wheels that remained on the pad. The Drehsockel mounting is still fitted in the center of the pad. This photo was taken immediately after the war.

57 The Regelbau 622 personnel bunker at WN 84 Maisy-Martinière in late June 1944 following the capture of the site by the 5th Rangers. In the background can be seen the base of the battery's observation tower as well as one of the Regelbau 612 gun casemates under construction at the site.

58 Eight men of the 5th Rangers are decorated with the Distinguished Service Cross in a ceremony in Normandy on June 22, 1944. From left to right they are Lt Col Max Schneider, Capt George P. Whittington, 1Lt Charles "Ace" Parker, 1Lt Francis Dawson, Sgt Wille Moody, T5 Howard McKissick, Sgt Denzil Johnson and Pfc Alexander Barber.

59 The naval gun battery at Longues-sur-Mer to the east of Omaha Beach was the most sophisticated gun battery in the area of the D-Day beaches. It was significantly damaged by preliminary aerial and naval bombardment, but managed to fire on the Allied fleet for much of D-Day before being captured by British troops on D+1. (Author)

60 This illustration compares the three types of field guns encountered by the Rangers. At the far left is the 155mm GPF gun deployed at Pointe-du-Hoc. In the center is the 155mm Schneider howitzer deployed at Maisy-les-Perruques. At the right is the 100mm vz. 14/19 howitzer that armed the battery at Maisy-Martinière. (Author)

MAPS

Introduction

The Ranger assault on Pointe-du-Hoc was one of the most daring missions of D-Day. As Lord Mountbatten later remarked, "Today we are used to the daring exploits of 007, James Bond, but the story of these gallant raiders, Commandos, Rangers... is even more exciting and gripping for these were real men facing real live dangers."[1]

The Ranger mission has become one of the core legends in American military lore. When President Ronald Reagan visited Normandy in June 1984 to celebrate the 40th anniversary of D-Day, he gave his primary commemorative speech at Pointe-du-Hoc. D-Day came to symbolize the American effort in Europe, and Pointe-du-Hoc became the iconic American symbol of D-Day.

The Rangers' place in D-Day mythology became further cemented in place a decade later with the release of Steven Spielberg's Hollywood blockbuster, *Saving Private Ryan*. Although depicting a different aspect of the Ranger mission on D-Day, it further enshrined the Rangers into American military legend.

Numerous accounts of the Rangers at Pointe-du-Hoc have been written, so is there a need for a new account? This book substantially amplifies the D-Day story in two important ways. Firstly, it provides a much more comprehensive account of the three Ranger missions on D-Day. In addition, it places the Ranger missions in a broader historical context by examining several critical but ignored subjects, such as the German side of the battle for Pointe-du-Hoc and the vital role played by the Allied navies and air forces in overwhelming the German defenses.

Many books about the Rangers on D-Day focus exclusively on Ranger Force A at Pointe-du-Hoc, but skip over the other Ranger missions on D-Day. The incredible tale of Goranson's Force B, and their mission to destroy the guns at Pointe-et-Raz-de-la-Percée, is often ignored or misunderstood. The vital role played by Schneider's Ranger Force C in redeeming the stalled American assault on Omaha Beach is seldom appreciated. The US Army landings in the Vierville sector came dangerously close to defeat, and could have been seen off but for the intervention of the Rangers and their determined defense of the right flank of Omaha Beach. These overlooked aspects of the Rangers on D-Day are investigated here in depth.

Besides amplifying the extraordinary tale of the Rangers on D-Day itself, this book broadens the perspective by examining many unexplored aspects of the Ranger story. It details the origins of the Rangers and explains why they were such a controversial new idea. For the first time, it provides a comprehensive account of how the Pointe-du-Hoc mission was planned, including many unexplored aspects such as early schemes to land paratroopers in support of the Rangers. The Ranger missions in Normandy after D-Day are also recounted from a fresh perspective. The controversial fighting for the German Maisy gun batteries is examined, based on fresh evidence long buried in the deepest recesses of the historical archives.

Why was the German gun battery at Pointe-du-Hoc such a threat that it justified sending the Rangers up a sheer cliff to attack the guns? This book explores not only what happened at Pointe-du-Hoc, but why it happened. It details previous Allied experiences with enemy coastal gun batteries during prior amphibious landings at Dieppe, on the North African coast, and during the landings in Italy. The earlier encounters provided Allied commanders with hard-earned lessons about the threat of coastal guns.

These lessons convinced D-Day planners that coastal gun batteries such as Pointe-du-Hoc had to be neutralized by firepower, followed by a bold special forces attack. As a result, Pointe-du-Hoc was the most heavily bombed site in Normandy, devastated by 40 tons of bombs per acre. This is the first book to provide extensive details about the air and naval role in the battle for Pointe-du-Hoc.

Amazingly, the German side of the Pointe-du-Hoc story is almost completely unknown. Why were the German guns never placed in their massive new bunkers? Why did this powerful gun battery remain silent on D-Day? In view of the fact the guns were moved away from Pointe-du-Hoc weeks before D-Day, was the Ranger attack even necessary? *Smashing Hitler's Guns* provides the first comprehensive description of the creation of the German strongpoint at Pointe-du-Hoc. The mysteries and controversies swirling around the performance of the German guns at Pointe-du-Hoc on D-Day are depicted in considerable detail for the very first time.

Author's Note

For readers unfamiliar with military jargon, I have used the normal conventions when referring to military units. The US Army traditionally used Arabic numerals for divisions and smaller independent formations (29th Division, 5th Ranger Infantry Battalion), Roman numerals for corps (V Corps), and spelled numbers for field armies (First US Army).

Infantry battalions are sometimes abbreviated in the fashion "2/116th Infantry," referring to the 2nd Battalion, 116th Infantry Regiment. I have used the usual simplified names for the two Ranger battalions. So, 2nd Rangers is often used rather than the more formal 2nd Ranger Infantry Battalion.

Within US Army infantry regiments, the three battalions had their companies lettered sequentially. So, 1st Battalion consisted of A, B, and C Companies; D Company was the battalion's heavy weapons (machine gun and mortar) company. The 2nd Battalion included E, F, G, and H Companies; 3rd Battalion included I, K, L, and M Companies; "J Company" was not used to avoid confusion with "I" Company. The company designations were used in three fashions: "A Company," "Company A," or "Able Company." The rifle platoons within an infantry company were numbered 1st, 2nd, and 3rd Platoons.

During amphibious operations, the US Army often formed temporary grouping of smaller units to carry out specific missions. For example, the 116th Infantry Regiment, 29th Division formed the core of the larger 116th Regimental Combat Team (RCT) that also included the Provisional Ranger Group, 743rd Tank Battalion, and other supporting units.

I have left most of the German unit designations in the standard German form. I did this to make it easier for the readers to distinguish German from American units. In a few cases where the meaning of the German designation was not obvious, I have used English for clarity. German unit designations generally place the unit number in front of the unit type for formations of a division or larger, but place them at the end of the unit type for those smaller than a division. We thus have 352.Infanterie-Division, but Artillerie-Regiment.352. Subunits within a small formation precede the unit designation, followed by a slash. In the case of German small unit designations, Arabic numerals indicate company/battery while Roman numerals indicate battalion. So, 2./GR.916 refers to the 2nd Company, Grenadier-Regiment.916, while II./GR.916 indicates the 2nd Battalion of Grenadier Regiment.916.

The Wehrmacht in World War II tended to use centimeter measurements for the gun calibers of artillery weapons and millimeters for small arms. I have used the contemporary NATO practice of millimeters for all types. So, 75mm instead of the wartime 7.5cm.

Regarding the times presented in this account, on D-Day, the Allies were on British Double Summer Time (B Time). This was Greenwich Mean Time (GMT) +2 hours. The Wehrmacht operated on the equivalent of GMT+3. So, an Allied report of a landing at 0630hrs would be reported by the Germans as 0730hrs. However, some German units in France used the local time that was the equivalent of British Double Summer Time. For clarity, the times in this book are those used by the Allies.

In order to help the flow of the narrative in this book, I have covered some of the technical issues in appendices at the end. I suspect that the general reader is not that interested in the nitty-gritty details of German coastal gun battery fire controls or the precise tables of organization and equipment of Ranger units. If so, these appendices can be avoided. But Osprey Publishing caters for specialist military history readers, and I think these subjects were well worth covering for those interested in these more specialized subjects.

Acknowledgments

The author would like to thank numerous people for help on this project. Maj Gen John C. Raaen Jr (US Army, Ret'd), commander of the headquarters company of the 5th Rangers on D-Day, was kind enough to discuss several aspects of the Ranger operations with me. Kevan Elsby has created a substantial archive of veteran interviews for a future book on the battle for Dog Green Beach. He has generously shared this material with me; it is identified in the notes as "Dog Green Insight/Kevan Elsby." Simon Trew of the Royal Military Academy at Sandhurst has generously shared many documents with me on this subject. Noel Mehlo Jr and Mark Reardon were kind enough to provide documents related to this project. Prof Thomas Hatfield, author of the splendid biography about Ranger commander Earl Rudder, was kind enough to comment on several issues. Chris Goss, Steven Coates, and Sven Carlsen provided material on the Luftwaffe actions near Pointe-du-Hoc on D-Day.

I

The Guns of Pointe-du-Hoc

Until 1942, Pointe-du-Hoc was an obscure promontory on the rural coast of the Calvados region in Lower Normandy. Many documents from World War II refer to it by an archaic Norman spelling, Pointe-du-Hoe. The Pointe-du-Hoe spelling was present on the standard military maps in use at the time.[1] The words Hoc and Hoe come from "*haugr*" in Norois, the language of the Norman Vikings, which means a mound.[2] After the war, the Pointe-du-Hoc spelling was standardized and remains so today.

The Pointe-du-Hoc headland edged up to the sea, and the narrow shoreline was cluttered with rocky shingle and large boulders that had fallen from the cliffs. The promontory was formed during the Middle Jurassic period, about 165 million years ago.[3] The cliffs are sedimentary formations of mixed composition, including limestone, lime-rich mud, and pebbles, and so are prone to coastal erosion.[4] Unlike the White Cliffs of Dover or the corresponding cliffs on the Pas-de-Calais on the French side of the English Channel, the cliffs are a rusty orange-brown color. While the geology of the cliffs may seem arcane, it would play a role in the Ranger mission on D-Day.

The cliffs near Pointe-du-Hoc gradually recede towards the sea around the small port of Grandcamp-les-Bains, 2 miles to the west, and the coastal village of Vierville-sur-Mer, about 4 miles to the east of Pointe-du-Hoc.*

The local economy of this area relied at the time on agriculture and fishing. The farmlands in the vicinity of Pointe-du-Hoc are typical of the bocage region of Lower Normandy. This refers to the agricultural practice of lining farm fields with hedgerows to shield the land from the strong coastal winds. The bocage consisted of an earth and stone perimeter, 1–2 yards high, topped with trees and thick undergrowth. From a defensive military standpoint, the bocage resembles an inverted trench system that can be very beneficial for defense. Besides agriculture, the small port of Grandcamp-les-Bains hosted numerous small fishing boats. Lobster pots were often set in the waters off Pointe-du-Hoc.

In 1942, the 30 acres of farmland on Pointe-du-Hoc were owned by three French families. The eastern section, facing the future Omaha Beach, was owned by the Le Normand family, the central section by the Valérie family, and the western section by the Guérin family. The lands south of the promontory were owned by the Guelinel family.

The nearest town was Saint-Pierre-du-Mont, about 2 miles to the southeast, which had a small church and a few shops. Many early Allied accounts of the Pointe-du-Hoc battery refer to it as the Saint-Pierre-du-Mont or Criqueville battery, since these were the largest towns nearby. This was notably the case with early Royal Air Force reports.

ESTABLISHMENT OF THE POINTE-DU-HOC BATTERY

The German artillery unit first deployed to Pointe-du-Hoc was 2.Batterie, Heeres-Küsten-Artillerie-Abteilung.832 (2nd Battery, Army Coastal Artillery Battalion 832), or 2./HKAA.832 for short. This unit was first formed on January 1, 1941, as part of Artillerie-Abteilung.832 (Küste).[5] It was not originally deployed in

---

*In 1972, the commune of Grandcamp-les-Bains amalgamated with the neighboring village of Maisy, and is currently called Grandcamp-Maisy.

Normandy; the 2nd Battery, along with its parent battalion, was assigned to defend the vital Pas-de-Calais, on the narrowest stretch of the English Channel. This was one of the first German artillery units assigned to this role.

Each of the battalion's three batteries was armed with six war-booty French Canon de 155 GPF modèle 1917.[6] In German service, they received the designation 15.5cm Kanone 418(f).[7] It's worth noting that this weapon was used by the American Expeditionary Force in France in 1918 and that the US Army license manufactured the gun in 1918–20 as the 155mm Gun Model 1918M1.[8] As a result, the US Army was very familiar with the technical characteristics of this gun. It was widely used in US Army coastal artillery batteries from 1941–44, in essentially the same role as the guns of Pointe-du-Hoc.[9]

These three German batteries were used mainly to engage British shipping in the English Channel and to defend the coast against British raids. The 2.Batterie was originally deployed at Le Portel on the outskirts of the port of Boulogne. The use of army gun batteries to defend the Channel coast, rather than the more sophisticated Kriegsmarine batteries, was simply due to the fact that there were not enough naval gun batteries available at the time.[10] The army batteries were inferior to the dedicated naval batteries since they were field guns and lacked the type of armor-piercing ammunition needed to combat warships.[11] They were better than nothing, but far from ideal. The Wehrmacht never had enough men or equipment to match Hitler's grandiose ambitions for the coastal defences.

In December 1941, British Commandos staged a major raid on the Lofoten Islands off the Norwegian coast.[12] Hitler became increasingly irate at these attacks, and on December 14, 1941, he issued a Führer directive to create a "New Westwall." The Westwall was the German fortification belt created along the Franco-German border in the late 1930s, often called the Siegfried Line by the Allies. Priority for the New Westwall was the Norwegian coast due to the frequent British raids. Next in order of priority were the French, Belgian, and Dutch coasts. At the time, there was little thought of deploying masses of infantry along the coast of occupied Europe due to the enormous personnel demands of the Russian Front. There simply weren't enough troops. Rather, the New Westwall would consist of artillery batteries positioned like "a string of pearls" along the coast. Artillery batteries did not require a great deal of manpower compared to infantry units. Furthermore, they could be created using war-booty artillery from France, Poland, the Soviet Union, and the other occupied countries. Each battery could typically cover a stretch of 12–25 miles of coastline, dependent on the range of the various guns in use.

The British Commandos struck again on the night of February 27/28, 1942, staging Operation *Biting*. This was aimed at grabbing the key components of a secret new German Würzburg radar located near Bruneval on the Normandy coast, north of the port of Le Havre. This was part of a string of new radar stations being established along the coast to provide surveillance of British naval and air traffic. As a result of this raid, the Wehrmacht decided to extend the coastal artillery batteries from the Pas-de-Calais westward down the Normandy coast.

On March 23, 1942, Hitler amplified his earlier instructions with Führer Directive No. 40, which ordered the construction of an Atlantikwall, the new name for the short-lived "New Westwall." With the ink hardly dry on the paper, on March 28, 1942, British Commandos staged their most daring raid yet, Operation *Chariot*. A specially modified old destroyer was packed full of high explosive and driven into the gates of the largest dry dock at the port of Saint-Nazaire in Brittany. The dry dock was severely damaged during the raid, which greatly impeded the ability of the Kriegsmarine to repair large warships on the Atlantic coast, most notably the battleship *Tirpitz*. As a result of Hitler's instructions, OB West began fortifying several critical ports in France and the Low Countries.[13]

GUNS FOR NORMANDY

As a consequence of these raids, in early May 1942, the HKAA.832 was instructed to prepare for movement from the Pas-de-Calais to Normandy. The 1.Batterie was assigned to Riva-Bella at the mouth of the river Orne; this was the future Sword Beach on D-Day. The 2.Batterie was assigned to Pointe-du-Hoc as part of the effort to reinforce defenses of the river Vire estuary, while the 3.Batterie was assigned to Sainte-Mère-Église, near the future Utah Beach and also part of the new Vire river defenses. The assignment of these batteries near the river outlets was due to the lack of deep-water ports on the Lower Normandy coast. The river estuaries had significant dock and cargo-handling capability that German intelligence believed might be essential to any potential Allied amphibious landing in Lower Normandy.

On May 24, the 2.Batterie arrived in Lower Normandy at Isigny-sur-Mer on a commercial freight train. On paper, the battery was horse-drawn. In reality, these coastal batteries were static formations to save precious equipment; horses were in great demand on the Russian Front. The 2.Batterie had only four draft horses for administrative duty. Special artillery half-tracks had to be sent from the army depot at Saint-Lô to tow the guns on the final 7-mile journey from the railhead at Isigny to their new home on Pointe-du-Hoc.

When 2./HKAA.832 was deployed to Pointe-du-Hoc, it also received a new commander, Oberleutnant Frido Ebeling.[*] Shortly after arriving at Pointe-du-Hoc, Ebeling sent a brief letter to an army friend, being careful to avoid any details that would incur the wrath of the army censor:

Thank you for the letter and the newspapers. Since then, my army postal code has changed and so too my location; I am with another unit which is being organized. My biggest concern is to start training 150 new men from scratch. You can well imagine that this is no lark! My former regimental commander writes me that he may need me in the East [Russian Front] urgently, which in truth, would be a questionable pleasure. But for the

[*]Oberleutnant: senior lieutenant. Ebeling had been born in Lehmke, Lower Saxony, and was twenty-seven years old, not much older than the rest of the men of the battery who were mostly twenty to twenty-five years old.

moment they don't want to send me there. Here, I am a young man amidst superior officers who are old and a bit feeble. But we can handle this. Duty is duty! We are now in one of the richest regions in France, in an agricultural area with cliffs, pastures and hedges all around. The peasants have cattle and small-scale farming, which makes life easier.[14]

Ebeling's 2.Batterie included three officers, 20 non-commissioned officers (NCOs), and 120 troops. The deputy chief of the battery was Oberleutnant Brotkorb and senior NCO was Hauptwachtmeister Appel. Each of the six guns had a crew of eight men; the remainder of the battery performed supporting duties. Many of the young soldiers were from central or southern Germany and had never seen the ocean before. They were pleased to receive a service posting along the scenic coast; while duty on Pointe-du-Hoc was austere, it was infinitely better than a posting to the brutal Russian Front.

The three French families farming on Pointe-du-Hoc were formally barred from the strongpoint by the local German Kommandantur, the occupation police. The Guelinel family in the farm south of the strongpoint was allowed to stay until September 1942, at which time the farm buildings were taken over for officer accommodations as well as being used as the canteen for the post.

For nearly six months, the battery was deployed under field conditions. Six gun-pits were dug, and the resulting piles of stone and dirt were used to create splinter walls around the guns. Nets were erected over the guns for camouflage. A variety of simple trenches were dug, including both communication trenches and covered pits for ready ammunition. At first, the troops had to sleep in the trenches or under tents, but that summer, the battery erected two wooden barracks on the south side of the strongpoint. The Pointe-du-Hoc battery was becoming permanent.

The German Army presumed that the main threat to Pointe-du-Hoc would come from the landward side, since the cliffs seemed to be an impregnable obstacle to enemy infantry. The strongpoint was thus shielded on the landward side by a barbed wire barrier and minefields. There was only a single entrance point to the strongpoint through these barriers, which made it easier to guard the post. These defenses were gradually improved as more equipment became available.

STRENGTHENING THE ATLANTIC WALL

At a Führer conference on August 13, 1942, Hitler ordered the creation of an "impregnable fortress along the Channel and Atlantic Coast," his Atlantic Wall. Days later, on August 17, the Royal Navy and largely Canadian Army forces staged Operation *Jubilee* against the fortified port of Dieppe in Upper Normandy.[15] The raid was a fiasco. German coastal artillery batteries on either side of Dieppe, along with fortifications inside the town itself, blasted the Allied landing force. Of the ten tank landing craft, all were sunk or severely damaged, and all the Churchill tanks were lost.

The Dieppe raid made it clear to both the Germans and the Royal Navy that a modest coastal artillery defense could confound an amphibious landing. This encouraged the Wehrmacht to deploy more coastal artillery along the French coast.[16] It was also the first reason that the Allied staff listed the destruction of the guns on Pointe-du-Hoc as one of their first priorities when they began planning a future invasion of the French coast.

The conversion of Pointe-du-Hoc from an ordinary, muddy field emplacement to a concrete-fortified strongpoint began in earnest in November 1942 as part of Hitler's new Atlantic Wall construction program. At this time, Pointe-du-Hoc was within the defense zone of the 716.Infanterie-Division (bodenständige), which issued an initial plan for the defense of the future Operation *Neptune* beach defenses.[17,*] It is interesting to note that the division commander concluded that "major landings in this sector are improbable." The Kriegsmarine concurred and argued, "In the

---

*The bodenständige (static) designation meant that the division lacked the usual organic transport equipment compared to a normal infantry division since it was configured for coastal defense. On the other hand, it was equipped with a much larger number of crew-served weapons associated with the various bunkers and strongpoints.

opinion of the Kriegsmarine, the area east of the mouth of the Vire river [from Pointe-du-Hoc through Omaha Beach and the Anglo-Canadian beaches up to the river Orne] was not suitable [for large-scale landings]. Although the coast northwest and north of Caen [Juno and Sword beaches] offered favorable landing conditions, it was too far away for close support with forces landed on the east coast of the Cotentin [Utah Beach]. Right from the start, it appeared out of the question that the center of gravity of a large-scale landing would be placed in the area of Caen."[18]

The Pointe-du-Hoc battery was part of this minimalist approach to the defense of the Lower Normandy coast. The battery, at least on paper, could cover a 25-mile swath of coast. Due to the range of its guns, the Pointe-du-Hoc battery was assigned to cover westward to defense nest WN 106 Redoute d'Audouville-la-Hubert near St Marie-du-Mont on the west side of the Vire estuary, encompassing the future Utah Beach.* Its eastward zone encompassed the future Omaha Beach as far east as defense nest WN 56 located on the pier in Port-en-Bessin.[19]

By 1944, the Atlantic Wall would become the largest military fortification program of the past century, substantially dwarfing other efforts such as the Maginot Line and Westwall. The Atlantic Wall program was managed by Organization Todt, named after its first leader, Fritz Todt. This was a paramilitary construction organization formed in 1933 to carry out various national engineering projects such as the Autobahn system and the Westwall.[20] Organization Todt conducted engineering design work and supervised construction projects. Part of the skilled workforce was subcontracted from large German engineering firms. Most of the labor came from prisoners of war or forced labor in the occupied countries. In France, there was an agreement in February 1943 between the German government and the collaborationist Vichy French government for the provision of labor for German projects: this was called the Compulsory Work Service.[21] In some cases,

---

*WN: Widerstandsnest (defense nest), usually of squad (Gruppe) size.

young men were sent to Germany to work in factories. In the case of the Atlantic Wall, local men were recruited for varying periods of time to carry out construction work on the new fortifications.[22]

The German engineers supervising the Pointe-du-Hoc construction did not trust the French laborers, assuming they would report their observations to the local French Resistance. This lack of trust was entirely justified, as French Resistance cells in Normandy regularly reported developments to British intelligence.[23] As a result, the French laborers at Pointe-du-Hoc were employed mostly for projects on the outskirts of the strongpoint, with prisoners-of-war used within the strongpoint itself. The first wave of construction used many Soviet prisoners of war. Rations were meager and the workers were often on the brink of starvation. The young artillery troops felt pity for these workers and slipped them the occasional potato. The composition of the workforce varied with time: in the late spring of 1944, many of the workers at Pointe-du-Hoc were Italian prisoners of war, imprisoned after Italy abandoned the Axis alliance in September 1943.

Organization Todt teams arrived at Pointe-du-Hoc in November 1942 to begin planning the layout of the strongpoint. For a time, Pointe-du-Hoc was the only heavily fortified strongpoint in the bay of the Seine from Cherbourg in the west to Le Havre in the east. For this reason, it stuck out in Allied intelligence briefings. Due to the increasing volume of work at the site, Organization Todt laid down a narrow-gauge railway line to facilitate the movement of concrete and other supplies into Pointe-du-Hoc.

The first major structure erected on the site was a first-aid bunker, which had a room added to serve as the temporary battery command post. The Atlantic Wall fortifications followed a set of standardized Regelbau (construction plans) that were designed by the German Army's Wa Prü Fest in Berlin.* These were given

---

*Wa Prü Fest (Waffen Prüfen Festung: Weapons Development-Fortification) was the German design office for fortifications and subordinated to the Heereswaffenamt (Army Weapons Department) of the OKH (Oberkommando des Heeres: Army High Command).

numerical designations, sometimes with a letter prefix such as R (Regelbau), H (Heer: Army), L (Luftwaffe: Air Force), or M (Kriegsmarine: Navy). The Pointe-du-Hoc medical shelter was based on the Regelbau 661 design. Most Atlantic Wall bunkers were built to construction standard B, meaning that they had walls and roof that were constructed of steel-reinforced concrete 6½ft thick. This was considered to be adequate to protect against the projectiles of warship guns up to 8in. and 1,000lb aircraft bombs. Standard A was 10ft thick, but was used mainly for the most substantial construction projects such as the U-boat pens along the Atlantic coast. Minor structures such as the Tobruk weapon pits were built to Standard B1, which was only 3½ft thick, but these were supposed to be buried and so shielded by the surrounding earth.*

Concrete gun-pits were built for the six 155mm guns, each about 200ft apart. The six positions were laid out in a trapezoidal shape. This was the standard configuration for German coastal batteries so that the guns would not have to fire over neighboring guns when aimed at their primary fire zones. The concrete gun-pits were called *Kesselbettungen* (kettle positions), so named for their pan-like shape. These had been used since World War I for German coastal artillery batteries such as those deployed along the Belgian coast in 1916–18. This was a fairly standard configuration for coastal guns around the world, and was essentially similar to the gun pits used by the US Army Coastal Artillery from the 1920s to the 1940s.

The kettle gun pits were 55ft in diameter, so that they could accommodate most medium field guns. On either side of the gun pit were two underground bunkers for projectiles and their separate propellant charges. Extending off one of these was another small underground shelter, about 8 x 13ft, to shield the eight-man gun crew in the event of enemy counterbattery fire.

---

*Tobruk was the nickname for a family of small bunkers that were more formally designated as a Ringstand. The essential feature was a circular opening on the roof that was used for a crew-served weapon such as a machine gun or mortar. The name stemmed from the use of concrete sewer pipes as improvised defensive positions during the fighting around Tobruk in 1942.

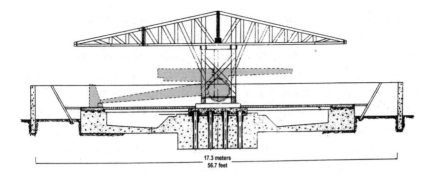

17.3 meters
56.7 feet

Kettle gun pit with camouflage umbrella

The kettle position was mainly intended to facilitate the employment of the gun; its protective features were largely secondary. It was built to a lower standard than the bunkers since it was to protect the gun and crew against splinters, not direct impacts. At the center of the pit was a raised concrete platform with a steel traverse platform bolted to it. This platform, called a *Drehsockel* (swivel socket), consisted of two main elements. The bottom of the platform was bolted to the concrete and helped absorb the gun's recoil. The upper platform was mounted on the lower platform by means of a central pivot and roller bearings to provide complete 360-degree traverse. The wheels of the 155mm gun were lashed to the top gun platform to hold the gun in place. This type of traverse system was necessary since the eight-man crew could not easily move the 9-ton gun without it. The trails of the 155mm gun rested on a ledge around the perimeter of the kettle.

A platform of wood planks was added behind the gun in the space between the open trails to provide a work platform for the crew over the concrete trench below. This was necessary since the guns were manually loaded and the projectiles were quite heavy, weighing about 100lb each. The loading process required a minimum of five of the gun crew: two men would carry the projectile to the gun breech on a loading pallet, and the third crewman would use a rammer to push the projectile into the gun. Another member of the gun crew would follow with the main propellant bag-charge,

29

which would be rammed into place behind the projectile, and a second charge-increment could be added behind it if needed for additional range. Once the loading process was completed, the screw-breech would be closed. The 155mm GPF had a maximum rate of fire of two rounds per minute, decreasing to one round per minute during prolonged firing. Additional men could be added to the gun crew, mainly to accelerate ammunition handling. For example, the US Army used a thirteen-man crew when employing the same 155mm GPF gun for coastal defense.

A variety of extemporized ammunition and stores bunkers were gradually added around Pointe-du-Hoc to increase the available supply of ammunition. Three of these were constructed of concrete and three more were simply trenches with a corrugated metal roof over them.

In late April 1943, Pointe-du-Hoc was attacked from the air for the first time. An unidentified Allied aircraft, probably an RAF night-fighter, strafed the site at night. As a result of the attack, greater priority was given to adding Flak protection to the site. In the summer of 1943, two L409A Flak bunkers were built on either side of the site. These may have been armed at first with 20mm Flak cannon, but by 1944, they had a 37mm Flak 36 automatic cannon. These bunkers had 3.5-meter-thick roofs, hence the "A" suffix to the designation. The Flak guns were mounted on the roof of the bunker. The interior of the Flak bunker contained a personnel shelter accommodating ten men, plus an adjacent ammunition room.

Another defense against air attack was the creation of a fake gun battery position to the west of Pointe-du-Hoc. This was of dubious value since the real gun battery was so obvious due to its location on the promontory. Indeed, the Allies quickly recognized the fakes once they spotted them that year.

Work continued on a variety of personnel bunkers to shelter the gun crews. These were modular designs for one or two sections (Gruppen) of ten men: Gruppenstand or Doppelgruppenstand. By 1944, four of these were completed, with two Regelbau 501 Gruppe bunkers as well as a Regelbau 502 and a Regelbau 621 Doppelgruppen bunker. These bunkers provided accommodations for at least 60 men – enough for the gun crews. For the first few months after their construction, the living conditions inside the personnel bunkers were not very pleasant. The concrete took months to dry out, and in the meantime, the cramped bunkers were uncomfortably damp.

The battery's troops were confined to post for most of the time, so Lt Ebeling permitted them to add a few creature comforts to the site. A wooden staircase was constructed on the cliff face that led to the wooden platform. Attached to this was a ladder that could be raised or lowered to the beach below, which permitted the battery troops to go down to the beach for swimming and fishing. A sauna was also created near the barracks.

With the site nearing completion, on August 19, 1943, the battery received a surprise visit by a high-ranking delegation led by General der Artillerie Erich Marcks, commander of LXXXIV. Armee-Korps, responsible for this sector of Lower Normandy. The delegation arrived unannounced in eighteen staff cars and began a thorough inspection of the new bunkers and gun-pits. One of the young soldiers assigned to the command post, radioman Albin Wienand, later described the scene:

> Each soldier took the position for which he was trained and waited to see what would happen. We saw all sorts of rank stripes, stars, decorations, and bands. Each of the generals inspected something different: the barracks, the camouflage, the ammunition, and all the different weapons. We [the command post] gave the guns the firing order, but the salvo did not occur due to a failure in the telephone connections.[24]

One of the last major bunkers built in the autumn of 1943 was also one of the largest, an H636a fire-control post located at the tip of Pointe-du-Hoc.* There had been a temporary entrenchment for a rangefinder at this location, but it was replaced by this massive new bunker. This command post was the centerpiece of the battery when completed.

---

* This was officially classified as a Befehlsstand für Heeres-Küsten-Batterie: fire-control bunker for an army coastal battery.

Part of the delay in constructing the bunker was that the area at the tip of the Pointe-du-Hoc promontory was riddled with underground cavities in the bedrock, so special reinforcement had to be added to the front of the bunker to prevent it from collapsing. Although the original plan was to construct the bunker as the standard Regelbau 636 with Standard B protection, it was later decided to upgrade the bunker to the Regelbau 636a design which had the much thicker Standard A level of protection. This meant that instead of requiring 960 cubic meters of concrete and 51 tons of steel, it needed 1,250 cubic meters of concrete and 75 tons of steel. This made the bunker almost impervious to naval gunfire, except for the heaviest battleship guns. Likewise, it was all but indestructible to air attack.

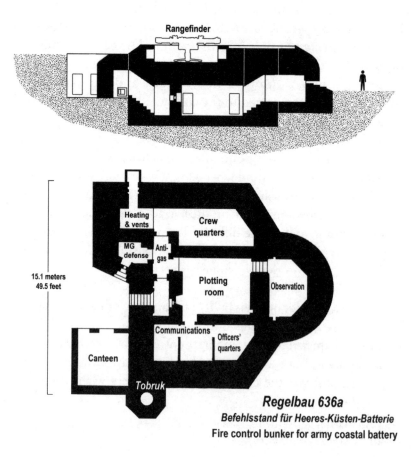

Regelbau 636a
Befehlsstand für Heeres-Küsten-Batterie
Fire control bunker for army coastal battery

The Regelbau 636a fire-control bunker was intended to include sophisticated fire-control devices to permit the battery to engage moving ships at sea. The bunker had an optical rangefinder on the roof for precisely measuring the distance to targets, and this data was fed into a mechanical calculator located in the plotting room in the center of the bunker. Additional data was obtained from forward observation posts east and west of Pointe-du-Hoc. Once the data was processed, firing instructions were relayed to the gun pits via buried electrical cables.[25]

COMMAND CHANGE

On October 22, 1943, unwelcome visitors appeared out of the dawn mist: three small Royal Navy warships approached the coast near Colleville-Vierville, the future Omaha Beach, to the east of Pointe-du-Hoc. Due to the morning fog, they could barely be seen, even through the battery's rangefinder. Lt Ebeling ordered the crews to their guns, but decided against firing on the ships since they could not be adequately tracked.[26] The battery had no forward observers near that part of the coast to report on the fall of shot, and the fire-control bunker was still under construction. The warships subsequently disappeared back into the mist. Troops of the 716.Infanterie-Division along the coast also reported the phantom warships, and the information went to the headquarters of HKAA.832 in nearby Carentan. The battalion commander called Lt Ebeling on the field telephone and asked him why the battery hadn't fired at the warships. Ebeling flippantly responded, "I can't hit sparrows with my guns." The chances of hitting moving targets were almost nil without adequate location data. The battalion commander responded, "I don't care, you should have fired," and slammed down the phone.

After the failure of the battery to fire during the August visit by Gen d.Art Marcks, followed by this incident, Ebeling was relieved of command and transferred to the Russian Front. He was assigned to command the 12./Artillerie-Regiment.389 and was later promoted to Hauptmann (captain) due to his leadership; he survived the war. Ebeling had been a very popular commander at Pointe-du-Hoc and his troops were sorry to see him go. His position was taken by the battery's executive officer, Lt Brotkorb. Very little is known about Brotkorb, and he does not figure at all in the surviving recollections of the soldiers of the battery.[27]

FINAL EVOLUTION OF THE
POINTE-DU-HOC BATTERY

One minor change was made to the Pointe-du-Hoc battery in December 1943. As part of a broader army standardization program, HKAA.832 was re-designated as HKAA.1260; the Pointe-du-Hoc battery consequently became 2./HKAA.1260. It would be known by this name on D-Day. The site identification also changed, with the battery being designated as defense nest WN 75. The neighboring fake gun battery to the west was designated as WN 76, and both areas constituted Stützpunkt Pointe-du-Hoc.*

The problem of spotting Allied warships in the bay of the Seine was addressed in late 1943 with a program to create a surveillance post at Le Guay, on the cliffs about 2½ miles to the east of Pointe-du-Hoc. The naval portion of the site received the codename "Imme" and consisted of a pair of FuMO 2 Calais surface-search radars to detect Allied warships and transports under all weather conditions and at night. It was manned by the Kreigsmarine's 2.Funkmess-Abteilung (radar regiment). It was expanded in March 1944 with an attached Luftwaffe post codenamed "Igel", gaining a pair of FuSE 65 Wurzberg-Riese air-search radars, manned by 9./Ln.Rgt. 53.[28]

This sophisticated surveillance site was linked by radio to Pointe-du-Hoc and higher commands by teams from the specialized Funkmess-Kompanie.369 communications unit that had radio personnel at both Le Guay and Pointe-du-Hoc. The entire complex was designated as Stützpunkt Le Guay and was able to provide alerts to the Pointe-du-Hoc battery long before visual spotting could take place. Neither type of radar was designed as a fire-control radar,

---

* Stützpunkt: strongpoint.

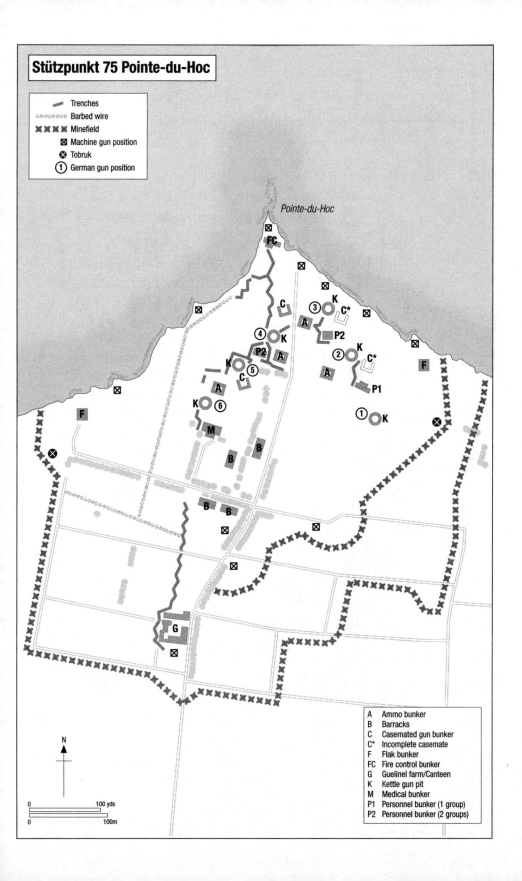

Stützpunkt 75 Pointe-du-Hoc

Trenches
Barbed wire
Minefield
Machine gun position
Tobruk
German gun position

Pointe-du-Hoc

A Ammo bunker
B Barracks
C Casemated gun bunker
C* Incomplete casemate
F Flak bunker
FC Fire control bunker
G Guelinel farm/Canteen
K Kettle gun pit
M Medical bunker
P1 Personnel bunker (1 group)
P2 Personnel bunker (2 groups)

N

0   100 yds
0   100m

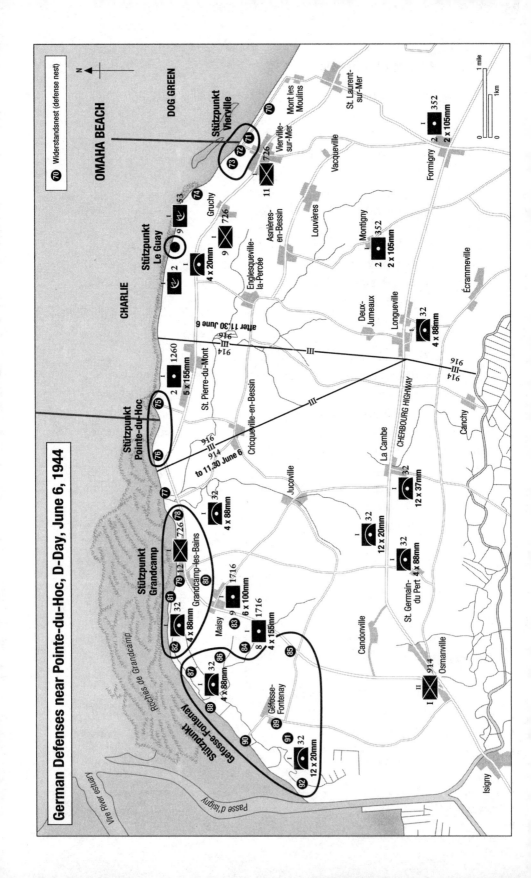

German Defenses near Pointe-du-Hoc, D-Day, June 6, 1944

70 Widerstandsnest (defense nest)

OMAHA BEACH

DOG GREEN

CHARLIE

Stützpunkt Vierville

Stützpunkt Le Guay

Stützpunkt Pointe-du-Hoc

Stützpunkt Grandcamp

Stützpunkt Géfosse-Fontenay

Vire River estuary

Roches de Grandcamp

Passe d'Isigny

St. Laurent-sur-Mer

Mont les Moulins

Vierville-sur-Mer

Vacqueville

Asnières-en-Bessin

Louvières

Gruchy

Englesqueville-la-Percée

Deux-Jumeaux

Longueville

Écrammeville

Montigny

Formigny

St. Pierre-du-Mont

Cricqueville-en-Bessin

La Cambe

CHERBOURG HIGHWAY

Canchy

Jucoville

St. Germain-du-Pert

Candonville

Osmanville

Isigny

Grandcamp-les-Bains

Maisy

Géfosse-Fontenay

352 — 2 x 105mm

352 — 2 x 105mm

32 — 4 x 88mm

32 — 12 x 37mm

32 — 12 x 20mm

32 — 4 x 88mm

1260 — 5 x 155mm

726

916 — after 11.30 June 6
914

916 — to 11.30 June 6
914

916
914

726 — 4 x 88mm

726

1716 — 6 x 100mm

1716 — 4 x 155mm

32 — 4 x 88mm

32 — 4 x 88mm

32 — 12 x 20mm

914

4 x 20mm

11 — 726

9 — 726

914

1 mile
1km

and so could not be automatically linked to the guns at Pointe-du-Hoc to provide them with precise aiming directions. Rather, they could provide only coarse bearing and range data while Pointe-du-Hoc itself had relatively simple fire controls.[29]

HARDENING POINTE-DU-HOC

Allied aircraft on missions over France would periodically make improvised attacks on Pointe-du-Hoc, if for no other reason than that its topography made it so obvious. The battery suffered its first casualties in late 1943 when a fighter strafed one of the barracks, killing and wounding several soldiers.

In January 1943, Hitler ordered that major Atlantic Wall coastal gun batteries should be enclosed with overhead concrete roofs to protect against air attack.[30] In reality, the fortification engineers in Berlin had not yet developed standardized plans for such construction, nor were resources immediately available. Priority went to the Pas-de-Calais and the Norwegian coast. Intensified Allied bombing attacks along the Lower Normandy coast in late 1943, as well as the growing probability of an amphibious landing somewhere in France in 1944, led to a plan to accelerate this effort in the autumn of 1943, including in Normandy. This was sometimes called the Schartenstand Programm, Schartenstand being the term for an enclosed gun bunker.

The new construction program envisioned rebuilding each coastal battery as a strongpoint able to defend itself against a seaborne attack. The open kettle pits would be replaced by fully enclosed casemates that would protect the guns against aerial bombing and naval gunfire. The batteries would be provided with close-defense weapons including machine guns, mortars, and anti-tank rockets. Communication links would be buried using protected cables.[31]

The decision to replace the kettle pits with enclosed casemates was a surprisingly controversial decision among the fortress engineers in Berlin. Many German fortification engineers argued that the guns in the kettle positions were nearly impossible to destroy, short of a direct bomb hit, since the field pieces were not especially vulnerable to the splinters from aerial bombs.[32] Furthermore, enclosed casemates would inevitably restrict the traverse of the guns from the 360 degrees of the kettle gun pits to about 120 degrees in the casemates. The Kriegsmarine favored an experimental solution of a traversing concrete turret using a new type of lightweight concrete reinforced with stressed wire.[33] The concrete turret was mounted on a metal turret race at the base of the structure, similar to those used on a warship. A prototype was built at Fort Vert in the Pas-de-Calais, but came too late for the Normandy batteries.

Instead, the German Army recommended that heavy batteries with casemated guns receive a few supplementary light or medium field guns for all-around site defense. Lower Normandy did not have a high-enough priority to get these supplementary guns, so medium batteries had a portion of their guns fully enclosed while leaving a few in the open kettle pits to provide all-azimuth traverse. In the case of Pointe-du-Hoc, the plan was to enclose four of the six guns in enclosed casemates and leave two in the kettle pits.

The Wa Prüf Fest in Berlin continued to design these new gun casemates into late 1943. One of the problems with using an unmodified 155mm GPF gun or similar field guns was that the trails of the gun carriage were so long that it would require an exceptionally large casemate to fully enclose the gun. This would waste tremendous amounts of concrete and steel. The solution to this problem was to adopt a new heavy platform mount for the 155mm gun that was sufficiently robust to absorb the recoil of the gun so that the carriage and trails would not be needed. The existing trunnion mount and gun barrel would be transferred to the new mount. Another advantage of the new type of heavy swivel mount was that it provided more precise traverse when targeting ships than the coarse corrections possible on an ordinary field gun mounting such as the 155mm GPF at Pointe-du-Hoc. The type selected for Pointe-du-Hoc was the new Schwere Drehbettung (32 ton) that had entered production in July 1943 specifically for medium guns such as the 155mm GPF.[34]

In the event, the final design for the Regelbau 694 casemate was not completed until March 30, 1944, so there was a rush to construct these casemates at Pointe-du-Hoc and other Lower Normandy strongpoints by early summer.[35]

Construction of the four Regelbau 694 gun casemates began at Pointe-du-Hoc in March 1944, about two months before D-Day. Allied intelligence picked up the first traces of this work in early March, when photo reconnaissance missions noticed that the camouflage umbrellas had been removed from two of the gun pits and the guns moved out of the pits.[36] The first signs of the actual construction did not appear until the April 10 photo mission.

The construction was supervised by the German construction firm W. Scheidt, which was also building the two big gun casemates in the Vierville area as part of WN 72 on Omaha Beach. The four Pointe-du-Hoc gun casemates received the designations Bauwerk (BW: Construction work) 465–468. The two casemates on the western side, BW 467 and BW 468, were oriented almost directly northward and out to sea. Those on the eastern side, BW 465 and BW 466, were oriented eastward. Had they been completed, their guns could not have fired on Omaha Beach due to the traverse limits of the casemates.

To speed up the process, an alternative form of construction was used. Most Atlantic Wall bunkers were built by first creating an elaborate steel rebar skeleton, resembling a gigantic jungle gym. Once completed, temporary wood panels were erected around the skeleton to create a mold. The lower levels of the bunker would be poured with concrete, with additional wood shuttering added up the side, followed by another concrete pouring. This process would continue until the complete bunker mold had been filled, at which point the wood forms would be removed and the process started on the neighboring bunker. To accelerate the building process, the modified technique used an outer shell of concrete cinder blocks instead of a wood mold, which permitted simultaneous construction of multiple bunkers without having to wait for the wood molds to be reused.

It took time to ship sufficient concrete blocks to Pointe-du-Hoc, since there was so much Atlantic Wall construction going on all over France in the spring of 1944. Indeed, April 1944 was the peak month for concrete consumption on the Atlantic Wall in 1944, totaling 607,600 cubic meters compared to 243,400 in January that year. As a result, only two of the four Regelbau 694 casemates were completed by late April: BW 467 and BW 468 on the western side of the site. Construction of the third and fourth casemates was started but never completed.

Allied air raids along the French railway network delayed the delivery of the ventilation ducting, electrical systems, and the gun's vital new swivel platform mount.* Consequently, no guns were ever deployed in Pointe-du-Hoc's two completed H694 casemates, even though the basic concrete shells were complete.

One of the last detachments to arrive at Pointe-du-Hoc in early 1944 came from Werfer-Regiment.84. This was a Nebelwerfer artillery rocket launcher unit stationed inland near Rouen at the time. Generalfeldmarschall Erwin Rommel, commander of Heeresgruppe B (Army Group B) in northern France, had insisted that units stationed away from the coast send detachments to reinforce the shoreline defenses. On March 23, a small forward observer team under Lt Stockinger from the 2.Batterie, Werfer-Regiment.84, arrived at Pointe-du-Hoc along with a detachment of about a dozen young soldiers.

This later group appears to have been a bunch of misfits who had run into trouble with their superior officers. They were assigned to dig a series of trenches and machine-gun pits along the cliffs on the eastern edge of the strongpoint, on either side of the eastern 37mm Flak bunker. They immediately earned the wrath of their officers after wandering around the outside of the strongpoint, trying to hunt down Calvados from the local French farmers. This was the local "moonshine," distilled by farmers from apples, and a very popular drink with German soldiers stationed in Normandy. As punishment, these troops were not stationed in the bunkers or barracks, but lived in field entrenchments near their firing positions.[37] They were sometimes called the "Werfer-Einheit" (launcher unit). This ad hoc group would play a surprisingly prominent role in the fighting with the Rangers at Pointe-du-Hoc on D-Day.

---

* One of the main bottlenecks in completing the bunker was that the heavy platform mount was being produced at a snail's pace of only twelve per month.

Chapter 2

The Coastal Gun Threat

Pointe-du-Hoc was the first fortified German coastal artillery battery to appear on the bay of the Seine in Lower Normandy. It immediately attracted Allied attention, and remained a focus of Allied concern during the planning for Operation *Overlord*. But it was not the first coastal artillery threat encountered by the Allies. Allied experiences with enemy coastal artillery batteries from 1942–44 strongly shaped the response to the threat of Pointe-du-Hoc on D-Day.

Indeed, the threat posed by coastal artillery batteries is a traditional problem for amphibious operations. In the age of sail, Admiral Horatio Nelson is reputed to have said, "A ship's a fool to fight a fort." The guns of a land fortress are in a fixed position, and well protected by stone and earth. In contrast, a ship's guns are on a moving platform, and thus more difficult to aim accurately. In World War I, the Turkish batteries overlooking Gallipoli were an important factor in the failure of the Anglo-French amphibious operation.[1] Throughout World War I, the presence of an extensive array of German coastal artillery along the Belgian coast was a major reason preventing Britain and France from making an "end run" around the German trench system in Flanders. The guns made an amphibious landing in the German rear too dangerous.[2]

LESSONS LEARNED: DIEPPE

The threat posed by coastal artillery batteries became painfully clear on August 17, 1942, when British and Canadian forces staged Operation *Jubilee* against the fortified port of Dieppe in Upper Normandy. The Dieppe raid was substantially larger than previous Commando raids on the French coast, including the use of tank landing craft to deliver thirty Churchill tanks to the beach in support of the large infantry force. The Dieppe planners were aware of the presence of German coastal artillery on either side of the port, and came up with special-operations tactics to deal with the threat.

Northeast of Dieppe near Berneval-sur-Mer was the 2.Batterie, HKAA.770, dubbed the "Goebbels battery" by British intelligence. It was equipped with three 170mm K18 Mrs.Laf. and one 155mm sFH 414 (f) howitzer. Southwest of Dieppe was a reinforced battery of the HKAA.813, called the "Hess battery" by British intelligence. It was equipped with four 220mm K532 (f) and four 105mm K35 (t) guns, and one 155mm sFH 414 (f).[3]

To thwart the German coastal batteries, Operation *Jubilee* included subsidiary raids by the Commandos. As would be the case with Pointe-du-Hoc two years later, the coastal batteries at Dieppe were perched on cliffs. The plan was to land Commando units at the base of the cliffs by landing craft. They would then scale the cliffs and eliminate the gun batteries before the main landings. The attack by No 4 Commando against the Hess Battery took place in the pre-dawn hours and was one of the few successes of the Dieppe raid. The Commandos scaled the cliffs without major incident, enveloped the battery on either side, and then overcame the barbed wire and minefields to attack and capture the battery. It was a model for raids of this type, including the later Pointe-du-Hoc attack.

The attack on the Goebbels battery by No 3 Commando, however, turned into a chaotic mess. The Commando flotilla of landing craft stumbled into a German coastal convoy, which included a number of armed vessels that brought the British landing force under cannon fire. After a brief skirmish at sea, only a small fraction of the landing craft arrived at the cliffs, and the remaining Commando force was unable to accomplish its mission.

During the main raid into Dieppe port, surviving German coastal guns wreaked havoc on the Royal Navy and Canadian landing force. Of the ten tank landing craft, all were either sunk or severely damaged. Of the 6,000 troops taking part in the raid, only about 2,100 returned to Britain. The Canadians lost 3,367 men killed, wounded, or captured; the Royal Navy suffered 550 casualties. While the coastal guns were only one of many contributors to the casualties, they severely restricted the ability of the Royal Navy to conduct the raid as planned.[4]

The stinging rebuke of Operation *Jubilee* haunted Allied commanders. It was the nightmare that motivated the schemes to smash the German battery at Pointe-du-Hoc on D-Day. The Dieppe raid suggested that Commando raids against coastal artillery could succeed even in the face of extreme terrain obstacles such as cliffs. However, they were extremely risky and success was not guaranteed.

In an after-action report on the Dieppe raid by the Combined Operations Headquarters, the first "lesson learned" was that such missions required "overwhelming fire support."[5] The elimination of the German coastal gun batteries by Commandos alone was too risky. The guns would have to be suppressed by a combination of naval gunfire, aerial attack, and finally a Commando raid to ensure success.

LESSONS LEARNED: OPERATION *TORCH*

The next combined operation for the Allies was Operation *Torch*, the amphibious landings in French North Africa on November 8, 1942. There were several separate landings on the Moroccan and Algerian coast, of which one, that near Oran, merits special attention.

On the western side of Oran was Mers-el-Kébir, the main French Mediterranean naval base. The Royal Navy had sunk several French warships in the harbor there on July 3, 1940, to prevent them from falling into German hands when they refused to hand themselves over to the British. Occurring only weeks after the defeat of the allied French and British armies in the Battle of France, this attack was regarded as a stab in the back by the French and remained a bitter grudge through the war. Due to the extensive losses at Mers-el-Kébir, the French naval force still operational on the North African coast was much weaker than in 1940.

Oran and Mers-el-Kébir had been fortified for over a century, including a number of coastal batteries. Under the Franco-Italian armistice agreement of 1940, Oran's defenses were scheduled to be demilitarized. This process was started in July 1940, and two of the four main gun batteries were disarmed. After the Royal Navy attack on Mers-el-Kébir, Germany and Italy suspended the disarmament. French naval defenses in North Africa were thereafter permitted to remain operational. The presumption was that after the Royal Navy attack on Mers-el-Kébir, the French Navy would enthusiastically defend the port against any future British naval action.

Two old batteries remained in Oran in 1942: Batterie du Santon was armed with four 194mm M1902 guns and Batterie Canastel had three antiquated 240mm M1884 guns. These were located within old fortifications built in the latter half of the 19th century.[6] The smaller port of Arzew to the east of Oran had two small gun batteries, Fort du Nord with four 105mm guns and Fort de la Pointe with two 75mm guns. The Arzew batteries were downgraded to reserve batteries in 1940, and so were only partly manned in late 1942.

The Allied attack on Oran was very complex and will only be summarized here, with an emphasis on the coastal artillery threat.[7] The easternmost landing sector was in the Golfe d'Arzew, assigned to two regimental combat teams of the US 1st Infantry Division. To deal with the threat of the two Arzew coastal batteries, the 1st Ranger Battalion, led by Lt Col William Darby, was to capture both forts in the pre-dawn hours prior to the main landing.

Darby's Rangers were split into two groups. The smaller of the forces, numbering two companies, was landed directly on the dock in Arzew harbor under the cover of darkness. The landing parties overcame a few sentries, and then caught the garrison of Fort de la

Pointe asleep, capturing about sixty French troops. The larger force, led by Darby himself, landed by boat on Cap Carbon and carried out a forced march of about a mile to the rear of Fort du Nord overlooking Arzew. Three companies attempted to surreptitiously breach the barbed wire perimeter, but were spotted by French sentries and came under fire. The Rangers then used four 81mm mortars to bombard the fort before rushing the defenses in the dark. Sixty prisoners were taken and the Rangers set up a defensive perimeter, preparing for a French counterattack that never came. The Ranger force's radios had been lost in the landing, so Darby shot off green flares in the dark early-morning sky to let the Center Task Force know that the battery had been neutralized.

In order to secure the vital docks in Oran, the Allies planned to conduct a *coup de main* under the cover of darkness directly into the harbor. This mission was codenamed Operation *Reservist*. The naval element of the force consisted of two small cutters, HMS *Hartland* and HMS *Walney*, supported by several motor launches. They were assigned to deliver a force of about 400 American troops of the 3rd Battalion, 6th Armored Infantry, 1st Armored Division direct to the docks.

Unfortunately, the French garrison had spotted the naval forces offshore and the port garrison had been alerted. As they approached the docks in darkness around 0300hrs, the assault teams on the Royal Navy cutters could hear sirens wailing in the city. The dock area had a significant number of antiaircraft gun batteries and heavy machine guns, and there were several French destroyers anchored nearby. These antiaircraft batteries included rapid-fire 75mm guns that could be used in an improvised anti-ship role. HMS *Walney* led the column but was raked with gunfire from the dock area and by an approaching French destroyer. All but one of the Royal Navy officers on the *Walney*'s bridge were killed and all its guns knocked out. The US Army team leader, Lt Col George F. Marshall, ordered his troops to abandon ship as the *Walney* began to sink. HMS *Hartland* followed and was similarly blasted while passing by the French destroyer *Typhon*. Two motor launches were able to extricate a few of the soldiers and sailors aboard. US casualties were 189 dead and 157 wounded. A total of just forty-seven troops landed on the docks and were taken prisoner by the French. The Royal Navy lost 113 dead and 86 wounded in the action.

Operation *Reservist* was a fiasco that was all too reminiscent of Dieppe. Boldness did not ensure success. However, although the attack into Oran harbor failed miserably, the landings on either side of the port succeeded and the US Army had a firm bridgehead on the Algerian coast.

While Operation *Reservist* was under way, the Center Naval Task Force was assigned to deal with the threat posed by the other two Oran coastal gun batteries. This force included the battleship HMS *Rodney* and three aircraft carriers – HMS *Furious*, HMS *Biter*, and HMS *Dasher*. Of the two French batteries near Oran, Batterie du Santon proved the more troublesome.

Batterie du Santon began firing at 0315hrs against several of the *Torch* landing sites. Around 0900hrs, it opened fire against the landing ships off Beach Y near Les Andalouses. The French gunfire struck two ocean liners that had been impressed into Royal Navy service as troop ships, the SS *Monarch of Bermuda* and MV *Llangibby Castle*. HMS *Rodney* tried to silence the battery with its 14in. guns, but none of the projectiles hit the fortified guns. Adm Sir Andrew Cunningham in his dispatches noted that "*Rodney* was frequently engaged with Du Santon from extreme ranges, and her fire, though it did not knock out the battery, was always sufficiently accurate to cause it to cease firing."[8] The duel subsided later in the day due to fog.

On November 9, Batterie du Santon provided fire support for the French troops defending La Sénia airfield against an advancing American tank column. This led to another counter-bombardment by HMS *Rodney*, again without effect. The Santon battery responded by firing against HMS *Rodney*. Consequently, an air attack was launched from the British carriers. Although one of the Albacore biplane light bombers managed to hit one of the gun batteries with a 500kg bomb, it failed to explode.

On November 10, the Allies conducted the final assault on Oran from both east and west. HMS *Rodney*, along with the cruisers

HMS *Aurora* and HMS *Jamaica*, was assigned to suppress Batterie du Santon as well as the battery at Cap Canastel. In spite of this bombardment, Batterie du Santon continued to fire in support of La Sénia garrison, and also fired at the Allied landing site at Les Andalouses beach. Naval gunfire and air attacks failed to silence the battery that day. An armistice was signed at 1215hrs, and gun crews of Batterie du Santon finally surrendered around 1310hrs.

As in the case of the landings near Oran, the other operations near Algiers also provide examples of the threat of coastal gun batteries. Algiers was defended by thirteen fortified batteries with sophisticated fire controls, including infrared thermal detectors and rangefinder stations. The three main threats consisted of the old fort at Cap Sidi Ferruch, another near Pointe Pescade at Fort Duperré, and Batterie du Lazaret on Cap Matifou near Fort d'Estrées. These were the targets of the main landing parties.

Batterie du Lazaret was armed with four 194mm Mle 1902 guns and was the target of No 1 Commando under Maj K. R. S. Trevor. The Commandos landed in the dark and managed to take their original objectives by surprise, reaching the approaches to the battery. However, the battery had been alerted, and searchlights on Cap Matifou illuminated the approaching landing force. The battery opened fire, but prompt counter-fire from accompanying British destroyers knocked out the searchlights, leaving the guns blind. French troops defended the Batterie du Lazaret and kept the Commandos at bay. Trevor was obliged to request naval gunfire support to deal with the French batteries, and around 1040hrs, the destroyer HMS *Zetland* began an hour-long bombardment of the battery, but without effect. This was followed around 1430hrs by a combination of naval gunfire from the cruiser HMS *Bermuda* and airstrikes from the carrier HMS *Formidable* using Albacore biplane light bombers. The Commandos began another land attack around 1600hrs, supported by a self-propelled 105mm howitzer from the US 39th Infantry. The fifty French naval troops of the battery finally surrendered around 1700hrs. Although the battery was eventually taken, it took precious hours to do so.

In retrospect, Operation *Torch* provided several important lessons about dealing with the threat of coastal gun batteries during amphibious operations. The inability of HMS *Rodney* to silence an old French gun battery protected by pre-modern fortifications was a clear reminder that warships alone were unreliable in overcoming fortified gun batteries. This was especially worrisome for future operations against the Atlantic Wall, since the German batteries used modern fortifications with steel-reinforced concrete that was much more resistant to naval gunfire than old masonry and unreinforced concrete forts. From the standpoint of special operations against fortified positions, Operation *Torch* reinforced the Dieppe lessons. The success of the Rangers at Arzew suggested that a commando raid on an exposed and weakly defended gun battery was feasible. But the attack directly into Oran harbor with its multitude of guns emphasized once again that a well-defended harbor was not a feasible objective for a lightly protected landing force. The prolonged fighting at Cap Matifou was a reminder of the limitations of elite light infantry if surprise was lost when facing a determined and fortified adversary. In contrast to the missions around Oran, the other *Torch* objectives at Casablanca, Safi, and Port Lyautey were more weakly defended and did not pose the hazards of a heavily defended port.

The failures at Dieppe and Oran encouraged Allied amphibious planners to avoid ports as principal objectives for amphibious operations. Up until 1942, ports had been a prized objective because the Allied navies did not have the means to land heavy equipment over open beaches during amphibious operations. But technical solutions to these tactical problems were already under way, as described below, and ports were no longer absolutely necessary for amphibious operations.

OPERATION *CORKSCREW*

One of the most obscure Allied amphibious operations in the Mediterranean, Operation *Corkscrew*, would have important ramifications for the D-Day landings. This operation was directed against the Italian island of Pantelleria, located between Tunisia and Sicily. Pantelleria was sometimes called the Italian Gibraltar or Italian Malta, alluding to the fortified British ports in the Mediterranean.

Following the defeat of the Axis forces in North Africa in May 1943, the Allies planned to invade Sicily as a stepping stone for an eventual conquest of Italy. Pantelleria was a significant obstacle to this, being home to a number of German radar stations and airbases. These stations could monitor Allied naval activity in the Tunisia–Sicily corridor. Allied amphibious doctrine depended on secrecy regarding the timing and location of operations to minimize the threat of the Axis forces moving reinforcements towards the vulnerable beachheads in the initial stages of the landings. Furthermore, Pantelleria's airfield could be used by Axis forces to attack the Allied naval convoys heading to Sicily.

Due to these factors, on May 9, Gen Dwight Eisenhower, the supreme commander of Allied forces in the theater, ordered an operation against Pantelleria as a preliminary step to the subsequent landings on Sicily. Italy had heavily reinforced the island with 21 coastal gun batteries and numerous bunkers. The operation would serve as a test case to determine the amount of aerial and naval bombardment needed to overcome a heavily defended coast.[9]

Starting on May 29, Allied aircraft dropped 14,203 bombs totaling 4,119 tons on sixteen of the most dangerous Italian coastal gun batteries. On May 31, a parallel campaign of naval bombardment began, reaching a crescendo on June 8. On June 11, the British 1st Division began amphibious landings on the island. The battered and shell-shocked Italian garrison surrendered later that day.

Assessments of the bombardment campaign were discouraging. A later USAAF report noted:

Despite the weight of the bombardment to which Pantelleria had been subjected, comparatively few of the coastal defense and antiaircraft batteries were damaged sufficiently to prevent their being fired by determined crews... Scarcely more than 3.3 percent of the bombs dropped by B-17s fell within a 100-yard radius of the battery on average. The corresponding figure for the medium bombers was approximately 6.4 percent and for the fighter-bombers about 2.6 percent. As a result of this lower accuracy, the bombing destroyed only about half the number of guns expected.[10]

Even though the bombing campaign failed to destroy very many guns, inspection of the batteries in the aftermath of Operation *Corkscrew* revealed that they had been effectively put out of action by the subsidiary effects of the bombing:

Gun platforms were upheaved, electrical connections severed, and many guns that could have been called serviceable were so covered with debris that one or two hours would have been needed for clearance... Because of the disrupted character of the terrain, the maintenance of an ammunition supply would have been a difficult matter, as merely walking from gun to gun required considerable effort... Although the material damage to the guns was slight ... the bombing attacks had produced a profound effect psychologically. No battery was provided with adequate shelter for detachments of ammunition – a state of affairs that led the crews to abandon their positions and seek cover at various distances.[11]

The lessons of Operation *Corkscrew* were intensely studied by Solly Zuckerman, a pioneer of operational research and the personal scientific advisor to Winston Churchill. Zuckerman prepared a detailed report on the Pantelleria bombing campaign that would later play an important role in the Normandy campaign against German coastal guns.[12] The assessments of Operation *Corkscrew* helped Allied planners to determine how much aerial or naval firepower would be needed to deal with the coastal gun threat. Most importantly, the studies concluded that it was not necessary to actually destroy a gun. Rather, a sufficient number of close hits would suppress the gun by demoralizing the crews and disrupting the proper servicing of the guns during the critical hours of the amphibious landings.

TECHNICAL INNOVATIONS FOR AMPHIBIOUS OPERATIONS

As mentioned before, early Allied amphibious operations tended to focus on ports due to the need for cargo-handling sites to support the subsequent land campaigns. However, innovations in landing craft were beginning to make the capture of ports less essential in amphibious operations. A new generation of amphibious landing craft, including new LCTs (Landing Craft Tank) and LSTs (Landing Ship Tank), would permit the landing of armored vehicles in the initial days of an amphibious operation. Other technical innovations such as the DUKW amphibious truck provided a means to rapidly move supplies onshore even without docks. The Allies were also on their way to developing substantial airborne formations that could be landed behind the enemy beach defenses. This meant that instead of attacking a port heavily defended by coastal guns, the amphibious operation could be conducted against less heavily defended beaches.

These technologies saw their fulsome debut during Operation *Husky* on Sicily in July 1943. *Husky* was the largest Allied amphibious operation in the Mediterranean to date and one of the largest in the war in Europe. The operation succeeded despite the Italians having substantial coastal defenses in Sicily, including some of the most powerful coastal gun batteries in the Mediterranean.[13]

After the Dieppe and North African experiences, the Allies were finally able to avoid the heavily defended ports altogether when they attacked Sicily. The new landing techniques made it possible to land substantial ground forces on weakly defended beaches and then wrest control of ports by seizing them from the landward side. This would be the core lesson for the ultimate amphibious operation in Europe, Operation *Overlord*.

EARLY *OVERLORD* PLANNING

Operation *Overlord* was the codename for the overall Allied plan to invade occupied France. *Overlord* contained several subsidiary plans. The two most important of these were Operation *Neptune*, the amphibious assault on the Normandy coast, and Operation *Anvil*, the amphibious landings in southern France. Other subsidiary plans included Operation *Bodyguard*, the deception plan to cloak *Neptune* and *Anvil*, and Operation *Rankin*, a contingency plan for an improvised amphibious landing in France in the event that Germany suddenly collapsed.*

Until 1943, Allied planning for operations on the French coast was primarily handled by the Combined Operations Headquarters (COHQ), led by Vice Admiral Lord Louis Mountbatten. This was largely a British organization and was focused on coordinating Commando raids with support from the Royal Navy and Royal Air Force. At the Casablanca conference in January 1943, US President Franklin D. Roosevelt and British Prime Minister Winston Churchill agreed, in principle, to staging an invasion of France in 1944. To prepare for such an operation, both sides agreed that a joint staff would be needed. This emerged in April 1943 as COSSAC (Chief of Staff to the Supreme Allied Commander).[14] It was headed by Lt Gen F. E. Morgan of the British Army, whose deputy was BrigGen Raymond W. Barker of the US Army.

The first draft of the *Overlord* plan was completed in July 1943. It was presented to the Combined Chiefs of Staff, as well as Roosevelt and Churchill, at the Quadrant conference in Quebec the following month. At this stage, the plan was limited to broad operational objectives rather than tactical details. The first hints of the potential use of the Rangers in *Overlord* were contained in a section on the assault landings, where it was noted that "subsidiary

---

* Under the early *Overlord* plans, *Bodyguard*'s military component was codenamed *Cockade* and consisted of three deception operations: *Tindall*, which pretended to be an operation by forces based in Scotland against the Norwegian coast; *Wadham*, an operation by US forces in southwest England against French ports on the Atlantic coast; and *Starkey*, an operation by forces on the southeast English coast against the Pas-de-Calais.

operations by commandos and possibly by airborne forces will be undertaken to neutralise certain coast defences."[15] These early plans assumed that two Ranger battalions would be assigned to *Overlord*.[16] At this stage, precise details of the landing beaches had not been selected, beyond the recommendation that the landings take place in Lower Normandy in the Caen area.

A more refined plan emerged later in 1943. The COSSAC *Overlord* plan envisioned an initial attack by three divisions against three beach sectors. This operation was smaller than Operation *Husky* in Sicily, but was forced on COSSAC by the limited size of the available amphibious landing fleet. However, the COSSAC staff felt that a larger landing was preferable. On New Year's Eve, Gen Bernard Montgomery was first shown the plan. Montgomery had been appointed as the land commander for *Overlord*, heading the 21st Army Group. He immediately recognized that the COSSAC plan was too feeble and that a bolder scheme was needed. During the first two weeks of January, he and his staff drafted a more ambitious plan that involved five divisional landings: two British, one Canadian, and two American.

In December 1943, Gen Eisenhower, fresh from his success in North Africa and Sicily, had been appointed to lead the Supreme Headquarters Allied Expeditionary Force (SHAEF), a joint command that included not only the land elements of *Overlord*, but also the air and naval commands. Eisenhower returned to Britain in mid-January 1944, where he met with Montgomery to discuss his revised plan. "Ike," as he was known, immediately saw the merits of Montgomery's modifications, and this became the basis for the "Neptune Initial Plan" that was presented to the Combined Chiefs of Staff on January 23. There was a broad consensus that a larger force would be needed, even if it required naval resources to be obtained from other theaters.

The revised plan had important consequences regarding Pointe-du-Hoc. There is widespread misunderstanding about the threat posed by the Pointe-du-Hoc battery. Many historical accounts assume that it was feared because it could bombard the landing beaches, yet this was only a small part of the reason for the anxiety over the Pointe-du-Hoc battery. Under the revised *Overlord* plan, the First US Army was now expected to land on two beach sectors: Utah to the west of the river Vire and Omaha to the east. Pointe-du-Hoc sat between these beaches, and its guns could reach the "Transport Areas" on the approaches to both. The Transport Areas were the zones where the Allied navies would conduct the transfer of troops and equipment from the larger transport ships to the smaller landing craft. A large concentration of transport ships and hundreds of small landing craft, milling about for several hours, would be a lucrative target for German coastal artillery. The neutralization of the Pointe-du-Hoc battery thus became the number one target for the US Army and US Navy.

THE GRAHAM REPORT

Although the early drafts of Operation *Overlord* assumed that a significant amount of aerial and naval fire support would be required for the Normandy landings, precise requirements were difficult to foresee. The German Atlantic Wall defenses were estimated to contain about 1,950 coastal guns over 75mm in caliber. The density of these gun batteries varied from a high of about 4.1 guns per mile in the Dunkirk–Somme area of the Pas-de-Calais to only about 0.7 guns per mile in Lower Normandy from Caen to Cherbourg, the future *Neptune* landing areas.[17] Even though the Normandy area did not have a particularly heavy concentration of guns, they were nonetheless sufficient to wreak havoc on Allied transport ships in the opening phase of Operation *Neptune*.

In August 1943, the Joint Technical Warfare Committee of the British War Cabinet set up the Fire Support of Seaborne Landings Sub-committee "to consider all existing means of providing fire support when landing forces on a heavily defended coast and to make recommendations, as a matter of urgency, for improving the degree of support." The sub-committee was chaired by Air Vice-Marshal Ronald Graham, and its key report is usually called the Graham Report. Graham was the Chief of Staff (Air) of the

Combined Operations Headquarters, and so particularly suited to examine combined arms requirements.

The sub-committee began by examining previous experiences in amphibious operations in the Mediterranean. Special attention was paid to Operation *Corkscrew* on Pantelleria, since Zuckerman's reports contained a great deal of quantitative data about the amount of bombs or naval gunfire required to destroy or suppress enemy coastal batteries.

The Graham Report, released on January 7, 1944, concluded that naval gunfire might cause significant damage to German coastal gun batteries, but would be more likely to temporarily neutralize the batteries rather than destroy them. In contrast, the study concluded that heavy aerial bombardment had a greater probability of destroying rather than just neutralizing the batteries. The Graham Report formed the basis for the subsequent Operation *Neptune* Joint Fire Plan.[18]

The report was careful to distinguish attacks on open gun pits versus guns in concrete casemates. Although the open gun pits were vulnerable to air and naval bombardment, the casemated guns were not. The report concluded that German gun casemates were impervious to typical 500lb or 1,000lb bombs. Likewise, naval guns were largely ineffective in engaging the casemate guns, except for 15in. battleship guns. Nevertheless, even if the guns could not be destroyed, engagement of casemated guns could be effective due to the secondary effects identified during Operation *Corkscrew* such as disruption of the battery communication, fire controls, and ammunition supplies.

The Graham Report concluded that air attacks which achieved a 12.5 percent chance of a hit on each gun pit could be expected to render the batteries ineffective for the coordinated fire that would be necessary for long-range engagement against Allied ships. This effect was achieved by direct hits on the guns, near misses on guns and emplacements that could not be repaired in time, destruction of fire-control posts, and destruction of communications between the gun batteries and fire-control posts. The Graham Report offered specific recommendations regarding the amount of firepower needed to achieve these results, based on past experiences such as Operation *Corkscrew*. For example, the report suggested that a typical coastal gun battery in open pits could be successfully neutralized by a daytime visual attack dropping 188 tons of bombs.[19]

In the case of naval gunfire, the Graham Report suggested that a battery could be temporarily neutralized by hitting the battery area for 10–15 minutes with a density of a half-pound of 6in. naval projectile per square yard per minute; roughly one 6in. projectile per 2,000 square yards per minute.

The Graham Report represented the culmination of Allied doctrinal thinking about fire support for amphibious operations in the Mediterranean and European theaters. Although the sub-committee did study US Navy gunfire support in the Pacific, this was of limited relevance in Europe. In the Pacific theater, the typical operation involved amphibious landings on heavily defended islands that could be isolated days or weeks beforehand. Under these circumstances, the fire-support plan often involved days of bombardment aimed at destroying key gun batteries rather than temporarily neutralizing them. In the European theater, such prolonged bombardments were not possible. Allied amphibious operations were invariably dependent on surprise to minimize the ability of the Germans to counterattack the beachhead. In consequence, pre-invasion bombardments had to be relatively brief to minimize the German identification of the intended landing zone. In the case of Operation *Overlord*, the principal objective was to temporarily suppress the German coastal gun batteries during the vulnerable landing phase.

The European planning assumed that the only way to permanently eliminate the German coastal gun batteries was to physically occupy them with ground troops. High-priority gun batteries could be eliminated in the opening phase of the landing operation using Commando/Ranger forces, as was demonstrated at Dieppe and in Operation *Torch*. However, there was a limit on the number of special operations that could be accomplished during

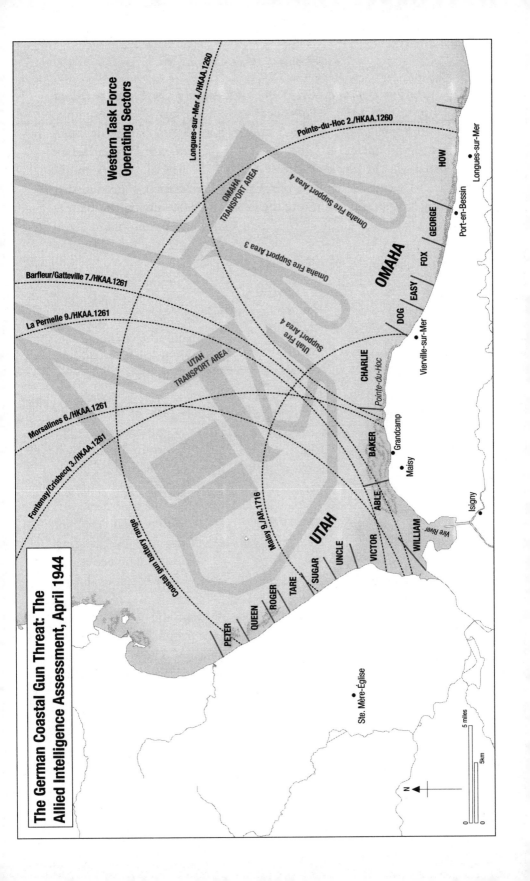

The German Coastal Gun Threat: The Allied Intelligence Assessment, April 1944

Operation *Neptune* due to the large number of German coastal batteries along the *Neptune* beaches.

Ultimately, only two high-priority gun batteries were earmarked for special operations missions during *Neptune*: the Pointe-du-Hoc battery in the Omaha/Utah sector and the Merville battery in the Sword sector. Otherwise, the *Neptune* fire-support plans aimed to only temporarily neutralize the German coastal gun batteries.

Chapter 3

"Hard Men for Dirty Work"

The mission of capturing Pointe-du-Hoc was assigned to two US Army Ranger battalions. The origins of the US Army Rangers in World War II can be directly traced back to the British Commandos. When the British Army was forced off the European mainland in 1940 following the defeat of France, Winston Churchill fostered the growth of a special operations force that could conduct small-scale raids along the coast of occupied Europe.

The role of the Commandos was twofold. One of their most important functions was to bolster British morale during the grim days of 1940–41 when Britain fought alone in Europe against the Nazi foe. Commando raids offered satisfying little victories that provided some solace to the embattled British public. Allies joined Britain in the struggle in 1941; the Soviet Union in June and the United States in December. Commando raids remained an important aspect of British military actions through 1942 and 1943 until larger campaigns in Europe were possible.

A second reason for the Commandos was the need to create versatile combined-arms tactics. The Commando operations invariably involved the support of the Royal Navy and the Royal Air Force, which was evident in the name of the Commando directorate: the Combined Operations Headquarters (COHQ).

The Commandos were ultimately a manifestation of Britain's traditional "peripheral strategy." Since Britain was primarily a maritime power, it depended on relatively small-scale land actions. Once Britain became allied to a continental power with a significant army, a major land campaign could commence.

The British Commandos staged a number of raids along the coastline of Nazi-occupied Europe in 1941 and 1942, as has been discussed previously. These received international press attention. In the United States, Gen George C. Marshall, the US Army's Chief of Staff, read such reports with considerable interest. The US Army had no such capabilities at the time, but he was convinced that an American Commando force was needed.

On a visit to London to meet senior British leaders in April 1942, Marshall met with Lord Louis Mountbatten, the leader of the Commandos. Mountbatten, a great-grandson of Queen Victoria and son of the Royal Navy's First Sea Lord at the start of World War I, served in the Royal Navy in the Great War. During the early years of World War II, he had three ships sunk beneath him. His naval exploits while in command of the HMS *Kelly* off Crete in 1941 were recounted in a thinly disguised manner in the popular film *In Which We Serve*, released in September 1942, starring Noël Coward. Churchill was a close friend and encouraged Mountbatten's appointment to COHQ in early 1942.

Marshall complimented Mountbatten on the Commandos' recent successes. He enquired whether Mountbatten would permit an American liaison team to visit COHQ, saying their aim was to learn about the British organization as the US Army wished to create its own Commando force in the future. Mountbatten enthusiastically supported the idea. Marshall was concerned that the US Army had no officers with any experience of fighting the Germans. Participation in Commando raids could thus help create a cadre of experienced officers who would be able to impart their knowledge throughout the US Army.[1] Furthermore, the Commandos epitomized a combined-service approach, fostering joint operations. This was an approach that Marshall recognized as essential to future amphibious operations in Europe. At the conclusion of his trip to Britain, Marshall visited the Commando Depot at Achnacarry in Scotland and left suitably impressed.

Marshall kept a "little black book" listing officers of special merit for future promotion. Several of the officers accompanying Marshall on his London visit had recommended 47-year-old Col Lucian Truscott for the Combined Operations posting. In April 1942, Truscott was ordered to report to Gen Mark Clark at the Army War College in Washington DC. Clark would later lead the US Army's campaigns in Italy.

Clark informed Truscott that he had been selected to lead an American team that would be assigned to Combined Operations. He was to report to Dwight Eisenhower at the Pentagon. At the time, Eisenhower was a relatively obscure planning officer, temporarily promoted to major general, and assistant chief of staff for War Plans. Combined Operations was clearly not a minor assignment, being seen by senior American commanders as a critical link in the growing British–American alliance.

Upon reporting to Eisenhower, Truscott learned why he had been chosen. Eisenhower told him, "I consider that your background as a cavalry officer, your experience with the Armored Force, your experience as an instructor at Fort Leavenworth, your experience at corps staff, and even your experience as a polo player especially fit you for this assignment... Did you know that Lord Louis [Mountbatten] wrote a book on polo?"[2]

Marshall and Eisenhower recognized that this posting was as much diplomatic as military. It required an exceptionally astute officer able to cooperate with the British and to serve as an early link between the British armed forces and the US Army.

Truscott was subsequently ushered into Marshall's inner sanctum for a personal briefing. It was not a typical "meet-and-greet." Marshall had prepared a daunting array of documents for Truscott to study, including plans for a future Anglo-American invasion of Europe. He also received extensive briefings on major British military personalities, differences between US and British military organizations, and likely problems that might arise in discussing future US–British operations. Truscott later wrote, "This interview made an everlasting impression upon me. General Marshall had removed any confusion in my mind as to what was expected of me. For the rest, it was up to me."[3]

After the meeting, Eisenhower suggested to Truscott that he pick a distinctly American name for the new American commando force: "I hope you will find some name other than 'Commandos.' The glamour of that name will always remain British."[4]

On April 30, now elevated to brigadier general, Truscott was formally directed to head a small liaison group to cooperate with Combined Operations in order to "study the planning, organization, preparation and conduct of Combined Operations, especially those of the Commando type, and to keep the Commanding Officer, War Department informed as to developments in the training techniques and equipment pertaining to these and related operations."[5]

Arriving in London on May 17, 1942, Truscott's team set up its office within COHQ on Richmond Terrace, Whitehall, at the very heart of the British government. Truscott was warmly greeted by Mountbatten and his staff, and the American team quickly set about work on learning about the Commando force before creating an American counterpart.

In response to Eisenhower's admonition to adopt an American name for the US Army commandos, Truscott decided to call them "Rangers." Rangers emerged in America in 1675 during King Philip's War in New England.[6] The early skirmishes between Metacomet's Wampanoag Indians and English settlers demonstrated that the Plymouth colony was unable to match the tactics of the Native Americans. Benjamin Church raised a force of about 200 men, including both Englishmen and Native Americans from tribes hostile to the Wampanoags. Church's force of "Rangers" used Native American tactics to defeat the Wampanoags and their allies. Although Church's Rangers fell into obscurity, they were the inspiration for the more famous Rogers' Rangers of the French and Indian War (1754–63). Truscott was probably inspired to use the Ranger name by the recent popular Hollywood film about Rogers' Rangers, *Northwest Passage*, starring Spencer Tracy and Robert Young, released in 1940. Mountbatten later claimed that he had come up with the idea, but whatever the case, it became a popular choice.[7]

The role of the Rangers was still under debate. On the one hand, Marshall envisioned the Ranger training as a means to create a seed of highly trained infantrymen who could then return to their home unit and spread their training and experiences. On the other hand, there was also an urge to create elite units that could carry out daring raids, closely modeled on the exploits of Britain's Commandos.[8] In 1942 and 1943, both approaches co-existed in a variety of Ranger units and Ranger training courses.

Truscott sent a cable to Washington on May 26, 1942, proposing to form the first Ranger unit in Britain. With Marshall's strong backing, the War Department agreed on May 28, and the 1st Ranger Battalion was duly raised in the United Kingdom in early June that year. At the time, the only major US units in Britain were the 34th Infantry Division and the 1st Armored Division. Truscott turned to the commander of the 34th Division, Maj Gen Russell Hartle, for suggestions for a possible Ranger commander. Hartle recommended one of his staff, Capt William O. Darby, who was formally appointed to head the 1st Ranger Battalion on June 8. Darby would prove to be an ideal choice; he was enthusiastic and charismatic, he got along well with superior officers, and he was idolized by his men. The initial Ranger force in the Mediterranean theater would be forever known as "Darby's Rangers."

Rangers were volunteers. Darby wanted men who were resourceful, independent-minded, courageous, and physically tough. The volunteers went through a screening process at the original battalion base in Northern Ireland, where officers questioned the men about their backgrounds, their proficiency in sports, and their willingness to use a knife in combat. This was not a job for the faint-hearted. Physical stamina was essential. From the outset, the Rangers placed an emphasis on endurance and determination in the face of adversity rather than sheer physical strength.

The first Ranger mission was the ill-fated Operation *Jubilee* raid on Dieppe in August 1942.[9] Fifty Rangers from Darby's 1st Ranger

Battalion were selected to participate as a means to gain seasoning in actual Commando operations. The Rangers were broken up into small groups and spread between No. 3 and No. 4 Commandos attacking the coastal gun batteries, and the Canadians attacking the main port. The Commando raids on coastal guns located on cliffs presaged the Pointe-du-Hoc mission two years later. The Commandos, with a small number of accompanying Rangers, were landed in the dark at the foot of the cliffs and had to scale the cliffs to reach their objective.

Of the fifty Rangers assigned to the Dieppe operation, most never made it to the shore. Of the roughly twenty who did, three were killed, three taken prisoner, and five wounded. This was the first combat action by US Army ground forces in Europe in World War II. The public reaction in the United States was wildly out of proportion to the miniscule American role in the operation, the American press making the minor Ranger role seem to be the highlight of the operation. Returning Rangers were interviewed for national radio programs; newspapers and magazines glorified "Truscott's Rangers."

The first combat mission for the entire 1st Ranger Battalion took place three months later during Operation *Torch*, the amphibious landings in French North Africa in November 1942. The mission, once again, was to eliminate coastal batteries and fortifications threatening the main amphibious landings. It was considerably more successful than Dieppe, and was explained in detail in Chapter 2. The 1st Ranger Battalion remained in action through the Tunisian campaign, winning a Presidential Unit Citation for their spirited performance at El Guettar in March 1943. This was the first major American victory in Tunisia, under the inspired leadership of a new commander, Gen George S. Patton Jr.

The success of Darby's Rangers led to the formation of two more Ranger battalions in the Mediterranean theater, the 3rd and 4th Ranger Battalions. These three battalions were later combined under Darby's command as the 6615th Ranger Force and were used in subsequent amphibious operations in the Mediterranean, including Operation *Husky* in Sicily in July 1943, Operation *Avalanche* at Salerno in September 1943, and Operation *Shingle* at Anzio in January 1944.[10]

29TH RANGER BATTALION (PROVISIONAL)

When the 1st Ranger Battalion was assigned to Operation *Torch*, the ETOUSA (European Theater of Operations, United States Army) headquarters in London realized that it would lack a force to participate with the Commandos in cross-Channel raids. As a short-term solution, the headquarters decided to create a provisional unit. In September 1942, the ETOUSA instructed the newly arrived 29th Division – a National Guard Division from the Maryland and Virginia region – to create a provisional Ranger force within the division. They would have a close connection with the Rangers on D-Day.

The provisional Ranger unit started as a cadre of three officers and fifteen enlisted men from Darby's 1st Ranger Battalion, combined with volunteers from the 29th Division.[11] This was unofficially called the 2nd Rangers, but the name changed after the official 2nd Ranger Battalion was formally created in the United States. On December 20, 1942, the Ranger unit in the 29th Division was re-designated as the 29th Ranger Battalion (Provisional) and put under the command of Maj Randolph Millholland. From the outset, the 29th Rangers were envisioned more as a training unit than a dedicated raiding force. The original ETOUSA direction described the battalion as "a training unit for a maximum number of officers and enlisted men of combat units to receive training and experience in actual combat after which they will return to their units."[12]

This battalion was trained within the divisional garrison near Tidworth in Wiltshire, southern England, until February 1943, when it moved to the Commando Depot at Achnacarry House in Spean Bridge in Scotland for a special five-week Commando course. After a period of leave, the battalion was attached to No. 4 Commando for further training as well as participation in Operation *Seaweed*, a series of simulated commando raids along the British coast. A small number of Rangers were also sent on three small Commando raids along the Norwegian coast.

Training intensified in the summer of 1943. On the night of September 3/4, troops of the 29th Rangers took part in Operation *Pound*. This raid was staged against German installations on the Île d'Ouessant, a rocky island off the tip of Brittany in western France. The Kriegsmarine's 3.Fu.M.Abt. (3rd Naval Radar Battalion) operated a FuMO.2 Calais-B maritime surveillance radar on the Pointe-du-Stiff outcropping. In this location, it could track British shipping exiting the English Channel and entering the Bay of Biscay. While the radar could have been bombed, Operation *Pound* had broader objectives. The plan was to destroy the German coastal radar station, possibly capturing German radar operators in the process, much like the earlier Bruneval raid. The planners also instructed the raiders to leave behind some US Army equipment to lend credence to the Operation *Wadham* deception operation. *Wadham* was part of the broader Operation *Bodyguard* deception plan, which was intended to convince the Germans that US Army units stationed in southwestern England were intended to land in Brittany.

The raiding force consisted of the British No. 12 Commando and twenty-nine men of the 29th Ranger Battalion led by Lt Eugene Dance. The force left Falmouth in Cornwall in dories* under the cover of darkness. After cutting through barbed wire barriers near the island's coast in the dark, the demolition team of the 29th Rangers blew up one of the radar's control huts and knocked down a radar mast. A firefight ensued with the German garrison, and in consequence, no German prisoners were taken. The Rangers deliberately left behind a US helmet and pistol belt as a token that the Americans had been there. The helmet was marked as that of the battalion commander, Maj Randy Millholland.

A one-hundred-man raid against German coastal gun positions on the Pas-de-Calais was planned for later in the autumn, staged

* A dory is a small, flat-bottomed fishing boat with a shallow draft, generally some 16–23ft in length.

from Dover. A dry run was made to within 6 miles of the French coast, but the actual raid never took place. At least one account suggests that one of these runs was an actual mission, but was called off due to the weather.[13] This was the swansong of the 29th Rangers.

On October 15, 1943, ETOUSA ordered that the battalion be disbanded and its men returned to their original regiments. The decision to disband the 29th Ranger Battalion was greeted with considerable anger within the 29th Division in view of the substantial effort and training put into the unit. The 29th Division felt that their extensive efforts would be wasted by deactivating the unit, and they released a staff study in the hopes that the issue would be reconsidered.

The issue of its de-activation had actually been under discussion since the late summer of 1943 for several reasons.[14] The head of Army Ground Forces,* Lt Gen Lesley McNair, was not keen on "private armies" and specialized units. He favored the "big battalions": standardized, mass-produced units for war in the industrial age. Although he acquiesced to a small number of elite infantry and paratrooper units, he limited their number. In his view, these types of units tended to sit idle waiting for specialized missions, or dreamed up missions tailored to their unique role. McNair felt they also attracted a disproportionate share of the most highly motivated young soldiers, at the expense of regular infantry units.[15]

At the time, there was no scientific data that measured the combat effectiveness of individual infantrymen, but there was certainly some intuitive sense that a "heroic minority" made a disproportionate contribution to an infantry unit in battle. One British officer in 1943 remarked that "a platoon is not made up of 30-odd fearless heroes, but of about a half dozen really good men,

---

*The Army Ground Forces was one of three principal branches of the US Army in World War II, responsible for organizing, training, and deploying Army ground units. Army Service Forces (ASF) was responsible for equipping and supplying the Army, and managing Army war production. The Army Air Forces (AAF), as their name implies, was the quasi-independent branch that became the US Air Force in 1947.

fifteen or so 'sheep' and the remainder would often as not 'lie dogo'*
or even retire but for the effort of junior officers and NCOs."[16]
McNair was concerned that elite Ranger and paratrooper units
siphoned off the heroic minority, leaving regular infantry units
with the sheep and the dregs. McNair wanted to keep the heroic
minority in the regular infantry units, and if possible, increase the
percentage of "really good" men through Ranger-style training.

By the summer of 1943, two dedicated Ranger battalions were
in formation in the United States and earmarked for Europe, as
is described in more detail below. In addition, the 99th Separate
Battalion (Norwegian) was scheduled to receive Ranger training
with the intention of deploying it on raids along the Norwegian
coast. This battalion had been formed from Norwegian-American
volunteers.† The 1943 Army Troop Basis authorized only five
Ranger battalions, with three earmarked for the Mediterranean
(Darby's Rangers) and two more for the European Theater of
Operations (ETO).[17] The two for the ETO were scheduled to
arrive in the UK in October and December 1943. It was as a result
of this cap on Ranger units that the 29th Ranger Battalion was
ordered to be disbanded.

Millholland went on to lead the 3rd Battalion, 115th Infantry,
29th Division during the campaign in Europe.‡ Most of these
erstwhile Rangers would land with the 29th Division on Omaha
Beach on D-Day, though not in a dedicated Ranger unit. Ironically,

---

* Slang term for lying low or in concealment.
† The 99th Battalion was one of five "ethnic" battalions formed in the US Army in 1942
to take advantage of the language skills of recent immigrants. They included a Filipino,
a Japanese, an Austrian, and a Greek battalion. The Austrian battalion was never actually
formed, and nor was a proposed Polish battalion. In the event, the 99th Battalion was
never used as intended and served as a separate infantry battalion in the ETO. The Office
of Strategic Services (OSS) selected eighty enlisted men and twelve officers from the
battalion for the OSS Norwegian Special Operations Group (NORSOG). NORSOG was
used in operations behind German lines in France. In early 1945, NORSOG operated
in Norway on railway sabotage missions called Operation *Lapwing/Grouse*. The battalion
was never formally designated as a Ranger battalion.
‡ The Maryland National Guard armory in Hagerstown, Maryland, is named in honor of
Randy Millholland.

the bulk of the D-Day Ranger force would serve alongside the 29th Division on Omaha Beach, as we shall see.

THE ROOTS OF THE 2ND RANGER BATTALION

In the summer of 1942, the Second US Army established a Ranger School at Camp Forrest in Tennessee. This program was entirely separate from the Ranger units being formed in Britain, and was the initiative of the Second Army commander, Lt Gen Ben Lear. In the autumn of 1941, Lear's Second US Army had served as the "Red Army" against Lt Gen Walter Krueger's Third US Army ("Blue Army") in the Louisiana maneuvers. Lear, who was disgusted by the poor physical stamina of the infantry in his formations, explained the aim of the Ranger School: "We are here to toughen men for dirty work."[18] The divisions of the Second US Army were instructed to send their most intelligent and physically fit junior officers and NCOs to the Ranger School "to train instructors in rough-and-tumble fighting tactics and in special techniques." Lear's intention was to train a cadre of the best infantrymen, who could then take those skills back to their original unit.

The new recruits were outfitted in US Marine Corps camouflage fatigue uniforms to set them apart from the regular Army troops. Lt Col William C. Saffarans was selected to lead the Ranger training course by Lear due to his background in rifle sporting competitions before the war.* He used Marine Corps close-combat training methods to improve the "alertness, smartness, aggressiveness, and esprit" of the new Rangers. The code of "Rangerism" was to be "tougher and nastier than the enemy." Saffarans created an innovative mock German village, dubbed "Naziville," for realistic close-quarter exercises. On January 23, 1943, the first class of Rangers put on an "art of killing" demonstration for Lt Gen McNair and a select group of senior Army and civilian officials.

---

* Saffarans had been part of the 1923 Georgetown University Intercollegiate Champion of Rifle Clubs, sponsored by the National Rifle Association.

A second class of 600 officers and NCOs rotated through the Second Army Ranger School in February 1943.

In December 1942, Maj Gen James E. Chaney, the ETOUSA commander, sent a message to the War Department in Washington, formally requesting the formation of a permanent 2nd Ranger Battalion for eventual dispatch to the United Kingdom. There was resistance to this request in Washington DC, especially, unsurprisingly, from Lt Gen McNair,[19] who had little patience for private armies and specialized boutique formations. As mentioned earlier, he was having a hard time getting adequate numbers of qualified personnel for the infantry since the more technical services, such as the Army Air Forces, were siphoning off many of the best men. He did not want to divert the best infantrymen into special "super-killer" units, but wanted improved training for the infantry as a whole. McNair favored Ranger training within the infantry divisions, not the formation of separate Ranger battalions.

Regardless of McNair's viewpoint, the Ranger concept had Gen Marshall's strong backing, and the ETOUSA request was approved. Planning for the 2nd Ranger Battalion began in February 1943, and was formally approved by Marshall on April 1 that year. Camp Forrest in Tennessee was assigned as its initial base due to Lear's innovative work there on Ranger training. As a result, the second class at the Camp Forrest Ranger School was its last; the base was now assigned the task of raising the new battalion.* Lt Col Saffarans was selected as the first commander of the 2nd Ranger Battalion. In view of his age and rank, it was expected he would eventually be replaced by a younger and more junior officer.

A battalion history explained the unit's identity:

> The whole idea behind this Ranger Battalion was to get a unit capable of enduring prolonged hardship, creating havoc amongst the enemy where he least expected trouble, and generally

---

*Other bases set up their own "Ranger" programs intended to improve the training.

speaking, to be twice as good and efficient as the men in the best army in the world. Each man was specially trained for his own specific job and at the same time, he had sufficient knowledge of all jobs in the battalion to take that job over and perform it efficiently in any case of emergency. Being all volunteers and eager for combat, these men expected to perform the most hazardous of missions.[20]

A call went out to the divisions of the Second US Army soliciting volunteers for the new unit. Some divisions viewed this as a good way to get rid of malcontents and troublemakers, and "volunteered" them for Ranger duty. The new battalion had a strict vetting process, starting with interviews to discover the motivations of the volunteers. Troublemakers dumped by their parent divisions were sent back without even going on the physical exams. The physical requirements were similar to those used in paratroop units; the battalion was looking for young soldiers with initiative and stamina. The physical winnowing process began with forced marches: 3 miles in 37 minutes; 5 miles in an hour; 9 miles in two hours. Volunteers who could not survive the physical challenges were washed out.

As expected, Saffarans was soon posted to a new training position in the Pacific, leaving the battalion without a leader. A succession of officers came and went as temporary commanders until replaced by an over-age National Guard officer, Maj Lionel McDonald. In the meantime, Gen Lear had been temporarily assigned to command Army Ground Forces after McNair had been wounded during a tour of the front in North Africa. Lear was replaced as Second Army commander by Lt Gen Lloyd Fredendall, who had recently been relieved of command in North Africa after the Kasserine Pass defeat in October 1943.

Fredendall had noted the exceptional performance of Darby's Rangers in North Africa and took personal interest in the new Ranger battalion. They had been issued tattered, hand-me-down uniforms, and the battalion was living in tents in muddy fields without proper sanitation. Some of the initial commanding officers had the idea that painfully spartan conditions were a principle to harden men for elite infantry units. Clearly, the battalion lacked suitable leadership. Fredendall's visits to Camp Forrest suggested that training and organization were a mess: "a rag-tag, orphan mob in want of military bearing and discipline."

One outcome of Lear's advocacy of "Rangerism" had been the establishment of special Ranger training companies in all of the infantry divisions in Second Army. While touring the 83rd Division at Camp Atterbury, Indiana, Fredendall had come in contact with Maj James Earl Rudder, who was supervising Ranger training in the division. The 83rd Division's Ranger program was the best he had encountered, and on June 18, 1943, he contacted the division and instructed them to transfer Rudder to Camp Forrest to lead the 2nd Ranger Battalion. Maj. Rudder assumed command on July 2.

EARL RUDDER

Much as was the case with Darby and the 1st Ranger Battalion, Rudder would become the heart of the 2nd Ranger Battalion. Behind his back, the Rangers called him "Big Jim"; family and friends called him by his middle name, Earl. He had grown up on a hardscrabble farm in Eden, West Texas. Another resident of the town, Ira Eaker, would go on to be a senior Army Air Forces commander during the war.* Rudder began to make his mark in the local community as a star high school football player. In the summer of 1927, a coach from John Tarleton Agricultural College visited Eden while recruiting for the college football team. Rudder was a mediocre student, but an avid football player, and took up the offer in spite of his family's poverty.[21] There's a popular expression in the state that "football is religion in Texas," and it was usually the center of community activity.

As was common at the time, the college required Rudder's participation in the Reserve Officer Training Corps (ROTC).

---

* General Ira Clarence Eaker was commander of the US Eighth Air Force from December 1942 and then deputy commander of US Army Air Forces by the end of the war.

Rudder did well in a course on athletic coaching and also showed an affinity for the mandatory ROTC military courses. He became team captain in his junior year of college. In 1930, he transferred to Texas A&M in College Station, Texas, eventually becoming a regimental staff officer in the Corps of Cadets and a star of the football team. He received his college degree in May 1932, and was commissioned a second lieutenant in the Army Reserve. With the advent of the Great Depression, jobs were scarce, but Rudder managed to win a high school coaching position in Brady, Texas, near his home town. Rudder married in June 1937, and the family prospered due to an inheritance of farmland from his wife's family. In August 1938, he was selected as the new football coach at his alma mater, Tarleton College.

With war brewing, the US Congress approved a call-up of the Organized Reserves, and Earl Rudder went on active Army duty on June 18, 1941, as a 1st lieutenant in the infantry. He was sent for further training to the Army's infantry school at Fort Benning for instruction on the new infantry weapons, including the M1 Garand rifle and BAR Browning automatic rifle. He was assigned to the 83rd Division at Camp Atterbury in May 1942.

Thirty-three years old when appointed to lead the 2nd Ranger Battalion, Rudder was a decade older than most of the men of his unit. He was given clear instructions from senior commanders: the Rangers were an elite unit. Any soldier who could not endure the physical and mental demands of the Rangers should be removed; plenty of replacement volunteers were willing and able to join the unit. Rudder's injunction to his men was simple: "First, I'm going to make men out of you. Then I'm going to make soldiers out of you. And then, I'm going to make Rangers out of you."

In contrast to previous commanders who rode in jeeps during Ranger field exercises, Rudder took part in the exercises himself. He had the physical build of a football center, being well over 6ft tall and weighing 235lb. Members of Darby's Rangers visited Camp Forrest and recommended speed marches as the heart of the physical training. Physical training of young men was Rudder's profession. He had been coaching championship football teams for over a decade, which consisted not only of physical conditioning, but instilling the competitiveness vital to victory.

Rudder was appalled by the wretched living conditions created by the previous Ranger commanders. The training regime was tough enough without resorting to tents in the Tennessee mud. Consequently, regular army barracks were erected. Wretched food prepared by untrained cooks using poorly washed utensils led to widespread dysentery; sickly troops could never become Rangers. Rudder thus insisted on proper cooking and hygienic practices. While he did not pamper his men, Rudder made certain that they could concentrate on the essentials of elite military training.

SPEARHEAD BATTALION

Were the 2nd Rangers a specialized raiding force or simply a way to improve the infantry? Although McNair and the Army Ground Forces favored the latter option, ETOUSA in London viewed them as a spearhead formation, especially for forthcoming amphibious operations. In some respects, this was an outcome of the decision early in the war to confine the US Marine Corps to the Pacific theater. Lacking specialized amphibious landing forces, ETOUSA saw the Rangers as one way to help fill that gap. The successful use of Darby's Rangers to spearhead amphibious operations in the Mediterranean theater reinforced this viewpoint.

As a result, the 2nd Ranger Battalion underwent specialized amphibious training as soon as their basic training was completed at Camp Forrest. In early September 1943, the 2nd Ranger Battalion was sent to Fort Pierce on the Florida coast. This Navy base was home of the joint-services Amphibious Scout and Raider School. The training included the use of inflatable rubber boats for amphibious missions as well as other specialized skills. The Rangers had been warned, half in jest, of the sharks and barracudas in the Florida waters, but they soon found that the main threat during seaborne exercises were the abundant stinging jellyfish. At Fort Pierce, the Rangers were introduced to the standard landing craft of the British Commandos, the LCA (Landing Craft Assault), that they would use nine months later on D-Day.

The culmination of the Fort Pierce training was a mock raid on the town of Fort Pierce against an opposing defense force of sailors and local police. The defenders were given advance warning of the time of the raid. The Rangers approached their objective unseen, using the cover offered by a barrier island. Upon reaching the island, they dragged their boats behind them, re-entered the water, and came ashore where least expected. They thus captured their objectives by surprise. The Navy commander of the school dubbed the Rangers the best trainees he had yet seen at the school.

Rudder rewarded his unit with a pass to visit the local town. A night of boozing and brawling ensued, including scuffles with the Navy's Shore Patrol. The US Navy was not amused. Rudder intervened and carried out discipline internally: several men were transferred out of the battalion, a few were court-martialed, others were broken in rank, and the rest were confined to quarters for the remainder of the battalion's stay in Fort Pierce. Rudder was not pleased with the brawling, but he had dealt with boisterous young men for all of his career and knew what to expect.

The successful completion of amphibious training at Fort Pierce led to the Rangers' transfer to Fort Dix, New Jersey, for advanced tactical training. When the 2nd Ranger Battalion left Camp Forrest, the newly formed 5th Ranger Battalion took their place there to start their training cycle. One of the key additions to the 2nd Ranger Battalion during their stay at Fort Dix was Capt Walter Block, a pediatrician from Chicago, who was assigned as the battalion medical officer. He was nearly two decades older than most of the troops, but fitted in comfortably with the rough-and-tumble of Ranger training. Dr Block became a popular fixture in the battalion. The troops turned to him daily for treatment of the numerous injuries and illnesses endured during training, and he became an amiable father figure for the young soldiers.

In early November 1943, the 2nd Ranger Battalion began staging forward, closer to the port of New York, for their eventual transfer to Britain. On November 11, they were transferred by train from Camp Shanks, New York, to the Hudson River docks in Manhattan, embarking on the Cunard Line's SS *Queen Elizabeth*. The once-elegant liner had been converted into a drab troopship. During the Atlantic voyage to Britain, the Rangers were employed as improvised military police to keep discipline among the 15,000 US Army troops aboard the liner.

As the 2nd Ranger Battalion made its way to Britain, the "Big Three" – Churchill, Roosevelt, and Soviet leader Joseph Stalin – were meeting at Tehran to make final strategic plans for 1944. On December 2, 1943, Dwight Eisenhower was formally selected to head SHAEF, Supreme Headquarters Allied Expeditionary Force, to command Operation *Overlord*. With a commander now in place, the final planning for the invasion accelerated. D-Day was tentatively scheduled for May 1, 1944.

The "Lizzie" docked in the river Clyde on the Scottish coast on December 1. Greeting them in Scotland was Maj Max Schneider, a battle-hardened company commander in Darby's Rangers who had taken part in the Algerian, Sicilian, and Salerno operations. He had been invalided out in late September 1943 after being injured by artillery near Salerno, suffering from concussion and hearing loss from the explosion. Exacerbating his recent injuries, he had a silver plate on his skull to repair injury from an airplane crash in 1933, and this was loosened by the blast.[22] Although Schneider was eligible to return Stateside due to his injuries, the need for experienced Ranger officers led to his appointment to the 2nd Ranger Battalion on November 11 while the unit was still in the United States.

After a short stop in the Scottish town of Greenock, the battalion was transferred by train to the village of Bude on the Cornish coast in the southwest of England, traveling across virtually the entire length of Britain from their landfall in Scotland. There was no military camp in Bude, so the troops were billeted in civilian homes. Exercises usually took place on the town's beaches or on the local golf course. The Rangers developed a fond attachment to the Cornish village, which was a total contrast to some of the rough camps where they had been billeted in the United States. The Rangers returned the kindnesses of the villagers by staging a Christmas party for the local children. At this time, Britain was on strict wartime rationing, but the Rangers were generously supplied with an assortment of candies and treats in their Army rations, which they hoarded for the party. There would be an enduring link between the 2nd Rangers and their adopted home of Bude. A Ranger later recalled that "England was good to us, especially Bude."[23]

THE MISSION

In early 1944, the battalion was transferred to England's south coast. With the battalion safely ensconced at their new camp at Sandown on the Isle of Wight, Rudder's first task was to make connection with his superior headquarters. The 2nd Ranger Battalion was subordinate to Lt Gen Omar Bradley's First US Army, and had been assigned directly to Maj Gen Leonard Gerow's V Corps. Rudder and Schneider traveled to Bradley's headquarters in London on January 4, a month after the battalion had reached Britain, to be briefed about their assignment.[24] This was the first time that any Ranger was informed of the D-Day mission to destroy a cliff-top German coastal gun battery.

Shortly after the London trip, Rudder submitted a request to Bradley's headquarters for Schneider's transfer back to the United States for medical reasons. There is a fine line between battle-hardened and battle-exhausted, and Rudder had come to realize that Schneider was suffering physical and mental problems from his earlier combat tour in the Mediterranean and his injuries near Salerno. It is not clear whether the request for transfer came from Schneider or was on Rudder's initiative. Nevertheless, Capt Block, the battalion medical officer, concurred with the request for transfer, fearing that Schneider might suffer a "mental crack up."[25] These problems today would be called post-traumatic stress disorder (PTSD). The decision was sent up the chain of command and ended up at Eisenhower's SHAEF headquarters. SHAEF, wanting experienced officers for Operation *Overlord*, vetoed the transfer.* Schneider would stay with the Rangers.

Advanced Ranger training began in Cornwall with the assistance of the Combined Operations Headquarters. Commando Lt Col Thomas H. Trevor was assigned as the liaison from COHQ to the 2nd Rangers. Trevor had taken part in Operation *Torch* and had been decorated with the Order of the British Empire for his actions there. COHQ dispatched special teams of Commandos to supervise Ranger training in close combat, including the use of their trademark Fairbairn-Sykes knife. Cliff climbing was an integral part of Commando training, since much of the French and Norwegian coasts were lined with cliffs. Trevor was instrumental in planning cliff-scaling training for the Rangers.

Small numbers of Rangers were detached and sent to participate in Commando raids along the French coast, notably against the German-occupied Channel Islands. Independent Ranger raids were planned, including an attempt to grab prisoners near Calais and a reconnaissance mission to the Isle of Herm, one of the smaller Channel Islands. These two missions were aborted due to the rough weather conditions in the Channel during the winter and early spring. The new head of the Allied land forces, Gen Bernard Montgomery, was opposed to Commando raids on the French coast for fear of alerting the Germans without gaining much useful intelligence. In February 1944, Eisenhower's SHAEF headquarters squashed any further Ranger raids.[26]

In the meantime, the new 5th Ranger Battalion had arrived in Britain. Their training had been compressed compared to the 2nd Ranger Battalion. It had followed the same basic progression from Camp Forrest to Fort Pierce on November 5, 1943, and then Fort Dix on November 20.[27] The 5th Ranger Battalion landed at Liverpool aboard the HMS *Mauritania II* on January 18, 1944, and were billeted first at Leominster in

* It is not clear from surviving records whether Eisenhower had anything to do with the decision or whether it was merely handled by the G-1 (Personnel) office.

Herefordshire, and then in Tighnabrauch, Scotland, in March for further Commando training.

In March 1944, the 5th Ranger Battalion was roiled by what became known as the "Captains' Revolt." The 5th Ranger Battalion was led by Lt Col Owen E. Carter, whose leadership style disturbed several of his company commanders.[28] His methods might have been acceptable for a regular infantry unit, but not for Rangers. Unlike charismatic leaders like Rudder and Darby, Carter did not always share the daily training torments of his subordinates. One Ranger recalled that "No [Ranger] officer was to ask anyone to do anything he wouldn't do. In Scotland, our Battalion Commander had the entire battalion walking in a ditch chest deep in water – but he led from the bank."[29]

Three of the company commanders were so infuriated with Carter's ineffectual leadership that they went outside of normal military channels. Viewing Rudder as the senior Ranger commander in the European theater, they explained the situation to him, asking that he take steps to have Carter relieved. News of this insubordination reached the 5th Ranger Battalion executive officer, Maj Richard Sullivan, who relieved the three officers on March 4 and ordered them to leave the unit. When Rudder learned of this, he brought it to the attention of senior commanders, presumably in Gerow's V Corps. In the event, Carter was relieved, and the three dismissed company commanders were offered their commands back.* Rudder recommended that Schneider take over the 5th Ranger Battalion, which was officially approved on March 24. In spite of Rudder's concerns over Schneider's health, he regarded him as a highly capable and effective leader. In Schneider's place, Capt Cleveland A. Lytle became the executive officer of the 2nd Ranger Battalion.

---

* Of the three captains, Eichnor declined reinstatement and was transferred to the 125th Cavalry Reconaissance Squadron. Whittington returned to his command of B Company and Heffelfinger became the 5th Ranger Battalion S-3 (operations) officer. A Company was assigned to 1st Lt Charles Parker and D Company to 1st Lt George Miller.

V Corps decided to combine both Ranger battalions into a Provisional Ranger Group (PRG). Rudder was officially placed in command of the group on May 19, though he had been acting commander since both battalions had been transferred at the Assault Training Center in April. Unlike most groups, the PRG did not have its own headquarters company. In most cases, the officers of the PRG served the same function in their parent battalion, with Maj Sullivan, executive officer of the 5th Ranger Battalion, having the same function in the PRG and Capt Richard Merrill, Rudder's adjutant in the 2nd Battalion, serving in the same role in the PRG.

One addition to the PRG was a Cannon Company, based on the experiences of the 1st Ranger Battalion in Italy.[30] The company was equipped with four M3 75mm Gun Motor Carriages (GMC). These consisted of an M3 half-track mounting the World War I-era French 75mm M1897 gun. These were developed as expedient tank destroyers in 1941, but by 1944, most had been retired from US Army service for more modern equipment. However, they were still useful for direct fire support.

In early April 1944, both Ranger battalions left their comfortable billets in Sandown and Tighnabrauch for the Assault Training Center at Braunton Burrows on Morte Bay along the north Devon coast. This facility had been established in 1943 for specialized amphibious training. It contained replicas of German coastal defense works, and the terrain resembled sections of the Normandy coast. The April training included the first use of rocket-propelled grapnels to assist in scaling the cliffs.

In the final week of April 1944, the 2nd and 5th Ranger Battalions took part in the largest training exercise to date, Exercise *Fabius I*, at the First US Army Assault Training Center at Slapton Sands in south Devon.[31] This exercise involved all the other units that would land as part of V Corps on Omaha Beach on D-Day, especially the 29th Division.

Most Ranger companies would be subordinate to the 116th Infantry, 29th Division, on D-Day, as is described in detail in subsequent chapters. Contact with the 29th Division was not an entirely happy one. Under the command of Maj Gen Charles H. Gerhardt, the 29th Division became a "spit-and-polish" unit. Some of the division officers were not pleased by the more relaxed standards among the Rangers regarding dress code and barracks maintenance. This led to complaints to Rudder and Schneider, who appear to have ignored the issue.

Fabius I was a dress rehearsal for the Operation *Neptune* landings. The exercises began on April 23 and lasted until May 7. Following the initial marshaling and embarkation training, the two Ranger battalions boarded their LCA craft in Weymouth harbor, which then converged with the LSI (Landing Ship Infantry) that would take them to the landing zone. This was identical to the process that would be followed on D-Day, involving the same ships and LCAs. Three Ranger companies landed at Blackpool Beach about 2 miles north of Slapton Sands to destroy enemy artillery installations, mimicking the D-Day assault at Pointe-du-Hoc. These were the same three companies assigned to the actual D-Day mission. Another company landed on the right flank of the regular assault beach, while other Rangers were landed with the infantry, advancing to the right to relieve the flanking company.[32]

The *Fabius I* exercise led to one of the iconic Ranger emblems, the orange diamond painted on the back of each Ranger's helmet. During the exercise, Rangers from both battalions became intermixed with troops from the 29th Division. To help avoid this problem, the orange diamond was adopted as a Ranger insignia, with the battalion number – either 2 or 5 – painted in the center of the diamond.[33] Orange was selected for the insignia instead of the blue of the normal Ranger shoulder patch as it was more visible on an olive drab helmet.

Following the conclusion of Exercise *Fabius I*, in mid-May the Ranger battalions moved to new billets near Swanage on the Channel coast in Dorset. The 2nd Battalion was billeted in a school building overlooking Swanage. The 5th Ranger Battalion was transferred to the Grand Hotel Swanage, which was perched on a cliff which provided a convenient location for further cliff-climbing exercises. At this point in the training cycle, troops from the Shore Fire Control Parties assigned to the Rangers conducted their first joint training. Much of this involved cliff-scaling and the use of the specialized equipment used for this purpose. On May 17, the Rangers moved to Camp D-5 in Dorchester, their final garrison before D-Day.

By this stage, the Ranger plan for Overlord had been approved, so the troops finally realized why they had been subjected to so many cliff-climbing exercises. Much of the training in the final weeks before D-Day involved the study of terrain maps and aerial photos to become accustomed to their mission. Once the Rangers were briefed on their mission, their camps were patrolled by military police; no one was allowed to leave base. The Pointe-du-Hoc mission was a closely guarded secret.

Chapter 4

Refining the Ranger Plan

Rudder was first informed of the Pointe-du-Hoc mission on Tuesday, January 4, 1944. Rudder, along with his executive officer Max Schneider, had been ordered to London to consult with Gen Bradley's First US Army headquarters, located on Bryanston Square, near Paddington railway station. At this stage, Rudder and Schneider had not yet been "Bigoted," or cleared to see the secret *Neptune* plans. Two security levels had been added above the usual "Secret" level: Secret-Security (later Top Secret) clearance was granted to personnel who needed to know about the plans in general terms;[1] Secret-Security-Bigot clearance was granted to only a select number of senior officers who were given more specific information about the *Neptune* plans, such as the timing, specific targets, and other important detail.[2]

Rudder and Schneider were not cleared for Bigot at the time of the January meeting. As a result, this early meeting covered only basic tactical issues but avoided the most sensitive information, such as the precise timing of the invasion. Both Rudder and Schneider were given the necessary Bigot clearance in March. Bradley's G-3 operations officer, Col Truman "Tubby" Thorson, conducted the first briefing. Thorson explained the importance of the Pointe-du-Hoc battery, showing Rudder and Schneider intelligence maps with the firing arcs of the German gun batteries. As Thorson explained, the guns posed a serious threat to the Transport Area off Beach 46, which in the future would be called Omaha Beach. Utah Beach – which was also in range for the battery – had not yet been added to the *Neptune* plan, and would not be until later in the month. At this time, the precise tactics for seizing Pointe-du-Hoc had not been selected.

Initially, it was expected that Pointe-du-Hoc would be attacked from the landward side, as the 1st Rangers had done at Arzew. Thorson directed Rudder, in conjunction with the Combined Operations HQ and V Corps, to come up with a suitable plan to rapidly secure and silence the Pointe-du-Hoc battery. Rudder was subsequently informed that his 2nd Ranger Battalion would be augmented by the newly arrived 5th Ranger Battalion. Together, they would constitute a Provisional Ranger Group under his overall command.

FEBRUARY 1944: THE GEROW RANGER PLAN

A variety of schemes were considered for the Pointe-du-Hoc mission. Since Omaha Beach was the responsibility of V Corps, the G-3 Operations section of V Corps began to develop a plan that would fit the broader corps objectives. V Corps commander Maj Gen Leonard Gerow had served earlier in the war as the Assistant Chief of the War Plans Division of the War Department General Staff; one of his subordinates there was then-Col Dwight Eisenhower. Gerow took personal interest in the Pointe-du-Hoc mission. His views about the Pointe-du-Hoc tactics were summarized at a V Corps *Overlord* planning meeting on February 4:

The Corps Commander [Gerow] desires that the bulk of the two Ranger battalions go ashore west of Beach 46 [Omaha Beach] to neutralize the enemy defenses on the cliffs as far west as the Passe d'Isigny, probably landing over the beaches in back of the Roches de Grandcamp. This, however, is subject to the ability of the Navy to land them in this area, possible interference with

Navy gunfire, and possibly with air support. This should be
fully developed... If they cannot be landed across the Roches
de Grandcamp, the plan should provide for their landing on
the right flank of the 29th Division RCT beach [Regimental
Combat Team]. It is suggested that the Commanding General,
1st Division, might wish to use a portion or portions of the
Ranger battalions elsewhere, as for example on his left flank.[3]

The Roches de Grandcamp are an expanse of rocky shoals
immediately off the Calvados coast, starting in the west near the
mouth of the river Vire and extending about 2 miles eastward
to within 500 yards of Pointe-du-Hoc. Passe d'Isigny is a
channel through the marshy Vire estuary entering the sea west
of Grandcamp, about 3 miles from Pointe-du-Hoc. Gerow was
presumably referring to other German defense works in this
sector, including the two German field artillery batteries near the
town of Maisy.

Bradley's First US Army released its initial *Neptune* plan on
February 25. It lacked any specific details of how the Rangers would
assault Pointe-du-Hoc. As a result, on February 27, Col Hewitt,
the V Corps Assistant G-3/Operations, requested that the V Corps,
Rangers, Combined Operations HQ, and Navy conduct a study
to establish the tactics for securing Pointe-du-Hoc.[4] The basic
parameters noted that the Ranger battalions would be limited to six
infantry landing ships, along with their associated landing craft. The
Ranger mission could not start before H-Hour, since it was planned
to conduct an aerial bombardment of Pointe-du-Hoc from H-4
to H-1½, followed by a naval bombardment from H-40 minutes
until the Rangers landed at H-Hour. A possible airborne operation
connected to the Ranger assault was also to be considered.

MARCH 1944: THE COHQ/RICHARDSON RANGER PLAN

Much of the initial planning for the Pointe-du-Hoc mission
was entrusted to a British Army staff officer, Lt Col Dermot L.
Richardson, assigned to the Combined Operations HQ. COHQ

had extensive experience with such operations and would also be essential in providing the Rangers with any specialized equipment that was necessary. Richardson's plan was based on Gerow's basic outline, and was presented to Gerow at the V Corps headquarters at Clifton College in Bristol on March 3. The COHQ plan proposed to land the Rangers at two locations, 4 miles east and west of Pointe-du-Hoc. This meant an amphibious landing over the Roches de Grandcamp in the east and in the Vierville sector of Omaha Beach. In addition, Richardson proposed landing an advance party of about 35 paratroopers immediately south of Pointe-du-Hoc.

Even though it was based on Gerow's previous outline, the Richardson plan was quickly rejected. By early March, the V Corps planners had realized that Gerow's scheme to land the Rangers over the Roches de Grandcamp was unacceptable to the Royal Navy, since the shoals could pose a hazard even to shallow-draft landing craft. Furthermore, the landings there would take place in the face of several German strongpoints on either side of the port of Grandcamp-les-Bains. Even if these defenses were overcome, such a plan would require the Rangers to march several miles through German defenses to reach Pointe-du-Hoc, delaying the attack on the battery for a few hours at least.

Gerow also rejected the idea of a paratrooper drop. Such a small force could not by itself seize Pointe-du-Hoc, and was insufficient to penetrate the defense belt that shielded the battery from the landward side. The problems of attacking from the Grandcamp area left a proposed march by the Rangers from the vicinity of Vierville to Pointe-du-Hoc. Once again, this would oblige the Rangers to fight their way through several miles of German defenses before reaching and attacking the Pointe-du-Hoc battery. Gerow's original concepts were unworkable in an acceptable time period.

In hindsight, the rejection of Gerow's original plan prevented a possible disaster on D-Day. Allied intelligence did not know it at the time, but on D-Day, this sector was one of the most heavily defended sectors of the invasion beaches. It included two significant German strongpoints, Stützpunkt Grandcamp and Stützpunkt

Gefosse-Fontenay, manned by a reinforced battalion of Grenadier-Regiment.914 of the 352.Infanterie-Division. This was the only first-rate German infantry division on the invasion coast.

REFINING THE TACTICS

The subsequent planning was largely handed over to Rudder and his staff, working in concert with COHQ and then consulting the operations staffs of Gerow's V Corps and Gen Huebner's 1st Division. The idea of landing forces on either side of Pointe-du-Hoc was studied again. COHQ was not keen on this idea, based on the experiences of the Commandos against the Batterie du Lazaret on Cap Matifou near Algiers during Operation *Torch* in November 1942. As described in Chapter 2, the Commandos had been unable to reach the battery before the landing and the French guns continued to bombard the amphibious force for nearly a day in spite of repeated air, naval, and Commando attacks. A COHQ Commando officer later wrote: "There it was demonstrated that even against light opposition, it is impossible to reach and reduce the battery quickly enough to prevent it engaging our shipping to considerable effect."[5]

Consideration was first given to landing in the small port of Grandcamp rather than across the Grandcamp shoals. Grandcamp was roughly 2 miles west of Pointe-du-Hoc, and study of aerial photos revealed that the Germans had created a flooded area between it and Pointe-du-Hoc.[6] Although this was intended to prevent Allied paratroop or glider landings, it would also hinder any advance over this route. Furthermore, there was evidence that the Germans had created ambush zones along the passages through the inundations. Even if the Rangers made it past the inundated areas, once they arrived at the southern perimeter of Pointe-du-Hoc, they would have to confront the defensive barrier of mines and barbed wire. This would take time to overcome and might result in substantial casualties. Once again, this would take precious time, during which the Pointe-du-Hoc battery might be firing on the invasion fleet. For this reason, the western route was rejected.

The next option was to land the Rangers at the cliffs east and west of Pointe-du-Hoc, but much closer than the previous options at Grandcamp and Vierville. The Commandos had already conducted cliff assaults in 1942–43, such as the Dieppe raid. However, there were a number of differences between the Dieppe cliffs and those at Pointe-du-Hoc. At Dieppe, the Commandos landed surreptitiously, under the cover of darkness, and the cliff edges were not heavily defended. Furthermore, there were clefts in the cliffs that gave the Commandos quicker and safer routes to the top than by climbing the entire cliff face. The Rangers would be landing in daylight against an enemy force that had been alerted by preliminary bombardments, and the landing craft would be plainly visible during the approach. The cliffs in this sector also lacked clefts or other features that might facilitate the climb.

While this option put the Rangers much nearer to Pointe-du-Hoc, with no forced marches from Grandcamp or Vierville, the problem remained that the Rangers would have to penetrate the heaviest defenses of the Pointe-du-Hoc strongpoint on its southern side.

At this point, the idea emerged to simply land at the base of Pointe-du-Hoc and scale the cliffs there. This was not as preposterous as it now may seem. The Commandos had, of course, already carried out such raids. An after-action report revealed, "A study of [the Pointe-du-Hoc] defenses showed they all faced inland and the enemy were relying for defense of the Battery to seaward on the sheer cliffs. If the assault force had to climb the cliffs under fire, it was obviously better to do so and get right into the objective without having to overcome any additional obstacles than climb the cliffs and then have to deal with prepared defenses."[7]

It is unclear who proposed to climb the Pointe-du-Hoc cliffs. It is often attributed to Rudder, but it is equally likely that it was reached by consensus of the Rangers and COHQ staff after ruling out other options. Another reason the cliff-scaling option seemed plausible was that there was a growing consensus that Pointe-du-Hoc would have to be heavily bombed and shelled prior to H-Hour

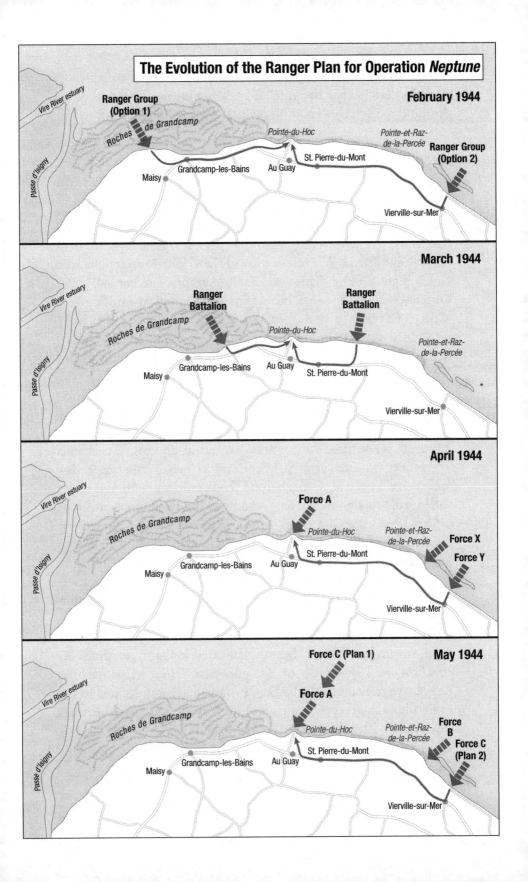

The Evolution of the Ranger Plan for Operation *Neptune*

February 1944

Ranger Group (Option 1)

Roches de Grandcamp

Pointe-du-Hoc

Pointe-et-Raz-de-la-Percée

Ranger Group (Option 2)

St. Pierre-du-Mont

Au Guay

Grandcamp-les-Bains

Maisy

Vierville-sur-Mer

Vire River estuary

Passe d'Isigny

March 1944

Vire River estuary

Roches de Grandcamp

Ranger Battalion

Ranger Battalion

Pointe-du-Hoc

Pointe-et-Raz-de-la-Percée

Au Guay

St. Pierre-du-Mont

Grandcamp-les-Bains

Maisy

Vierville-sur-Mer

Passe d'Isigny

April 1944

Vire River estuary

Roches de Grandcamp

Force A

Pointe-du-Hoc

Pointe-et-Raz-de-la-Percée

Force X

Force Y

St. Pierre-du-Mont

Au Guay

Grandcamp-les-Bains

Maisy

Vierville-sur-Mer

Passe d'Isigny

May 1944

Force C (Plan 1)

Force A

Roches de Grandcamp

Pointe-du-Hoc

Pointe-et-Raz-de-la-Percée

Force B

Force C (Plan 2)

St. Pierre-du-Mont

Au Guay

Grandcamp-les-Bains

Maisy

Vierville-sur-Mer

Vire River estuary

Passe d'Isigny

to make certain that the guns did not fire on the Transport Areas during the disembarkation phase, prior to the Ranger landing.[8]

SCALING THE CLIFFS: THE SPECIAL COMMANDO DEVICES

For this plan to succeed, the Rangers would need to be able to surmount the cliffs quickly. Fortunately for the Rangers, COHQ had its own Department of Miscellaneous Weapons Development under Capt Francis W. H. Jeans, Royal Navy. He was an experienced naval engineer and had been the Assistant Director of Naval Ordnance from 1936–37. His department had been working on a variety of devices to assist the Commandos in rapidly scaling cliffs, since these were a common obstacle during Commando raids along the Atlantic coast. By 1944, no fewer than nine such devices had been developed.[9]

Two of these were of special interest to the Rangers. COHQ had developed rocket-projected grapnel hooks with attached ropes or rope ladders. These consisted of a 2in. "J" rocket with a grapnel hook fitted to the head instead of an explosive charge. The rocket was fired from a J-projector at a 45-degree angle. The rocket was attached to plain rope, rope ladders, or toggle ropes with small wooden toggle bars attached. The toggle rope and rope ladders were generally easier to use than plain rope, though the plain rope had the advantage of being lighter and therefore easier to fire to greater heights. The ropes were up to 45 fathoms in length, or 270ft. This was adequate for the Pointe-du-Hoc cliffs. Early experiments mounted the projector in a small dory so that they could be launched from offshore.

To facilitate the use of these devices for Pointe-du-Hoc, Jeans' team organized Project Scam. This developed a method for attaching six J Projectors on the gunwales of the LCAs that the Rangers were assigned for D-Day. Eventually, it was decided to use a mixture of rope types, two each of the plain rope, toggle rope, and rope ladders. The projectors could be dismounted from the landing craft and fired from the beach if necessary. A lightweight, mobile

Schermuly rocket/rope projector was also added to the arsenal of each craft.

The second device available was the light tubular steel ladder, which came in 4ft sections. It was not especially quick or easy to erect, and so was intended for the follow-on waves rather than the first wave of assault troops. A single soldier could assemble a 100ft ladder, and it would then be erected up the cliff using a rope from another soldier already on top of the cliff.

A third device was developed specifically for the Pointe-du-Hoc mission. COHQ had been experimenting with the use of 100ft power-operated ladders of the type used by the London fire brigades. The original configuration used a conventional fire truck. For D-Day, the idea emerged to fit a Merryweather Turntable Ladder in the cargo hold of a DUKW amphibious truck. This was codenamed a "Swan." As an added feature, three Vickers "K" machine guns were added to the top of the ladder. The idea was that once the Swan reached the beach, a Ranger would man the machine guns on the top of the ladder as it was erected up the cliff face. The machine guns could then be used to clear the top of the cliff face of enemy troops. A total of four Swans were built for use by the Rangers at Pointe-du-Hoc.

Another climbing aid was the Fairbairn-Sykes fighting knife. This double-sided knife was widely used by the British Commandos for close-quarter fighting. During the Dieppe mission, the Commandos also found that the chalk cliffs were soft enough that the knives could be used as a climbing aid. Some Rangers obtained these knives prior to D-Day.

These ingenious technical aids convinced Rudder and the other Ranger officers that the Pointe-du-Hoc cliffs could be scaled in a relatively speedy fashion if the Rangers received robust training beforehand. Aerial reconnaissance photographs of Pointe-du-Hoc indicated that the Germans were not anticipating an attack from the sea and there were no major defenses facing the sea.

Once the issue of the assault tactics at Pointe-du-Hoc was settled, it was necessary to calculate how much force would be needed to take Pointe-du-Hoc. The beaches at the foot of the Pointe-du-Hoc cliffs were limited. Rudder and his senior officers felt that the initial assault could be conducted by just a few companies of Rangers, with follow-on waves landed either at Pointe-du-Hoc or farther east near Omaha Beach. Gen Clarence Huebner, commander of the 1st Infantry Division, was concerned about the threat posed by a pair of German field gun positions that had appeared in recent aerial photographs on the cliffs to the west of Omaha Beach near the Pointe-et-Raz-de-la Percée. Rudder met with Huebner at the 1st Division headquarters on two occasions in late March 1944 to discuss these issues.[10] As a result, a mission to eliminate these gun positions was added to the Ranger plan.

APRIL 1944: THE V CORPS RANGER PLAN

The evolving Ranger plan now contained three missions: Force A would directly attack Pointe-du-Hoc; Force X would climb the cliffs nearer to Omaha Beach to eliminate the Pointe-et-Raz-de-la Percée gun batteries; and Force Y would land on the far-right flank of Omaha Beach and march westward to attack Pointe-du-Hoc from its southeast side. The final mission was essentially an insurance policy in case the riskier *coup de main* against Pointe-du-Hoc failed.

After receiving approval from Gerow's V Corps headquarters, the Ranger plan was released on April 20 as Annex 19 of the V Corps Operation *Neptune* Plan. It is worth quoting in detail:

Ranger Force A, consisting of the HQ detachment of the 2nd Ranger Battalion as well as Cos. D, E, and F of the 2nd Ranger Battalion will land at H-Hour, D-Day on Beach Charlie [Pointe-du-Hoc], companies abreast. One company will land on the west portion of Pointe du Hoe.[*] Two companies and a naval fire support command party will land on the east portion of Pointe du Hoe. The force will assault Pointe du Hoe directly, destroy

---

[*]The Americans tended to refer to Pointe-du-Hoc as Point du Hoe.

the shore batteries, and assist the advance of the remainder of the force.

Ranger Force X (Co. C, 2nd Ranger Battalion), will land on the right of Beach Omaha Dog Green at H-Hour, D-Day advance rapidly to Pointe et Raz la Percée, destroy installations at the Pointe and continue to advance west covering the flank of the remainder of the Ranger Group.

Ranger Force Y, consisting of Co. A and B, 2nd Ranger Battalion and the 5th Ranger Battalion, will land in two waves at H+28 and H+30 [minutes] at Beach Dog Green, proceed rapidly in a column of companies, along the route paralleling the shore line, avoiding all unnecessary action, to seize Pointe-du-Hoe from the rear and destroy battery installations. The two companies of the 2nd Ranger Battalion will provide advance guard and flank protection for Force Y from the beach to objective.

The Cannon Platoon will land at H+120, D-Day, on Beach Dog Green and will proceed along the road Vierville sur Mer – Grandcamp les Bains to the vicinity of Pointe du Hoe and be prepared to support the assault of Force Y in the capture of Pointe-du-Hoe.

Upon accomplishment of the primary mission, the [Ranger] group will reorganize in preparation for future missions on the right flank.[11]

MAY 1944: THE FINAL 1ST DIVISION RANGER PLAN

Bold missions can have equally extravagant results: stunning success or crushing defeat. If Force A did succeed in quickly taking the Pointe-du-Hoc battery, why send Ranger Force Y to Omaha Beach and have them fight their way through 4 miles of German defenses to Pointe-du-Hoc? On May 11, there was a final and significant change to the Ranger plan that addressed these issues. This change was introduced during the preparation of the final 1st Division *Neptune* Plan. Under this plan, Rudder's Provisional Ranger Group was subordinated to the 116th Regimental Combat Team, so the Ranger plan was incorporated into the 116th RCT

Plan. One minor change was to simplify the designations of the various groups, with Force X becoming Force B and Force Y becoming Force C.

Under the final plan, the missions of Force A at Pointe-du-Hoc and Force B at Pointe-et-Raz-de-la-Percée remained the same. The change mostly concerned the largest element of the Provisional Ranger Group, Force C. This force, consisting of Schneider's 5th Ranger Battalion and two companies of the 2nd Rangers, was given two options on D-Day to take advantage of battlefield circumstances:

Force A, consisting of 3 companies (reinforced), at H-Hour D-Day land on Beach Charlie, capture Pointe du Hoe, prepare to repel counter-attack, and cover advance of remainder of Ranger Group.

Force B, consisting of 1 company, land at H+3 minutes D-Day on Beach Omaha Dog Green, move rapidly through breach in wire on western edge of Dog Green Beach, destroy defenses at Point et Raz de la Percée. Continue advance along coast, assist 1st Bn, 116th Infantry in destruction of fortifications from Pointe et Raz de la Percée to and including Pointe du Hoe. On arrival at Pointe du Hoe revert to Ranger Group.

Force C, (Ranger Group less detachments), land at H+60 [minutes] D-Day and execute one of following plans:

Plan 1. If success signal is received prior to H+30 [minutes] from Force A, Force C will move to and land at H+60 minutes D-Day on Beach Charlie. Gain contact with Force A, destroy fortifications at Pointe du Hoe and along coast from Pointe du Hoe to Sluice gate (563933). Reorganize, prepare to repel counter-attack. Cover advance of the 1st Bn, 116th Infantry to Pointe du Hoe. Upon arrival of 1st Bn, 116th Infantry at Pointe du Hoe, Ranger Group is attached to 1st Bn, 116th Infantry.

Plan 2. Force C land on Beach Omaha Dog Green commencing at H+60 minutes D-Day move rapidly to Pointe du Hoe. Capture Pointe du Hoe. Destroy fortifications from Pointe du Hoe to sluice gate (563937-563933) reorganize, prepare to repel counter-attack. Cover advance of 1st Bn 116th Infantry to Pointe du Hoe. Upon arrival of 1st Bn, 116th Inf at Pointe du Hoe, Ranger Group is attached to 1st Bn, 116th Infantry.

The sluice gate mentioned in the plans was located about 2,500 yards west of Pointe-du-Hoc, where the coastal road intersected the Ruisseau Fontaine-Sainte-Marie stream. It was selected since this sluice gate had been used by the Germans to flood the farm fields in this vicinity, creating an obstacle to the western advance out of the Omaha Beach sector. It was also chosen as a convenient point of departure for further D-Day operations, since it was clearly marked on the standard Army map of the time.[12] The overall *Neptune* plan expected the 116th RCT, along with the attached Provisional Ranger Group, would pass beyond the sluice gate, capture the town of Grandcamp-les-Bains and the German defenses in the sector including the two Maisy artillery batteries, and reach a point north of the town of Isigny by D-Day evening.

As the 19th-century Prussian military commander Helmuth van Moltke once quipped: "No plan survives first contact with the enemy." This would certainly be the case on D-Day.

Chapter 5

Spying on Pointe-du-Hoc:
The Intelligence Battle

On August 18, 1942, a photo-reconnaissance Mosquito took off from RAF Benson outside Oxford in southern England for a sortie over the Manche and Calvados coastlines of Normandy at an altitude of 31,000ft.* It covered the coastline from the vicinity of Cherbourg on the Cotentin peninsula across Lower Normandy to Le Havre, a distance of 120 miles. This was the first reconnaissance mission in the area since the Pointe-du-Hoc battery had been deployed in late May 1942. By this stage, construction of the kettle gun pits had begun. After the aircraft's film was processed and interpreted, the RAF Medmenham Interpretation center released a report that identified the new battery with geographic specifications and a description of the new position: "A three-gun battery facing NE [northeast] and right on the cliff edge. Each gun appears to have a 360-degree traverse. There are two areas [about 70–80 feet by 100 feet] covered by camouflage netting with [motor transport] standing outside. The whole site is enclosed by well concealed wire; this also encloses some farm buildings. There is a remote possibility of a fourth emplacement under construction."[1]

---

* The Manche department in France covers the Cotentin peninsula, including the major port of Cherbourg.

Once the Pointe-du-Hoc site was identified, it was periodically overflown to monitor progress on its construction. The Allied understanding of Pointe-du-Hoc received a major boost in late June 1943 with the arrival of a map from France that detailed the German Atlantic Wall construction program in Normandy. Not only did the map include existing sites, but also sites that were intended for construction later in 1943 and 1944. It was one of the most important discoveries of the French Resistance in Normandy.

THE DUCHEZ MAP

The French Resistance in 1943 was an amalgamation of small local organizations, with very limited central direction. The groups were of many types: some were extensions of local political organizations, while others were organized by French Army veterans. In many cases, several organizations operated in the same area without any knowledge of each other.

This was certainly the case in the Calvados area of Basse Normandie (Lower Normandy) where Pointe-du-Hoc was located.[2] Postwar French histories suggest that during the war, about 135–180 people were involved in Resistance intelligence activities in the Calvados area. The Resistance units in Normandy were loosely coordinated by the BCRA (Bureau Central de Renseignements et d'Action: Central Bureau of Intelligence and Operations), the primary intelligence agency of Gen Charles de Gaulle's Free French government in London. The BCRA was closely connected with the British SOE (Special Operations Executive) that managed Allied intelligence operations in occupied Europe.

The first major intelligence coup took place in Caen in the late spring of 1943 courtesy of the Confrérie Notre-Dame (CND) group.[*] It managed to put one of its members, René Duchez, into the offices of the Organization Todt construction group in Caen. Duchez, who had been contracted by the Germans to paint and

---

[*] CND was led by Gilbert Renault, alias Colonel Rémy, and had twenty-six cells and about 1,500 agents at its peak. It was part of the larger OCM (Organisation civile et militaire).

wallpaper several rooms in the office building,[3] found a detailed map of the German construction plans for the Atlantic Wall, covering Cherbourg to Honfleur, and including the Pointe-du-Hoc battery. He managed to sneak it out of the building while moving his wallpaper supplies. After the war, Duchez was honored by the French government with both the Medal of Resistance and Croix du Guerre.

The map was carefully copied so that the original could be returned to the office. In June 1943, an opportunity to smuggle the map out of France occurred when the BCRA arranged to exfiltrate several people and some documents out of France, under Operation *Marie-Louise*. The Resistance members departed on a small fishing boat, *Deux Anges* (*Two Angels*), from a small port near Pont-Aven on the southern Breton coast. They were met at sea by the trawler N.51, manned by SOE agents, operating out of the Isles of Scilly off southwest England.[4]

The map was delivered to the top-secret "Martian Room" in Storey's Gate, St James's Park, London, on June 22. The "Martians," or more formally the Theatre Intelligence Section (TIS), GHQ, Home Forces, was a combined intelligence agency under the direction of the Oxford don John L. Austin, created in 1942 to collect data for the forthcoming *Overlord* invasion.[*] Its weekly product, the "Martian Report," listed all the latest intelligence news about German defenses along the occupied French coast. The Duchez map was a critical breakthrough, as it identified the Atlantic Wall batteries being built along the French coast, as well as the types of guns and their resident unit.

In the case of Pointe-du-Hoc, it identified the resident unit as HKAA.832 and the guns as 155mm GPF. This was important for two reasons. First, it made it clear that it was a coastal artillery battery due to its designation, and was therefore a potential threat to naval vessels. Second, it clarified the type of gun positioned there. Although RAF photo-reconnaissance planes had photographed

---

[*] The TIS was later subordinated to Montgomery's 21st Army Group.

the Pointe-du-Hoc battery, the resolution of the photos was not high enough to identify the specific type. The guns were identified generically as medium/heavy guns in the 150–170mm range. The map specifically identified the type, and therefore their technical characteristics were immediately understood in detail.

With the Duchez map in hand, intelligence organizations in London could better manage RAF photo-reconnaissance missions over the French coast. Just as importantly, SOE and the BCRA now had a better grasp of intelligence targets to help direct the collection activities of French Resistance agents.

THE ALLIED INTELLIGENCE ASSESSMENT OF POINTE-DU-HOC

Aerial reconnaissance, in conjunction with the information from the French Resistance, gave Allied intelligence agencies a relatively complete picture of the Pointe-du-Hoc battery. But why was this particular battery regarded as such a threat? As one historian has written, "At the beginning of World War II, naval planners were convinced that the coastal defense gun would be a major hazard to surface combatants; so much so that pre-war doctrine specified that ships would deliver counterbattery and fire support from long ranges while maneuvering at high speed to avoid damage."[5] The threat of the Pointe-du-Hoc battery was amplified since Allied naval planners feared its effectiveness against the vulnerable transport ships of the invasion fleet, as summarized in a report by the US Navy's Western Task Force:

> Pointe du Hoe battery was considered the number one priority in the bombardment plan for it was the only enemy position which covered both of the beaches [Utah and Omaha] and transport areas. Originally there were six 155mm guns (French type GPF) with an estimated range of 25,000 yards, in open concrete emplacements. It was strategically located atop a 90-foot-high coastal bluff, remote from any large landing beach, surrounded by wire and mine fields and extremely well protected

on the flanks by prepared strongpoints, [while] personnel and ammunition shelters were underground and constructed of heavily reinforced mass concrete. Machine gun positions were well dug in and camouflaged. The observation and command post on the seaward edge of the bluff was constructed of heavily reinforced concrete, partially earth banked.

Early in March casemates began to be built near four of the positions; two guns having been removed from their emplacements. It was estimated that by D-Day the enemy would probably have two guns in casemates (sited to fire on Utah) with 4 guns, possibly only 2 guns, with unrestricted arcs of fire remaining in open positions. [6]

As a result of these factors, Pointe-du-Hoc was Target Number 1 on the naval Gunfire Support Plan.[7] From the naval perspective, the Pointe-du-Hoc battery could engage the naval invasion force at its most vulnerable moments, when the transport ships were located in the Transport Area. This was the term for the area off the coast where transport ships unloaded the troops into the small landing craft that would take them ashore. At this moment, the transport ships made a prime target since they could not maneuver while the troop transfer took place. There had been many examples of the threat of coastal batteries in previous amphibious operations. German coastal guns had been a primary reason for the Dieppe debacle. Even when they failed to stop an amphibious operation, such as the Vichy-French coastal guns during Operation *Torch*, they could force transport ships to abandon their unloading process.

Pointe-du-Hoc posed a double threat. Not only could it engage the vulnerable transport ships, but it could also bombard two of the invasion beaches during the landing operations. During the *Overlord* planning process in late 1943 and early 1944, the Pointe-du-Hoc battery was the main German field artillery battery identified near Omaha Beach.

One of the more curious aspects of Allied intelligence assessments of the threat of the Pointe-du-Hoc battery was that they tended to overestimate the range of the guns. This was due to overcautious assumptions about the guns rather than any lack of technical data.

Some US Army documents listed the maximum range of the 155mm GPF gun as 26,000 yards,[8] while most Allied intelligence assessments in *Overlord* planning documents indicated that the 155mm GPF guns stationed at Pointe-du-Hoc had a range of 25,000 yards. These figures indicated the extreme performance of the gun, not the normal performance. The 26,000-yard figure was possible if the gun was at an elevation of 45 degrees with an initial muzzle velocity of 2,800ft-per-second. However, the actual maximum elevation of the gun was only 35 degrees.[9] The additional elevation was possible only if the gun was positioned on a ramp, but the German guns at Pointe-du-Hoc did not have this feature. The extreme velocity could be fostered by the use of unusually large propellant increments.

A more realistic range for the Pointe-du-Hoc guns, as provided in French Army documents, was 17,800 yards when using a more typical charge with a muzzle velocity of 2,350ft/s and a 35-degree elevation.[10] Standard Wehrmacht data tables list the maximum range as 21,325 yards at an initial muzzle velocity of 2,410ft/s. The differences between the French and German data were due to differences in the type of ammunition and propellant charge in use; the 155mm GPF fired several different types of ammunition with different weights and ballistic characteristics. To summarize, the Allied intelligence assessments tended to exaggerate the effective range of the 155mm GPF gun by about 40 percent.

The exaggeration of the range of the guns was actually a policy established in January 1944 during discussions between the intelligence analysts and the naval planners. The planners were unhappy with the analysts' tendency to waffle about the range of German coastal batteries in their assessments. On January 18, 1944, they held a meeting in the "Martian Room," home of the Theatre Intelligence Section. The TIS analysts asked the Navy planners whether they would prefer that intelligence reports indicate the effective range or maximum range of German coastal guns. Maximum range is the outer limit that can be reached by a field gun; however, at maximum range, the gun is so inaccurate as to be nearly useless in hitting the target. Effective range is the outer range at which a gun has a reasonable chance of hitting a specific target.* The accuracy issue is detailed below. Commander G. W. Hawkins, Royal Navy, stated emphatically that maximum range was the criterion they preferred.[11] Hawkins was a member of Admiral Ramsey's ANCXF (Allied Naval Command Expeditionary Force), and so his preference prevailed.

This data was used in establishing the Transport Areas where the assault transports would transfer the troops to the landing craft. The US Navy's Western Naval Task Force decided to establish the Transport Area for Omaha Beach about 11–12 miles from shore, specifically due to the threat posed by Pointe-du-Hoc. This area was within the maximum range of the Pointe-du-Hoc battery, but outside its effective range. So, on paper, the Transport Area could be reached by the Pointe-du-Hoc battery. However, it was outside the effective range of the Pointe-du-Hoc battery, so beyond the range at which the battery would have any accuracy.

ASSESSING THE ACCURACY OF THE POINTE-DU-HOC GUNS

The threat of the Pointe-du-Hoc battery was also heavily dependent on its accuracy. Field guns firing at long range are not especially accurate, due to the vagaries of gun performance. Repeated firings of the gun wear down the rifling in the gun tube and reduce its maximum range. The number of firings was usually recorded for each gun to compensate for barrel wear in ballistic calculations. In addition, World War II projectiles were influenced by yaw (oscillation about a vertical axis) that was induced by imperfections in the manufacture of the shell, variations in the propellant temperature, inconsistencies in the propellant burn, cross-wind,

---

*The criterion for effective range is usually established by the firing charts in a field gun's technical manual. For example, the criterion might be a 15 percent chance of hitting a target of 10 x 10m at a specified range.

and other small but significant factors. The probability of hitting a 1 square yard target was 18 percent at 3,000 yards, requiring on average five and a half rounds. But at 10,000 yards, its probability was only 0.32 percent, requiring 310 rounds.[12] In other words, a 155mm GPF gun firing against a target about the size of a landing craft would take about fifty-five times more ammunition to hit it at 10,000 yards than at 3,000 yards. Clearly, the 155mm GPF gun was not intended for precision shooting against small targets at long ranges. The probability of hitting targets significantly decreased when engaging moving targets such as ships.

Allied planners were aware of these factors. As a result, the Transport Areas off the *Neptune* invasion beaches were positioned at the edge of the effective range of the principal German guns, rather that farther out beyond their theoretical (but inaccurate) maximum ranges.

NEWS FROM THE FRENCH RESISTANCE

French Resistance organizations in the Calvados region took on new importance in the second half of 1943 when the Allies settled on the Calvados coast in Normandy as the location for Operation *Neptune*. One of the largest French Resistance networks was the OCM (Organisation civile et militaire). Its most significant cell in the Calvados region of Lower Normandy, codenamed "Centurie," was headed by R. Delente and Guillaume Mercader, based in Bayeux. Mercader was a well-known figure in the local community as he had been a professional cyclist before the war and had won numerous national prizes. He had served in the French Army in 1940, and after the armistice he returned to his bicycle shop in Bayeux. His prewar sporting achievements were known to the Germans, who gave him a special pass which allowed him to practice racing on the small country roads in Normandy. He used this as a means to communicate with other members of the Centurie cell.

The two members of the Centurie cell most familiar with Pointe-du-Hoc were Jean Marion, a sailor and member of the municipal council in Grandcamp-les-Bains, and his friend André Farine, who ran the Café L'Étanville near Grandcamp. German troops from Pointe-du-Hoc visited his cafe, as did many of the other German soldiers in the area. Farine received permission from the Germans to purchase firewood from the farms along the coast. These farms were in the coastal zone that was otherwise off limits for French civilians. He frequently visited a M. Fouché's Les Perruques farm southeast of Maisy. Some of the farm fields were high enough to obtain a view over Pointe-du-Hoc. On a number of occasions, he surveyed the construction work at Pointe-du-Hoc and passed on the information through the Centurie network. Farine was probably the first French Resistance member to discover that the Pointe-du-Hoc guns had been moved away from the site in April 1944. Marion and Farine conveyed this information to Mercader to forward it to London.[13]

Another active group in Lower Normandy area was the "Alliance" network formed by Commander Georges Lacau Loustanou, alias "Navarre," and later run by Madeleine Fourcade and Léon Faye.[14] The group's "Ferme" sector in Normandy was led by Jean Roger, alias "Sainteny," who owned a villa in Vierville and so had connections in the area. The future Omaha Beach was in the group's Bessin sector, headed by Marcel Couliboeuf, alias "Bison noir" (Black Bison), a teacher in Formigny. This sector had a radio transmitter, operated by M. Rodriguez, alias "Pie." The Bessin sector had three cells in the area: in Bayeux, in Port-en-Bessin to the east of Omaha Beach, and in the Omaha Beach area around Vierville. The Vierville group was headed by Desiré Lemière, alias "Chordeille," and included three other members, most of whom were postmen in the town. There were about 15–20 people associated with the Alliance network.

Lemière's group was responsible for scouting the German beach defense construction in the area, made somewhat easier by their occupation as postmen. Many of the construction workers in the area were young Moroccans, recruited by the Germans in southern France and used as workers in Normandy because of their lack of local connections. However, they spoke French and had contact with the postmen because of their mail sent back home to French

North Africa. Lemière's cell scouted out most of the major sites in this area, including the artillery batteries at Maisy, Pointe-du-Hoc, and Longues-sur-Mer, as well as the shore defenses on Omaha Beach. In late April 1944, the group discovered the movement of the Pointe-du-Hoc gun battery when in contact with Farine. They attempted to warn the Allies of these developments by sending messages via pigeons.

On March 14, 1944, a liaison officer of the Alliance network was arrested in Paris. The German counterintelligence service then began to roll up the group. Suspects were tortured, and as more names were revealed, the operatives in Normandy were arrested. On May 5, Lemière's group was arrested and sent to the prison in Caen for interrogation and torture. On D-Day, many of the prisoners there were shot and others were sent to concentration camps; none survived.

THE WANDERING GUNS OF POINTE-DU-HOC

One of the lingering controversies about Pointe-du-Hoc is whether Allied intelligence knew that the guns there had been removed from the strongpoint prior to D-Day. Several French Resistance cells insist that they sent messages to London warning of the movement of the guns. The Ranger Force commander, Col Earl Rudder, was informed a few days before D-Day that "French civilians" had informed Allied intelligence that the guns had been moved. Rudder's biographer, Tom Hatfield, discussed this issue with several of the participants, including Rudder and Eikner, who insisted that they had been told that the guns had been moved. This confirms that at least one of the messages from the French Resistance was received by London.

This has led to arguments in recent years that the Pointe-du-Hoc mission was not necessary and should have been called off. One reason the controversy lingers is that none of the Allied intelligence reports about the movement of the guns have been discovered in the archives. It is possible that the original French reports may still exist in the archival records of the BCRA or SOE, but if so, they have yet to be found. Available archival records such as the G-2 (Intelligence) records of First US Army and V Corps do not contain any information about the movement of the guns. Furthermore, it is not clear when the French Resistance transmitted these reports to London, or when they were received.

The Pointe-du-Hoc guns were moved in late April 1944 after the first major bombing raid. It would take time for the French to pass the initial reports through their networks and then transmit the information to London, either by radio or courier pigeon, so the earliest that Allied intelligence might have learned about the movement probably would have been early May.

Radio transmission would seem to be the ideal method to inform London of the movement of the guns. However, the French Resistance in Normandy had limited numbers of radio transmitters and a long list of subjects of interest from the BCRA/SOE. Radio transmission times had to be minimized because German counter-intelligence operated a vigorous radio-detection service in France to track down and eliminate French Resistance broadcasters.[15] The Abwehr set up a special program in France, codenamed Operation *Donar* after the mythical god of thunder in Valhalla. This effort revolved around specialized direction-finding teams, dubbed KWU (Kurzwellenüberwachung: Short Wave Monitoring).

The French radio teams knew that they had to move their radios to avoid the German detectors. They were careful to limit the broadcast time, knowing that it took the German teams only a few minutes to identify the radio signal and initiate the triangulation process. This led to a cat-and-mouse game pitting the German teams against the French radio broadcasters, a chase that often ended with tragic consequences for the French operators. Of the approximately 100 radio teams operating in France, at least ten were arrested by the Germans.[16] The French had no way of knowing that the movement of the Pointe-du-Hoc guns was of any particular urgency, and no information exists about whether the Normandy cells ever informed London of the guns' movement via radio. As already mentioned above, one of the main Calvados Resistance cells was rolled up in early

May 1944, exactly the time that the Pointe-du-Hoc information would be passing through the network.

The other transmission method, and one that was used extensively by the smaller Resistance cells, was homing pigeons. The British SOE delivered large numbers of homing pigeons into France for communications between the Resistance and London.[17] The Germans were well aware of the use of pigeons for intelligence communications, and numerous divisions along the Atlantic Wall set up special pigeon patrols. Soldiers armed with shotguns patrolled along the coast with orders to shoot down any unfortunate bird that was seen. The Pointe-du-Hoc strongpoint conducted regular pigeon patrols. For example, on February 27, 1944, Uffz Müller was awarded a one-day special pass for having downed a courier pigeon.[18] In the Omaha Beach sector, the 352. Infanterie-Division's pigeon patrols downed no fewer than twenty-seven courier pigeons between March 20 and May 20, 1944.[19] It has been suggested that one of the downed pigeons may have carried one of the Pointe-du-Hoc messages. Furthermore, some pigeons returned to England but failed to reach their roost. The remains of one were found in 2012 in the chimney of an English house, with its message still intact.[20]

Even if London received reports that the guns had been moved, this information would not necessarily lead to the cancellation of the Pointe-du-Hoc mission. To some extent, the impact of this information would have depended upon when it arrived in London. Due to the sheer complexity of Operation *Neptune*, last-minute tactical changes would have been difficult.

But last-minute changes were not impossible. This can be seen in the case of the late arrival of the 91.Luftlande-Division on the Cotentin Peninsula in May 1944. Ultra intelligence decrypted a strategic appreciation of the situation in his command by the German commander-in-chief in the West (OB West), Generalfeldmarschall Gerd von Rundstedt, from May 8, 1944, that identified the transfer of the division. This information was distributed on May 13 and 14[21] and led to changes in the planned drop zones of the 82nd Airborne Division from

St Sauveur-le-Vicomte to the river Mederet area. So intelligence information could lead to changes in Allied planning, even in late May 1944; but why didn't it result in changes to the Pointe-du-Hoc plan?

Assuming for a moment that the French information about the Pointe-du-Hoc guns arrived in the first half of May, the reports would have to survive the scrutiny of the Allied intelligence handlers. The basic question was whether it was valid or not. It should be kept in mind that Allied intelligence did not always accept information from European intelligence networks at face value. The most glaring reason for this was the success of the Germans in turning the Dutch intelligence network, which passed false information back to London.[22] The British were at this very moment carrying on a similar counterintelligence operation against the German spy networks in Britain. Consequently, intelligence from foreign agents always was handled with a degree of skepticism.

Even assuming that Allied intelligence accepted the French data as valid, this did not invalidate the Ranger mission at Pointe-du-Hoc. To begin with, if the guns could be moved out of the Pointe-du-Hoc strongpoint, they could also be moved back there prior to D-Day. In March 1944, two of the guns had been temporarily moved away due to the construction of the gun casemates at Pointe-du-Hoc. As is detailed in Appendix D here about the neighboring Maisy batteries, the guns for one of the batteries were moved away from the strongpoint for several weeks during the construction of the new gun casemates; they returned prior to D-Day. This also happened with the Pointe-du-Hoc's sister battery at Riva-Bella. In other words, the movement of the guns away from Pointe-du-Hoc would have fitted the existing pattern of moving guns out of a strongpoint during the casemate construction phase. The critical question was whether the guns would be back in the battery positions prior to D-Day.

Allied intelligence believed the guns had returned to the strongpoint as late as May 31, when the final overall assessment of the German coastal batteries was conducted. The Top-Secret/Bigot report prepared on May 31 and circulated on June 1 indicated that there were at least five guns active at the Pointe-du-Hoc battery.[23] The report concluded that:

- four casemates were nearing completion;
- three open emplacements were intact and occupied;
- two open emplacements were damaged but still occupied;
- one gun was not accounted for, but not believed to have been destroyed.

If the French information had arrived after June 1, it would have been extremely difficult to make last-minute changes to the Ranger mission, simply because of the sheer bureaucratic inertia in such a massive undertaking. Late-arriving information would have encountered skepticism on the part of Allied intelligence regarding its timeliness and accuracy. It may have been dismissed as dated news dealing with the movement of the guns earlier in May prior to their return in late May.

Given the high levels of uncertainty when dealing with unconfirmed French intelligence, it would appear that Rudder was briefed about the information. However, the information was not judged significantly worrisome to consider altering the Ranger mission.

Even if the guns were not present, the Rangers' task still had a place in the *Neptune* mission. Aside from dealing with the Pointe-du-Hoc guns, the Ranger mission served to cover the right flank of Omaha Beach by securing the passage of the 116th RCT from the Vierville draw to the Isigny area on D-Day. This was the first step in the important operational goal of linking Omaha and Utah beaches.

Chapter 6

Softening Pointe-du-Hoc

Early planning by COSSAC for Operation *Neptune* presumed that the most threatening German coastal batteries, such as Pointe-du-Hoc and the Merville guns, would be dealt with by Ranger and airborne operations. The main problem with the Rangers' dawn attack on Pointe-du-Hoc was that the vulnerable transport ships of the Royal Navy and US Navy would already be in range of the Pointe-du-Hoc battery for several hours before the Rangers struck the site. In the debates over *Neptune* planning in early 1944, increasing attention was paid to suppressing the coastal batteries by air attack and naval bombardment before the Ranger units landed.

Lt Gen Carl Spaatz, the commander of the United States Strategic Air Forces in Europe (USSTAF), was adamantly opposed to diverting the heavy bombers for use against tactical targets such as the coastal batteries. The USSTAF was in the process of Operation *Pointblank*, a campaign to smash the Luftwaffe fighter force prior to D-Day.[1] Spaatz was in part opposed to the attacks on the gun batteries due to the dispersion of effort from *Pointblank*, but also because he felt his heavy bombers were poorly suited to attacking hardened, pinpoint targets such as gun bunkers. To demolish a bunker would require a direct hit, and the chances of hitting these very small, very well-protected targets was very, very unlikely.*

On April 3, 1944, a conference of senior Allied commanders was held at Widewing, the SHAEF headquarters in Bushy Park, southwest London. Air Chief Marshal Arthur Tedder, Gen Eisenhower's deputy, argued that bombing raids were ineffective against steel-reinforced concrete coastal artillery bunkers, and would be valuable only if staged before the concrete had been set or in a last-minute raid to disrupt the operation of the battery. Allied intelligence was aware that these gun sites relied on buried underground cables for communication between the command posts and gun positions that was essential for fire-control purposes. Heavy bombs could reach and damage the communication cables, disrupting the functioning of the battery. These arguments largely echoed the findings of the Graham Report.

The initial Joint Fire Plan for Operation *Neptune* was released on April 8, covering air support before and after D-Day.[2] According to the directive: "First priority is given to the neutralisation or destruction of [gun] batteries that might interfere with the approach of the Naval Forces. For this reason, the effort of the Heavy Night Bombers and Medium Oboe Bombers is allotted entirely to this type of target."[3]

On April 10, at another Widewing conference, Admiral Bertram Ramsay, the senior Allied naval commander for Operation *Neptune*, complained that no specific plans had been formulated to deal with the threat of the coastal batteries in a timely fashion. Ramsay had served in the Mediterranean theater and was well aware of the disruption caused by coastal batteries in amphibious landings such as those during Operation *Torch* and at Dieppe. After further arguments with Tedder and the *Neptune* air commander, Air Chief Marshal Sir Trafford Leigh-Mallory, the air commanders finally

---

* The Graham Report estimated it would take a force of about 90 B-17 bombers to have a 50 percent chance of hitting every gun pit in an eight-gun battery; for Pointe-du-Hoc's six-gun battery, the requirement would have been somewhat less. Attacks against casemated guns were not considered since at the time, the usual 500lb or 1,000lb bombs were incapable of penetrating the steel-reinforced concrete of the casemate roof.

agreed that a detailed program would be established to deal with the naval concerns.

To sort out the controversy, on April 13, a conference was held at RAF Bentley Priory northwest of London. Leigh-Mallory indicated that the coastal batteries were still in the process of construction, so it would be an ideal time to hit them.[4] The air commanders had been briefed by construction engineers, who noted that the concrete casemates presented a difficult target once the concrete had hardened. However, the concrete took weeks to harden after it had poured, and so was especially vulnerable during this interval.

Due to the resistance of the heavy bomber commands, the Allied Expeditionary Air Force agreed to use the medium bombers of the USAAF 9th Air Force and the RAF's 2nd Tactical Air Force (TAF) in the preliminary attacks on the gun bunkers on the presumption that lower-altitude raids had a greater chance of actually hitting the targets. Heavy bombers of both the USAAF and RAF would not be brought to bear until the final raids immediately preceding D-Day.

These final heavy bomber attacks were codenamed Operation *Flashlamp*. They focused on ten coastal batteries, with four singled out as posing a special hazard to the landing force: Pointe-du-Hoc, Houlgate, Villerville, and Ouistreham.

To avoid identifying the location of the *Neptune* landing area, SHAEF instructed the RAF and USAAF that it would be necessary to attack two targets outside of the *Neptune* area for every target bombed near the Normandy beaches. These were generally coastal gun batteries on the Pas-de-Calais. This policy was tied to an element of the overall *Bodyguard* strategic deception plan called Operation *Fortitude*. *Fortitude* was intended to convince the Germans that the main invasion would take place on the Pas-de-Calais, thereby tying down vital German resources and keeping defenses in Normandy as weak as possible. Operation *Fortitude* proved to be exceptionally effective, partly because it reflected the Germans' preconception that the Pas-de-Calais was the most natural invasion location.[5]

The need to conduct additional raids against the Pas-de-Calais resulted in a restriction of air attacks prior to D-Day to only the most important German gun batteries. Pointe-du-Hoc was one of these priority targets. Aside from the diversion of missions associated with the *Fortitude* deception, both the 9th Air Force and 2nd TAF had been assigned the politically sensitive mission of bombing German V-weapon sites in France, codenamed Operation *Crossbow*.[6] These attacks were absorbing from 25–50 percent of their missions. By the middle of May, *Crossbow* targets were reduced from 25 percent of the tactical bomber missions to only 10 percent in order to shift to the *Neptune* missions.

THE AIR ATTACKS BEGIN

The Pointe-du-Hoc battery was bombed for the first time in the early evening of April 25, 1944. Two A-20 Havoc medium bomber units were involved in the attack, the 409th Bombardment Group (BG) flying from RAF Little Walden and the 416th BG from RAF Wethersfield, both in Essex north of London. The attack was conducted in the early evening, with the first aircraft arriving over the site at 1659hrs (GMT). To minimize Flak damage, the formations flew across the French coast and away from Pointe-du-Hoc, then swung north again towards the target, striking from the rear of the strongpoint.

The attacks on the coastal batteries usually consisted of a mixture of 500lb general-purpose, high-explosive/fragmentation bombs and 1,000lb semi-armor-piercing (SAP) bombs. The 500lb bombs, when fitted with a delayed-action fuze, could create a crater about 5ft deep and 20ft wide. The 1,000lb SAP bombs, intended to penetrate the concrete structures, were fitted with a specially hardened steel nose cap. These required a direct hit on the concrete structure to do any significant damage. In the event that they landed on the ground near a bunker, they could be expected to create a crater 13ft deep and 45ft in diameter,[7] which was sufficient to rip up buried communication cables.

When the bombers arrived over Pointe-du-Hoc, many of the troops of 2./HKAA.1260 were queuing up for supper at the canteen in the Guelinel farm. The skies were clear and cloudless. One of the German soldiers recalled the scene:

> When we entered [the canteen], there are only a few men there. By custom, we waited a little while until the others arrived. Suddenly we heard a loud hum and then a roar. It sounded [like] a steam locomotive coming into the station… Immediately after, the first large bombs fell on the farm. We heard the bomb bursts rapidly approaching us. Everything trembles and shakes. We ran towards the exit, Otto Keller at the head. But we can't go any further. A few meters ahead of us, the next bomb falls on the barracks. I can still see the flame and the dust.[8]

The soldier mentioned in the account, Otto Keller, was one of two men killed during the attack when he was hit in the head by a steel fragment from the bombs. The first wave of bombers hit the rear of the strongpoint, mostly around the Guelinel farm, while the following two hit the battery positions themselves. In total, the 51 A-20 bombers dropped 49½ tons of bombs, more than a ton per acre, including 193 500lb general-purpose bombs and five 200lb general-purpose bombs. The bomber crews assessed their accuracy as generally good. An assessment the following day recorded: "Practically the entire target area with the exception of Nos. 3 and 4 gun positions is blanketed with bursts… A building just south of the target area has received a direct hit and is seen burning in later photos."[9] Another report indicated that overall it was an accurate attack: 60 bombs struck in the target area, damaging three emplacements, with unclear damage on the gun casemates, and several buildings damaged.[10]

From the German perspective, the attack was both accurate and devastating. A German higher headquarters report stated: "Pointe du Hoc: 1800 hours. During the attack on army coastal battery 2./1260 (east of Grandcamp) by 50 bombs, 1 gun was destroyed, communication cable cut. Remaining guns operational after clean-up work. Personnel casualties were 2 dead, 1 heavily wounded, 2 lightly wounded."[11]

The April 25 USAAF raid was followed up with a photo-reconnaissance sortie. The resulting images were interpreted by the RAF and a report on the raid issued on April 28:

No. 1 emplacement: Crater 14 yards from centre – some damage to outer part.

No. 4 emplacement: Possible direct hit; craters 10 yards and 14 yards from centre, bed of emplacement destroyed.

No. 1 gun casemate: Direct hit on completed foundations. Extensive damage.

No. 2 gun casemate: Crater 30 ft from SE corner. No apparent damage.

No. 3 gun casemate: Crater 14 ft from NE corner. Crater 28 ft forward of casemate causing partial demolition of front wall.

No. 4 gun casemate: Crater 28 ft from centre on NNE side appears to have demolished front wall of casemate.

Command Post: A crater is seen 14 yds from NW corner of the probable command post, which is apparently undamaged, and at least one direct hit and two near misses on the probable crew accommodation in farm buildings in the rear of the battery. The road serving the battery is blocked by a direct hit between the farm buildings and the command post.[12]

The Allied assessment of the raid slightly exaggerated the damage. The apparent collapse of the front wall of the two gun casemates was due to the non-standard construction technique, with some of the concrete cinder-blocks having been knocked loose by the bomb detonations. The actual core of the building was not significantly damaged.

A Swedish artillery officer who visited Normandy immediately after the war to study the German coastal defenses reported that the Germans had moved the guns away from the site immediately after this first bombing attack. The process of moving the guns took two evenings, since only a single vehicle was available to tow them to a new location.[13] German historian Helmut Konrad von Keusgen interviewed veterans of 2./HKAA.1260 and confirmed that the battery pulled the guns away from Pointe-du-Hoc on the night of April 25/26 after this first attack.[14] The guns were moved to a tree line about 1,000 yards south on the Guérin farm. It also seems likely that the battery officers shifted their accommodations from the heavily damaged Guelinel farm buildings to the Guérin farmhouse that was farther to the southwest.

The second air attack took place just over two weeks later at 1139hrs on May 13. The 322nd BG ("Nye's Annihilators"), flying 35 B-26 Marauders, departed RAF Andrews Field in Essex, with two aircraft aborting the mission before reaching Pointe-du-Hoc. Unlike the first strike, the mission on May 13 encountered rainy and cloudy weather conditions along the Normandy coast.[15] The 33 B-26 Marauders dropped sixty-nine 2,000lb bombs.

Flak over Pointe-du-Hoc was described as "weak and inaccurate." At the time, the site was protected by two 37mm automatic cannon and two 20mm automatic cannon. A single 88mm gun was later added, but the site never received a fire-control radar or other sophisticated air defense equipment.

A P-38 Lightning photo-reconnaissance aircraft was sent over the battery that afternoon to conduct a post-strike assessment. The raid was judged as unsuccessful, probably due to the rain. A German assessment of the attack estimated the scale of the attack as forty bombers dropping thirty light and twelve heavy bombs. The communication trenches between the main positions were buried, but no guns were destroyed or damaged and there were no personnel casualties.[16] Later Allied assessments of this mission suggest that it was the least successful of the pre-D-day attacks, with only a handful of near misses on the western side of the site.[17] An RAF report based on a later photo-reconnaissance sortie indicated that "Mines were set off by sympathetic detonation."[18] This was in the minefield south of the strongpoint and about 100 yards north of the D514 main road. Subsequent photo missions confirmed the existence of the east–west minefield on the southern perimeter of the strongpoint due to several mine detonations.

A minor mystery about this bombing mission was a short and cryptic note in the war diary of the German 7.Armee that reported that on May 13, there was a bombing attack in the 352. Infanterie-Division sector, and that three guns were ready to fire at "2./1261 Pointe du Roc."[19] There are two obvious problems to this report. First, 2./1261 was not the Pointe-du-Hoc battery (which was 2./1260), but the Azeville battery, which was not in the 352. Infanterie-Division sector but on the east coast of the Cotentin peninsula. Also, there is a Pointe du Roc on the Cotentin peninsula near Granville, but once again, not in the 352.Infanterie-Division sector. These are most likely just typing or spelling mistakes. If so, this note confirms other German reports that indicate that by mid-May, only three guns were functional at Pointe-du-Hoc, with one destroyed and two damaged by the first bombing attack.

On May 21, Pointe-du-Hoc was hit by an impromptu strike by several P-47 Thunderbolt fighters which strafed the strongpoint around 1345hrs. The Flak guns at Pointe-du-Hoc hit at least one fighter, which departed the area trailing smoke. A German report indicates that at the time, two guns were still damaged but that the battery was ready to fire, presumably from the improvised location along the Guérin farm path.[20]

Due to the poor results of the May 13 mission, another bomber attack was launched the following week on May 22 by the 323rd BG "White Tails" from RAF Earls Colne, Essex. The mission involved 32 B-26 Marauder bombers, three of which aborted before reaching the target. Weather conditions over Normandy were clear. A total of 56 tons of bombs were dropped between 1928 and 1950hrs, consisting of 54 2,000lb and eight 500lb general-purpose bombs. The results were reported to be "fair to poor."[21] Post-strike assessments counted only thirteen hits on the site and four below on the cliffs.[22] One bomb struck near the No 2 gun pit without causing any damage, but most of the bombs missed or hit at the foot of the cliff. Five guns appeared to have been in their emplacements.[23]

The battery reported that the attack had been conducted by between sixteen and eighteen bombers. According to a German report, the No 4 gun position was destroyed and the gun pit of the No 3 gun was severely damaged.[24] The third of the new gun casemates that was under construction was so badly damaged that Organization Todt gave up any attempts to complete it. There were no personnel casualties. Due to the heavy cratering around the site, Organization Todt ceased any further construction on the site, and was mainly involved in cleanup actions after the raids. A Kriegsmarine summary of damage to coastal batteries between April 10 and May 30, 1944 indicated that the 2./HKAA.1260 had suffered one gun destroyed and two damaged.[25]

The largest medium bomber raid to date was staged on June 4, just two days before D-Day. This was conducted by two A-20 Havoc bombardment groups. The 416th BG from RAF Wethersfield, flying 37 A-20Gs and six A-20Hs, dropped 50½ tons of bombs, starting around 1502hrs, with results judged "good to fair." The 409th Bomb Group, flying from RAF Little Walden followed at 1522hrs with 42 A-20 Havoc bombers, delivering 51 tons of bombs with the results judged "poor to fair." A subsequent photo-reconnaissance mission assessed the damage that day as including "60 new craters in target area. Near misses on command post and gun positions 1, 4, 5, 6." A German report that day indicated that three of the personnel bunkers had received direct hits, causing only insignificant damage. The gun pit of the No 6 gun was destroyed. A decontamination room and a weapons storage room were also destroyed, but there were no personnel losses.[26]

PRE-D-DAY BOMBER ATTACKS AGAINST POINTE-DU-HOC

Date	Attack Time	Unit	Aircraft	Bomb tonnage
Apr 25	1659hrs	416th BG	35 (2)* A-20s	33¾
Apr 25	1731hrs	409th BG	16 (4) A-20s	16
May 13	1139hrs	322nd BG	33 (2) B-26s	66
May 22	1928hrs	323rd BG	29 (3) B-26s	56
Jun 4	1510hrs	416th BG	43 A-20s	50½
Jun 4	1522hrs	409th BG	42 A-20s	51
Jun 5	0921hrs	379th BG	35 B-17s	104¼

Data in parentheses indicate aircraft which sortied but aborted

While the five 155mm guns remained near Pointe-du-Hoc, there is still some mystery about whether the Germans planned to move these guns back into the casemates when completed or to install fresh new guns. A US Navy report compiled after D-Day, based on prisoner interrogations, stated that "it was the enemy's intention to install new guns, which were momentarily expected. A captured document from Admiral Hennike's [sic] headquarters revealed that the position was intended to house 6 155mm guns."[27]

Chapter 7

Obliteration

The April 13 AEAF directive authorized the use of heavy bombers against key coastal gun positions immediately before the start of the D-Day landings. These missions were codenamed Operation *Flashlamp*. The original plan was to launch the Operation *Neptune* landings on June 5, but they were postponed for a day due to poor weather conditions in the English Channel and along the Normandy coast. However, *Flashlamp* raids began on June 5 as originally planned.

The first *Flashlamp* mission against Pointe-du-Hoc was executed by the 379th BG, one of the 8th Air Force's best units, given the "Operational Grand Slam" award for its performance in April 1944.* This mission departed from RAF Kimbolton in Cambridgeshire at 0614hrs on June 5. A total of forty B-17 bombers plus one pathfinder were involved in the mission, but five aircraft were designated as spares and did not actually drop bombs. The thirty-six "active" aircraft dropped a total of 427 500lb bombs, starting around 0921hrs, and were judged to have hit about 500ft right

---

*The Grand Slam was awarded when a group met five criteria for a month of operations: best bombing results, greatest tonnage dropped, largest number of aircraft, lowest losses, and lowest abortive rate of aircraft dispatched. It was awarded only once by the 8th Air Force, to the 379th Bombardment Group for its April 1944 performance.

of the target area but with "fair-to-good" results. An assessment the following day based on film taken during the raid concluded that "more than 50 bursts blanket the target area and there are probable hits on 2 or more [of] the six 15.5cm French guns and other installations. Concentrations are also seen in the fields immediately adjacent to the target area and in the water to the north."[1] A German report indicated that one of the new gun casemates under construction was damaged during the raid.[2] Information on this raid from the German perspective is not very detailed, since it would have arrived at high command headquarters on June 6, D-Day, and so was presumably lost in the chaos of the invasion.

The next mission occurred in the pre-dawn hours of D-Day and was by far the largest bombing attack to date, exceeding the tonnage of all five previous missions combined. It was also the only RAF mission against Pointe-du-Hoc. The role of the RAF in obliterating the Pointe-du-Hoc battery has been obscured by the fact that most RAF documents of the time refer to the raid as being directed at St Pierre-du-Mont, the village south of Pointe-du-Hoc. However, this was the common British identification for the Pointe-du-Hoc battery at the time.

Since the mission was conducted in darkness, the attack was preceded by Pathfinder Mosquitos. The tactics used at Pointe-du-Hoc had been perfected over the past year during night attacks against German cities. The Pathfinders were equipped with the Airborne Radio A.R.5513 navigation aid, better known as Oboe. An Oboe radio station, codenamed Cat, emitted a radio signal that was received and retransmitted by a radio transponder on the Mosquito. When the Mosquito reached a specified range, the Cat station ordered the Mosquito pilot to turn south to follow the circumference of the circular track emitted by the station that would bring the aircraft directly over the target. The Cat signal gave the pilot audio cues about whether the aircraft was right or left of the track so that course corrections could be made. The second Oboe station, codenamed Mouse, created a second circular track of radio signals that crossed the Cat track at a point over the target. When the Cat and Mouse tracks intersected each other, the

Mosquito crew was instructed to drop its payload. This could of course be supplemented by visual sighting.

The payload for the Pathfinder Mosquitos were brilliant illumination flare dispensers, known by the abbreviation TI (Target Indicators).[3] On the Pointe-du-Hoc mission, the Pathfinders used a tactic called "sky-marking" in which the Target Indicator containers opened up in the air, usually at around 1,500ft, and then spread dozens of "candles" that slowly drifted to the ground below.[*] These remained illuminated for seven to twelve minutes, even after they had reached the ground.

The first flight of two Oboe-equipped Mosquitos arrived at Pointe-du-Hoc around 0445hrs. A Mosquito IX flown by Flt Lt Gordon from 105 Squadron, 8 (Pathfinder) Group, began dropping red illumination flares over the headlands. A second Mosquito piloted by Wing Commander Cundall was unable to drop its markers. As these aircraft exited, three more Mosquitos from 109 Squadron arrived: two of these dropped green markers from altitudes of 30,000ft and 18,000ft; the third Mosquito brought back its markers due to an unspecified technical glitch.

Cloud cover that night varied, but was estimated at about 5/10ths, with denser cloud cover over 10,000ft. Some bombers encountered a cloud layer around 7,000ft along with icing, and so descended below this. The bright markers provided the aiming point for the subsequent waves of Lancaster bombers, while the colored markers provided an eerie illumination over Pointe-du-Hoc as they slowly drifted downward. French farmers in neighboring villages recalled that the "sky was on fire" as the brilliant markers cascaded down through the clouds.

Within moments, the first stream of Lancaster bombers flew over Pointe-du-Hoc. The first aircraft began bombing around 0451hrs, aiming at the points illuminated by the TI markers. Eight Lancaster squadrons from 5 Group totaling 115 aircraft, along with four Mosquitos, bombed Pointe-du-Hoc for about half an

---

[*]The number of candles depended on the type of TI. The 250lb TI contained sixty 9in. candles, while the 1,000lb TI had 200.

hour. The aircraft arrived at altitudes ranging from 6,000–12,000ft. Typical payloads for the bombers were eleven 1,000lb SAP bombs and four 500lb bombs each.

The Operations Record Book of one of the squadrons recalled the mission:

> Today must be recorded as one of the most eventful days in the [97] Squadron's history. The target had been given us at about 1pm. It was a battery of coastal heavy guns on the French coast at a point called St Pierre du Mont, which is situated just on the south eastern base of the Cherbourg Peninsula... It seemed quite a normal target until various other things came trickling in – things such as convoys to be avoided – keeping strictly on track, news of impending naval actions to the East, and many other things, until one became aware of the obvious that the invasion of Europe was about to commence... Everyone was delighted and excitement was at fever pitch... Eighteen of our aircraft were detailed. The attack started at 4.50am – about 30 minutes before dawn – with a red TI which was accurately dropped by an Oboe Mosquito on the target. It was instantly backed up by green TI dropped visually by Mosquito aircraft of 627 Squadron. These TI were not so accurate as those dropped by Oboe. However, by the time Main Force came in to bomb, the target was well marked. The Main Force bombing was extremely accurate and the whole point was flattened. Crossing the Channel on the return journey thousands of landing craft were seen proceeding towards the French coast."[4]

The large number of aircraft converging over the small target led to some near collisions over Pointe-du-Hoc. Two aircraft failed to bomb after their pilots were forced to take evasive action to avoid mid-air collisions. Several of the pilots later reported that they could see the target area, and at least one noted that he had spotted Pointe-du-Hoc's distinctive headland. In total, 5 Group's *Flashlamp* mission showered the site with more than 634 tons of bombs, over 20 tons of bombs per acre.

A later report by 463 Squadron stated: "This very large position was wiped out, and the results of our bombing, which was staggering, had never been excelled, and paved the way for successful landing on the beachheads by our troops. The concentration of our bombing was really outstanding."[5]

AERIAL DUEL OVER POINTE-DU-HOC

The attacking RAF bombers did not escape unscathed. The first Allied D-Day casualties near Pointe-du-Hoc were not American, but British, Australian, and Canadian bomber crews from the *Flashlamp* raid. Around 0500hrs, the Lancaster bombers on the Pointe-du-Hoc mission were confronted by Focke Wulf Fw 190 fighters in the first large aerial battle of D-Day.

There is a widespread public perception that the only significant Luftwaffe action on D-Day was the sortie by "Pips" Priller and his wingman over the D-Day beaches on the morning of June 6.[*] This was certainly not the case. This legend can be traced back to Cornelius Ryan's bestselling book, *The Longest Day*, and the associated motion picture which highlighted Priller's adventures. In the case of Pointe-du-Hoc, the aerial battles pitted some of the elite members of the RAF's Bomber Command against one of the Luftwaffe's most obscure and audacious fighter squadrons, preceding Priller's more famous mission by several hours.

The Luftwaffe unit involved in the Pointe-du-Hoc air battles was I.Gruppe, Schnell-kampfgeschwader.10 (I./SKG.10: 1st Squadron, Fast Attack Wing 10).[6] This squadron was not a normal fighter unit, but a ground-attack squadron equipped with Fw 190G fighter-bombers. In 1943, most of the wing was sent to the Italian Front, but I.Gruppe remained in France to conduct hit-and-run bombing raids against the English coast under the cover of darkness. The

---

[*]Oberst Priller and his wingman from Jagdgeschwader.26 departed from the airstrip around 0800hrs and conducted their famous strafing run over Sword Beach shortly afterwards.

squadron paid a heavy price for these raids, since it was often targeted by radar-equipped RAF night-fighters.

In April 1944, the squadron's higher headquarters, II.Fliegerkorps, gave it a new mission. Since there were so few dedicated German night-fighters in France, the squadron was assigned to carry out "Wilde Sau" (wild boar) missions on nights where there were clear skies and a full moon. These missions were mainly aimed at RAF bombers conducting pre-*Overlord* strikes against targets in France. The missions were called Wild Boar since they did not have the aid of airborne interception radars of the type fitted to dedicated Luftwaffe night-fighters. The Fw 190 was too small for the airborne radars of the day, which were fitted to larger twin-engine night-fighters such as the Messerschmitt Bf 110 and Junkers Ju 88C that were spacious enough to accommodate a dedicated radar operator.

At best, the Wild Boar fighters would sometimes receive navigational cues from ground-based Luftwaffe radar stations. Ground control of these Wild Boar missions became increasingly useless in late May 1944 due to the Allied campaign to wipe out Luftwaffe radar stations prior to D-Day.[7] As a result, the pilots had to show considerable individual initiative to locate and attack RAF bombers, using their eyesight alone. Many missions were futile because of the difficulty of finding targets in the dark. But occasionally, the Wild Boars were successful in their hunt: on the night of May 3/4, the Wild Boars of SKG.10 struck RAF bombers that were attacking the Panzer training center at Mailly-le-Camp east of Paris, shooting down six bombers that night.

Due to these previous Wild Boar missions, I./SKG.10 was unusually well prepared to conduct night sorties against Allied bombers. The squadron's air strip was already busy because its 2.Staffel (2nd Flight) had conducted a hit-and-run bombing raid over Portsmouth earlier on the evening of June 5. The Gruppe commander, Maj Kurt Dahlmann, first ordered the squadron into action around midnight on D-Day. There were reports of intense Allied aerial activity in Lower Normandy, including possible paratrooper drops. The pilots were a bit skeptical about the reports of paratroopers as there had been several false alarms on previous evenings. In the event, the squadron scrambled from its forward base at Evreux, a simple grass airstrip about 150 miles from the American paratroop drop zones behind Utah Beach. The mission was as much a reconnaissance sortie as a fighter sweep. So many German radars had been bombed or jammed that the Luftwaffe had no clear picture of what was happening off the Normandy coast. A storm was still passing through the Calvados coast, so there was broken cloud cover with occasional areas of moonlit sky. One of the pilots in the 2.Staffel, Oberfähnrich (NCO) Wolfgang Zebrowski, later recalled:

> We were ordered to get all available aircraft ready to attack and destroy the transport gliders and their four-engine tugs reported to be near Saint-Lô. The night was dark and the visibility not very good when we took off again. On arriving in the sector, I stared into the darkness like a lynx, looking from side to side, expecting to see the tell-tale signs of tracers from machine guns or from aircraft cannons. But there were no signs of heavy gliders! When I only had the fuel for the return trip, I headed back to Evreux. I was frustrated and disappointed that I had not been successful. The other pilots didn't do any better and everyone returned without having seen or done anything.[8]

The Allied transports were not over Saint-Lô, but farther to the northwest past Carentan, near the outer range of the German fighters. By the time that the German fighters reached the area, the C-47 Skytrain transports had departed back to Britain and the Wild Boars were low on fuel. After this futile and confusing mission, the German fighter-bombers returned to their forward base to refuel. Their timing was extremely lucky, as their base was being monitored by radar-equipped RAF Mosquito night-fighters that were on the prowl for German aircraft operating from the Évreux and Saint-André-de-l'Eure air-strips. When the Mosquito intruders passed over the SKG.10 base at Évreux a short time earlier, the base was dark and there was no evidence of air activity. An Me 410 of 4./Kampfgeschwader.51 was not so lucky and was shot down when returning to its base at nearby Saint-André around 0130hrs.[9]

Reports continued to arrive of extensive Allied air activity all along the Calvados coast. Shortly before dawn, Maj Dahlmann ordered his squadron airborne again with the mission to try to determine what was happening along the coast. The 3.Staffel, led by Hauptmann Helmut Eberspächer, was instructed to conduct a sortie towards the coast from Caen to Carentan. Eberspächer, 29 years old at the time, was the scion of a successful German automotive parts manufacturer. He had served as a reconnaissance pilot until May 1943, when he was posted to SKG.10. In May 1944, he was appointed as a flight commander in the squadron. He eventually became an ace with seven aerial victories, and was highly decorated for his actions in Normandy.[*] Eberspächer's 3.Staffel had four Fw 190G fighter-bombers ready for operations. The distance from their forward base at Evreux to the Carentan area was about 125 miles, taking under 30 minutes at cruising speed. Eberspächer later recalled:

> It was still pitch-black, we were all excited – you could also call it fear – of what would await us up front. There was a full moon in the night sky. You buckle up, let [the ground crew] tell you about any problems with the engine, the weapons, or anything else, you pressed the start button, the BMW 801 engine started, the ground crewman hopped from the wing onto the ground, waved 'ready to go' – and you sat wedged in the narrow cabin… Taking off from an auxiliary airfield in the dark with a single-engine fighter plane, which is designed for day missions, was a tricky moment in wartime, because the pilot initially had no view to the front and could therefore hardly assess whether the machine was moving straight ahead or in a curve.[10]

---

[*] Eberspächer was awarded the German Cross in Gold (Deutsches Kreuz in Gold) on July 23, 1944, and the Knight's Cross of the Iron Cross (Ritterkreuz des Eisernen Kreuzes) on January 24, 1945, after 170 ground-attack missions over the Western Front. His aerial kill claims included the three night kills claimed on D-Day and four daylight victories later in 1944. His squadron was assigned as a night-attack squadron later in the war.

Due to their training as fighter-bomber pilots, Eberspächer's flight flew at low altitude under the cloud cover. Flying at night with only intermittent moonlight through the clouds, it was too dangerous to stay in formation. Once they left Evreux, the four Focke Wulfs flew to the combat zone on their own. Eberspächer flew over the water along the Calvados shoreline to simplify navigation in the dark, and later described the scene:

> Gradually it became brighter on the horizon. With every minute it became clearer to see what was going on below me. It was stupendous. On the sea below, the contours of hundreds of ships of various sizes emerged from the gloom. In the vanguard, directly along the coast, parallel to the beach, lay the heavy warships, which fired broadsides from all their guns at the German bunkers of the Atlantic Wall. In between, as if on a string of pearls, the landing craft struggled towards the coast, led by a motor boat at the tip of the string. For me from the air, flying at 450 km/h, the scene down there hardly seemed to move. But my imagination was enough to guess what was going on – and I was right in the middle of it all – in the tumult of muzzle flashes, bombs and flares… In order to see as much as possible, I threw caution to the wind and descended to a few hundred meters. I flew over a heavy warship at low altitude, but [it] didn't fire a shot at me, in spite of its dozens of anti-aircraft guns.[11]

By the time he passed over Omaha Beach, Eberspächer's fuel gauge indicated that the Focke Wulf was running low on fuel and he would soon have to turn back. As he started to make the turn back to Evreux, "I saw a row of what were obviously British bombers above me, below the moonlit cloud cover. They stood out against the clouds like in an unworldly shadow play, a magic lantern show. But they couldn't see me against the dark ground below."

Eberspächer had stumbled into part of the RAF bomber stream from 5 Group as it was finishing its bomb-run over Pointe-du-Hoc around 0500hrs. The original RAF plan had been to attack from 9,000ft or higher. However, as we have seen, the bombers encountered cloud cover and icing around 7,000ft and so flew lower to avoid these issues. This was unusually low for Lancaster night missions, but German Flak defenses on the Normandy coast were quite feeble compared to the deadly night skies over their usual targets in Germany. The bombers approached Pointe-du-Hoc from the northeast, and after their bomb run they continued south towards Isigny for a short distance. They tried to minimize flying over the invasion fleet on the return trip for fear that the trigger-happy antiaircraft gunners on the ships below might fire at them, as had happened to Allied aircraft over the Sicily invasion fleet in July 1943. So instead of taking the shortest route home to Britain, they flew west past Carentan and Cherbourg before heading north.

The RAF aircraft in Eberspächer's gunsight were a loose stream of Lancaster Mk III heavy bombers of 97 Squadron. This was a high-tech squadron that had belonged to the Pathfinder Force (PFF) until April 1944, when it was attached to 5 Group. The crews of the PFF were the elite of Bomber Command, trained in advanced night navigation to serve as the spearhead for night missions deep into the heart of the Reich. Their aircraft were equipped with specialized night-bombing aids, including Oboe and the revolutionary H2S ground navigation radar.

Probably the first aircraft that Eberspächer attacked was Lancaster ND501, squadron code OF–Q, piloted by Flt Lt G. F. Baker. Baker later reported that he was attacked about five minutes before his bomb run over Pointe-du-Hoc, so around 0500hrs. Eberspächer made his first victory claim for an engagement at 0501hrs at an altitude of 2,000 meters.[12] Although he claimed to have shot down this first bomber, it was in fact only damaged.

Eberspächer continued his attack through the bomber stream, shooting down two Lancasters of 97 Squadron in the area around Isigny and Carentan. The entire engagement lasted only three minutes, from 0501 to 0504hrs. The next Lancaster attacked by Eberspächer was probably ND815/OF–G, which crashed near Osmanville on the eastern side of the Vire estuary. The crew of this aircraft was mainly Norwegian, and it was piloted by Lt F. V. Jespersen. None of them survived.

The third of the 97 Squadron Lancasters attacked by Eberspächer that morning was piloted by Wing Commander E. J. (Jimmy) Carter, the commander of 97 Squadron and deputy commander for the *Flashlamp* mission against Pointe-du-Hoc.

Carter had taken over command of the squadron six months earlier, in January 1944, and had already been decorated with the Distinguished Flying Cross for his combat service. Prior to take-off, Carter had remarked to other squadron members, "Thank God I'm still on ops [operations] and not at an O.T.U. [operational training unit]." Like most other 97 Squadron pilots, Carter anticipated a relatively brief and uneventful mission, since the target was so near to Britain. Compared to missions deep into Germany, the Normandy sites were not heavily protected by either Flak or fighters. Most pilots expected to be back home for breakfast. Carter's seven-man crew was exceptional; among them were holders of four Distinguished Flying Crosses and three Distinguished Flying Medals.*

Carter's Lancaster III bomber, serial number ND739, squadron code OF–Z, was fitted with H2S ground navigation radar. This substantially increased the accuracy of the bomb run when there was cloud cover. As deputy commander for the mission, Carter was obliged to remain on the radio with the rest of the force through the operation, relaying orders from the mission's Master Bomber, who was flying in a specially equipped Mosquito. Carter was last heard on the radio by the mission's Deputy Controller at 0504hrs, with his voice ending abruptly in mid-sentence. This time corresponds with that given by Eberspächer for his final interception of the Lancasters.

Ahead of Carter's aircraft was another Lancaster from his squadron, ND961/OF–N, piloted by Squadron Leader Charles B. Owen, whose rear turret gunner saw Carter's aircraft burst into flames. Owen later recalled: "We bombed at 0500 just as it

---

*There was a total of eight men onboard his aircraft that day, the extra crew being a "Special Air Bomber" to operate its specialized equipment. Of the eight men, six were British, one Australian, and one Canadian.

was getting light and had a grandstand view of the Americans running in on the beach. First class prang on the battery, but saw Jimmy Carter shot down by a Ju 88 over the target."[13] Owen was mistaken about the identity of the German fighter, unsurprisingly considering the clouds and dull dawn sky. Owen did not see if the crew had escaped by parachute before the aircraft crashed. Eberspächer later stated that some crew had parachuted from at least one of the bombers he shot down.

Carter and his crew were listed as "missing" later on D-Day when they failed to return to RAF Coningsby in Lincolnshire. Months later, the RAF made enquiries to the International Red Cross in Geneva, acting as an intermediary to the Luftwaffe prisoner-of-war camps. There were no traces of any of the members of Carter's crew in the Luftwaffe records, which suggested that they had been killed and not captured.

The wreck of Carter's aircraft was not discovered until 2010, when aviation archeologist Tony Graves located an unidentified aircraft wreck in a marsh near Brucheville, a small French farming community on the western side of the Vire estuary about 2 miles northeast of Carentan and 15 miles from Pointe-du-Hoc.[14] It was a short distance from the crash site of the Norwegian Lancaster shot down moments before. It took time for Graves to obtain French government permission to excavate the site and organize the use of specialized excavation equipment, so the wreck was not dug out until 2012.

Like many aircraft wrecks, the Lancaster disintegrated due to the violent, high-speed impact. The smashed debris was buried deep in the marshy ground, with few features to confirm the identity of the aircraft. Obvious identification features such as the unit codes or serial number on the fuselage were shattered beyond all recognition. No bodies of the crew were discovered during the excavation. It was presumed that they had been located and buried by one of the local French communities, like so many others during the war, in graves marked simply as "unknown." The mystery of the wreck's identity was solved after a ring from one of the crewmen was discovered.

The story of the wreck recovery went largely unnoticed except within the community of aviation specialists. Curiously enough, it stirred up some controversy in Australia. The popular weekly TV news program "60 Minutes-Australia" broadcast a sensationalistic episode in April 2013 suggesting that there had been an official cover-up of the crash, perhaps connected to its top-secret radar. Australian TV was interested in the story because the Lancaster's navigator, R. J. Conley, was Australian.

The third bomber lost on the Pointe-du-Hoc mission was Lancaster ND874/VN-R from 50 Squadron, piloted by Pilot Officer Roland G. Ward of the Royal Australian Air Force. Another German pilot, Feldwebel Eisele, claimed a Lancaster over Carentan on this mission, and it was probably this one.[15] Only a single member of this Lancaster crew survived, Sgt S. K. Reading, the mid-upper gunner. He was closest to the fuselage door, which probably saved his life, although he was badly burned while attempting to escape the aircraft. Reading later recalled that his aircraft was hit near Pointe-du-Hoc by 20mm light Flak, but in view of the confusing circumstances that night, it more likely was 20mm fighter cannon fire when the Focke Wulf attacked, unseen, from under the bomber.

Reading was captured by German troops after landing by parachute, probably by the 352.Infanterie-Division which was conducting patrols in this area to deal with the scattered American paratrooper drops from earlier in the morning. His captors took him to Balleroy, about 25 miles to the southeast of Pointe-du-Hoc. Over the next few days, he was bundled up with a number of other Allied prisoners and sent farther south to Caumont l'Eventé. This town was in the path of US forces advancing southward from Omaha Beach in the days after D-Day. Troops of the US 1st Infantry Division reached the outskirts of the town on the evening of June 12. Reading and some of the other prisoners had convinced their captors to leave them behind when they retreated, and they were freed the following day when the 26th Infantry Regiment, supported by the 743rd Tank Battalion, liberated Caumont.

Eberspächer escaped without a scratch from his encounters with the Lancaster bombers near Pointe-du-Hoc, but on returning to his squadron's base at Evreux, his Focke Wulf was hit by trigger-happy German Flak gunners in a village on the approaches to his airbase. There was a German Army saying at the time that if an airplane was blue it was American, if red it was British, and if it was invisible it was German! In view of all the Allied air activity that morning, such mistakes were inevitable. Eberspächer managed to reach the grass strip in his crippled aircraft, but one of its landing gears collapsed and the Focke Wulf swung wildly around before coming to a stop. Uninjured from the crash, he was rushed to the squadron's headquarters in a nearby chateau and put on the telephone to the Luftflotte 2 headquarters in Paris. He reached the chief of staff, Generalleutnant Ernst Müller, and described his experiences over the Allied invasion fleet. This was the first detailed information that the Luftwaffe had about the D-Day landings. Moments into the phone conversation, Müller was joined by the air fleet commander, Generalfeldmarschall Wolfram Freiherr von Richthofen, cousin of the Red Baron and a World War I ace in his own right. The senior commanders peppered Eberspächer with questions for over an hour. It became very obvious from Eberspächer's experiences that the invasion had finally started.

THE SKY ON FIRE

In the days before D-Day, the mood of the German garrison at Pointe-du-Hoc was grim. The composition of the garrison had changed over the past several months. Due to the heavy troop losses on the Russian Front in the summer of 1943, many units in France were combed for young, fit soldiers. Pointe-du-Hoc was no exception, where several younger troops were replaced by older artillery veterans from World War I. One of the soldiers at Pointe-du-Hoc later recalled: "Towards the end of 1943, increasingly old soldiers, up to 50 years old, arrived at our Strongpoint. They thought a lot about their families in the country, and their morale suffered." Those who were transferred were not all replaced, and the battery's personnel strength fell from a high of 220 in the summer of 1943 to about 120 by the end of May 1944. A senior German artillery officer later complained:

> It became increasingly difficult to train these physically deficient and older men for the multifaceted duties of the coast artillery. This service required adaptability since each man had to be trained on both heavy artillery weapons and as infantry, and some as communication troops, forward observers, or supply services. The number of men in a battery had to be reduced as low as possible on account of the personnel shortage [on the Russian Front].[16]

The declining quality of the troops at the Pointe-du-Hoc battery was evident even to the local French civilians who encountered them in the local cafés in Grandcamp. Jean Marion, a member of the municipal council in Grandcamp, recalled that, "From the beginning of 1944, it was a different caliber of troops. They were terrified. They told the French people 'we are going to be chopped up.'"[17]

The ultimate sign of the demoralization of the Pointe-du-Hoc garrison occurred three weeks before D-Day. The battery officers had moved to the Guérin farm in late April after the Guelinel farm had been damaged in the first Allied bombing attack on Pointe-du-Hoc on April 25. Around noon one day, a German soldier entered the building while the officers were sitting around a table eating lunch. The soldier had recently been informed that his family in Germany had been killed in an air raid. Distraught at the news about his family, he decided to kill the battery officers and himself using an explosive device.[18] Among the dead was probably the battery commander, Oberleutnant Brotkorb.[19] A new replacement commander was sent only a week before D-Day, hardly enough time to become accustomed to his new command. His name remains unknown.

When the Lancaster bombers arrived on D-Day morning around 0445hrs, the Pointe-du-Hoc garrison was already in the bunkers due to alert warnings that started three hours earlier. The night sky was filled with tracer fire, flares, and unexplained explosions. Over 800 USAAF C-47 Skytrain transports had arrived over the Cotentin peninsula around 0130hrs and dropped paratroopers behind Utah Beach to the west. A few of these aircraft missed their objectives and flew near Pointe-du-Hoc. As will be detailed later,[20] at least one C-47 dropped paratroopers very near to Pointe-du-Hoc and was shot down by Flak guns at, or near, the battery. The Germans at Pointe-du-Hoc did not initially realize that these were transport aircraft, presuming that they were yet another bombing attack. There had been bomber raids about once a week since late April, most recently the day before. Another was expected.

Shaken by the incessant bombing, the troops of the gun battery were stunned and demoralized. Many of the men were probably suffering from shock, trauma, and the concussive injuries caused by the previous bombings. Very few combat units have ever undergone such severe and prolonged bombardment. The Allied aircraft had been dropping 1,000lb bombs, usually with a delay fuze, which allowed the bomb to penetrate into the soil before detonating in order to rip up hardened communication wire between the fire-control bunker and the outlying gun pits and bunkers. A typical 1,000lb bomb detonation could create a crater 13ft deep and 45ft in diameter. Any troops caught out in the open were likely to be killed or seriously wounded. Troops who survived the bomb impacts while inside the bunkers could still suffer traumatic brain injury and lung damage due to the pressure waves of the bomb blasts. Adding to the physical injury was the mental stress and anxiety. Troops sheltering in the personnel bunkers were often buried for hours or even days until the entranceways could be dug clear from all the soil of the collapsed access trenches leading to the doors.

Trapped at Pointe-du-Hoc, the troops of the battery were frightened and despondent. They were powerless to stop the attacks, and more attacks seemed inevitable. The gun crews south of the main strongpoint decided to drown their sorrows with whatever alcohol they could find. Benno Müller, a radioman located in the fire-control bunker at the tip of Pointe-du-Hoc, later recalled: "They couldn't fire the guns anymore because they were all completely drunk. We knew this because we were still in radio contact with them. That night, some of the artillerymen had carried large amounts of alcohol to their position in the rear. Later, they also went to get anything remaining, even when all that was still available was sparkling wine." The gun commander of the No 6 gun told the battery officers, "Screw this!" and had fled the area around 0300hrs along with the rest of his crew, two hours before the RAF bombers struck.[21]

It is not clear how many German troops remained in the Pointe-du-Hoc strongpoint when the RAF bombers began their attack on Pointe-du-Hoc. No records survive to indicate how many men had been killed or wounded by previous attacks, or who had deserted after the repeated bombing attacks. Nevertheless, some rough estimates can be made. The senior commanders, a forward observer team from Werfer-Regiment.84, and the associated headquarters staff are known to have remained in the main command bunker. They probably numbered less than twenty men. With the gun crews gone, it is not clear how many other personnel remained in the bunkers at the center of the post. There were probably some Organization Todt workers in the area, since several were captured later that day by the Rangers. Both 37mm Flak bunkers were probably manned, along with two 20mm Flak guns and a sole 88mm Flak gun. This may have totaled an additional thirty men. There was probably also an assortment of troops assigned to guard duty near the strongpoint entrance and at various other positions. The Werfer-Einheit, manning their machine guns near the eastern cliff sides, numbered around fifteen men. So in total, there were probably about seventy German troops still in the immediate vicinity of Pointe-du-Hoc.

One of the Werfer-Einheit soldiers, Wilhelm Kirchhoff, later recounted the start of the bombing:

When the bombers arrived, we, the 15 men of the Werfer-Einheit, crouched in our little earthen fox-holes. There were so many bombers that you couldn't count them. They were coming from the northeast direction and they began dropping powerful stuff. You could see the red flashes of the explosions constantly, and everything trembled. I really did not notice that I suffered permanent ear damage during the bombing. It then lasted well over half an hour… We, the fifteen men, nothing happened to us during this bombardment. The explosions completely buried a lot of trenches and tore camouflage nets everywhere. Then, in the dark, we dug out as much as possible so that we could move again. Then we ate something. We said to ourselves: "Who knows what awaits us today".[22]

The bombs also fell on the many small French villages south of Pointe-du-Hoc. One bomb hit the small village church of Criqueville-sur-Bessin, destroying the altar and shattering the stained-glass windows. A young French woman in the village of Saint-Pierre-du-Mont, Gerette Coulmain, recalled the terrible dawn:

All the houses on the whole property were shaking. Grandmother and I hugged each other and crouched in a corner of the house. A German soldier suddenly appeared in the house. Blood flowed from his head, all over his uniform that was coated in thick white dust. He was completely stained with blood and only spoke German. He kept saying "Alles Kaputt, Alles Kaputt…" [all is finished, all is finished]. The soldier was very upset and from what he kept saying, I could deduce that everything was destroyed on Pointe-du-Hoc, the commander and all the soldiers killed. Then he left.[23]

It is unknown how many German soldiers were killed or injured in the bombing. The headquarters troops in the forward command bunker did not suffer any casualties because the bunker was not hit and there was only one near miss behind it. Its "Standard A" steel-reinforced concrete was strong enough to prevent penetration, even by 1,000lb bombs. The munitions bunker on the west side suffered one or more direct hits and was badly damaged. The whole east side of the site was thoroughly demolished. Curiously, Kirchhoff and the Werfer-Einheit, huddled in their dirt foxholes, suffered no casualties. However, two large bombs had struck very close to their positions at the edge of the cliff, gouging out two deep crevices in the cliff face. These would play an important role in the Ranger attack later that morning. It seems likely that the eastern Flak bunker was directly hit, since photographs from later in the day show no evidence of the 37mm gun mounted there. It was presumably obliterated by a direct hit. There was also no evidence of the two 20mm guns or the 88mm Flak gun, and presumably they were destroyed in the attack as well.

FIRE FROM THE SEA

To further savage the strongpoint, Pointe-du-Hoc was listed as Target No 1 for the US Navy's Bombardment Force C. This flotilla included the battleships USS *Texas* and USS *Arkansas*, as well as a number of cruisers and destroyers.

When it entered service in 1914, USS *Texas* was the most powerful ship in the US Navy. It was the first American ship armed with the new 14in. guns. It served in World War I, and was a veteran of the many amphibious operations in the Mediterranean theater in 1942–43. It had undergone continuous modernization, mainly to deal with contemporary threats such as air attack. Although it was no longer the most modern battleship in the US Navy, it was still a very powerful warship when used in the shore bombardment role. On D-Day, it served as the flagship of Rear Admiral Carleton F. Bryant, commander of the Gunfire Support Group of Assault Force O, "O" standing for Omaha Beach.

At 0550hrs, USS *Texas* began pounding the Pointe-du-Hoc with its 14in. guns from a range of 12,000 yards. To ensure accuracy, a Spitfire spotter plane orbited over Pointe-du-Hoc to call in artillery corrections. The *Texas* fired 262 rounds of 14in. ammunition, consisting of ninety-eight High-Capacity projectiles and 164 Armor-Piercing.[24] The High-Capacity projectiles were filled with high-explosive, while the Armor-Piercing shells were intended to penetrate the concrete casemates and bunkers. The salvo from USS *Texas* totaled 177 tons of projectiles, containing 14 tons of high explosive.* Given the high level of damage inflicted on Pointe-du-Hoc by bombs and naval gunfire, it is difficult to precisely assess the damage inflicted by the *Texas*. However, some of the surviving structures on Pointe-du-Hoc bear the scars typical of heavy-caliber naval gunfire.

While the *Texas* pounded Pointe-du-Hoc itself, the destroyer USS *Satterlee* attacked known pillboxes on the western side of Pointe-du-Hoc, including the dummy batteries. Farther east, another destroyer, HMS *Talybont*, bombarded the Strongpoint Le Guay radar station and other German defensive positions to the east of Pointe-du-Hoc. The destroyer USS *Thompson* was assigned to bombard WN 74 at the tip of Pointe-et-Raz-de-la-Percée. The naval bombardment lifted at H-5 minutes, 0625hrs, in anticipation of the arrival of the Rangers at H-Hour.

As if this was not enough, seventeen B-26 Marauder bombers of the 391st BG left RAF Matching in Essex shortly after dawn. Six aborted their mission due to icing problems. Pointe-du-Hoc was enveloped in clouds and smoke from the naval bombardment when they arrived over the battery. This was anticipated by the weather forecasters, and the bomber group was accompanied by a Pathfinder equipped with radar to permit blind bombing. Starting at 0630hrs, they dropped 16 tons of bombs. The results were unrecorded, since the crews could not see the ground. This was the last of seven bombing missions against Pointe-du-Hoc.

Pointe-du-Hoc was the most heavily bombed target on the Normandy coast, and one of the most heavily bombed sites in all of Europe. In the aftermath of these attacks, it was a hellish lunar landscape, cloaked in clouds of smoke and dust, and heavy with the stench of burnt explosive. The surface of the strongpoint had been deeply gouged by bomb craters. Some craters consisted of

---

*The 14in. High-Capacity projectile weighed 1,275lb and contained 104lb of high explosive; the Armor-Piercing shell weighed 1,400lb, including a 23lb high-explosive burster charge.

multiple impacts from the several air raids. In total, Pointe-du-Hoc had been hit by almost 1¼ kilotons of bombs. On average, every acre of Pointe-du-Hoc had been hit by about 40 tons of bombs. To put this in perspective, the Hiroshima atomic bomb was the equivalent of 15 kilotons and destroyed an area of about 3,200 acres, or less than 5 tons per acre.[*] Of the ten Normandy coastal batteries given priority for bomber attack, Pointe-du-Hoc ranked number one in density of bombs and number two in tonnage, as shown in the charts below.[†]

BOMBING ATTACKS AGAINST PRIMARY *NEPTUNE* COASTAL BATTERIES[25]

Location	Battery	Tons to D-1	Tons D-Day	Total tons	Density to D-1*	Density D-Day	Total
Pointe-du-Hoc	2./1260	487	696	1,183	6.4	4.5	10.9
St Martin-de-Varreville	1./1261	398	611	1,009	9.1	0	9.1
Longues-sur-Mer	4./1260	176	707	883	5.2	1.9	7.1
Houlgate	3./1255	117	524	641	3.2	2.6	5.8
La Pernelle	10./1261	419	663	1,082	5.7	0	5.7
Merville	1./1716	917	380	1,297	5.1	0	5.1
Mont Fleury	3./1260	164	611	775	3.8	0	3.8
Fontenay-sur-Mer	3./1261	137	597	734	2.5	1.1	3.6
Maisy	8. & 9./1716	293	649	942	0.6	2.5	3.1
Ouistreham	4./1716	217	669	886	1.0	1.3	2.3

*Density = Strikes per acre. Tons = short tons (2,000lb)

[*] This is only a rough comparison, since the Hiroshima blast was equivalent to 15 tons of TNT; the Pointe-du-Hoc tonnage refers to bomb weight, of which only a fraction was high explosive. However, it does not include the damage to Pointe-du-Hoc caused by the kinetic energy of bomb impacts or the radiation damage at Hiroshima.
[†] It should be noted that in many British accounts, Pointe-du-Hoc is named as St Pierre-du-Mont or Cricqueville due to the neighboring villages, while it is usually called Pointe du Hoe in US wartime records.

By the time that the Rangers landed, the Pointe-du-Hoc battery was no longer combat-effective. Only three of the original six 155mm gun crews were still functional, all pointed toward Utah Beach. The battery was inoperative because the drunk and demoralized gun crews had abandoned the site. The battery headquarters was still in operation, but it controlled nothing. The western 37mm Flak bunker had escaped destruction. There were a few dozen soldiers still alive within the strongpoint, including the Werfer-Einheit on the eastern side of the promontory. The *Neptune* Joint Fire Plan had proven completely successful in neutralizing Pointe-du-Hoc even before the Rangers arrived. It would be up to the Rangers to ensure that it remained neutralized.

Chapter 8

Assault Group O-4

The naval element of the Ranger mission to Pointe-du-Hoc was designated Assault Group O-4.* This force was provided by the Royal Navy and was led by Commander Stratford H. Dennis, RN. He was forty-five years old at the time and had already seen extensive service in amphibious operations. He had received his first Distinguished Service Cross (DSC) when serving as the liaison officer on the Polish destroyer ORP *Burza* while covering the evacuation of British forces from Dunkirk in 1940. He served on a number of landing ships before being appointed commanding officer of HMS *Prince Charles* on April 16, 1942. This landing ship took part in the Dieppe raid, and then landed elements of Darby's Rangers on Sicily during Operation *Husky* in July 1943. Dennis was decorated with the DSC again while commanding the *Prince Charles* during Operation *Avalanche* at Anzio in January 1944. He served as the commanding officer of this ship on D-Day as well as leading Assault Group O-4.

Assault Group O-4 was based around five LSIs (Landing Ship Infantry) that served as the motherships for the LCAs (Landing Craft Assault) that were taking the Rangers ashore. These came in two varieties. Force A employed two LSI(H)s that were converted British Channel passenger steamers; the "H" indicated "hand-hoisting," referring to the type of davits used to unload the craft.

* O-4 indicated "Omaha-4." Naval forces operating off Utah Beach used codenames with a "U" prefix.

Force B and Force C used the LSI(S)s that were converted Belgian cross-Channel ferries; the "S" indicated "small" to distinguish them from the medium LSI(M) and large LSI(L) landing ships. The steamers had been converted into landing ships by adding davits suitable for launching the LCAs.

The SS *Ben My Chree* had belonged to the Isle of Man Steam Packet Company prior to being taken into Royal Navy service at the start of the war.* It was the fourth ship of this firm to carry the name. Curiously, its predecessor, converted into a seaplane tender during the Great War, was sunk by Turkish coastal artillery during the Gallipoli campaign in 1917. The current *Ben My Chree* was originally used as a troopship by the Royal Navy and served during Operation *Dynamo*, the evacuation of British forces from Dunkirk in 1940. It was converted into an LSI in 1944 specifically for D-Day. The TSS *Amsterdam* was a passenger and freight vessel of the London and North Eastern Railway until requisitioned by the Royal Navy in September 1939. As in the case of the *Ben My Chree*, it was converted into an LSI in 1944.

The three LSI(M) craft were sister ships built for the Belgian Marine Administration (Regie voor Maritiem Transport) before the war in Cockerill's Hoboken yards. Before the war, all three served on the Ostend–Dover route. They were taken over by the Royal Navy in 1940. HMS *Prince Leopold* saw extensive combat with the Commandos, including the Operation *Sunstar* raid on Houlgate in Normandy in November 1941, the raid on Vaagso in Norway in December 1941, and the Operation *Jubilee* raid on Dieppe in August 1942. It subsequently served in most of the amphibious landings in the Mediterranean, including Operation *Husky* on Sicily and Operation *Avalanche* at Salerno. The *Prince Charles* also saw use in early Commando raids, including Operation *Anklet* at Floss in Norway and the Vaagso raid in December 1941, followed by the Dieppe raid in 1942. It landed part of the Ranger force on Sicily in July 1943. Unlike the other two ships, *Prince Baudouin*

---

* *Ben my Chree* means "Woman of my heart" in the archaic Manx language of the Isle of Man, where this ship was based.

mainly served as a troopship in the Mediterranean until early 1943, when it began conversion into an LSI.

Each LSI carried an LCA Flotilla, the size of which varied. Although a standard Royal Navy LCA Flotilla was twelve craft, in practice it depended on the capacity of the landing ship. The LSI(H) used by Force A carried six LCAs each; the LSI(S) carried seven or eight. The flotillas were commanded by junior officers of the Royal Navy Volunteer Reserves (RNVR)

The LCA was the standard British landing craft.[1] It differed from the American LCVP (Landing Craft Vehicle and Personnel), better known as the Higgins boat. The LCA had a very narrow ramp in the bow, 4½ft wide, only wide enough for a single soldier to disembark. This was a disadvantage when under fire. In contrast, the LCVP had a wider, almost 8ft ramp in front, so that three soldiers could disembark at a time. The LCA was lightly armored around the troop compartment to provide some protection against enemy small-arms fire for the embarked troops; the Higgins boat had light armor only on the bow ramp. There were varying opinions about which craft was superior.

The crew of each LCA was four sailors: a coxswain in charge, two seamen, and a stoker to operate the engine. The crew layout was different between the LCA and LCVP. The coxswain position on the LCA was in a forward compartment toward the bow on the starboard side, whereas it was in the rear on the LCVP. The stoker was located in the rear engine compartment of the LCA. One of the seamen was usually assigned to the port compartment opposite the coxswain's in the bow, and this station was usually armed with a Lewis light machine gun or a Bren gun.

The British Army was not entirely happy with the quality of Royal Navy landing craft crew early in the war due to a lack of training and experience. The Royal Marines had been contributing personnel to Combined Operations to man the armament of landing craft and ships. In 1943, there was a major policy change and Royal Marines began to be qualified for LCA crews. As a result, about two-thirds of the LCA crews during Operation *Neptune* were Royal Marines.[2] Generally, a flotilla had either Royal Navy or Royal

Marines personnel. Flotillas assigned to the COHQ were usually Royal Marines, but the LCAs used at Pointe-du-Hoc were mostly Royal Navy personnel.

The LCA could carry a thirty-two-man platoon. In Assault Group O-4, the number was usually less due to added equipment. In Force A landing at Pointe-du-Hoc, the average was closer to twenty-two troops due to the added weight of the rocket-grapnel projectors on the Project Scam LCAs. The troops inside the LCA sat in three rows on simple bench seats.

The only US-crewed vessel in Assault Group O-4 was LCT 413. This was an LCT(5) (Landing Craft Tank), commanded by Lt Commander A. Hayes. It was needed to deliver the four Swan Ladder DUKWs. Force C was supported by two LCTs of Assault Group O-2 assigned to the 116th RCT. These were used to land vehicles such as the M3 75mm GMC of the Ranger Cannon Company as well as the Rangers' administrative vehicles such as jeeps and ¾-ton trucks.

Each landing force was assigned an accompanying Fairmile motor launch (ML), which provided navigation to steer the flotillas to their destination. The two flotillas of Force A were accompanied by two LCS(M)s – Landing Craft Support, Medium Mark III. These were LCAs converted into fire-support craft.[3] There was a single 4in. smoke mortar in a gun pit in the bow, a power-operated turret with twin Vickers .50 cal heavy machine guns on top of the new superstructure in the center of the craft, and two Lewis guns.

ASSAULT GROUP O-4, D-DAY

Ranger Force A					
Ship	Flotilla	CO	LCA	Troops	Units
ML 304		Lt Colin Beever	-		Fairmile navigation launch
LCT 413	Flotilla 18	Lt Cmdr A. Hayes	-		Swan Ladder – DUKWs
LSI(H) 1 *Ben My Chree*	520 LCA Flotilla	Lt C. W. R. Cross	6 LCA	112	Co F, Co E (-), Bn HQ 2nd Ranger Battalion, 58th AFAB Det

LSI(H) 2 *Amsterdam*	522 LCA Flotilla	Lt R. E. Dobson	6 LCA	105	Co D, Co E (-), Bn HQ 2nd Ranger Battalion, NSFCP-1
LCS (M) 91	507 LCA Flotilla	Lt N. E. Fraser	-	-	Fire-support gunboat
LCS (M) 102	504 LCA Flotilla	2nd Lt W. I. Eccles	-	-	Fire-support gunboat
Ranger Force B/C					
ML 163		Lt J. James	-		Fairmile navigation launch
LSI(S) 1 *Prince Charles*	501 LCA Flotilla	Lt R. D.Turnbull	8 LCA	262	Cos A, B, C, HQ 2nd Ranger Battalion, NSFCP-2, 58th AFAB Det
LSI(S) 2 *Prince Leopold*	504 LCA Flotilla	Lt J. M. F.Cassidy	7 LCA	244	Co A, Co F, HQ 5th Ranger Battalion
LSI(S) 3 *Prince Baudoin*	507 LCA Flotilla	Lt E. H. West	7 LCA	246	Co C, Co D, Co F, HQ 5th Ranger Battalion

The Rangers arrived near the port of Weymouth in the first week of June 1944 following the *Fabius I* exercises. The original schedule was for D-Day to occur on June 5. As a result, much of the boarding process to load the assault transport ships took place days before, with the Rangers arriving on the ships of Assault Group O-4 on Thursday, June 1. Col Rudder and the headquarters of the Provisional Ranger Group were stationed onboard Commander Dennis's command ship, the LSI(S) *Prince Charles*.

Although Rudder had wanted to go ashore on Pointe-du-Hoc on D-Day, 1st Division commander Clarence Huebner reminded him that his duty was as group commander, so they both agreed that he would go ashore with Schneider's Ranger Force C. Consequently, Rudder had selected the executive officer of the 2nd Rangers, Capt Cleveland A. Lytle, to lead the main mission of Ranger Force A at Pointe-du-Hoc. On Saturday, June 3, Rudder visited Lytle onboard the LSI(H) *Ben My Chree* to let him know that he had been promoted from captain to major. To help celebrate the promotion, Rudder gave Lytle a quart of gin before returning to the *Prince Charles*. Lytle had the reputation of being a hard drinker, though it does not seem to have interfered with his performance until that evening.

On the Saturday evening, Lytle and several other officers of Ranger Force A congregated around the ship's bar on the *Ben My Chree*. During the course of the evening, Lytle got thoroughly drunk and began to bitterly complain about the Pointe-du-Hoc mission. He revealed that Rudder had confided in him about a message from French sources that claimed that the guns had been removed from Pointe-du-Hoc. He told the group around him that it was a pointless suicide mission to scale the cliffs and attack the battery. When some of the other officers tried to calm him down, Lytle got surly and took a swing at the battalion surgeon, "Doc" Block. Block was significantly older than the rest of the Rangers and an extremely popular figure in the battalion. Lytle's attempt to punch Block did not sit well with the other officers, and he was put under detention by the ship's commanding officer, Lt C. W. R. Cross, for being drunk and unruly.

That evening, the command ship *Prince Charles* was in a holding pattern off the Isle of Wight awaiting confirmation of the start of the invasion, but Eisenhower called off the June 5 start date at 0430hrs on June 4 due to deteriorating weather conditions off Normandy. The *Prince Charles*, with Rudder aboard, returned to Weymouth harbor late on Sunday, June 4. By this point, Rudder having learned about the drunken episode on the *Ben My Chree*, instructed three captains – his adjutant Richard Merrill, Harvey Cook (operations and intelligence), and Frank Corder – to visit the *Ben My Chree* to discover what had happened.

After hearing their report that evening, Rudder decided to remove Lytle from command of Ranger Force A as he obviously had lost faith in the mission. Cook recommended against relieving him. Instead, Rudder had Cook and Merrill take him ashore and place him in a hospital under military police supervision. Although Rudder could have subjected Lytle to court martial, he did not want to end his military career over the incident. Lytle was released from the hospital on June 7, and later became a battalion commander in the 90th Division.[4]

Under the circumstances, Rudder felt that the only possible solution was for him to lead Ranger Force A at Pointe-du-Hoc in place of Lytle. Since this issue had already been contentious, he visited Maj Gen Clarence Huebner aboard the command ship USS *Ancon* at 0200hrs on June 5 to discuss the matter. In his memoirs, Gen Omar Bradley depicted a dramatic scene at the meeting, during which Huebner refused to allow Rudder to go ashore during the first wave for fear of losing him at the outset of the mission, to which Rudder allegedly threatened to disobey him.[5] Rudder's biographer, Thomas Hatfield, is skeptical of Bradley's account, noting that it meant Rudder would go ashore only an hour earlier than planned.[6]

In the event, Huebner acquiesced to Rudder's decision. Maj Richard Sullivan, the Provisional Ranger Group executive officer, took over Rudder's role as PRG leader on the *Prince Charles* while Rudder led the Pointe-du-Hoc attack. Before Assault Group O-2 departed Weymouth harbor for Normandy later on Monday, June 5, Rudder took a motor launch to the various infantry landing ships to talk to the unit commanders and give brief talks to the Rangers on board. Rudder had been warned to expect 60 percent casualties among the Ranger force, and at the end of a short but inspirational talk on the *Prince Leopold*, he ended with a melancholy rhetorical question, "What better way to die than to die for your country?"

Chapter 9

Carnage on Charlie Beach

The first of the three Ranger forces to land on D-Day was Force B. It was the first unit of V Corps to get off Omaha Beach and reach the bluffs over the beach. But it was also one of the costliest missions, with three-quarters of the Rangers killed or wounded in the attack.

Ranger Force B was the smallest of the three Ranger groups, consisting of sixty-four men of Charlie Company, 2nd Ranger Battalion. It was led by twenty-four-year-old Capt Ralph E. Goranson. Like many of the Ranger officers, Goranson was not a professional soldier. He had received military training in the ROTC (Reserve Officer Training Corps) while in high school, and worked in a sales promotion firm in the Chicago area prior to the war. He was drafted a few days after the Pearl Harbor attack. His ROTC training served him well and he quickly became an NCO. His company commander appreciated his performance and directed Goranson to Officer Candidate School at Fort Benning; he became a "90-day wonder" 2nd lieutenant. He was assigned to the 98th Division in Kentucky, serving with the division during the 1942 Tennessee maneuvers. He volunteered for the Rangers, arriving in May 1943 as a 1st lieutenant. Although with the 2nd Rangers only a short time, Col Rudder was confident enough in Goranson to post him as the C Company commander on June 10, 1943. One of the battalion headquarters' officers later recalled, "Goranson was one of the finest officers you'll ever see anywhere."[1]

The mission of Force B was to attack and clear the German strongpoints along the Pointe-et-Raz-de-la-Percée. These cliffs jutted out from the western side of Omaha Beach, and so could fire into the flank of the 116th Regimental Combat Team, one of the two RCTs in the first wave on D-Day. The 116th RCT was based around the 116th Infantry Regiment of the 29th Division. Although part of the 29th Division, the regiment was subordinate temporarily to the 1st "Big Red One" Infantry Division during the initial phase of Operation *Neptune*. Rudder's Provisional Ranger Group was subordinate to the 116th RCT.

Goranson and the other officers of Force B had developed two plans to carry out their mission. They were scheduled to land at H+3 minutes, three minutes after the 1st Battalion, 116th Infantry. If it appeared that the 1/116th Infantry made a successful landing on Dog Green Beach, then Force B would follow immediately behind. Under Plan 1, Force B would proceed up the Vierville draw, one of the few good roads off Omaha Beach. After exiting the beach, they would turn westward and proceed over the bluffs to their objectives at Pointe-et-Raz-de-la-Percée. They were supposed to be supported in this mission by a platoon of M4 medium tanks of the 743rd Tank Battalion.

In the event that the landing by the 1/116th Infantry was strongly contested, then Force B would execute Plan 2. They would land a few hundred yards to the west, at the junction of Beaches Dog Green and Charlie, climb the cliffs there, and proceed to their objective. In this case, they expected fire support from the 743rd Tank Battalion, though obviously the tanks could not follow them if they used the cliff route. Once they assaulted and secured the strongpoint at Pointe-et-Raz-de-la-Percée, they were to proceed farther west and capture the German radar station at Le Guay.

Force B was carried in two Landing Craft Assault: LCA 418 and LCA 1038, which were based on HMS *Prince Charles*. LCA 418 contained Capt Goranson and the 1st Platoon led by Lt William Moody. LCA 1038 had the 2nd Platoon under Lt Sydney

Salomon. Force B was equipped in the usual fashion, with most of the Rangers armed with the M1 Garand rifle. Seven of the Rangers instead had the M1A1 Thompson submachine gun. Other weapons in the company included four BARs, two 2.36in. bazookas, and two 60mm light mortars. The group was also allotted twenty bangalore torpedoes, a 5ft-long tubular explosive device weighing 13lb that could be used to breach barbed wire entanglements. They also carried 160lb of C-2 plastic explosive for demolition work.

Unlike the LCAs of Force A, the two LCAs of Force B were not fitted with the J Projectors to launch rope ladders. This was partly due to the expectation that Force B would execute Plan 1 and land at the Vierville draw, thereby not needing specialized cliff-scaling equipment. In addition, Force B had only two LCAs allotted, so the craft were fully loaded with 32 Rangers each. Force B did, however, bring along toggle ropes in case they were needed.

The two LCAs had a difficult approach to Omaha Beach in the pre-dawn hours due to the rough seas. "Doc" Block had recommended a light breakfast of coffee and pancakes. However, even with this modest meal, many of the Rangers became seasick. Capt Goranson recalled that the seasickness was a contributing factor to the losses suffered on the beach since it prevented the men from operating effectively when they landed. Goranson had the men take turns standing up in the LCA during the approach to prevent them from becoming cramped. In the darkness, they witnessed the air attack on Pointe-du-Hoc as recalled by Ranger Edwin Sorvisto: "Over to our right, we could hear the bombs from our bombers, crumping as they poured down on Pointe du Hoe and caused the sky to turn a brilliant reddish orange hue."[2]

Shortly before sunrise, the destroyer USS *Thompson* began firing against targets on the beach ahead of the Rangers. At 0550hrs, its four 5in. guns started firing at Target 74.[3] This was the German defense nest WN 74, the primary objective of Ranger Force B. After a half-hour bombardment, the *Thompson* shifted the fire of its guns to Target 75, the WN 73 defense nest which was very close to the intended landing sector for Goranson's Ranger Force B.

As the *Thompson's* gunfire screamed overhead, the two Ranger LCAs passed an LCVP of the 1/116th RCT that was sinking off Dog Green Beach due to the sea conditions. This was from the Command Group of the 1/116th Infantry off HMS *Princess Maude*, and this particular craft contained the Beachmaster. This waterlogged group eventually landed later than Ranger Force B, around 0720hrs.[4]

It was evident that the LCAs of A Company, 116th Infantry, were taking very heavy fire when they landed immediately in front of the Vierville draw. As a result, Goranson and the Royal Navy crew agreed to execute the second option and land farther west. The two Ranger LCAs proceed to the junction of Dog Green and Charlie Beaches, landing to the right, west of the 1/116th RCT. Force B was twelve minutes late landing, around H+15 (0645hrs) instead of the planned H+3. USS *Thompson* spotted the Ranger craft heading toward the beach around 0635hrs. The *Thompson's* commanding officer, Lt Cdr Albert Gebelin, ordered the guns to hold fire at 0646hrs due to the amount of dust and smoke along the shore that made it difficult to see where the landing craft had reached the beach.

THE MASSACRE OF A COMPANY, 116TH INFANTRY

A Company, 116th Infantry, the first wave of the 1/116th RCT, landed shortly before Ranger Force B. Its LCA landing craft disembarked its troops immediately to the left of the Rangers and in front of the Vierville draw. This was one of the most strongly defended sectors on Omaha Beach, designated as Stützpunkt Vierville.

To the right of the landing area was WN 72, one of the most formidable defense nests on all of Omaha Beach. Its most powerful bunker was an enclosed casemate, armed with an 88mm PaK 43/41 antitank gun. The gun was oriented to fire eastward in enfilade along the beach, and its embrasure was shielded from the sea by a large wall. A high antitank wall emanated off the bunker's eastern corner, preventing any access off Omaha Beach by vehicles. Next to it was another fully enclosed gun bunker with a pivot-mounted 50mm gun able to fire either east or west; it was defended on top by a war-booty Renault tank turret. Invisible to the American troops was a pair of Tobruks on the bluff to the right, each armed with 81.4mm mortars.* Besides these weapons, there were several trenches with MG 34 or MG 42 machine guns.

To the left of the landing area was WN 71, a complex of trenches and machine-gun pits located on the bluff overlooking the Vierville draw. Although it lacked the powerful weapons of WN 72, the ample assortment of machine guns and its high perch made it a potent anti-infantry strongpoint.

The preliminary bombardment of the Vierville strongpoint had been largely ineffective. WN 72, the German defense nest on the west side of the Vierville draw, was engaged by the LCT(R)-464 firing 1,064 5in. rockets. The rocket barrage failed to reach the beach, a common problem with these bombardment craft on D-Day. As a result, WN 72 was largely undamaged when the 1/116th RCT landed. Defense nest WN 71 on the east side of the Vierville draw had been hit by 5in. gunfire from USS *McCook* starting at 0550hrs.[5] This destroyer engaged three prearranged targets for twenty minutes, expending 220 rounds of ammunition. Assessing the targets as neutralized, the *McCook* ended its bombardment at 0616hrs, about fifteen minutes before the arrival of the first wave of landing craft.

Expecting only weak resistance, A Company, 1/116th RCT landed immediately in front of the WN 71 and WN 72 defense nests. The landing craft began receiving mortar and machine-gun fire before even hitting the beach. It was a massacre. Within moments of landing, Able Company, 1/116th RCT lost three of its four company commanders and sixteen junior officers. Unlike later landing waves, A/116th Infantry landed from LCAs, so disembarking was slow and deadly. The narrow ramps restricted exit to one soldier at a time. Once the armored ramps went down,

---

* These were war-booty French Brandt mortars, designated as 81.4mm Granatwerfer 278 (f) by the Germans.

German machine gunners on the beach and overhead fired directly into the open landing craft. The mortar Tobruks overhead began raining bombs on the beach. These mortars had been preregistered, and there were colored stakes on the beach to further assist in precise aiming. A later British study estimated that the mortars were three times as lethal as the MG 42 machine guns. The A Company after-action report described the gruesome scene:

Within 7–10 minutes after the ramps had dropped, [A Company] had become inert, leaderless and almost incapable of action. The company was entirely bereft of officers. Lieutenant Edward N. Garing was back where the first boat had [floundered]. All of the others were dead, except Lieutenant Elijah Nance who had been hit in the heel as he left the boat, and then in the body as he reached the sands. Lieutenant Edward Tidrick was hit in the throat as he jumped from the ramp into the water. He went on to the sands and flopped down 15 feet from Private Leo J. Nash. He raised up to give Nash an order. Nash saw him bleeding from the throat and heard his words: "Advance with the wire-cutters!" It was futile. Nash had no wire cutters, and in giving the order, Tidrick had made himself a target for just an instant. Nash saw MG bullets cleave him from head to pelvis. German machine gunners along the cliff directly ahead were now firing straight down into the party. [A Company commander] Captain Taylor N. Fellers and Lieutenant Benjamin R. Kearfott had come in with 30 men aboard LCA 1015, but what happened to that boat team in detail will never be known. Every man was killed; most of the bodies were found along the beach.

In those first 5–10 confused minutes, the men were fighting the water, dropping their weapons and even their helmets to save themselves from drowning, and learning by what they saw that the landing had deteriorated into a struggle for personal survival. Every sergeant was either killed or wounded. It seemed that enemy snipers had spotted their leaders and had directed their fire so as to exterminate them. A medical boat team came in on the right of Tidrick's boat. The Germans machine-gunned every man in the section. Their bodies floated with the tide. By this time the leader-less infantrymen had foregone any attempt to get forward against the enemy and where men moved at all, their efforts were directed toward trying to save any of their comrades they could reach. The men in the water pushed wounded men ahead of them so as to get them ashore. Those who had reached the sands crawled back and forth into the water, pulling men to the land to save them from drowning, in many cases, only to have them shot out of their hands or to be hit themselves while in these exertions. The weight of the infantry equipment handicapped all this rescue work. If left unhelped, the wounded drowned because of it. The able-bodied who pulled them in stripped themselves of equipment so that they could move more freely in the water, then cut away the assault jackets and the equipment of the wounded, and dropped them in the water. Within 20 minutes of striking the beach, [A Company] had ceased to be an assault company and had become a forlorn little rescue party bent on survival and the saving of lives. Orders were no longer being given by anyone; each man who remained sound moved or not as he saw fit.[6]

By the time B Company, 116th RCT landed behind A Company at H+26 (0656hrs), about two-thirds of the men of A Company were casualties. Some elements of B Company landed to either side of A Company, sparing them the worst of the German fire.

FORCE B LANDS

Until Ranger Force B was near the shore, the Germans did not seem to notice the approach of the two Ranger landing craft. "Two hundred yards to go and no enemy opposition, looked like a pushover. Suddenly in LCA 1038, 1st Sgt. Golas exclaimed 'Gee fellows, they are shooting back at us!'"[7] Goranson's Ranger Force B landed to the right of the doomed A Company, 116th Infantry. The two Ranger LCAs encountered fewer obstacles as they were farther west of the Vierville draw where the obstacle belts petered out. The Ranger craft landed within 125 yards of each other, near defense nest WN 73.

WN 73 consisted of an array of trenches and small personnel bunkers. It was manned by about seventy troops, mostly from the 9.Kompanie, Grenadier-Regiment.726, 716.Infanterie-Division. On the eastern side of the defense nest was a 75mm PaK 97/38 antitank gun, built into a cave on the side of the bluff, aimed eastward toward the Vierville draw to provide enfilade fire along the beach. As a result, it fired mainly against A Company, 116th Infantry, not against the Rangers, who landed too far west and so were not in the gun's arc of fire. The strongpoint's two mortars had been preregistered against targets along the beach and were one of the reasons for the carnage inflicted on A Company there. These mortars, mostly preoccupied with the A Company landing in front of the Vierville draw, fired a few mortar bombs at the two inbound Ranger LCAs, but without a single hit.

Farther to the right was WN 74, the ultimate objective of Ranger Force B. The most potent weapons in the defense nest were a pair of World War I-era Austro-Hungarian 76.5mm FK 17 regimental guns, called 76.5mm FK17 (t) by the German Army.* These two guns were deployed in earthworks at the top of the cliffs, with log roofs for overhead protection. They had an effective range of 7 miles, and from their elevated position they could hit any point along the western side of Omaha Beach.

The Rangers' 1st Platoon in LCA 418 bore the brunt of the fire from these two guns. Within moments of grounding, the LCA received four rounds of 76.5mm fire from the cliffs of Pointe-et-Raz-de-la-Percée. The first round missed, but the second struck the bow and ripped off the ramp. The third struck the rear and the fourth exploded amidships.[8] These initial impacts killed about a dozen Rangers. Capt Goranson and four other Rangers nearby were dazed and suffered concussion injuries from the explosions.

---

* This type of FK (Feld Kanone) had been manufactured at the Škoda arsenal in Plzeň (Pilsen) in the Czech provinces of the former Austro-Hungarian Empire, hence the "t" (Tschechoslowakisch) in their designation.

Along with the remaining Rangers, they managed to escape from the wreck of LCA 418.

The 2nd Platoon under Lt Sydney Salomon landed to the left in LCA 1038, grounding on a sandbar in waist-deep water. The German machine-gun teams on the cliffs above began firing on the craft before the front ramp went down. Salomon was the first out of the craft, followed by Sgt Oliver Reed. Reed was hit by machine-gun fire and slipped under the ramp. Salomon managed to extricate him and drag him forward onto the beach.[9] While running across the beach, a mortar round struck amidst Salomon and the accompanying Ranger mortar team, killing the head of the mortar section and wounding most of the rest. Lt Salomon was hit by fragments in the back. After reaching the base of the cliff, the platoon medic extracted the larger fragments from Salomon's back and quickly dressed the wounds.

Salomon estimated that half the men on the craft, about fifteen, were killed or wounded by the initial machine-gun fire. Several of the wounded tried to crawl forward, but were killed by further machine-gun and mortar fire. Of the twenty-three Rangers of Charlie Company killed on D-Day, nineteen were killed in the first few minutes of landing.

The two craft landed about 250–300 yards from the base of the cliff. The tide created two runnels in the sand along the shoreline, so the troops had to wade through these waist-deep water obstacles, slowing their advance to the safety of the cliffs. The Rangers had been taught to run immediately to the security of the cliff, and not to stop and organize. Some of the Rangers later recalled that the soldiers of A Company, 116th Infantry, immediately to their left, followed assault training procedure and tried to organize a firing line before advancing off the beach. According to a later report, this resulted in the men "being cut to pieces with machine gun and mortar fire." Salomon later recalled that the "116th men looked up in surprise" when they saw the Rangers continue to run for the cliffs. In addition, the Rangers were much more lightly equipped than the soldiers from the 116th RCT, with only about half their load.

Goranson later recounted the race to the cliffs:

> Running across the beach was like in a dream. As I went across, I saw men down. However, we had trained that if a man went down, leave him alone. He stayed down. Your job was to get across the beach intact, with your weapons, and the knowledge of the job to be accomplished. Then set out to do it. Every man in the company was trained to achieve the company objective. So, no matter who fell, the job would get done.[10]

One of the Ranger BAR gunners, T-5[11] Jesse Runyan, had been hit in the groin and lost the use of his legs. He managed to keep firing against a German machine-gun position to the left near the Vierville draw. Capt Goranson later praised his actions for holding down Ranger losses during the race across the beach. Runyan survived and was later decorated with the Silver Star for his heroic actions that day.

It took the Rangers some three or four minutes to reach the shelter of the cliffs. In the process, about thirty-five of the original sixty-four men were wounded or killed, many of them still lying on the beach. Charlie Company lost both mortars. Only one bazooka remained. Three of the four BAR gunners had made it to the cliffs. Casualties amongst the squad leaders were high. Upon reaching the safety of the cliff, Capt Goranson counted several hits to his equipment:

> Later on, I found that I had picked up nine rounds of shrapnel and bullets in my gear, some of which took care of all my food in my backpack. My canteen had a couple of bullets in it, the flare projector on my patch pocket on my right leg had two bullets in it, but they didn't detonate them. The morphine bag for the aid man strapped to my chest was shot away by machine gun bullets and was all in tatters. So in all, I think I collected eight or nine pieces of metal from all this gear. I thank God I didn't have any [injuries] – not even a scratch.[12]

The thirty surviving Rangers of Force B were stretched along 200 yards of the cliff, with the largest clump of up to eight men off

1. In commemoration of the 75th anniversary of D-Day, in June 2019 the 75th Ranger Regiment scaled the cliffs of Pointe-du-Hoc. (US Army photo by Markus Rauchenberger, Training Support Activity Europe. DoD)

2. President Ronald Reagan's commemoration of the Ranger memorial on top of the observation bunker at Pointe-du-Hoc was the centerpiece of the American D-Day 40th anniversary in Normandy in June 1984. (DoD)

3. A C-47 Skytrain transport aircraft in D-Day invasion stripe markings passes over the west side of the Pointe-du-Hoc promontory on June 8, 2019 during the 75th anniversary ceremonies. (US Air Force photo by Senior Airman Devin M. Rumbaugh, 86th Airlift Wing/ Public Affairs. DoD)

4. A view of the eastern side of Pointe-du-Hoc from the eastern Flak bunker overlooking the cliffs climbed by the Rangers on D-Day. (Author)

5. An aerial view of Pointe-du-Hoc looking eastward with the town of Grandcamp and the Vire river estuary visible in the background. (US Air Force photo by Tech. Sgt. Stacia Zachary. DoD)

6. A view of the eastern side of Pointe-du-Hoc from the command bunker overlooking the cliffs climbed by the Rangers on D-Day. (Author)

7. An aerial view looking eastward with the Pointe-du-Hoc promontory in the upper left. In the foreground is the WN 76 defense nest, which contained dummy artillery batteries.

8. One of the 155mm GPF guns in its kettle gun pit on Pointe-du-Hoc in August 1943.

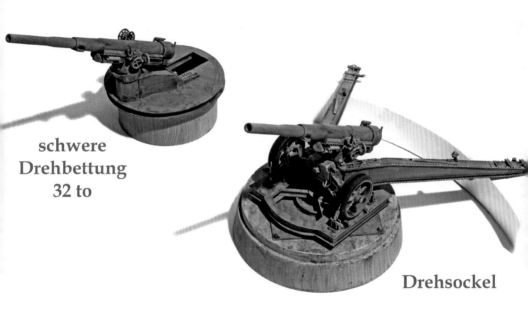

schwere
Drehbettung
32 to

Drehsockel

9. The 155mm GPF guns used a Drehsockel (swivel socket) mounting in the kettle gun pits as seen on the right. To conserve space in the enclosed casemates, the guns were supposed to be re-mounted on the more compact schwere Drehbettung 32.To, but these were in short supply. (Author)

10. The US Army was very familiar with the 155mm GPF gun deployed at Pointe-du-Hoc, since the American Expeditionary Force had been equipped with the same weapon in 1917–1918. (Author)

11. The Regelbau H636a command post bunker on Pointe-du-Hoc in August 1943 as construction was nearing completion.

12. The Regelbau H636a command post bunker at Pointe-du-Hoc after its capture by the Rangers.

13. Kettle gun pit No. 6 is the least damaged example at Pointe-du-Hoc. (Author)

14. Bauwerk 468 is one of two surviving Regelbau 694 gun casemates at Pointe-du-Hoc. (Author)

15. The western Regelbau H502 Doppelgruppenstand personnel bunker, located between gun pits No. 4 and No. 5. (Author)

16. This is the interior of a restored Regelbau 502 Gruppenstand bunker at Stützpunkt Lohengrin near Vlissingen. (Author)

17. The only element of the Pointe-du-Hoc strongpoint to remain in German hands through June 8 was the western Regelbau L409A Flak bunker. (Author)

18. A view of the back side of the Regelbau H636 command post bunker with the Ranger memorial on top. (Author)

19. A Ranger exercise at Hive Beach, Burton Bradstock, Dorset in the spring of 1944.

20. Able Company, 2nd Rangers on the march to the embarkation area in Weymouth harbor on June 1, 1944 with Col Earl Rudder in the lower right.

21. The Project Scam LCA were fitted with six J-Projectors to fire rocket-propelled grapnel hooks up the cliffs of Pointe-du-Hoc as shown in these illustrations. (Author)

22. This is LCA 1377 of the 507 LCA Flotilla from LSI(S)-3 *Prince Baudoin* seen during pre-invasion exercises.

23. The LCAs assigned to Ranger Force A were fitted with special J-Projectors under Project Scam.

24. This LCA is seen launching its grapnels during pre-invasion exercises off the British coast.

25. Teams from the 5th Rangers and the 507 LCA Flotilla are loaded aboard LSI(S)-3 *Prince Baudoin* off the English coast.

26. The Swan DUKW had a machine gun position fitted to the top of the ladder to sweep the top of the cliff once the ladder was elevated.

27. Four DUKW amphibious trucks were fitted with Merryweather 100-foot Turntable Ladders obtained from the London fire brigade.

28. Pointe-du-Hoc was subjected to its first major bombing attack on the evening of April 25, 1944 by the A-20 Havocs of the 409th and 416th Bomb Groups.

29. Pointe-du-Hoc was subjected to an intense bombardment by RAF Bomber Command in the pre-dawn hours of D-Day as shown in this illustration of the Operation *Flashlamp* raid. (Author)

to the right. Salomon tried to deploy the BAR gunners to the left side, facing the Vierville draw. He told them to suppress the German machine gunners in the defense works to allow some of the wounded Rangers to crawl across the beach to the base of the cliff. Five of the wounded eventually managed to drag themselves to the safety of the cliff.

The base of the cliff offered the surviving Rangers some cover. The German infantry in the trenches above could not see them, and so were unable to hit the Rangers. The German mortars were unable to drop their rounds close to the bottom of the cliff, and in any event, were busy slaughtering A Company, 116th Infantry. The German infantry on the cliffs overhead began lobbing "potato-masher" hand grenades over the cliff. These were thrown randomly, since the Germans had a hard time seeing the Rangers below. They often exploded some distance from the Rangers.

Shortly after reaching the cliffs, one of the bazooka crewmen began yelling at Capt Goranson: "Mashed potatoes, mashed potatoes!" Goranson yelled back "What the hell are you talking about?" The bazooka man replied "Right between your legs." Goranson looked and saw a German grenade in the sand next to him, with its fuze still smoldering. Goranson tried to get away from it. The grenade detonated, but the sand absorbed much of the blast and Goranson was not severely injured. The Rangers became contemptuous of these grenades since they seldom caused more than "a few cuts and scratches."

Goranson ordered the Rangers to help the wounded into a small cavity at the base of the cliff to provide them with some shelter. He then turned to the leader of the 1st Platoon, Lt William Moody, and they both agreed it would be impossible to execute Plan 1 via the Vierville draw since A Company, 116th Infantry had been slaughtered on the neighboring Dog Green Beach. Plan 2 meant climbing the cliffs.

Moody then took two of his men, Sgt Julius Belcher and Pfc Otto Stephens, to try to find a suitable place to climb the cliff. The cliff was largely vertical for the first 40–50ft, followed by another 40–50ft that was slightly inclined and an easier climb. Stephens found a spot about 350 yards away to the west and began climbing, using his bayonet to create successive holds in the soft sedimentary rock. Belcher followed behind him, trying to push him up using his rifle. The German infantry in the vicinity did not see them, and an after-action report described the climb as "routine" in view of their extensive cliff-scaling training.

Moody followed the two Rangers, bringing along four lengths of toggle rope. The trio found some stakes at the edge of a German minefield on the plateau above, and used these to tie down the four ropes. By this stage, the group was beginning to receive rifle fire from Germans troops in the trenches near the "fortified house" to the left of their position.

The "fortified house" was a stone villa, locally called the "Folie Gambier," the Gambier Folly. Part of the seaside hamlet of Vignotière, it was in a deep gully in the cliff face. The house had an associated stone barn above it on the rise to the east of the gully. The Gambier stone house served as the main building for WN 73, with a wooden barracks erected next to it along with a field kitchen for the troops of the defense nest.

Moody and his men had the ropes in place by 0700hrs, about 15 minutes after Force B had landed. Moody shouted down to Goranson, and the two-dozen uninjured Rangers began climbing up the cliffs using the ropes. It took about half an hour of "monkey walking" to get the men up the cliffs. In the meantime, Moody and his men fanned out over the cliff to scout the location of the German positions.

Upon arriving at the top of the cliff, Goranson could see that the Force B objective, WN 74, was at least 1,000 yards farther west. With only two-dozen men under his command, advancing that distance against an undetermined amount of resistance seemed suicidal. He decided instead to clean out the German resistance around the "fortified house" before proceeding any farther, sending out patrols around the house to determine the defenders' location. They found that the Gambier villa had been struck by several rounds of naval gunfire from USS *McCook* and was partly collapsed.

When he reached the top of the cliff, Lt Salomon counted only nine men from his LCA; all but two had been lightly wounded during the run across the beach. Moments after reaching the cliff top, his group was shaken by gunfire from the destroyer USS *Harding* off shore. The crew on the *Harding* had presumed that "it was impossible that anyone could have survived that landing, let alone reached the top of the cliffs."[13] Salomon reached into his pack, pulled out a fluorescent orange identification panel, and waved this over his head, which convinced the *Harding*'s crew to cease fire.

Six soldiers from A Company, 116th Infantry, had landed immediately to the left of the Rangers, and two of them, Pvts Shefer and Lovejoy, joined the Rangers and climbed the cliffs up to the Gambier villa. B Company, 116th Infantry, landed around 0656hrs, just as the Rangers were starting up the cliffs. One of these landing craft, carrying men led by Lt Leo Pingenot and SSgt Odell Padgett, landed within sight of the Rangers. They lost one man killed and three wounded before reaching the security of the cliffs. Goranson sent a runner to the group to show them the location of the scaling ropes. Pingenot's surviving twenty-eight men joined the Rangers and climbed up the ropes to the Gambier villa.

The unexpected arrival of the infantrymen from the 116th Infantry's B Company doubled the size of Ranger Force B. Goranson assigned them to occupy the German trenches around the house, and positioned their invaluable .30cal Browning light machine gun in a trench to cover the approaches to the house toward the south.

Lt Moody continued to spearhead the efforts of the Ranger force to reconnoiter the German strongpoint. Moody's patrol encountered a German patrol advancing toward them on the slopes below, and engaged them with BAR fire, killing two and discouraging the rest. Moody jumped into a crater near Lt Salomon. After describing the situation, Moody raised his head over the edge of the crater and was immediately killed by rifle fire. Nearby, Pfc Stephens was creased in the head by a rifle round and suffered a head wound. Another Ranger patrol heading south came under a hail of grenades from German troops in the vicinity of the Gambier barn. However, the grenades had been thrown prematurely, and the Rangers threw them back at the Germans.

In the meantime, Sgt Julius Belcher had crept to the edge of a trench near the barn, stuck his rifle over the edge, and then attempted to get into the trench. As he raised himself over the top of the trench, he was confronted by a German rifleman with his weapon pointed directly at him. Both soldiers pulled the trigger; both rifles misfired. The German soldier ran away to the safety of a mortar Tobruk nearby.

Belcher had a reputation amongst the 2nd Rangers as being one of the most belligerent squad leaders, a real berserker. One of the battalion officers later recalled:

> God, he was one of the most aggressive, even vicious guys. His technique was to kick open the door of these bunkers and throw in a grenade and then shoot the Germans when they came out. He didn't yield. He'd let 'em have it. [Later in Normandy] he and a lieutenant buddy of his, when everybody else would be trying to bed down for the night in the hedgerows, would go scouting into enemy territory. You could hear them back there with the brrrtt ... brrrtt of their machine guns, shooting things up. He would jump back over the hedge, just laughing, telling about what a good time they had.[14]

After his misadventure with the German soldier, Belcher was joined by another Ranger. They proceeded down a neighboring trench near the mortar Tobruk, shooting three German riflemen. Belcher lobbed a white phosphorus grenade into a neighboring dugout, which flushed out two German riflemen whom he shot as they tried to escape. Realizing that the trench system was complex and full of German infantry, Belcher and his partner returned to the Gambier villa. Goranson subsequently put together two larger patrols to flush out the trench system around the mortar Tobruk.

Lt Salomon had followed the same route as Lt Moody. As they rounded the barn, a German machine gun fired at Sgt Charles Flanagan, who aimed a rifle grenade at the machine gunner, killing him when the grenade detonated against the German's helmet. The grenade launch damaged Flanagan's rifle, so he picked up a German machine pistol, probably an MP 40, from a dead German officer in the trench. Farther along the trench, Flanagan stumbled into four Germans advancing down a connecting trench toward the Gambier villa. One German fired a machine pistol at him but missed; Flanagan returned fire and killed two Germans, with the other two fleeing back up the trench.

Flanagan, joined by several other Rangers, advanced back toward the German mortar Tobruk. One of the Rangers then tossed a white phosphorus grenade toward the entrance of the Tobruk. A German soldier came out of the trench with his clothes on fire. He turned out to be a Polish conscript, and promptly surrendered.* He told the Rangers about the strength of the German strongpoint, and warned them about the large amount of mortar ammunition stored in the anteroom to the Tobruk. The Rangers decided against throwing another grenade inside the Tobruk for fear of detonating the ammunition cache. The mortar Tobruk was subsequently cleared on a later patrol.

Another patrol led by Sgt Belcher tried to skirt around WN 73 by using communication trenches closer to the cliff edge in front of the house. The Rangers did not have enough troops to clear out the extensive trench network. German troops continued to infiltrate into the strongpoint through the early afternoon, and a stalemate ensued. Additional Ranger casualties in this phase of the fighting were low, with just two men wounded. Days later, when US Army teams began clearing up the bodies in the area, they found sixty-nine dead Germans in the position.

The US Navy attempted to help the Rangers by engaging German targets. At 0716hrs, USS *Thompson* spotted one of the 76.5mm

---

* The 716.Infanterie-Division had a significant number of "Volksdeutsche" Poles from the western Polish provinces absorbed into Germany. They were drafted into the German Army even though many of them spoke little or no German. The Rangers had a significant number of Polish-Americans and German-Americans from recent immigrant families, so prisoner interrogations were not a problem.

guns in WN 74, and began engaging it with 5in. gunfire. It ceased fire at 0755hrs, with the destroyer's deck log reporting "Target destroyed."[15] The *Thompson* expended 106 rounds of ammunition on the target, but hit only one of the two guns.* The destroyer remained off Dog Green Beach for most of the morning and early afternoon, engaging the various bunkers and defense nests in the Vierville draw.

One of the problems with naval fire support in this sector was that no Shore Fire Control Party managed to establish radio communications with the warships offshore through the morning. This had unfortunate consequences and led to a string of "blue-on-blue" incidents. One of these involved the 1/116th RCT Command Group, led by Major Thomas Dallas, which had set up a small headquarters to the west of the Vierville draw in a small gully. USS *McCook*, thinking that Dallas's group were Germans, began to shell the gully. Dallas ignited an orange smoke grenade to identify the group as friendly, but the *McCook* fired at the smoke. Later in the afternoon, around 1635hrs, when the Dallas group was moving around, the *McCook* again thought they were German. The Dallas group waved white flags and tried to contact the *McCook* with semaphore signals. The *McCook* thought they were German troops trying to surrender. The USS *McCook* war diary noted: "1635–1735 Trying to signal German troops in German and English. Troops could not receive or transmit legibly until advised in English that ship was resuming pointblank fire. Received message Cease Fire. Ordered troops to march eastward and surrender."[16]

The after-action report by the 116th RCT Command Group recorded, "The men made sets of signal flags from their handkerchiefs and waved them to the destroyer: We are Americans. Cease Firing. They got messages back from on the ship's blinker (light): 'Surrender to the Americans.'" This tragi-comedy continued through most of the day, with the result, according to Dallas, that he lost more men that afternoon to the destroyer than to the

---

* Several photos of one of the two guns were taken in the days after D-Day, indicating that at least one of them was not hit.

enemy.[17] A similar incident involved the Rangers at the Grenier villa, with the *McCook* sending several rounds into the house before being convinced to cease fire.

In the early afternoon, around 1400hrs, Goranson and a few Rangers walked westward to make a closer observation of the WN 74 strongpoint, the principal Force B objective. As they watched, a destroyer came close to shore and fired again on the position.* A patrol led by S/Sgt Elijah Dycus reached nearest to the strongpoint and reported that it was destroyed and abandoned.[18] Goranson thus "wrote off that mission." USS *Carmick* mentions attacks on the cliff positions on D-Day, but does not specify at what times they took place.[19] USS *Thompson* returned to the Pointe-et-Raz-de-la-Percée area in the early evening to bombard WN 74 again, beginning an engagement at 1836hrs and ceasing fire at 1848hrs, when the strongpoint's gun aperture was reported to have caved it in.

Goranson's Ranger Force B remained isolated from the main body of the 116th RCT for most of the day. As a result of its SCR-300 radios having been waterlogged or lost during the morning, no radio contact was possible. In the afternoon, Goranson sent out a patrol towards the village of Vierville-sur-Mer. The patrol was caught up in a firefight between US and German troops, so prudently withdrew westward back to the bluffs. Around 1600hrs, a Ranger came up from the beach and told Goranson that he had encountered Dallas's command group from the 116th RCT on the beach below, and that they had a functioning SCR-300 radio. Goranson sent a runner to ask the 116th RCT command group to contact the other Ranger forces for them, but they were unable to do so because of lingering problems with the radios. Instead, Goranson sent a runner to Vierville-sur-Mer in an attempt to reach Lt Col John Metcalfe, commander of the 1/116th Infantry. However, the runner was unable to find Metcalfe.

---

*This does not appear to have been USS *McCook*, since its logbook notes that at this time, it was farther east bombarding targets in the Vierville draw along with USS *Harding* and USS *Thompson*.

At 1900hrs, Goranson climbed down the cliff and met Maj Thomas Dallas at the base of the cliffs. By the early evening, Dallas had finally made radio contact with the 116th RCT and had told them about the situation with the Rangers. Metcalfe instructed Goranson, via Dallas, to march his unit to Gruchy, a hamlet to the southeast of the Grenier villa. Ranger Force B reached Schneider's 5th Rangers near Gruchy shortly before dark.

By the end of the day, Ranger Force B had been reduced to less than twenty men of the original sixty-four. A total of twenty-one men had been killed and eighteen seriously wounded.[20] Of the three officers and twenty-four NCOs in the company, two officers and seventeen NCOs became casualties during the fighting on D-Day and the next few days. Some of the walking wounded remained with Goranson when they joined the 5th Ranger Battalion at Gruchy that evening.

The actions by Goranson's Force B on D-Day illustrate why the Rangers were selected for these special missions. Few infantry units survive 70 percent casualties and still remain functional. Yet Goranson's stalwart force, outnumbered and suffering heavy casualties, managed to overcome a significant German strongpoint. They remained combat-ready at the day's end and took part in the subsequent efforts to reach Pointe-du-Hoc.

Chapter 10

The Stormy Voyage to Pointe-du-Hoc

The flagship for Assault Group O-4, HMS *Prince Charles*, left Portland harbor on the afternoon of June 5 around 1645hrs. Other elements of the group left nearby Weymouth at about the same time. The assorted ships and craft were part of a much larger convoy heading for the Omaha Transport Area, a zone about a dozen miles off the Normandy coast. The procession took place under the cover of total darkness, with the vulnerable transport ships preceded by minesweepers and escorted by destroyers. The weather was overcast; the visibility poor.

The massive convoy began reaching the Transport Area in the pre-dawn hours of June 6 around 0250hrs. The *Prince Charles* arrived in the Transport Area at 0328hrs.[1] Since Col Rudder would go to Pointe-du-Hoc with Ranger Force A, he left the *Prince Charles* around 0353hrs by motor launch to transfer to HMS *Ben My Chree*. This landing ship hosted about half of Ranger Force A. "Doc" Block urged the men to have a light breakfast to avoid seasickness, only two small pancakes and coffee. The Rangers were not happy with such a meager meal as they readied for action.

Since the Rangers were expected to climb the cliffs at Pointe-du-Hoc, they were lightly equipped; the regular infantry landing at Omaha Beach were overburdened with 60lb or more of equipment. The 2nd Rangers were issued assault vests, a new type of battle dress influenced by British jerkins used in place of the normal combat belt, straps, and haversack. The vests had pouches built into them to carry the various and sundry items carried by the Rangers. The 5th Rangers were not issued the assault vest.[2]

A typical Ranger combat load was an M1 Garand rifle, ten clips of ammunition plus a clip in the rifle (80+8 rounds), a bayonet, two "pineapple" fragmentation grenades, a water canteen, and an enriched chocolate bar. Many Rangers had also purchased Commando daggers. In a Ranger platoon, the platoon leader and platoon sergeant were armed with M1A1 Thompson submachine guns.

Each LCA designated their best climbers as "Top Monkeys" who would go up the cliff first. These men were armed with M1 carbines and pistols instead of the M1 Garand rifle. Most platoons substituted the BAR Browning automatic rifle for the Browning .30cal light machine gun since they were easier to carry up the cliffs. Each company had four BARs and two 60mm light mortars. Two 81mm mortars were carried on the two supply LCAs. To deal with the 155mm guns, each company was issued with ten thermite grenades. There were additional explosives carried on the supply LCAs.[3]

The Rangers began to load into their assigned LCAs around 0400hrs while the craft were still mounted on the davits of the infantry landing ships. Rudder was in LCA 888, along with the 2nd Rangers HQ Company leader, Lt James "Ike" Eikner. At the last minute, they decided to separate in order to avoid having two of the senior leaders lost on a single craft. The LCAs were gradually lowered into the water, and the craft then pushed away from the *Ben My Chree* and *Amsterdam* to avoid congestion. The weather was not as severe as the day before, but there was still a 20mph wind and 5ft waves. The small LCAs wallowed in the high seas, and many Rangers gradually became sea-sick. Shortly after 0430hrs, the two accompanying LCS(M) gunboats arrived and the two LCA flotillas began their run to shore. At the head of the LCA flotillas was the guide vessel, Fairmile Motor Launch (ML) 304. The LCAs followed in two columns, with Rudder's LCA 888 in the lead of the starboard column.

ML 304 was commanded by Temporary Lt Colin Beever, RNVR. The 40-year-old Beever had been stationed on ML 304 since December 1943. The trailing LCAs had a hard time following ML 304 in the dark, since the operation was conducted in blackout conditions. To make matters worse, there was early morning mist and fog, further complicating the approach to the beach. The coxswains on the LCAs had to carefully search for the slightly phosphorescent wakes of the craft in front of them.

Beever did not consider the usual method of dead reckoning to be of much use due to "the slow speed of advance, the relatively strong effect of wind and tide, and the difficulty of steering an accurate course in the sea which was running."[4] Consequently, the initial navigation on ML 304 was conducted using the Q.H. 2 "Tree" radio navigation set. This relied on radio cross bearings from land-based transmitters in Britain. On paper, it offered an accuracy of about 50 yards. The motor launch also had a Type 970 radar, but this was not helpful in providing directions against a shoreline that was featureless on a radar scope.

As dawn slowly broke around 0530hrs, the coastline became visible, but Beever found it difficult to make out any landmarks since much of the shore was obscured by thick clouds of smoke from the preliminary aerial and naval bombardments. Around this time, H-60 (0530hrs), the radio navigation set and radar began to fail. This was due to a faulty power supply that eventually crippled both navigation aids. As a result, Beever had to resort to dead reckoning and visual identification. He had expected that the location of Pointe-du-Hoc would be obvious due to the firing cannon, but no muzzle flashes were evident. Furthermore, the navigational photos available gave very few visual clues. He had a hard time distinguishing the Pointe-du-Hoc promontory from Pointe-et-Raz-de-la-Percée, which looked very similar from the sea.

While still about 3 miles from shore, Beever changed course to port and began heading for Pointe-et-Raz-de-la-Percée, mistaking it for Pointe-du-Hoc. Around 0540hrs, and 4,000 yards from shore, LCT 413 received the codeword "Splash." On this signal, it prematurely disgorged its four Swan Ladder DUKWs into the water and they joined the LCA flotilla. The DUKWs had a hard time keeping up with the LCAs due to the added weight of the ladders and the harsh sea conditions.

Due to the duration of the voyage, many of the LCAs took on a considerable amount of seawater, sometimes overwhelming the capacity of their bilge pumps. The Rangers on board were forced to use their helmets to keep their landing craft from flooding. Around 0515hrs, LCA 914, one of the two supply LCAs, sank; only one crewman survived after nearly four hours in the frigid water. LCA 1003, the second supply craft, nearly suffered the same fate. To prevent it from swamping and sinking, all the packs for E and F Companies were thrown overboard, along with much of their supplies. These two craft contained all of Force A's food and water, spare ammunition, and the explosives for demolishing the bunkers. Little remained on the waterlogged LCA 1003, so the Rangers at Pointe-du-Hoc would have to fight with what they carried in their packs. Around 0530hrs, LCA 860 – carrying Capt Harold Slater and 20 Rangers from D Company – was swamped and sank; the troops were not rescued for several hours and suffered hyperthermia from exposure in the cold water.

As the coastline started to clear after 0600hrs, Rudder became convinced that the motor launch was leading them in the wrong direction. Once they were about 1,000 yards from Pointe-et-Raz-de-la-Percée, he suggested to the coxswain on LCA 888 that they swing west. Beever by now recognized his mistake, being unable to see any evidence of the distinctive gun casemates on the point. The flotilla consequently turned 160 degrees to starboard to reach the original point.

HMS *Talybont*, a Royal Navy Hunt-class escort destroyer, was in Fire Support Area No 3 as part of the Gunfire Support Group. It was assigned to bombard Targets 81 and 82, the Le Guay radar strongpoint east of Pointe-du-Hoc. The *Talybont* began to engage the targets around 0550hrs, just as Ranger Force A was arriving off Pointe-et-Raz-de-la-Percée. *Talybont* moved eastward to bombard the German fortifications there, and its deck log noted that around 0630hrs "ML 204 [*sic*] and Rangers had realized their mistake and were making for Pte. Du Hoe parallel with the shore at a range of 05* [500 yards] and 010* [1,000 yards]." The commander of the *Talybont*, Lt Commander Edmund Baines, later wrote, "The mistake in identification of the target by ML 204 [*sic*] is difficult to understand as *Texas*' fall of shot on Pte. Du Hoe was obvious. Their course from Raz de la Percée to the shore of Pte. Du Hoe was suicidal."[5]

The Rangers should have been landing at Pointe-du-Hoc by 0630hrs, but instead were 3 miles away at H-Hour. This westward turn of Ranger Force A exposed the LCAs and DUKWs to the machine guns on the cliffs above. The sharp turn proved to be the undoing of the gunboat LCS(M) 91. As it turned parallel to the sea swells, the waves swamped the forward mortar well and the craft began going down at the bow:

> After about five minutes, her screws were almost clear of the water and she became unmanageable. Six of the crew got swept into the sea and almost immediately, a [German] light machine gun in a cliff position opened up on them. A rapid reply from the .5 Vickers and Lewis guns stopped his fire whilst they were pulled inboard. Almost as the last one came in, a short burst from a heavier weapon [20mm?] hit the craft in three places aft. This gun and the light machine gun supporting it were at once engaged and after about 1,000 rounds of .5", lost all further interest.[6]

The force's second gun-boat, LCS(M) 102, also was swamped during the turn westward, with the forepeak flooding and the mortar-well cover caving in, leaving the craft dead in the water. The crew attempted to turn the boat into the waves and began bailing out the forward hold. This took between 45 minutes and an hour, during which the craft drifted toward Dog Green Beach. A US Navy cutter noticed the craft and offered assistance, but by this time, control had been regained. Around 0815hrs, it slowly made its way back out to rejoin its mothership, HMS *Prince Leopold*.[7] The loss of these two craft deprived Rudder's Rangers of the expected fire support during their landing at Pointe-du-Hoc.

At the head of Ranger Force A, ML 304 encountered only light machine-gun fire and responded with its own 20mm Oerlikon. However, the craft further behind in their trail received more fire, including some bursts from a 20mm Flak gun. At 0640hrs, Lt Cdr Baines on the *Talybont* noted that two German machine guns on the cliffs were firing at the Ranger LCAs and DUKWs to the rear. The *Talybont* closed to 2,100 yards and began firing at the machine-gun nests with its four 4in. guns, adding 2-pdr pom-pom fire once within range. The *Talybont* deck log noted, "Two DUKWs were hit – one badly. Shortly afterwards, a further 2 LMGs [light machine guns] opened fire from shore and another DUKW was put out of action." The German machine-gun fire hit DUKW Swan-II and disabled the engine, leaving it adrift below the cliffs. From 0646 to 0700hrs, the *Talybont* tried to shield the Ranger Force by firing on any identifiable German position. The *Talybont* deck log noted that after 0700hrs, "Rangers sustained no further casualties from these [German] sources."

There are a number of minor mysteries about the actions that morning. The G-2 Journal of the 1st Infantry Division has an entry at 0700hrs from V Corps indicating "5 white flares vic[inity] Pont Du Hoe." No action was taken on this disclosure beyond the journal entry. There is no evidence that the flares were fired by the Ranger force. In view of the enormous amount of ordnance being fired along the coast, the 1st Division's apparent indifference to this message is understandable.

As the *Talybont* accompanied Ranger Force A, it noticed the destroyer USS *Satterlee* that was on station in this sector. At 0710hrs, HMS *Talybont* withdrew from this Fire Support Area, leaving the Rangers in the hands of the *Satterlee*.

USS *Texas* arrived off Pointe-du-Hoc before daylight and began its bombardment at 0453hrs, shortly after the departure of the last Lancaster bombers. It was accompanied by the *Satterlee*, a Gleaves-class destroyer, commanded by Lieutenant Commander Robert W. Leach. The *Satterlee* arrived off Pointe-du-Hoc at 0535hrs in the dim early morning light, and began firing on the promontory at 0548hrs from ranges of 2,500–3,000 yards.[8] The ship's war diary reported, "From daylight until the Rangers approached the beach, there were no signs of life or activity around Pointe du Hoe. It looked as if the bombardment had knocked them out completely. There were no visible targets. Fire was reduced to conserve ammunition because we did not know for how long the weather would delay the landing." The *Satterlee* continued to fire until 0618hrs, when "small and medium caliber guns" in the vicinity of Pointe-du-Hoc began returning fire. These were most likely surviving Flak guns from the Pointe-du-Hoc strongpoint. The *Satterlee* returned fire against these guns for nine minutes, silencing them. The destroyer suffered no hits during the engagement.

Immediately before H-Hour, 0630hrs, USS *Texas* lifted its fire in anticipation of the landing of Ranger Force A. It was now up to Rudder's Rangers to redeem the situation.

Chapter 11

Force A Strikes Pointe-du-Hoc

Earl Rudder, in the lead LCA, looked back at his diminished force. Two LCAs had been lost, including one of the supply craft. Both fire support craft had also been left behind. The Swan DUKWs were in bad shape after having been raked with machine-gun fire; one of the four had been sunk. The landing was more than half an hour behind schedule.

Due to the delayed arrival of Ranger Force A, the Pointe-du-Hoc garrison had been given a brief respite to recover from the dawn bombardments. It is unclear just how many Germans survived the air and naval attacks. One of the members of the Werfer-Einheit on the eastern side of the promontory recalled that most of his fifteen-man unit was still intact, even if deafened and suffering from concussive blasts. This unit still had three MG 42 machine guns, and were located on the eastern side of the promontory where the Rangers were intending to land. The command post bunker had survived without major structural damage, though the stereoscopic rangefinder on the roof had been blasted away. Other isolated groups of German troops may have survived, but no accounts remain. The 37mm Flak gun on the bunker overlooking the Rangers' landing beach had been destroyed by bombs or naval gunfire.

Rudder decided that instead of executing the original plan with LCAs landing on both the eastern and western sides of Pointe-du-Hoc, the nine surviving landing craft should all concentrate on the closer eastern side. Dog Company, scheduled to land on the western side, was instead directed to land between Easy and Fox Companies.

Ranger Force A arrived at Pointe-du-Hoc around 0708hrs, according to the *Satterlee's* deck log. ML 304 sent the radio codeword "Crowbar" as soon as the landing took place. The command ship HMS *Prince Charles* recorded this signal in its deck log at 0709hrs.[1]

On the bridge of USS *Satterlee*, the sailors could see some signs of enemy activity on the top of Pointe-du-Hoc for the first time: "As these [LCAs] neared the landing point on Pointe du Hoe, enemy infantry were observed assembling on the cliffs overlooking the point, obviously to repel the landing. We closed to within 1,500 yards of the beach and opened fire with the main battery and heavy machine guns on enemy infantry on the cliff-tops. Results were good. During the period, we were under ineffective fire from enemy machine guns."[2]

From his foxhole along the edge of the cliff, Wilhelm Kirchhoff watched as the LCAs approached the beach below: "The American barges were approaching to the right, completely stuffed with soldiers and equipment."[3] There were no officers among the German troops, and the various soldiers began firing at random as soon as the LCAs landed on the beach below. Kirchhoff continued:

When the Americans started to disembark from their barges, we targeted them as they were getting off. By firing at the crowd, from overhead, they were completely defenseless… The first soldiers out of the barges fell, pushed by the others behind them. The dead were floating in the shallow water, and among them were some wounded who I could hear screaming and screaming. From the first barges, the Americans did not shoot at us at all. We only suffered from naval gun fire.

Lt Beever on ML 304 recalled:

The landing was effected without opposition and at this point the top of the cliff became clearly visible. The smoke had cleared away and several huts and concrete emplacements could be observed. While the landing was in progress, I engaged these targets with 3 pdr. and 20mm Oerlikon fire at ranges of 700–1,000 yards: 20 rounds of 3 pdr. HE [high-explosive] were fired into the huts and emplacements, and 1,000 rounds of Oerlikon were used to spray the top of the cliff until the ascent was complete. A few figures were discerned moving about the top of the cliff, but these were fired on and appeared to take cover.[4]

The lead Ranger craft was LCA 888, with Rudder along with six men from the headquarters and fifteen from Easy Company. The J Projectors were fired before landing, about 35 yards from shore. The ropes had become so soaked with seawater during the waterlogged trip to shore that none of the grapnel hooks reached the top of the cliff. The beach where the LCA landed was full of deep craters which the men waded through, neck deep in water. Getting out of the craters was a challenge because they were slick with churned-up clay. LCA 888 made landfall slightly to the left of the German command bunker. A few German soldiers were seen at the cliff edge, but Sgt Domenic Boggetto shot one of them off the cliff-edge with his BAR; the rest disappeared. A few "potato-masher" grenades followed, but were inaccurate and caused no injuries.

Two of the "Top Monkeys" tried climbing the cliffs using only their Commando knives or bayonets, but the clay was not firm enough and gave way. In the meantime, four ladder extensions were assembled into a 16ft section. The bombardment had dislodged a heap of clay about 35ft tall at the base of the cliff, reducing the height that had to be climbed. A 50ft length of toggle rope was attached to the bottom of the ladder, and one of the Rangers climbed to the top. He then cut a foothold into the clay of the cliff, pushed the ladder upward, and enabled another Ranger to climb 16ft farther. This leapfrog process was continued until T-5 George Putzek was able to reach the top. The toggle rope was secured firmly and the remainder of the Easy Company squad reached the cliff top over the course of about 15 minutes. At this point, no German troops were evident, in part due to the enormous spoil heaps ringing the bomb craters. Rudder and the headquarters team remained on the beach to supervise the landings.

To the right of LCA 888, Easy Company's LCA 861 landed at the extreme right, immediately under the German fire-control bunker. During the approach to the beach, three German soldiers were spotted firing down at the landing craft, but were forced to hide by BAR fire. Four of the J Projectors on the LCA were fired, but these ropes were also too wet and failed to reach the cliff. The German soldiers on the cliff above were led by Unteroffizier Rudolf Karl, in charge of the communications crew of the fire-control bunker. He sent most of his men into the bunker to shield them from the naval gunfire. After being forced back from the cliff by American small-arms fire, Karl and a few of the radio and telephone operators began throwing stick grenades over the cliff: "We threw hand grenades down from the top – until we ran out of them… The effect on the Americans down on the beach was devastating. They had no cover there."[5]

The Rangers on the beach below were led by 1st Lt Theodore Lapres Jr. According to Ranger accounts, the German grenades were not very accurate and the detonations caused only two casualties. A rocket projector was then brought to the shore and finally managed to secure a grapnel on the cliff above. The slippery clay cliff was not entirely vertical, inclined at about 80 degrees. The team's "Top Monkey," Pfc Harry Roberts, climbed up. After reaching about 25ft up, the rope either came loose or was cut from above; Roberts fell to the beach below. A second rocket carried another grapnel to the top, and Roberts managed this time to climb up to a slight niche in the cliff edge. He tied the rope to a section of wire picket, but the soil gave way, and again the rope fell down to the beach. This time, Roberts managed to cling to the cliff face. One of the Rangers climbed up a 20ft mound of clay spoil knocked off the cliff by the bombardment and managed to throw a rope to Roberts, some 60ft above him. Roberts then secured the rope to a piece of metal stake. This allowed five more Rangers quickly to reach the top of the cliff. By this point, Karl and the other German soldiers had retreated inside the fire-control bunker.

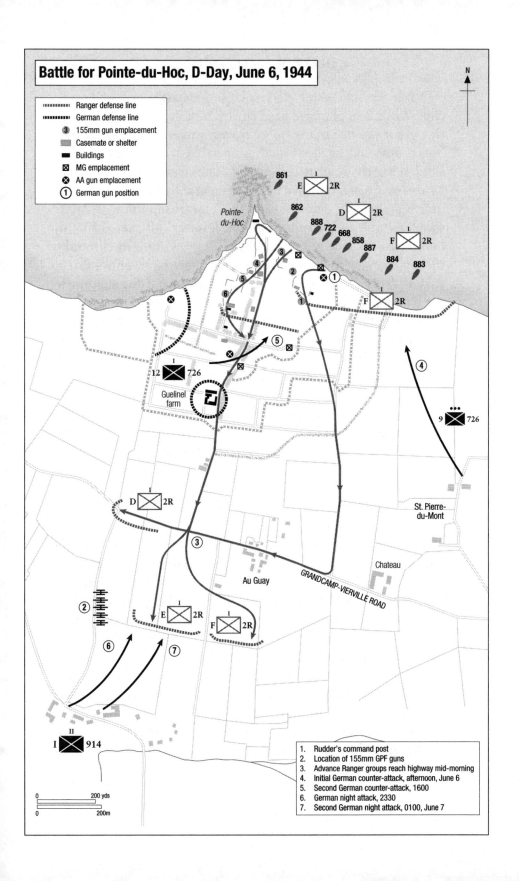

Battle for Pointe-du-Hoc, D-Day, June 6, 1944

N

Legend:
- Ranger defense line
- German defense line
- ③ 155mm gun emplacement
- Casemate or shelter
- Buildings
- ⊠ MG emplacement
- ⊗ AA gun emplacement
- ① German gun position

Pointe-du-Hoc

861
862
888 722 668 858 887
884 883

E | 2R
D | 2R
F | 2R
F | 2R

① ①

12 | 726
Guelinel farm

⊗

⑤

④

9 | 726

D | 2R

St. Pierre-du-Mont

③
Au Guay

Chateau

GRANDCAMP-VIERVILLE ROAD

②
⑥ ⑦
E | 2R   F | 2R

I | II | 914

0   200 yds
0   200m

1. Rudder's command post
2. Location of 155mm GPF guns
3. Advance Ranger groups reach highway mid-morning
4. Initial German counter-attack, afternoon, June 6
5. Second German counter-attack, 1600
6. German night attack, 2330
7. Second German night attack, 0100, June 7

While this was taking place, a large detonation occurred on the cliff. While it might have been an errant naval round, the Rangers thought it was one of the "roller mines" suspended along the cliffs. These were old artillery shells suspended by cable on the cliff sides, remotely detonated from the command bunker. Corp Paul Madeiros was nearly buried by the ensuing collapse of clay and rock. This was the only detonation of this type of munition at Pointe-du-Hoc, most of them having been knocked off the cliff by the bombardment. The rest of the Easy Company Rangers climbed to the top, along with the five members of Shore Fire Control Party-1 (SFCP-1) who were assigned to coordinate naval fire support for the Rangers.

To the left of LCA 861, Easy Company's LCA 862, led by 1st Lt Joseph Leagans, landed with another group of fifteen Rangers and seven SFCP-1 men. Four J Projectors were fired, with three reaching the top, although one fell off the cliff without getting a firm hold. This group was subjected to grenades and machine-gun fire, suffering one man wounded and one killed by the grenade blasts. Since two ropes had successfully reached the top, this Easy Company squad was able to reach the cliff top relatively quickly.

LCA 722, which landed about 20 yards left of Rudder's LCA 888, included an Easy Company squad of fifteen Rangers, five headquarters personnel including Lt Eikner, Commando liaison officer Col Trevor, and a *Stars and Stripes* reporter. This craft also included the group's main SCR-284 radio and two communication pigeons. The J Projectors were fired shortly before landing, and two ropes reached the top of the cliff. One Ranger was wounded by small-arms fire shortly before landing, with another lightly wounded during a short rain of grenades. When Sgt E. P. Smith climbed to the top of the bluffs, he noticed some five or six Germans throwing grenades over the cliff. He was joined by Sgt A. Robey, who opened fire with his BAR, hitting three Germans and causing the others to retreat to nearby bunkers.

Dog Company's LCA 688 landed to the left of Easy Company, to the immediate left of LCA 722. A large spoil heap knocked off the cliff prevented the craft from reaching the beach, and the troops had to swim in. Sgt Leonard Lomell brought a projector and rope to shore. He was lightly wounded by machine-gun fire in the process, but managed to reach the shore. Three ropes were launched up the cliff, but two were precariously attached under an overhang. Bill Von, the squad's "Top Monkey," reached the top by the toggle rope, but was killed almost immediately by German small-arms fire. Lomell instructed the men to get extension ladders from the LCA, and two were duly erected. Due to the gouge in the cliff, about a dozen men were able to quickly climb to the top. A few grenades "caused some annoyance" but did not result in any further casualties.

The neighboring Fox Company LCA 858, under Lt Robert Arman, faced the same problem as LCA 688, coming ashore against a huge crater that forced the men to wade and swim through the head-high water to shore. Their bazooka was ruined in the process when its launch battery was soaked. This area received no grenades from the Germans on the cliffs, but was within range of the machine guns of the Werfer-Enheit. Two Rangers were wounded. One of the two forward J Projectors managed to get a grapnel up the cliff, but Arman decided to dismount the others and fire them from ashore. The coxswain did an admirable job keeping the craft steady for the 10–15 minutes it took to accomplish this.

In the meantime, Sgt William "L-Rod" Petty and three other Rangers attempted to make the climb on the plain rope. However, the Rangers' boots were covered in slick clay mud and the rope was slippery and lacked footholds, so in spite of their best efforts, the Rangers could not hold on. Sgt Petty tried a ladder and got up about 30ft before he too fell. T-5 Carl Winsch tried the other ladder, with machine-gun fire striking nearby. Petty followed him up the second ladder, expecting to find him wounded. However, he had succeeded in reaching a shell hole at the top unscathed. Two more Rangers from Dog Company joined them moments later. Without waiting for the rest of the squad, Petty and the group headed off to their objective. The projectors were by now finally assembled on shore, but the proper ignition system was missing, so T/Sgt John Cripps manually ignited them using a "hot-box" trigger from about a yard behind the projector. This blasted sand and exhaust into Cripps' face and "he was looking a hell of a mess" after four rockets were ignited.[6] The rest of the squad gradually made their way to the top.

Easy Company's LCA 884, led by Lt Jacob Hill, was the craft closest to the machine guns of the Werfer-Einheit. German machine-gun fire began hitting near the landing craft before it beached, with the Rangers firing back with a BAR and the Royal Navy seaman firing his Lewis gun. Of the six J Projectors fired, four managed to reach the cliff top. The two plain ropes were useless since the men's boots were too muddy to provide grip on the rope. Pfc William Anderson got part way up by free-climbing, but attempts to use the other ropes were fruitless. This section of the beach was particularly vulnerable to the Werfer-Einheit machine-gun fire, and three Rangers were wounded. Consequently, Lt Hill ordered the squad to shift to the left, where LCA 883 had beached, since the area offered shelter from the overhead machine-gun fire.

Easy Company's LCA 883 under Lt Richard A. Wintz was the final craft in the flotilla and landed the farthest to the southeast. There was a small protrusion of cliff face that offered protection from the machine-gun fire from the Werfer-Einheit. All six J-Projectors were successful, and ladders were also erected. When the first teams from the squad reached the cliff top, they encountered no opposition. The Werfer-Einheit was farther to the right, and the huge craters blocked the view along the edge of the cliff. As with the other squads, Wintz's men set off toward their objectives as soon as they reached the top of the cliff.

The surviving Swan Ladder DUKWs were a total disappointment. They had been damaged by machine-gun fire on the way to Pointe-du-Hoc, and the beach was too narrow and too badly disrupted by craters and debris for the DUKWs to get a firm foothold. Sgt William Stivison's DUKW attempted to erect the ladder, with Stivison manning the Vickers K machine guns at the top. Lacking a firm grounding, the ladder swung drunkenly from side to side. The effort was finally abandoned as pointless and too dangerous. The enormous effort put into the Swan DUKWs had been wasted.

RANGERS ON THE CREST

By 0730hrs, most of Ranger Force A was on the crest of the Pointe-du-Hoc promontory. What was expected to be the most dangerous phase of the operation had gone flawlessly, largely due to the superb preparation of the Rangers. The cliff scaling had seemed almost effortless due to their extensive and realistic training. The German resistance had been weak, consisting mainly of ineffective and inaccurate grenade tossing. The machine-gun fire from the Werfer-Einheit was disruptive, but the Germans did not have very good fields-of-fire from their trenches due to the irregular features of the cliffs. In total, the Rangers estimated the casualty toll of the climb to be about fifteen men, including a handful killed, with some of the injuries due to falls rather than German fire.

Climbing the cliffs had been a messy but ultimately successful enterprise. The J Projectors generally worked well if their ropes had remained dry during the voyage to the beach. However, many of the LCAs had been swamped by waves during the journey, and the sodden ropes became too heavy for the rockets to carry them over the cliff edge. The ladders were occasionally used to good results. An unanticipated result of the bombardment had been that many sections of cliff had been dislodged, creating huge heaps of spoil that shortened the distance of the climb. This feature, more than any other, accelerated the scaling of the cliffs.

The most dangerous sectors of the beach during the landing were at the two extremes: towards the tip of the promontory where there were a number of German soldiers operating from the fire-control bunker, and at the eastern base of the promontory where the three machine guns of the Werfer-Einheit inflicted the majority of the Ranger casualties.

The situation on top of the cliffs was completely unexpected. The flat surface of the promontory had been churned up and cratered by the bombs and naval gunfire, with enormous heaps of soil and debris creating a lunar landscape. The devastation made it very difficult to see for any distance. Wilhelm Kirchhoff and the Werfer-Einheit were only a few hundred yards farther south from Rudder's command post. He later recalled that he never saw an American on the top of the Pointe-du-Hoc cliffs, even though Ranger teams had climbed the cliffs on either side of him, only a few dozen yards away.

Rudder established his headquarters in a shell crater on the southeastern side of the eastern Flak bunker. The rest of the headquarters company and 60mm mortar teams remained on the beach for about an hour. "Doc" Block set up a temporary medical aid station on the beach, nestled in a small cavern for protection against sporadic German fire from the cliffs to the east. Among the wounded was Commando Lt Col Thomas H. Trevor. He was struck in the head by rifle or machine-gun fire, but his helmet saved him. He walked around Pointe-du-Hoc with a bloody bandage over his gashed forehead for the next few days. His aide, Sub Lt Ronald F. Eades RNVR, survived the fighting on Pointe-du-Hoc, only to be killed several days later after returning to the British sector.

The main "snafu"* to strike the mission was the failure of the communications. If the mission had gone in on schedule, Rudder was supposed to instruct Schneider's Force C to land at Pointe-du-Hoc. If not successful, they instead would land at Dog Green Beach. Since Force A had landed so late, Force C had already headed for Dog Green. As a result, Rudder's Force A would have to fend for themselves until the rest of the Rangers marched from Omaha Beach to Pointe-du-Hoc. Under the *Neptune* plans, it was expected they could reach Pointe-du-Hoc by noon on D-Day. This proved to be wildly optimistic.

Eikner tried without success to contact the outside world by SCR-300 walkie-talkie radio at 0725hrs. There is no record of

---

*The sarcastic term "snafu" stands for "Situation Normal: All Fucked Up", but originally stood for "Status Nominal: All Fucked Up." It was coined during World War II by US troops.

his transmission being received; it is possible it was sent on a frequency not being monitored by USS *Satterlee* or other ships. The larger SCR-284 radio took time to assemble on the beach and failed to make a connection with anyone.[7] Lt Eikner had shown the foresight to include an EE-84 signal lamp along with the radio equipment. Unlike the bulky and complicated SCR-284 radio, this could be quickly set up. The first connection between Ranger Force A and the outside world occurred at 0728hrs when the SFCP-1 established communications with the *Satterlee* immediately off Pointe-du-Hoc using Eikner's signal lamp.[8] The SFCP was a twelve-man Army and Navy team led by US Army officer Capt Jonathan H. Harwood of the 293rd Signal Company and Lt (jg) Kenneth S. Norton from the US Navy. The Rangers usually referred to this group as their "FOO Party," slang for Forward Observer Officers.[9]

Subsequently, once the SCR-284 radio was assembled again on top of the cliff with better transmission potential, the *Satterlee* was able to send the SFCP-1 the proper radio frequencies to establish radio links. Even so, the battalion after-action report noted that Eikner's signal lamp proved to be more reliable than the radio. At 1100hrs, a courier pigeon was dispatched from Pointe-du-Hoc to the headquarters of the 1st Division carrying the message, "Enemy battery on Pointe du Hoe destroyed." Whether the pigeon arrived safely is unrecorded. Radio contact with the 116th Infantry Regiment at Vierville was finally established via an SCR-300 radio at 1400hrs with the message, "Many casualties, need reinforcements, my position Pointe du Hoe." No return message was received until the following morning. As mentioned in the previous chapter about Ranger Force B, radio communications with the 116th RCT were very poor all day long.

News that the Rangers were at Pointe-du-Hoc spread through the various senior Army commands through the morning, usually based on naval reports. For example, the G-2 (Intelligence) and G-3 (Operations) Journals of the 1st Infantry Division both acknowledged a message from the *Prince Leopold* at 0930hrs that "Rangers landed safely, [heavy] opposition. Beach not cleared of [enemy] – very dangerous for LCA's." Most of the senior US Army commanders – Bradley, Gerow, and Huebner – were preoccupied with the difficulties on Omaha Beach and paid very little attention to Pointe-du-Hoc. There were no reports of heavy gunfire from its guns, and so little reason for any concern.

The Rangers' main lifeline was their tenuous connection to the naval bombardment group, and in particular the destroyer USS *Satterlee*. The gunfire support from the *Satterlee* on D-Day would keep the Germans at bay.

The first targets assigned by SFCP-1 were Targets 88 and 89, located immediately west of Pointe-du-Hoc. Target 88 was the 37mm Flak bunker at the western extremity of Pointe-du-Hoc. It had been spared during the bombardment and was the only major German weapon still functional near the strongpoint. It duly began firing at Rangers along the western side of Pointe-du-Hoc. The *Satterlee* started firing at it from 0739hrs and ceased fire at 0744hrs once the Flak bunker went quiet. According to photographs taken after D-Day, the 37mm gun itself was not hit, but there were several impacts nearby that probably killed or injured the Flak crew.[10]

AIRBORNE GUESTS

Rangers were not the only US troops on Pointe-du-Hoc, nor were they the first to arrive. As Rudder and the rest of the headquarters team prepared to move off the beach and climb the cliffs around 0745hrs, a pair of unexpected visitors arrived from farther down the coast. They were two paratroopers from the 101st Airborne Division who had been dropped in the wrong location earlier that morning, and had made their way to Pointe-du-Hoc.

The paratroopers were Privates Raymond Crouch and Leonard Goodgal. They had been among nineteen paratroopers from I Company, 506th Parachute Infantry Regiment, 101st Airborne Division, on a C-47 Skytrain of the 96th Troop Carrier Squadron, 440th Group, heading for a drop zone north of Carentan in the early morning hours of D-Day.[11] The aircraft was hit by heavy machine-gun fire and the pilot became disoriented. When the green light was turned on, the jumpmaster, Lt Floyd Johnston, looked out of the doorway. The sky was moonlit and he could see that the aircraft was over the ocean. He told the pilot, Lt William Zeuner, to turn the aircraft back around so that they could drop over land. The aircraft made a wide turn, but ended up over Saint-Pierre-du-Mont, about 15 miles from their intended drop zone. The plane was hit by further heavy machine-gun and also 20mm Flak fire, and just four paratroopers got out of the aircraft before it headed out to sea and crashed around 0140hrs. The four were Lt Johnston, Sgt Neil Christensen, Crouch, and Goodgal. Other paratroopers possibly made it out of the aircraft but drowned at sea; bodies were found along the shore over subsequent days.

Johnston and Christensen landed on Pointe-du-Hoc and, after a short firefight, were captured by the German garrison.[12] They both survived the pre-dawn bombardment of Pointe-du-Hoc. Johnston had broken his arm during the jump, but in the chaos he managed to escape captivity. Christensen ended up in a German prisoner-of-war camp until the end of the war.

Crouch and Goodgal, meanwhile, had landed in shallow water near the shore about 1,000 yards to the east of Pointe-du-Hoc. They tried to find an area to climb the cliffs, but without success. They remained to the east of Pointe-du-Hoc and witnessed the pre-dawn Operation *Flashlamp* bombardment. The fumes and smoke from the bombing attack were so intense that they put on their gas masks. After dawn, they saw the Rangers land at Pointe-du-Hoc, so decided to join them. They avoided German fire by walking close to the base of the cliffs. The paratroopers spent the next two days alongside Rudder, guarding the command post. They remained with the Rangers for six days, finally leaving on June 11 to rejoin their unit near Carentan.

At least two British soldiers also joined the Rangers on D-Day. Cpl Joseph J. Good and Pte Colin E. Blackmore were drivers on two of the Swan DUKWs. They dismounted the Vickers K machine guns from the tops of the useless ladders, and then climbed up the cliffs to join the Rangers. Their performance over the next few days was so exceptional that Rudder sent letters to the British Army recommending awards for their gallantry. They later both received the Military Medal, the second-highest British gallantry award.[13]

The first phase of the Rangers' operation, scaling the cliffs, had been accomplished in unexpectedly speedy fashion with casualties much fewer than expected. Now they had to locate and destroy the guns.

Chapter 12

Spiking the Guns

As the Rangers surveyed the top of the Pointe-du-Hoc, they faced a major problem: where were the guns? They had been thoroughly briefed about the location of each of the six guns, but the scene on top of the promontory was one of hellish devastation. The enormous heaps of spoil and debris encircling the numerous bomb craters made it very difficult to see across the otherwise flat surface. As each Ranger team reached the top, they went off to their objectives. There was no effort made to congregate and discuss options. As per the original plan, the individual Ranger boat teams began advancing through the strongpoint.

The three Ranger companies each had specific objectives. Easy Company was assigned the fire-control bunker and the No 3 gun position. Dog Company was assigned the three western gun positions, Nos 4, 5, and 6, while Fox Company was assigned the eastern gun positions, Nos 1 and 2, as well as the machine-gun positions occupied by the Werfer-Einheit. In most cases, the Rangers from each LCA advanced together.

The gun pits were a jumble of camouflage net, timbers, and debris. Several of the pits had suffered direct bomb hits and were a wreckage of huge slabs of concrete. Others had been spared direct hits, and from these, it was clear that the "guns" on Pointe-du-Hoc were simply dummies made from telephone poles and covered with camouflage net. Only one 155mm gun was still within the strongpoint. This was the one that had been destroyed during the first April bomber attack. The gun tube had been removed and sent off for repair; all that remained was the gun carriage. It had been further ripped apart by the pre-dawn *Flashlamp* bombing. The only recognizable features amidst the blasted landscape were the two completed gun casemates and the command post bunker. Most of the other bunkers were subterranean and had been completely covered by dirt and debris during the bombing attacks.

There were still isolated groups of Germans active in the ruins of the strongpoint. The Werfer-Einheit had been forced away from the eastern cliff edge by naval fire and were huddled in some craters on the southeastern corner of the strongpoint. They eventually escaped southward around noon. There were still about a dozen headquarters staff and other troops in the fire-control bunker. Some isolated groups of German soldiers were operating from the scattered personnel bunkers, and would pop-up every now and then, take shots at the Rangers, then disappear underground.

The Rangers from LCA 861, who had landed nearest the tip of Pointe-du-Hoc, began the attack on the fire-control bunker. SSgt Charles Denbo and Pfc Roberts managed to approach the bunker using a communication trench. The German bunker troops had set up an MG 34 or MG 42 machine gun in the forward observation room, and began firing at the Rangers. Denbo and Roberts responded by throwing four grenades at the bunker embrasure. Three fell inside, silencing the machine gun. Sgt Andrew Yardley then appeared with a bazooka and fired two rockets. One hit above the bunker embrasure to no effect, but the second went inside the embrasure and exploded. The observation room at the front of the command post bunker was isolated from the bunker interior by an armored door. Even though the machine-gun team had been killed by the grenades and bazooka rocket, the troops inside the plotting room and personnel room had not been injured.

Additional Rangers began to congregate around the bunker. A group from LCA 862 saw a German throwing grenades over the cliff from a position near the command post and chased after him. They threw grenades at him, and the German disappeared into the bunker through the rear door. This was presumably one of the troops under Unteroffizer Rudolf Karl, and may have been Karl himself. At this point, Corp V. Aguzzi took up position in a crater where he could keep an eye on the rear door of the bunker, trapping the Germans inside. Another two Rangers from LCA 861 kept watch over the front of the bunker from a trench toward the front. These three Rangers observed the fire-control bunker throughout the following day and the nine Germans still inside made no effort to sally out. T-5 Thompson could hear radio chatter from within the bunker, so he fired at the antenna on the top of the bunker, knocking it down. With the bunker contained, the other Rangers headed off to find the guns.

Some of the isolated Ranger groups became involved in close-quarter skirmishes with German troops who had survived in the various underground shelters. A group of about ten Rangers of Easy Company from LCA 858 engaged isolated German soldiers on the west side of the strongpoint near gun pit No 6. This area of the strongpoint was the most dangerous for the Rangers because the western 37mm Flak bunker was still active. Not only did movement in this area attract 37mm fire, but the bunker was presumably in contact with neighboring German units and would call in mortar and artillery fire whenever Rangers appeared. The team from LCA 858 disappeared in this sector except for one survivor, Sgt William Crug. It was unclear whether they had been captured or killed. As mentioned earlier, USS *Satterlee* targeted the 37mm Flak bunker before 0800hrs, silencing it for a time.

The original plan had been that once the guns were found and destroyed, the three companies would move southward, cross the Vierville–Grandcamp road, and set up a defensive position blocking the road. One platoon of Easy Company was assigned to remain behind with the headquarters to maintain a perimeter guard. Since the guns were missing, the scattered Ranger teams set off on the secondary mission of blocking the Vierville–Grandcamp road.

The lead squads came from Easy Company's LCA 888 and Dog Company's LCA 858. The LCA 888 group under 1st Sgt Robert Lang located the shattered ruins of casemate No 3 and decided to proceed south. One of the main problems was that prearranged destroyer fire was blocking their way, and Lang used his SCR-538 "handy-talkie" to try to contact the platoon leader, Lt Bell, to stop the naval fire. These small radios did not have much range, and as often as not were water-damaged. Lang's group ran into a patrol from Fox Company led by Lt Robert Arman from LCA 887, and they continued south as a group.

Much the same situation took place with an Easy Company team under 1st Lt Theodore Lapres. They were joined by a patrol of a dozen men from Dog Company, forming a larger group about 30 strong. This group began moving down the main road from Pointe-du-Hoc toward the D514 Vierville–Grandcamp road and past the Guelinel farm. There were far more German troops active to the south of the strongpoint, since this area had not been as hard hit by the bombardment. The farm had been used as barracks and canteen for the strongpoint, but by now was in ruins. Skirmishing with the scattered German troops cut the size of the force in half while traversing a few hundred yards of terrain, with seven killed and eight wounded. In fact, the Rangers suffered worse casualties in this short skirmish than they did during the cliff climb.

Once this team fought its way past the farm buildings, the passage to the Vierville–Grandcamp road was less costly. Upon reaching the road, Lapres's group met a Fox Company patrol led by T-5 Davis. Also arriving at the road was the mixed patrol under Lt Arman, which had cleared out the tiny hamlet of Au Guay during the advance southward. By 0815hrs, the Rangers on the main road numbered about 50 men. The German defenses had been most heavily concentrated in the various buildings on the southern side of the strongpoint, and resistance abruptly faded once the road was reached.

The Ranger spearhead was expecting that Schneider's Ranger Force C and the 116th RCT would be arriving up the road from the east at any moment. The German resistance seemed to be coming mainly from the south and west, so defenses were set up appropriately. About twenty Rangers under Sgt Lomell were assigned to secure the western side of the road toward Grandcamp.

Once the defenses were set up, the Rangers began active patrols to the south and west.

LOCATING THE GUNS

The Pointe-du-Hoc guns were discovered about 45 minutes later, around 0900hrs, during a patrol by Sgt Lomell and SSgt Jack Kuhn. All five surviving guns were well camouflaged on the Guérin farm along a country lane edged on both sides with hedgerows. The guns were aimed westward toward Utah Beach. As mentioned earlier, the guns had been abandoned more than five hours previously when the crews had got drunk and fled the site. Fuzed artillery ammunition and propellant charges were found nearby, so the guns were still ready to fire. Lomell, who had two thermite grenades, placed these in the recoil mechanism of two of the guns, disabling them.[1] A third gun was damaged by smashing its sight with a rifle butt. Kuhn and Lomell then headed back to the Ranger perimeter on the road to get additional grenades.

Moments after Lomell and Kuhn left, an Easy Company patrol under SSgt Frank Rupinski also located the guns. Rupinski's patrol had more grenades, and placed a thermite grenade down the barrel of all five guns. They also dismounted the sights from several of the guns and threw grenades into the stores of propellant charges, starting a ferocious fire. Rupinski dispatched a runner back to Pointe-du-Hoc to inform Rudder that the main objective of locating and disabling the guns had been accomplished. As Lomell was returning with more grenades, he saw Rupinski's Easy Company team disabling the guns, so he returned to the Ranger defense perimeter. Lomell returned to the guns in the afternoon to make certain that all had been disabled, placing a thermite grenade in one of the guns' recoil mechanism.[2]

Details of this action have become muddied over the years. According to Lomell's testimony to Army historians within a few weeks of D-Day, he and Kuhn had placed grenades in only two guns and damaged the other three by bashing their sights. In later years, Lomell would begin to claim that he had returned to the site with additional grenades and finished off the remaining guns.[3] This contradicted his wartime testimony and made his role appear to be more central. Rupinski never gave an account of his actions that day to Army historians because he was captured during the nighttime fighting and didn't return from a German prisoner-of-war camp until after the war's end. The actions by Rupinski's Easy Company patrol that morning were related to Army historians by other members of Easy Company. After the war, Rupinski shunned publicity, while Lomell courted interviews and TV appearances. As a result, Lomell's later embellished accounts have predominated in the depictions of the discovery of the guns.

Regardless of who deserved credit, by mid-morning, Range Force A had accomplished its primary mission of eliminating the Pointe-du-Hoc guns. The 2nd Rangers were in the process of accomplishing their secondary mission of holding the Vierville–Grandcamp road in anticipation of the arrival of the rest of the Provisional Ranger Group and the 116th RCT. Although the Rangers had established a perimeter along the road, the Pointe-du-Hoc strongpoint was not entirely secure. A deadly game of cat-and-mouse continued for most of the day as Ranger patrols tried to clean out isolated groups of German soldiers in the shattered ruins of the strongpoint.

German troops located in one of the observation posts along the cliffs to the southeast of the strongpoint were still firing machine guns at the Rangers on the eastern side until mid-morning. These were probably the southernmost elements of the Werfer-Einheit. A number of small defense works had been set up along the cliffs, outside the eastern end of the Pointe-du-Hoc strongpoint,[4] and these machine guns posed a special hazard to Rudder's command post. There were several efforts by small Ranger patrols to deal with the machine guns. The area where the promontory met the eastern cliffs also contained several minefields. One of the patrols got to within grenade range of the machine-gun nests, but there were numerous scattered German riflemen in the vicinity. Several Rangers were wounded during these skirmishes.

Rudder finally pulled back the patrols and instructed Eikner to signal USS *Satterlee* to deal with the problem. The *Satterlee* had already attempted to deal with this target, starting at 0758hrs. The destroyer had fired for about three minutes but was urgently requested to shift its fire to the Guelinel farm buildings that were holding up the Ranger advance to the road. After firing at targets near the Vierville–Grandcamp road until 0836hrs, the *Satterlee* then turned its attention to a German gun on the cliffs northeast of Grandcamp that was shooting at naval vessels near the coast.* It returned to firing on targets near the Guelinel farm from 0933–1004hrs. At this time, the SFCP-1 team instructed the *Satterlee* to deal with the machine guns on the cliff. After two corrections, its 5in. rounds began to impact the machine-gun nest at 1011hrs; after five salvoes, it was instructed to cease fire at 1012hrs.[5] The Rangers recalled afterwards, "The destroyer pulled close in, and 7 salvoes from the main batteries blew the whole top off the cliff at the right spot. That ended the trouble from flanking automatic fire to the east."[6]

Rudder's command post was in a large crater at the rear of the eastern Flak bunker, immediately above the cliffs. The 37mm Flak gun originally located on the roof of the bunker had been completely obliterated by the early-morning bombardment, and the doors into the bunker were covered with dirt, chunks of concrete, and other debris. During the course of the day, the Rangers under the direction of Col Trevor, the Commando liaison, cleared away enough debris to get into the interior of the Flak bunker. It then was used as a protected aid station by "Doc" Block.

Rudder's headquarters became the main link between Force A and the outside world. Eikner, in conjunction with Capt Harwood and Lt (jg) Norton of the Shore Fire Control Party, kept in touch with the ships off the coast via the signal lamp and radios. Their primary source of support for most of the day was USS *Satterlee*. Communications between the headquarters and the Rangers in the forward outpost along the Vierville–Grandcamp road were patchy. Although the platoons had received the SCR-536 "handie-talkies," the performance of these battery-operated devices proved to be

---

* These were probably 88mm Flak guns of Kistowski's Flak-Regiment.32.

very erratic. Many of the hand-held radios had become water-damaged during the trip ashore, or had failed for other reasons. The supplies located on the two supply LCAs had been lost, so other communication methods such as field telephones were not available. Runners could be used between the headquarters and the forward outpost, but this was time-consuming and dangerous in view of the number of Germans lurking in bomb craters around Pointe-du-Hoc.

Rudder instructed Harwood and Norton to set up the main SFCP-1 radio center inside gun casemate No 2, about 125 yards from his command post. Rudder was visiting with the fire-control party near the casemate in mid-morning when he was struck in the leg by a rifle round. The bullet cut clear through the muscle without hitting a blood vessel or a bone. "Doc" Block dressed the wound, and Rudder remained at the casemate. About half an hour later, Rudder was inside the casemate embrasure along with Harwood, Norton and Pfc Theodore Wells, an SCR-300 radioman. As they were standing there, a stray naval round struck the wall of the casemate. The impact killed the SFCP leader, Harwood, and injured the Naval Gunnery Liaison Officer, Norton, and Wells. Rudder, who was deeper inside the casemate when the projectile struck, suffered from concussion and a spray of concrete and steel fragments to his chest and right arm.[7] He was covered with a thin yellow powder by the blast, which has led to the idea that the projectile may have been a yellow dye marker rather than a high-explosive round. However, John Raaen Jr, the HQ Company commander of the 5th Rangers and a senior Ordnance officer after the war, believes that it was a high-explosive round containing a picric acid burster charge, which also leaves a distinctive coating of yellow powder after detonation.[8] Norton and Wells were later evacuated to USS *Texas*, but Rudder remained in command in spite of his growing list of injuries. He was later awarded two Purple Hearts for his actions on D-Day. Command of SFCP-1 was then assigned to Lt (jg) Ben Berger, now the senior member of the team.

The number of wounded Rangers and German prisoners around the command post increased as the day went on. Rudder requested assistance from the destroyers offshore to help evacuate the wounded and prisoners as well as to bring in supplies. The destroyer USS *Barton* arrived in Fire Support Station No 3 shortly after noon, and first established contact with SFCP-1 after 1300hrs via Eikner's signal lamp. The *Barton* dispatched one of its whaleboats to shore to pick up the most seriously wounded around 1435hrs. Upon approaching the shore, the whaleboat came under fire from a German machine-gun nest east of Pointe-du-Hoc. One of the Navy medics aboard was wounded, while a US Army soldier fished out of the water earlier in the afternoon from a sinking LCT was hit in the helmet. As the fire intensified, the lieutenant commanding the whaleboat ordered the coxswain to head back to the *Barton*. The whaleboat returned to the destroyer at 1519hrs, ending the first relief attempt. In response, the *Barton* fired 130 5in. rounds at the German machine-gun positions. The *Barton* managed to contact Bradley's First US Army headquarters staff about the deteriorating situation at Pointe-du-Hoc at 1542hrs.

With the state of affairs on Pointe-du-Hoc becoming desperate, SFCP-1 tried contacting the *Barton* again, but was unable to do so. However, SFCP-1 did manage to maintain contact with USS *Satterlee* and asked it to facilitate an evacuation of the wounded and, if possible, a dispatch of replacements. This message was forwarded to the command ship, USS *Ancon*, at 1626hrs. At 1633hrs, Gen Huebner's staff of the 1st Division relayed a message to Rudder saying, "All Rangers have landed Dog Green. No other troops available."[9] It is not clear if this message was ever received. In the early evening, SFCP-1 contacted USS *McCook* by signal light and this was forwarded to the *Ancon* at 1824hrs, indicating an immediate need for reinforcements, ammunition, and evacuation of prisoners and wounded. The message was repeated to USS *Thompson* at 1930hrs. At 1928hrs, Omaha Beach's Task Force 124 commander Rear Admiral John L. Hall's staff on USS *Ancon* ordered LCI(L) 86 (LCI: Landing Craft Infantry) to send two LCVPs to Pointe-du-Hoc to evacuate the wounded. For unknown reasons, this did not take place. No relief for Ranger Force A came on D-Day.

Chapter 13

The Germans Strike Back

Aside from the artillery troops of 2.Batterie, HKAA.1230, there were very few German troops in the immediate vicinity of Pointe-du-Hoc on D-Day morning. Allied intelligence estimates before D-Day expected the Rangers to encounter about 125 troops, roughly an understrength company, from the 716.Infanterie-Division. The actual forces were significantly smaller.

As mentioned previously, the 716.Infanterie-Division was a bodenständige (static) division intended for coastal defense. It was perennially understrength. In February 1944, for example, it had only 7,197 troops compared to a nominal strength of 9,859 troops, about three-quarters of full strength. Only a single battalion from the division, the III./Grenadier-Regiment.726, was in the sector from Grandcamp-les-Bains to the western side of Omaha Beach. The battalion headquarters was at the Chateau de Jucoville south of Pointe-du-Hoc. The battalion had two of its four companies deployed on either side of Pointe-du-Hoc: to the west was the 12./GR.726 headquartered in Grandcamp-les-Bains, and to the east the 9./GR.726 located in the Pointe-et-Raz-de-la-Percée area. The 9./GR.726 was headquartered in the chateau in Gruchy and commanded by Hptm Grünschloss. These two companies were understrength, with only about one hundred men each, covering some 7 miles of defense line, less than thirty men per mile. There was a detachment in St Pierre-du-Mont from 9./GR.726, numbering about fifty men.

Two artillery batteries of the 716.Infanterie-Division were to the west of Pointe-du-Hoc near the village of Maisy. Although neither battery had Pointe-du-Hoc in their assigned control zone, both batteries were in range of Pointe-du-Hoc. It is not clear whether the batteries fired on Pointe-du-Hoc on D-Day.[1]

The 352.Infanterie-Division had moved forward from its training area around Saint-Lô toward what became Omaha Beach in March 1944. This division did not deploy in the Pointe-du-Hoc area, but the two battalions of GR.726 in this sector were put under its control.* The most important consequence of the arrival of the 352.Infanterie-Division here was that one of its battalions, the I./Grenadier-Regiment.914, took control of the defenses of the Vire estuary west of Grandcamp-les-Bains, while two of the division's artillery battalions were deployed within range of Pointe-du-Hoc. The IV./Artillerie-Regiment.352 was located south of Pointe-du-Hoc supporting GR.914, while I./AR.352 was to the east behind Omaha Beach, supporting GR.916.†

The German command post at Pointe-du-Hoc remained in contact with elements of the 352.Infanterie-Division in the early morning hours of D-Day, reporting on the bombing attacks and the approach of the Allied fleet. From these reports, the 352. Infanterie-Division deduced that the "commando attack" consisted of about two companies of enemy troops.[2] Around 1015hrs, GR.916 reported that no more messages from the strongpoint

---

*Grenadier-Regiment.914 was based around the Vire estuary, with I./GR.914 holding the coast west of Grandcamp/Isigny. Grenadier-Regiment.916 was farther east, covering Omaha Beach toward Gold Beach. The division's third regiment, GR.915, was in LXXXIV. Armee-Korps reserve and the division's Fusilier battalion was in divisional reserve. The only significant addition to the defense of Pointe-du-Hoc by the 352.Infanterie-Division was the deployment of two of its artillery battalions, I./ and II./AR.352. The I./AR.352 was located south of Grandcamp and its twelve 105mm field guns were in range of Pointe-du-Hoc. This unit was probably responsible for most of the artillery fire directed against Pointe-du-Hoc on D-Day. The II./AR.352 was behind Omaha Beach, and so was probably preoccupied with targets on the beach on D-Day.

† Both of these battalions were equipped with the standard German 10.5cm le.FH 18/40.

at Pointe-du-Hoc had been received. As mentioned earlier, the Rangers had knocked out the radio antenna on the command bunker, and presumably the field telephone trunk line had been ripped up by the bombardment.

The headquarters of Grenadier-Regiment.916 instructed the garrison at St Pierre-du-Mont to counterattack Pointe-du-Hoc. A platoon of 40 men from 9./GR.726 advanced towards the eastern side of Pointe-du-Hoc around 0900hrs[3] in an attack supported by artillery and mortar fire. The artillery fire probably came from one of the batteries of IV./AR.1352 near Asnières-en-Bessin.[4] The German platoon set up its machine gun and began firing at the Fox Company defenses. The Rangers could not request naval gunfire support since the Germans were located very close to Fox Company, and overshots might hit the Rangers advancing toward the Vierville–Grandcamp road. The firefight lasted for about an hour. The Rangers later reported, "The attack was stopped by rifle fire; after a time, the German fire slackened and they could be seen drifting back. The Rangers had sustained no casualties."[5]

The Rangers on the highway defense line spent most of the morning and afternoon sending out patrols that usually consisted of six or seven men. There were sporadic contacts with isolated groups of German troops; in some cases, there were minor skirmishes. In many other cases, the Germans were caught walking along the Vierville–Grandcamp road, escaping from Omaha Beach toward the west. Some of these may have been elements of the 2.Batterie who had fled southward during the pre-dawn bombardment, such as the gun crews. About forty prisoners were captured by the Rangers, while the forward teams estimated that they had killed or wounded another thirty German troops during the scattered skirmishes.

Around 1300hrs, the headquarters of the III./GR.726 at the Chateau de Jucoville was ordered to counterattack Pointe-du-Hoc again. Since it was so short of troops, it took a few hours to pull together an attack force, which swung into action in the late afternoon around 1600hrs. The attack emanated from the area of the western Flak bunker and probably consisted of platoons from 12./GR.726 from Grandcamp.[6] The counterattack struck the right side of the Fox Company defense line, which had only a small number of riflemen but included two BARs and a 60mm mortar section. An initial probe by the German infantry was temporarily halted by BAR fire. The Rangers used the opportunity to move a few more riflemen into the area. SSgt Eugene Elder then hit one of the German patrols with 60mm bombs at only 60 yards. Spotting another group in a crater, Elder shifted his aim and flushed out the Germans. As they escaped, they suffered further casualties from BAR fire. This largely ended the attack on the Fox Company right flank, though sporadic small-arms fire continued after dark.

Around the same time, a large German patrol of about fifty men – including two machine guns and a mortar – passed by the Dog Company outpost near the highway. The Rangers in this area, heavily outnumbered, held their fire as the Germans exited to the southwest. This German patrol may have been part of the group attacking the Fox Company line which became lost or disoriented in the bocage terrain of the farm fields.

PARKER'S PATROL ARRIVES

In one of the most incredible events of the day, a patrol of twenty-three Rangers from 1st Platoon, Able Company, 5th Rangers Battalion, arrived from Omaha Beach at the Ranger defense line at about 2100hrs, an hour before sunset. The Ranger on guard demanded the password, and the platoon's leader, Lt Charles "Ace" Parker, responded with "Tally-Ho!"

Parker's company had landed on Omaha Beach with the rest of Ranger Force C that morning. The 5th Ranger Battalion eventually made it up the bluffs overlooking Omaha Beach and headed inland in the late morning.[7] Parker went up the bluff with about thirty soldiers from his company, mainly from the 1st Platoon. Two men were wounded during the process, Lt Suchier and Pte Bernard Berkowitz. After arriving at the top of the bluff, Parker organized the men around him and set off for the rendezvous point, the Ormel farm, marked as the Chateau de Vaumicel on Army maps, south of the town of Vierville-sur-Mer. The column came under scattered small-arms fire, with the lead scout, T-5 William Fox, and 1st Lt Woodford Moore being wounded; Fox later died, but Moore survived in spite of a serious head wound. At this point, Parker's force had been reduced to twenty-seven men.

When Parker and his men arrived there in the afternoon, around 1400hrs, there were eleven soldiers from the 116th Infantry in the farm buildings, but no sign of the 5th Ranger Battalion. Parker recalled: "I imagined that the rest of my Ranger battalion had been there and gone on, not being able to wait for us... So we took off. We figured that maybe we would catch them."[8] Before they set off, three Rangers serving as guards south of the farm were discovered to be missing; two had been captured and one killed in encounters with scattered German patrols.[9]

Around 1430hrs, Parker's platoon headed westward along the farm trails through the bocage. In many cases, the trails resembled foliage tunnels, with a narrow path enclosed between two hedgerows and the branches of the trees and shrubs almost enveloping the trails. Some trails were wide enough for a cart but others were passable only by a single person on foot. During the advance west, the platoon had numerous small skirmishes with isolated groups of German troops. They eventually collected sixteen German prisoners, and about a dozen curious French civilians followed along. The civilians were left behind in the village of Englesqueville-la-Percée.

During their march to Pointe-du-Hoc, Parker's platoon almost became trapped when the front of the column was halted by an emplaced German machine gun and there was fire from toward the rear of the column. On the narrow bocage path, neither the Germans nor the Americans could see one another, but they could hear each other speaking. Eventually, the Germans began throwing stick grenades over the hedgerows at the Rangers. But the German troops were inexperienced, and threw their grenades immediately after pulling the cord at their base. The grenades had a nominal delay time of 4½ seconds, so the Rangers usually managed to pick them up and throw them back at the Germans. Many of the grenades simply failed to detonate.[10]

Parker realized his platoon might be trapped by a larger German force, and it was still accompanied by German prisoners of war. Leaving the captured Germans in a neighboring barn, Parker and the Rangers scurried back down the bocage path as fast as they could, trying to reach a path to Pointe-du-Hoc that was shown on their map. About 100 yards down the trail, the Rangers crossed over the hedgerow, realizing it could become a trap. They saw no signs of any German unit ahead.

For the remainder of the evening, they headed to Pointe-du-Hoc across farm fields and avoided the enclosed farm paths. They eventually made their way to St Pierre-du-Mont. The local German garrison had left the village earlier in the day during the counterattacks against Pointe-du-Hoc, and Parker's men moved through without incident.

After Parker's platoon finally reached Pointe-du-Hoc, Rudder was informed of its arrival. Rudder wanted to know whether the remainder of Ranger Force C was following him. Parker replied that he had not been in contact with the rest of the Rangers since morning, but that the 5th Rangers were probably just behind them.[11] In fact, the remainder of Ranger Force C did not arrive at Pointe-du-Hoc until D+2.[12] Parker's platoon was incorporated into the defense line along the Vierville–Grandcamp road. They did not have long to wait before the first major German attack began.

Chapter 14

Night Attack

For most of D-Day, German attacks against Pointe-du-Hoc were small-scale and disorganized. The III./Grenadier-Regiment.726 assigned to this sector was thinly spread along the Vierville–Grandcamp corridor. Much of its strength was frittered away in the series of minor counterattacks conducted in the morning and afternoon, as detailed in the previous chapter. At the start of D-Day, this battalion was subordinated to Oberst Ernst Goth's Grenadier-Regiment.916. Goth's regiment was itself badly overextended, covering the area from Omaha Beach in the west to Gold Beach in the east. All of its resources were being concentrated against the two Allied invasion beaches. During the late morning, the 352. Infanterie-Division headquarters agreed to shift responsibility for the counterattack on Pointe-du-Hoc from Goth's GR.916 to the I./Grenadier-Regiment.914.[1]

In the early evening of D-Day, Generalleutnant Dietrich Kraiss, commander of the 352.Infanterie-Division, visited Goth at his headquarters in Trévières, about 6 miles south of Omaha Beach, to discuss options for repelling the Allied landings. Given the lack of reserves, this seemed all but impossible. During the discussion of the situation around Vierville, the matter of Pointe-du-Hoc came up. Goth's initial attempts earlier in the day to use the understrength III./GR.726 to crush the invaders had failed.

Reports indicated that Pointe-du-Hoc was being held by about two companies of Allied "commandos."

Since responsibility for Pointe-du-Hoc had been transferred to I./GR.914 earlier in the day, Kraiss instructed his operations officer, Oberstleutnant Fritz Ziegelmann, to contact the headquarters of I./GR.914 in Osmanville and tell them to counterattack the enemy commandos at Pointe-du-Hoc.[2] Osmanville is about 6 miles southwest of Pointe-du-Hoc, and most of the battalion manned coastal defenses along the Vire estuary to the west of Grandcamp and Maisy. The I./GR.914 was not heavily involved in the D-Day fighting, aside from sending patrols to deal with scattered US paratroopers accidently dropped on the eastern side of the river Vire.

This battalion would be the principal opponent of the Rangers at Pointe-du-Hoc over the next few days. The instructions from Kraiss were transmitted around 1925hrs, and it took some time for I./GR.914 to mobilize its forces.[3] German accounts indicate that the attack force was a reinforced battalion, so presumably the battle group for I./GR.914 included troops from other units. This probably included surviving elements of 12./GR.726 that had been involved in the fighting on the southwestern side of Pointe-du-Hoc earlier in the afternoon.

RANGER DEFENSES

By nightfall, around 2300hrs, a third of the troops of Ranger Group A were casualties. Most of the wounded were located in shelters near Rudder's headquarters or down on the beach. Of the remaining men, about half were deployed within the Pointe-du-Hoc strongpoint, while the remaining eighty-five men were with the forward detachment on the Vierville–Grandcamp road. Ammunition was low due to the loss of one of the two supply LCAs. Although the second supply LCA reached Pointe-du-Hoc, the crew had been forced to throw much of the equipment overboard during the trip when it was nearly swamped by waves. The shortages were most extreme with regard to grenades and

30. The devastating power of the Operation *Flashlamp* bomber attacks on Pointe-du-Hoc can be seen in this image of one of the numerous bomb craters that pockmarked the site.

31. The World War I-era battleship USS *Texas* (BB35) was assigned the primary naval bombardment mission to suppress the German gun battery at Pointe-du-Hoc.

32. The savior of the Rangers on Pointe-du-Hoc was the destroyer USS *Satterlee* (DD626) that provided fire support through most of D-Day. *Satterlee* is in the foreground with her sisters of the Gleaves-class, USS *Baldwin* (DD624) and USS *Nelson* (DD623).

33. The destroyer USS *Thompson* seen off the coast of Normandy on D-Day while being refueled by the battleship USS *Arkansas*.

34. The 1st Platoon of Charlie Company, 2nd Rangers in LCA-418 in Weymouth harbor on June 1, 1944 prior to their boarding the HMS *Prince Charles*.

35. Much of the fighting by Goranson's Ranger Force C took place around the "Folie Gambier," nestled in the cliff face to the west of the Vierville draw.

36. This overhead view of the Vierville draw area was taken in 1947. The 1/116th Infantry landed on Dog Green Beach (1), dominated by the bunkers in defense nests WN 72 (2) and WN 71 (3). Schneider's 5th Rangers landed further east and surmounted the bluffs east of WN 71 (4). Goranson's Ranger Force B landed on Charlie Beach (5) and saw most of their fighting around the Gambier farmhouse and WN 73 (6).

37. This 76.5mm FK17(t) at Pointe-et-Raz-de-la-Percée survived the repeated naval shelling on D-Day.

38. Goranson's Force B spent much of D-Day trying to overcome the numerous trench defenses and bunkers of the WN 73 defense nest. On top of the hill are the remnants of the Gambier stone barn used as a barracks by the 11./GR.726.

39. The D-Day bombardment of Pointe-du-Hoc dislodged a large chunk of the cliff, creating a heap of rocky soil beneath. This facilitated the Ranger scaling effort in this sector.

40. The climb of the 75th Ranger Regiment at Point-du-Hoc for the 75th anniversary commemoration took place in the same part of the cliff used by the Rangers on D-Day. (US Air Force photo by Master Sgt. Andy M. Kin, Regional Media Center AFN Europe. DoD)

41. A good impression of the height of the Pointe-du-Hoc cliffs can be seen in this photo during the 2019 commemoration. This provides some idea of the German soldier's perspective on D-Day. (US Army photo by Photo by Sgt. Henry Villarama, US Army Europe. DoD)

42. Col. J. Earl Rudder at the Ranger Force A command post on Pointe-du-Hoc. Behind him is Eikner's EE-84 signal lamp, the essential tool for contacting the Navy warships off shore on D-Day.

43. On D-Day, the critical link between Army units and Navy warships was the Shore Fire Control Party like this one near Les Dunes de Varreville on June 10, 1944.

44. The most persistent threat to the Rangers at Pointe-du-Hoc was this 37mm Flak 36 located in an L409A emplacement on the far western side of the strongpoint.

45. When the Rangers reached the kettle gun pits on D-Day, they found a jumbled mess of camouflage net and the shattered wooden frame of the camouflage umbrella over the fake timber guns.

46. One of the surviving five 155mm GPF guns after their capture by the Rangers on D-Day.

47. Rangers in a crater near the Pointe-du-Hoc command post. The Ranger to the right is armed with a tripod-mounted Browning M1918 air-cooled light machine gun.

48. Brig Gen Norman Cota, assistant commander of the 29th Division, receives the Distinguished Service Order from Gen Bernard Montgomery on July 7, 1944 for his heroism on D-Day.

49. A contemporary view of the Vierville draw showing Dog Green Beach (**1**), the 88mm gun bunker of WN 72 and now the US National Guard Memorial (**2**), the WN 71 defense nest (**3**), Charlie Beach (**4**), defense nest WN 73 (**5**), and the ultimate objective of Goranson's Force B, the Point-et-Raz-de-la-Percée (**6**). (Author)

50. Ranger Force C landed here on Dog White Beach in front of the seaside villas of Hamel-au-Prêtre. They surmounted the bluffs in this area, to the east of the WN 71 defense nest, before proceeding to the village of Vierville-sur-Mer. (Author)

51. Troops of the communication section of the 2nd Rangers headquarters company play with "Ranger," a puppy they adopted while in bivouac after D-Day.

52. A view of the Ranger command post taken by a US Navy photographer after the relief of Pointe-du-Hoc.

53. Rudder's Rangers prepare to depart Pointe-du-Hoc on D+2 after the arrival of the 116th RCT relief column. Rudder is in the center facing the camera, while in front of him is Capt Harvey Cook, searching a German prisoner.

54. Rudder's command post on Pointe-du-Hoc was established in a crater on the edge of the cliff near the eastern Flak bunker. Several German prisoners can be seen under escort above the crater, being led down to the beach for transfer to ships offshore.

55. The fields east of Pointe-du-Hoc were converted into Emergency Landing Strip (ELS) A-1 starting on June 7 by the 834th Engineer Aviation Battalion even before the strongpoint was secured.

56. One of the Schneider 155mm howitzers of 9.Batterie, Artillerie-Regiment-1716 in WN 83 at Maisy-Les Perruques was knocked off its concrete pad by the preliminary Allied bombardment.

57. The Regelbau 622 personnel bunker at WN 84 Maisy-Martinière in late June 1944 following the capture of the site by the 5th Rangers.

58. Eight men of the 5th Rangers are decorated with the Distinguished Service Cross in a ceremony in Normandy on June 22, 1944, with Lt Col Max Schneider at the left.

59. The naval gun battery at Longues-sur-Mer to the east of Omaha Beach was the most sophisticated gun battery in the area of the D-Day beaches. (Author)

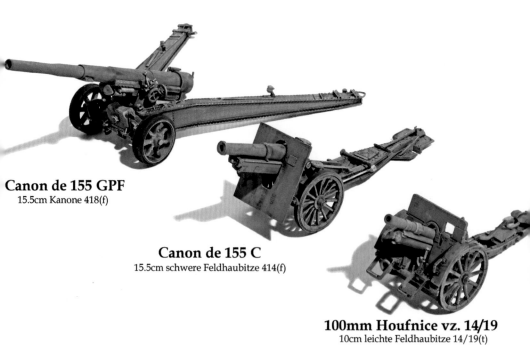

Canon de 155 GPF
15.5cm Kanone 418(f)

Canon de 155 C
15.5cm schwere Feldhaubitze 414(f)

100mm Houfnice vz. 14/19
10cm leichte Feldhaubitze 14/19(t)

60. This illustration compares the three types of field guns encountered by the Rangers – the 155mm GPF gun, the 155mm Schneider howitzer, and the 100mm vz. 14/19 howitzer. (Author)

60mm mortar ammunition. Some Rangers were having to use captured German weapons and ammunition; Easy Company had three German machine guns, either MG 34s or MG 42s. There was also an ample supply of German "potato-masher" grenades, but the Rangers had a poor opinion of these from their own experiences that day. The forward detachment was located in three fields south of the Vierville–Grandcamp road in a roughly "L"-shaped deployment, some 300ft long on either side, oriented toward the southwest. Aside from the main defense line, the Rangers had deployed smaller outposts farther to the west and south.

The Rangers had observed German troops to the southwest around dusk. Around 2330hrs, as night fell, the Rangers heard the first signs of a German attack. As was the usual German practice, small-unit leaders began blowing whistles to signal the beginning of the attack. The German troops also started shouting, a method to increase unit cohesion and keep unit control in the dark. Once the attack began, German machine guns opened fire on the Rangers' defense line. In some cases, they began with tracer fire, hoping to pinpoint the American positions when they returned fire. The German forward positions were only 25–50 yards from the Ranger lines, the terrain being compartmented into small, enclosed fields.

The initial attack struck at the junction of the "L" in the southwest corner. Corporals Thompson and Hornhardt, in an outpost about 35 yards forward of the main defense line, had a squad of Germans walk right through the bocage hedge into their position. In a close-quarter skirmish, Thompson killed three Germans with his BAR, but was injured in the face by grenade fragments. Hornhardt took over the BAR and they both withdrew into the main defense line. Moments after the start of the attack, there was a large explosion in the vicinity of the five spiked German 155mm guns. It seemed to be an eruption of artillery propellant, but the exact cause of the explosion was unknown. The German attackers, startled by the blast, were illuminated for an instant by the flames behind them. In the confusion, the German troops retreated into a nearby orchard. Some of the Rangers thought that the initial attack was simply a probe to identify their defenses.

During this first German attack, Lt Kerchner, positioned at the junction of the "L," decided to put together a small group, move back towards the highway, and then swing back to the southwest behind the Germans. In the darkness and chaos, Kerchner found himself at the northwestern end of the defense line with only two accompanying Rangers, having lost the rest of them in the dark. With Kerchner's impromptu counterattack scheme and Ranger casualties, the junction of the "L" in the southwest corner had been weakened. The forward outposts thus pulled back into the main defense line near the road.

The second German attack began around 0100hrs in much the same fashion. German squad leaders blew whistles, their men shouted their names to provide some measure of control, and supporting machine guns fired at the Ranger positions with a heavy mix of tracers. By this time, the corner of the "L" was held only by BAR gunner T-5 Henry Stecki and one other Ranger. The Rangers in positions nearby heard Stecki's BAR fire for about two minutes, then heard German voices in the corner behind the bocage hedgerow. After several minutes of fighting, the German attack ceased. Stecki's position had been overrun. There were no reinforcements to plug gaps in the defenses, and most of the platoon leaders were back at the detachment command post on the eastern end of the "L" discussing what action to take. Some of the platoon leaders recommended pulling back to the north side of the road because the "L" defense line was badly overextended and the men were short of ammunition.

The third German attack started at 0300hrs in the same manner as the first two: German NCOs began blowing whistles, followed by the troops in their squads calling out their names. Once this process was complete, the supporting machine guns opened fire on the Rangers' defense line. However, this time the German Kampfgruppe was significantly larger and had machine guns positioned against a broader swath of the Ranger defenses. The focus of the attack was also about 50 yards farther east, at the base of the "L" defense line. Easy Company's defensive line at the middle of base of the "L" was overrun after a German squad advanced through the hedgerow in the dark, then rolled up the Ranger defenses from behind. In the skirmish, Lt Leagans was killed and about twenty Rangers, many of them wounded, were captured. They were taken to the command post of the I./GR.914 battle group, located about a mile to the south.

The German attack continued down the base of the "L" defense line toward the east. At Lt Arman's command post near the eastern end of the "L", it was evident that the Germans had got into the neighboring field and overwhelmed the forward Ranger line in that area. Arman and Lt Zelepsky from the 5th Rangers decided to withdraw their men back to the Vierville–Grandcamp road. This was difficult to do in the darkness and chaos of a firefight, but word went around as NCOs hastily told their men to get ready to move back to the road.

Upon reaching the road, the officers and NCOs tried to take a headcount. Most of the Fox Company men were present, but there were few Rangers from Easy Company and none from Dog Company. About fifty of the original eighty-five Rangers reached the road by 0400hrs. Some Rangers remained isolated in their foxholes, while about a dozen men from Dog Company didn't receive any instructions to withdraw but managed to find refuge in a deep drainage ditch. They remained there until June 8. A few other scattered survivors infiltrated back to the road later in the morning. One account put the night's casualties as one officer killed and nineteen NCOs and enlisted men missing.[4] The surviving Rangers set up a new defense line within the Pointe-du-Hoc strongpoint stretching between the No 5 and No 3 gun positions, but they were desperately short of small-arms ammunition and food. There was very little naval fire support that night due to the proximity of the attacking Germans and defending Americans.

With no sign of relief, a last-ditch battle seemed inevitable. Indeed, Rudder "thought we were goners."[5] What they did not realize was that they had inflicted such heavy losses on the German Kampfgruppe that no further attacks would take place that day.

Chapter 15

Ranger Force C on Dog Green Beach

The largest of the Ranger formations, Force C, was the last to land on D-Day. Max Schneider's Force C consisted of the entire 5th Ranger Battalion, plus two companies of the 2nd Rangers, as well as the group's Cannon Company.

As detailed previously,[1] Force C had two optional plans. If Rudder's Force A successfully landed and eliminated the Pointe-du-Hoc guns, Force C would follow behind them and land at Pointe du Hoc. In the event that this did not happen by H+30 minutes, then Force C would head to Dog Green Beach and land behind the 116th RCT before heading westward to Pointe-du-Hoc by an overland route.

Onboard the flagship HMS *Prince Charles*, Lt R. D. Turnbull waited anxiously for the "Crowbar" message from the navigation launch ML 304 that would indicate that Rudder's force had successfully landed at Pointe-du-Hoc. Although this was expected around H-Hour (0630hrs), it didn't arrive until 0709hrs. If the mission had gone as planned, Turnbull should have received the second codeword "Bingo" at H+30 (0700hrs) that would have indicated that the mission was successful and the guns eliminated. Turnbull decided to wait a few more minutes in the hope that the success messages might arrive, even if slightly delayed.

A parallel series of messages were supposed to be delivered to Schneider. Around dawn, Schneider's LCA did pick up Rudder's message "Splash" to LCT 413, the codeword to disembark the Swan Ladder DUKWs. Schneider tried to get in touch with Rudder by radio, without success.[2] All of the Ranger companies were outfitted with the new SCR-300 walkie-talkies.* As a back-up, the Royal Navy LCAs carried their own radios. Most of the SCR-300 radios with Rudder's Force A had been damaged by seawater during the trip to shore or upon landing. Rudder was supposed to send the radio message "Praise the Lord" to Schneider around H-Hour, when Ranger Force A was scheduled to land at Pointe-du-Hoc. In the event, Schneider never received such a message.[3] Another codeword, "Tilt," was supposed to be sent if the Pointe-du-Hoc mission failed or if Rudder decided to have Ranger Force C land at Dog Green Beach. There is some dispute in surviving documents as to whether Schneider received any such message.

The 2nd Ranger Battalion after-action report cryptically noted that "Group notified not to land at Pointe-du-Hoc," presumably referring to the "Tilt" message to Ranger Force C. The report by Force C later noted, "Listening Watch was maintained in the Headquarters craft for signals from Force A. An unintelligible message was received at 0715; the only recognizable word was 'Charlie.' The SCR-284 [radio] was set up but failed to contact either Force A, or the Force headquarters ship, the *Prince Charles*. The radio communications on the Guide craft [ML 163] also failed."[4] The report's mention of an unintelligible radio message at 0715hrs reinforces the idea that Rudder did attempt to inform Schneider, but that the message was not understood. This is entirely plausible, since the nominal range of the SCR-300 was 3 miles and Schneider was on the margins of this range when the message was sent. To add further confusion about this issue, one of the US Army official histories suggests that Schneider did in fact receive

---

* The hand-held SCR-538 is popularly called a "walkie-talkie," as are similar commercial radios. During the war, it was called a "handy-talkie" and the backpack SCR-300 a "walkie-talkie."

the "Tilt" message at 0710hrs, prompting his decision to proceed to Dog Green.[5]

In the face of the communications confusion, Turnbull and Schneider both concluded that the Pointe-du-Hoc mission had not succeeded on time. They thus decided to execute Plan 2 and land Ranger Force C behind the 116th RCT on Dog Green Beach. Although not apparent at the time, the fifteen-minute delay in deciding to execute Plan 2 saved Force C from catastrophe on Dog Green Beach. Due to its size, Force C was delivered to Omaha Beach in three LCA flotillas. Able and Baker Companies, 2nd Ranger Battalion, were carried across the Channel on the LSI *Prince Charles* and delivered to the beach by LCA Flotilla 501. Able and Fox Company, 5th Ranger Battalion, along with most of the 5th Rangers HQ Company, were carried aboard the LSI *Prince Leopold* and taken to the beach by LCA Flotilla 504. The remainder of the 5th Ranger Battalion was carried by LSI *Prince Baudouin* and delivered by LCA Flotilla 507.

The LCA flotillas left their motherships about 10 miles from Omaha Beach at around 0615hrs in a sea "choppy enough to turn the stomach of Sinbad the Sailor."[6] In the lead flotilla, the Royal Navy report noted, "During the run-in, the Rangers became soaked, and at least half in LCA 421 were sea-sick. The remainder, however, were quite cheerful and in good spirits, and were allowed to stand up in the craft until within about 2 miles of the beach."[7] One of the flotilla leaders later stated, "Station-keeping was quite good under the conditions, swell and a following sea making it difficult to control the craft."[8]

The three flotillas arrived at point "Queenie" off Omaha Beach about H+30 (0700hrs), where they remained until 0715hrs, when Schneider and Turnbull decided to proceed to Dog Green Beach instead of Pointe-du-Hoc. The navigation leader, motor launch ML 163, moved in front of the three flotillas to direct them to the beach. LCA Flotilla 501 with the 2nd Rangers aboard was in the vanguard. The two other flotillas carrying the 5th Rangers followed behind at four-minute intervals. About 1,300 yards from shore, the LCA flotilla deployed from column to line-abreast formation.

FLOTILLA 501

The LCAs received little fire until they reached the first line of German beach obstructions. About 200 yards from the outer layer of Belgian Gate obstacles,* LCA Flotilla 501 came under German mortar fire. LCA 401, carrying troops of the 2nd Platoon, Baker Company, was hit by a German mortar at 0740hrs and had its bow blown off. Lt Bob Fitzsimmons was struck by the ramp and presumed killed. The Rangers were thrown into the sea and had to swim ashore from 100 yards out. At least five of the Rangers were killed and several wounded. In spite of the growing intensity of the fire, the Royal Navy coxswains maneuvered their LCAs between the Belgian Gates and other obstacles. Subsequent Ranger accounts noted the considerable skill of the British seamen in avoiding the forest of beach obstructions.

The surviving LCAs of Flotilla 501 beached on Dog White from 0745 to 0752hrs. They landed about a thousand yards east of their intended landing spot near the Vierville draw on Dog Green. This minor error saved many Rangers' lives, since the German fire was far more concentrated in the kill-zone in front of the Vierville draw, where Able Company of the 116th RCT had been slaughtered just half an hour before. Remarkably, the Royal Navy crews did not notice any Ranger casualties as the LCAs beached and withdrew. Nevertheless, the casualties would soon come. A young private in Able Company, 2nd Rangers, recalled the landing:

> Small arms and machine gun bullets began to bounce off our bullet-proofed sides. The shore began to take on new and larger aspects. We could clearly view the beach and surrounding terrain... We seemed to be on top of the beach when a scraping and searing sound cut through the air. Our craft came to an abrupt stop that marked the finish to our ride. Ramps were quickly lowered. Men

---

*A Belgian Gate was a heavy steel fence, about 3 meters wide and 2 meters high, usually mounted on steel rollers, heavily used as an anti-tank beach obstacle along the Atlantic Wall in Normandy. They were also known as Cointet-elements or C-elements.

hastily jumped and dived into the icy, waist-deep water. We were about seventy-five yards from the shore. Bullets ware really flying about now. Cleverly concealed and smartly defended enemy positions gave the Jerry a decided advantage over us… Men were being hit while in the water. It was a struggle to maintain balance in the surf and to dodge the withering hail of enemy fire. We were helpless, like ducks in a shooting gallery. Our Navy and planes hadn't completely neutralized these positions at all… It was up to us, the footsloggers alone now.

On the left, a breached LCI stood smoldering and burning. On all sides of us dead bodies of American GIs were floating around. We had no feeling for them. But now we had a score to settle with those dirty Nazi bastards… Our return fire was inadequate and inaccurate. Our only hope lay in reaching cover on land and storming the enemy in a frontal attack.

Enemy mortar and small arms fire were causing us many deaths and other casualties. We gained shore and found momentary respite behind a pile of rocks that ran parallel to the water's edge, about one hundred yards across the beach. But before we had reached this cover, we had to go through a curtain of lead, and to chance a continual artillery barrage which covered this entire section of open beach. Men were stripping themselves of their packs and excess ammunition. They had become too waterlogged and were too much of a hindrance to carry. Lifebelts were also shed as we dashed to the precarious safety afforded us by the rockpile. Anyone that reached this cover did so by sheer luck rather than skill. Murderous close-range automatic fire was sweeping everything in sight and mowing down soldier after soldier.

We were exhausted and tired on reaching the rockpile. There seemed to be no end to the enemy resistance… We were fighting mad. We dashed into the fray, shooting up anything that looked like the enemy.[9]

Six LCAs remained: two from Able Company on the left, two headquarters LCAs in the center, and two from Baker Company on the right. The landing area was on Dog White Beach, almost directly in front of the WN 70 defense nest. This position was built above the seaside villas of Hamel-au-Prêtre and was separated from the beach by a narrow coastal road and a low seawall. It included at least three light machine guns, three heavy machine guns, and two mortars. Both mortars and three of the machine guns were shielded within Tobruks. The defense nest, one of the less formidable on Omaha Beach, was held by less than a platoon of German troops. The Ranger unit after-action report provides a terse description: "Touchdown at 0745 under heavy MG and mortar fire. Direct MG and artillery fire laid on ramps of LCAs. Beach covered by MG crossfire, mortars and 88s. Many men, dropped in deep water, floated in with the tide until footing could be gained for dash to cover of the seawall."

One of the Baker Company LCAs blew up about 300 yards from shore from either a direct mortar hit or a mine. The coxswain was killed and the platoon leader wounded. Sgt Maj Manning Rubenstein yelled "Abandon ship," and the rest of the men went over the side. At least five of the men were killed in the water by small-arms and machine-gun fire, the rest floating in with the tide. The remaining Baker Company landing craft reached the shore near the most concentrated German defenses and took heavy casualties. The Baker Company commander, Capt Edgar Arnold, had his carbine shot from his hands; the 1st Platoon leader, Lt Robert Brice, was hit in the head and killed.

The rangers later reported, "Debarking in waist-deep water, the men began to fall under small-arms fire and casualties were heavy all the way to the sea-wall. When the two platoons of B Company joined along the wall, there were 2 officers and 25 men present of the [original] 68. Not all of the others were casualties as some of the Rangers who swam in were carried further down the beach."[10]

Able Company landed farther to the east, where a number of M4A1 Duplex Drive amphibious tanks of B Company, 743rd Tank Battalion, had landed. Several of these tanks had been knocked out by an 88mm antitank gun located in the bunker in defense nest WN 72 on the right side of the Vierville draw. With his platoon under German machine-gun fire, Lt Stan White tried to get fire support from the tanks. At the first tank, he banged

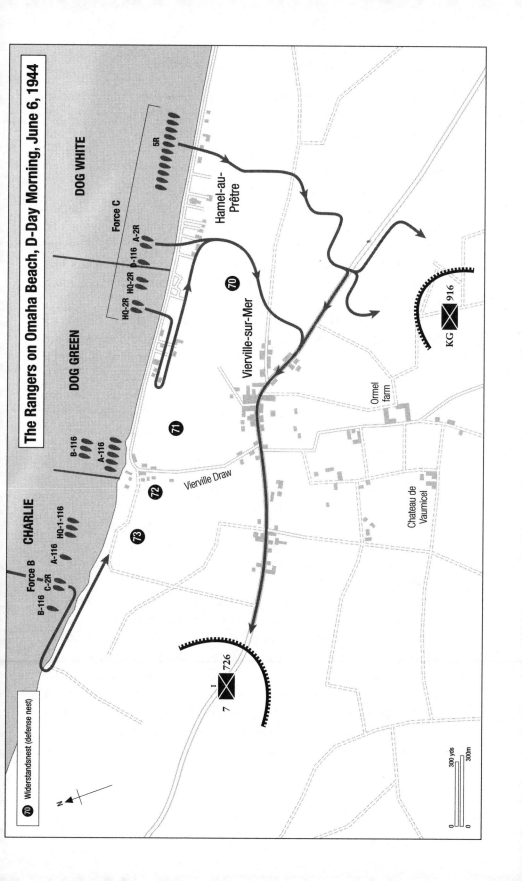

The Rangers on Omaha Beach, D-Day Morning, June 6, 1944

70 Widerstandsnest (defense nest)

DOG WHITE

DOG GREEN

CHARLIE

Force C

5R

A-2R

D-116

HQ-2R

HQ-2R

B-116

A-116

Hamel-au-Prêtre

Vierville-sur-Mer

70

71

72

Vierville Draw

73

Force B

B-116

C-2R

A-116

HQ-1-116

KG 916

Ormel farm

Chateau de Vaumicel

7 726

N

300 yds
300m

on the hull with his pistol, but got no response. At the second tank, the commander opened the hatch and White pointed out the German machine-gun nest. The tank fired, destroying the nest but attracting the attention of the 88mm gun. Lt White was still on its left side when the DD tank was hit and destroyed; White suffered concussive injuries and didn't wake up until in hospital.

The Able Company commander, Capt Joe Rafferty, reached the shore. Upon seeing that some of his men were still in the sea, hiding behind obstacles, he headed back into the water, screaming, "For God's sake men, get off this beach!" He was hit in the legs by machine-gun or rifle fire, fell to his knees, and was killed when then hit in the head.[11]

The other Able Company LCA contained the 1st Platoon, led by Lt Bob Edlin. On the approach, one of the British seamen on the LCA had his head blown off. The LCA then became trapped on a sandbar. Edlin later recalled, "The British coxswain on our LCA was one of the bravest men I ever saw in my life. We hit a sandbar about 75 yards out. I screamed at him to get us in closer. With tears streaming down his face he said 'I can't get off the sandbar but I will go in with you.'"[12] Of the thirty-four Rangers on the craft, only fourteen reached the protection of the rocky shingle on shore. Lt Edlin also returned to the water's edge to encourage his men to get out of the water and to the protection of the shingle. He was wounded in the legs, but was saved when Sgt Bill Klaus, himself wounded, dragged him back to the shingle. With all the company's officers now wounded or dead, leadership of Able Company fell to platoon sergeant Bill White.

Survivors from the 2nd Rangers congregated along the shingle and the seawall that edged the coastal road for protection from German machine-gun fire from the WN 70 defense nest on the bluffs across of the coastal road. With smoke from a burning LCI on the beach offering some modest cover, Sgt White, along with less than a dozen Rangers, began running across the road, taking advantage of the protection provided by the ruined buildings on the other side. Other small groups from Baker Company did likewise. Slowly, they began advancing up the bluffs. This first attempt by the 2nd Rangers to reach the bluffs involved only about fifteen men. After they reached the top of the bluffs, they began to clear out the German defense nest, as recounted in the after-action report:

> Men of Co. A were the first up hill, destroying the MG that killed their CO [commanding officer]. Together with six men of Co. B, these seven started on [their] assigned mission, meeting the 5th Ranger Battalion and attaching themselves to it. Remainder of Force on beach attempted to advance thru beach exit but stopped by enemy fire, ascended hill and contacted 5th Battalion. Companies began re-forming; detail from HQ Company remained on beach to assist in caring for wounded.[13]

Most of the two companies from the 2nd Rangers were badly dispersed and remained pinned down by heavy fire along the seawall. Capt Arnold was with a group of about eighteen men from the 2nd Rangers nearest the Vierville draw. He decided to try to go through the Vierville draw as planned. They crossed the road quickly due to a lack of barbed wire in this sector, and tried to advance to the right along the base of the bluff. As they reached the edge of the villas, Arnold saw three M4 DD tanks of the 743rd Tank Battalion and instructed Sgt Rubenstein to contact one of the tanks to get their support for a further advance into the draw. As Rubenstein climbed back over the seawall on to the road, he was hit in the throat by small-arms fire. Realizing that this sector was too hot for any further advance, Arnold directed the remaining Rangers to retreat back along the same route and rejoin the other Rangers. Arnold thought that Rubenstein had been killed and left him on the beach. However, remarkably, Rubenstein had survived, but lay in shock on the road for nearly an hour. After regaining consciousness, he got up, went over to one of the tanks, and asked for a cigarette. The tanker threw him a pack, and Rubenstein walked calmly back down the road to rejoin Arnold and his men. Arnold and the other 2nd Rangers with him then climbed up the bluff without encountering any German positions.

Another group from the 2nd Rangers under Sgt Fuda took advantage of grass fires caused by the earlier bombardment to advance up the bluffs. The troops from Able Company, 2nd Rangers, were scattered along the seawall in small groups and made their way over the road and to the bluffs. A group under Sgt James was one of the few Ranger teams to receive fire support from the M4 DD tanks of the 743rd Tank Battalion. Signaling to the tanks, the Rangers pointed out German positions on the bluffs. The tanks engaged two of these targets with their 75mm guns and machine guns. James climbed up the bluff on his own, saw the various groups of Rangers there, and went back down to the beach to convince soldiers huddled along the seawall to follow him: "Get the hell off the beach! The hill is ours! They are going to hit the beach with mortars and 88s!" The WN 70 defense nest on top of the bluffs was largely secure by 0830hrs, about half an hour after the landing of Flotilla 501.

The Royal Navy's LCA Flotilla 501 that brought the Rangers to shore lost at least three of its landing craft. One of these was commanded by 19-year-old Sub Lt Hilaire Benbow RNVR. After he and his crew abandoned their damaged LCA, Benbow reached the protection of the seawall, where he realized that there were a number of Royal Navy crew from other damaged craft mixed in with American troops along the shore. During the morning, he collected sixteen Royal Navy seamen and led them to a more sheltered area of the beach.[14] He finally found an American LCT that was about to return to the Transport Area offshore, and convinced the crew to take his wayward sailors onboard. The after-action report of the mothership HMS *Prince Charles* noted that "Benbow's courage and initiative deserve special commendation." He was subsequently awarded the Distinguished Service Order for his actions on D-Day.

5TH RANGER BATTALION AT DOG WHITE

The 5th Ranger Battalion followed the 2nd Ranger companies in two waves, with a four-minute interval between them. The next wave was brought ashore by LCA Flotilla 504, led by Lt J. M. F. Cassidy RNVR in seven LCAs. This flotilla had departed HMS *Prince*

Leopold before dawn, so many of the Rangers were seasick from the slow, gut-wrenching, 12-mile journey through seas with a 5ft swell.

Shortly after the navigation launch HML 163 departed around 0715hrs, the flotilla came under German mortar fire about 1,300 yards from shore. Both Schneider and Cassidy could see the enormous volume of firepower smashing Able Company, 116th RCT, on Dog Green Beach, which was also the planned landing sector for the 5th Rangers.

One of the few radio messages picked up during the trip to the beach was from the Beachmaster on Omaha Beach, indicating that Dog White Beach was empty; G Company of the 116th RCT had landed much farther east. Schneider consulted with Cassidy and they agreed to land farther east, which seemed to be under less German gunfire.[15] Four minutes ahead of them, LCA Flotilla 501 had landed left of the Vierville draw on the boundary with Dog White. Cassidy could see that those LCAs could not clear the beach in time for his flotilla to land. As he recounted in his after-action report, Flotilla 501 was suffering "several hits on their craft, so I decided to land 504 Flotilla to the left [of Flotilla 501], because this part of the beach provided more cover from the fire that was sweeping across... This sector of the beach was also covered with smoke."[16] The smoke mentioned by Cassidy came from grass fires on the bluffs over the beach that had been ignited by the naval bombardment.

The 5th Rangers account describes the scene that greeted Flotilla 504 on the approach to the beach:

The beach was protected by a large number of under-water obstacles consisting of Element C [Belgian Gates], hedgehogs and tetrahedra, many of which had Teller-mines attached. Mortar and artillery shells were bursting in the area of these obstacles and a heavy concentration of small-arms fire swept the beach. A four-foot sea-wall ran laterally along the beach about 75 yards from the water's edge. Friendly troops were observed utilizing the protective cover afforded by this wall. A pall of smoke obscured the sharply rising ground immediately in the rear of and overlooking the beach.

About 30 yards from shore, the formation of seven LCAs separated to allow the individual coxswains to maneuver their craft through the numerous German obstacles. They managed to do so without losing a single craft. The flotilla report indicated that "the Rangers landed without any casualties and only had to wade ashore in water up to their knees."

Flotilla 504 delivered the first wave of the 5th Rangers, consisting of half the battalion headquarters, as well as Able, Baker, and Easy Companies. According to the unit's after-action report, "The first wave crossed the beach in good order with few casualties, halted temporarily in rear of the sea wall, and immediately reorganized."

Following the first wave was Flotilla 507, commanded by Lt E. H. West RNVR. About 5 miles from shore, LCA 578 containing the 1st Platoon and part of the headquarters of Fox Company began to slow down due to water flooding its engine compartment. Although the coxswain suggested returning to the mothership, Capt William Runge ordered him to continue to shore. Within moments, the Rangers onboard were in water that was chest high, and the engines were flooded. The Rangers on this craft later transferred to LCT-88, arriving on Omaha Beach in mid-morning.

The six remaining LCAs headed to Dog White Beach behind Flotilla 504. About half a mile from shore, the formation broke up to allow the individual craft to maneuver around the obstacles. Lt West later recalled that "the officers and coxswains all showed utmost presence of mind and kept a cool head in beaching their craft in these extremely difficult conditions. All the craft found their way to the beach and the Rangers were disembarked at 0805 into between one and two feet of water; and I must say that after a very rough passage and certain amount of sea-sickness, the Rangers went ashore in exceptionally good spirits."[17]

Flotilla 507 encountered less fire than the other Ranger flotillas. This was in part due to the fact that they arrived after two larger LCIs, which attracted most of the German fire. LCI(L) 91 landed about 25 minutes before the arrival of the 5th Rangers, around 0740hrs. While wallowing in the water as the troops disembarked, the LCI struck one of the beach obstructions that was fitted with a Teller mine. The mine damaged the starboard ramp, so the troops disembarked from the port side. Moments before Flotilla 507 reached the beach, the LCI burst into flames: "The remaining troops had disembarked over the port ramp when what appeared to be an '88' struck the center of the well deck and exploded in the fuel tanks below. A blast of flame immediately followed and within seconds the entire well deck was a mass of flames. Water pressure was inadequate to fight the flames. Small caliber enemy fire continued near the beach and intermittent '88' fire near the ship."[18] Moments after the start of this conflagration, three LCAs from Flotilla 507 landed downwind of it on its left side, partially shielded by the billowing plumes of black smoke. The LCAs of this flotilla helped rescue a number of burn casualties from the stricken LCI(L) 91.

By the time that Flotilla 507 began landing, the tide had come in and covered many obstacles. One LCA was lifted by a wave and smashed into one of the obstacles sideways, dislodging the Teller mine off the top. To the relief of the Rangers, it failed to explode and sank beside the craft. The later Ranger accounts noted that, "In general, the Rangers spoke with admiration of the nerve and skill of the coxswains."[19]

The second wave of the 5th Rangers arriving with Flotilla 507 consisted of the other half of battalion headquarters and Charlie, Dog, and Fox Companies, minus the one platoon from Fox Company in the disabled LCA. Unlike the 2nd Rangers at Pointe-du-Hoc and Dog White, the 5th Rangers landed with minimal casualties. This was in no small measure due to the delay in landing, combined with Schneider's and Cassidy's prudent decision to land on Dog White and Dog Red, where the German defenses were much less substantial than in the Vierville draw to the west. Another advantage was that this area of the beach had wooden breakwaters extending off the seawall that offered some measure of cover for the troops.

On the beach, the 5th Rangers from Flotilla 507 encountered numerous troops of Charlie Company, 116th RCT. This company was supposed to have landed directly into the kill-zone of the Vierville draw on Dog Green. Fortuitously, it had landed to the left on Dog White, saving many lives. In stark contrast to the experience of the 2nd Rangers in Forces B and C, there were only four or five casualties among the 5th Rangers during the landing. It is worth noting that Charlie Company, 116th Infantry, which landed in this sector, also suffered very light casualties.

One platoon from Fox Company landed much farther east than the rest of the battalion, near the St Laurent draw. This was the center of another major German strongpoint, Stützpunkt St Laurent, with a significant concentration of bunkers and crew-served weapons. The isolated platoon attempted to join the rest of the battalion by moving east about 600 yards, but it was eventually forced to ground by artillery and small-arms fire. The platoon remained pinned down in this sector through to the end of the day. As we shall see they eventually ended up on Pointe-du-Hoc by a circuitous route.[20]

RANGERS LEAD THE WAY!

The 5th Ranger Battalion huddled behind the seawall on Dog White Beach for several minutes as the platoon and squad leaders put their men in some order. Striding down the beach in their direction was a stocky old officer smoking a cigar. The first Ranger he encountered was Sgt Richard Hathaway of the 1st Platoon, Able Company, who was preparing a bangalore torpedo to breach the concertina wire blocking access over the road. The officer, standing on the road overhead, yelled to him, "What outfit is this?" Preoccupied with his dangerous explosive charge, Hathaway responded, "We're the Rangers." The officer replied, "Let's get off this beach!" To which Hathaway shouted, "As soon as we blow this fucking wire!" Hathaway looked over his shoulder to discover the officer wore a single star – a brigadier general.

The general was Norman Cota, the assistant divisional commander of the 29th Division. Cota had landed on the beach around 0745hrs as part of the follow-on wave of the 29th Division. He had been exhorting the men of Charlie Company, 116th RCT, to move off the beach before he encountered the Rangers. On his first meeting with the Rangers, he shouted to them, "We're getting murdered down here. Let's get murdered up there," pointing to the bluffs above.[21] Cota subsequently encountered Capt John Raaen and asked him where the Rangers' headquarters was located. Raaen offered to escort him to Schneider, but Cota continued eastward along the beach on his own after exhorting the men, "You men are Rangers! I know you won't let me down!"[22]

Capt Luther of Easy Company was preparing to move his unit when an unidentified officer – Cota again – appeared at a distance and began telling the men to move across the road. Not seeing his rank insignia, Luther put up a warning hand and yelled, "Hey bud! Take it easy – don't get excited. This is my outfit – I'll take care of it!" Cota told him, "Well, you've got to get over that wall!" To which Luther replied, "Quit bothering my men. You'll disorganize them. The colonel's over there if you want to see him. But stop bothering me!"

Walking farther to the east, Cota found the headquarters of the 5th Rangers. Schneider and his staff were lying in the sand behind the seawall as Cota approached. Schneider, seeing Cota, walked over to him. Cota, convinced that much of the artillery falling on the 116th RCT was coming from German gun positions on the Pointe-et-Raz-de-la-Percée, ordered Schneider to take his men over the bluff, pass through Vierville, and knock out the guns overlooking Omaha Beach.[23] He concluded the conversation with the legendary words that would echo through Ranger history, "Colonel, we are counting on the Rangers to lead the way!" "Rangers Lead the Way" has subsequently been the Ranger motto to this day.

Schneider returned to his staff, and Sgt Herb Epstein, the intelligence NCO for the headquarters, asked him why in the world he was crazy enough to be standing up with all the German small-arms fire in the vicinity. Schneider replied, "Well, he was standing and I wasn't going to be laying down there!"

Schneider issued his final instructions to his company commanders. The approaches to the bluffs were lined with concertina wire that would have to be blown with bangalore torpedoes for passage. With the breaching teams in place, and the bangalore torpedoes detonating, Schneider gave the signal to begin the assault up the bluffs with the cry "Tally Ho!" This was the codeword for the Rangers to advance to the rendezvous point near Vierville. The plan was for the Ranger squads and platoons to advance on their own initiative, and not to consolidate or regroup before moving south. Four gaps were blown with bangalore torpedoes, three using a single charge and one a double charge. The battalion after-action report summarized the attack:

> At a signal from the Battalion Commander, the leading echelon scrambled over the wall, blew gaps in the protective wire, and protected from enemy observation by the curtain of rising smoke advanced unhesitatingly to a point near the top of the hill. Here the smoke had cleared and the topographical crest was being swept by effective automatic weapons fire. First Lieutenant Francis W. Dawson, Company D, led his platoon over the top and wiped out a strongpoint thereby enabling the battalion to advance.[24]

The bluffs were quite steep and slowed down the Rangers. In spite of their extensive physical training, the pace had been reduced to a slow crawl near the top of the bluff. The slope was covered with acrid smoke from the grass fires; while the smoke shielded the Rangers, it was thick enough that the advance up the bluff became very disorganized. In one case, a lieutenant began the ascent with his entire platoon, but he reached the crest with only two men. Capt George "Whit" Whittington, leading Baker Company, 5th Rangers, was one of the first Rangers to the top of the bluff. Along with Pfc Carl Weist, he maneuvered behind a German machine-gun nest, attacking from behind, and killed its three-man crew. A later report estimated that the 5th Rangers lost only eight men in the advance from the seawall to the top of the bluffs. Most of the 5th Rangers were on top of the bluffs by 0830hrs, about half an hour since landing.

Although Schneider's "Tally-Ho" at the beginning of the ascent had been the signal for the squads and platoons to advance on their own without reorganization, the disruption caused by the smoke led him to reconsider. Instead, Schneider sent runners out to the various platoons and companies and told them to try to get their units in order before proceeding.

The survivors from the decimated Able and Baker Companies of the 2nd Rangers joined the 5th Rangers on the crest, and Schneider consolidated them into a provisional company under their sole officer, Capt Arnold. Parts of this group, mainly from Able Company, 2nd Rangers, became engaged with surviving German machine-gun nests in WN 71, located to their right on the eastern edge of the Vierville draw. Small groups of Rangers made their way into the German trench system and gradually cleared it out, killing several Germans and capturing six prisoners.

At the same time that the 5th Rangers conducted their advance up the bluffs, elements of Charlie Company, 116th Infantry, also crossed the road and climbed the bluffs. This attack finished clearing the German defenses between WN 70 in Hamel-au-Prêtre and the WN 71 defense nest on the top of the bluff overlooking the eastern side of the Vierville draw. The 5th Rangers continued on their mission toward the town of Vierville-sur-Mer, while Charlie Company, 116th Infantry, began the process of clearing out the Vierville draw from behind.

While advancing along the top of the bluffs, the Rangers began to encounter scattered minefields. Rather than advance on a broad front, Schneider decided to switch to a column. Whittington's Baker Company had reached the top in good order, so Schneider ordered Whittington to take the lead. Lt Bernard Pepper's 1st Platoon took point at the head of the column. There were numerous encounters with small groups of German troops during the advance, though this sector was devoid of major German strongpoints. As mentioned previously, one platoon from Able Company, led by "Ace" Parker, had already become separated from the main body of the 5th Rangers and made their way to Pointe-du-Hoc on their own.[25]

Baker Company eventually reached the Vierville–Grandcamp road about a thousand yards east of Vierville-sur-Mer, where they began to encounter significantly more German small-arms fire from the village. By this time, the Germans, realizing that the American forces had penetrated their forward line of defense in this sector, had begun to bring artillery to bear on the Ranger column. The artillery fell most heavily on the platoons from Fox and George Companies at the rear of the column, causing a number of casualties.

Easy Company attempted to push south off the road, but almost immediately ran into entrenched German troops. Charlie Company attacked these defenses using an 81mm mortar, but the Germans kept reinforcing their line. Schneider attempted to get artillery support to clear out the German defenses, but an accompanying forward observer indicated that the Rangers were too close to the German positions for a fire mission to be safely conducted.

By the late morning, German reinforcements had begun to arrive. The beach defenses in this sector of Omaha Beach were manned primarily by 10.Kompanie, Grenadier-Regiment.726, with elements of Hauptmann Grimme's 2.Bataillon, Grenadier-Regiment.916, in reserve positions.[26] Two of the battalion's four companies had already been deployed into the defenses of Omaha Beach, with Lt Hahn's 5.Kompanie in reserve in Surrain, Lt Heller's 6.Kompanie in neighboring Trévières, and Lt Berthy's 7.Kompanie at Asnières-en-Bessin.

The 7.Kompanie was nearest to Vierville, and at 1100hrs, Berthy was ordered to counterattack the American forces besieging Stützpunkt St Laurent and retake defense nest WN 68 which had reportedly been captured. The 7.Kompanie consisted of three rifle platoons and an 81mm mortar squad; it had a strength of 160 men, twelve MG 42 machine guns, two 81mm mortars, and six of the new "Panzerschreck" anti-tank rocket launchers. Eighteen of the men in the company were former Soviet soldiers, mostly from Turkmenistan; the rest were Germans. The advance from Asnières to St Laurent took the company directly into the path of the advancing Rangers. It seems likely that Berthy's company was the primary opponent of the Rangers on D-Day, along with scattered elements of 10./GR.726.[27]

Schneider's intention upon reaching the edge of Vierville was to skirt around the town to the south to avoid becoming entangled with snipers in the village. However, the lead companies ran into stiff resistance immediately south of Vierville, probably Berthy's 7.Kompanie. Lt Pepper's lead squad was midway across a wheat field when it came under small-arms fire. Using fire and movement, Pepper reached the edge of the hedgerow ahead and worked his way behind the German positions, shooting them up before the Germans could react.

Due to the increasing mortar fire, Whittington ordered Baker Company back to the Vierville–Grandcamp road and they began heading westward through Vierville rather than around it. There was scattered small-arms fire outside the village, but the Rangers did not encounter the level of opposition they faced in the farm fields to the south. Vierville-sur-Mer was entered around noon by Baker Company, and the remainder of the 5th Rangers arrived around 1400hrs. The easy passage through Vierville was probably due to the fact that elements of Charlie Company, 116th Infantry, had passed through the village, some squads as early as 1000hrs.[28]

To the west of the village, Whittington, Pepper, and 1st Sgt Avery Thornhill took cover behind a hedgerow after receiving sniper fire. An officer approached them and yelled, "Get up and start moving! We'll never win this war on our tails!" It was the indefatigable Gen Cota, who had reached Vierville with the 116th Infantry. After Whittington explained that they were trying to clear the snipers, Cota growled, "There's no snipers!" Moments later, a round hit the ground near Cota, who sheepishly admitted, "Well, there may be one!"[29]

In all likelihood, the forces facing them were Berthy's 7.Kompanie, along with some troops of 3./GR.914 that had been shifted into the Vierville area in the days before the landings. Once the village was cleared and secured, Schneider decided to push three companies westward to reach Pointe-du-Hoc. Whittington's Baker Company remained in the lead. The advance ground to a halt about 500 yards west of Vierville near the hamlet of Gruchy around 1700hrs after encountering heavy small-arms fire.

Shortly after Baker Company passed through Vierville, the commander of the shattered 116th Infantry, Col Charles Canham, arrived in Vierville. At this point, Canham had only about 150 men immediately on hand near Vierville after his regiment's horrific casualties that day. With so few of his own men available, Canham instructed Schneider to abandon his mission of marching to Pointe-du-Hoc and instead to set up a perimeter defense of Vierville. The Rangers were not at all happy about this order, but Force C was directly subordinated to the 116th RCT, so they had no choice. The 29th Division commander, Maj Gen Charles Gerhardt, later confirmed Canham's orders.

The Rangers set up their defenses, with the remnants of the three companies of the 2nd Ranger Battalion to the west on the outskirts of Gruchy. As mentioned earlier, Capt Goranson's battered Force B joined them before nightfall.[30] Of the 192 men of the 2nd Rangers who had landed on Omaha Beach on D-Day, there were only about eighty men still bearing arms at nightfall. Schneider's 5th Rangers had suffered far fewer casualties.

Aside from small outbursts of fighting, there was no concerted German counterattack near Vierville on D-Day night. According to the communication logs of the 352.Infanterie-Division, Gen Kraiss viewed the threat as far greater in three other sectors: St Laurent, Colleville, and Asnelles. This was due in part to reports from a forward observer in WN 74 on the Pointe-et-Raz-de-la-Percée that overlooked Dog Green. This officer was a friend of Oberstleutnant Fritz Ziegelmann, the divisional operations officer.[31] The forward observer reported that the landings in the Vierville draw had apparently been stopped, based on his observation of two burning LCIs, damaged LCTs, and a number of burning tanks. The divisional reserves – Grenadier-Regiment.915, Fusilier-Bataillon.352, and Schnelle-Brigade.30 – had all been sent to the division's eastern sectors. Even Berthy's 7.Kompanie, giving Schneider so much trouble near Gruchy, had in fact been directed to St Laurent. Furthermore, the meager resources available in the division's western sector, mainly I./GR.914, were ordered to smash the Ranger intrusion at Pointe-du-Hoc.

Although Force C did not reach its intended objective of Pointe-du-Hoc on D-Day, it was instrumental in redeeming the landings in the Vierville sector. The excellent training and unit cohesion of the Rangers enabled them to quickly surmount the bluffs and shield the Vierville area from German counterattacks, such as those by Berthy's company. In view of the battered shape of the 116th Infantry after the massacre on the Vierville beach, Force C provided an essential reserve to defend the shaky American hold on the western side of Omaha Beach.

Chapter 16

The Crazy March on D+1

The intention of the Rangers to reach Rudder's trapped forces at Pointe-du-Hoc on D+1, June 7, was largely frustrated due to counterattacks by the German 352.Infanterie Division around Vierville. A brief summary of the 352.Infanterie-Division on June 6–7 is necessary to help understand the German reaction to the Omaha Beach landings.

The 352.Infanterie-Division had three infantry regiments: GR.914, GR.915, and GR.916. It also had two battalions from GR.726 of the static 716.Infanterie-Division and attached Ost (Eastern) battalions.

In the early morning hours of D-Day, after the first reports of Allied paratroop drops, GR.915 and the division's Füsilier-Bataillon.352 were combined to form Kampfgruppe Meyer.[1] This was named after the regiment's commander, Oberst Karl Meyer, and was headquartered in St Saveur-Lendelin, well to the southwest of Omaha Beach. Before dawn on D-Day, KG Meyer was ordered by LXXXIV.Armee-Korps to counterattack the paratroop landings near the mouth of the river Vire. As a result, it began a wild goose chase for much of D-Day morning. After dawn, when the amphibious landings took place, control of KG Meyer reverted back to the 352.Infanterie-Division.

From the perspective of the divisional headquarters, the main threat was on the division's right flank in the St Laurent–Colleville–Asnelles area of Omaha Beach and Gold Beach. KG Meyer was sent to deal with the threat emanating from Gold Beach around Asnelles, and suffered heavy casualties in the process; Meyer himself was killed during these battles.

Of the 352.Infanterie-Division's other two regiments, GR.914 was concentrated on the division's left flank near the mouth of the Vire. German pre-invasion planning placed far more emphasis on this sector than on Omaha Beach. There were two reasons for this. One of the main German concerns was that the Allies might try to seize the port of Cherbourg by landing at the base of the Cotentin peninsula, cutting it off and capturing Cherbourg from the landward side. This was in fact one of the operational goals of Operation *Overlord*. However, the Germans were also concerned that the Vire estuary would make an attractive objective because of its small ports such as Grandcamp, as well as its access to the Normandy river network via the Vire. Consequently, German defenses in this sector were particularly strong, including the left wing of the 352.Infanterie-Division, the 709.Infanterie-Division (bo.) on the western side of the Vire, and the 91.Luftlande-Division in reserve behind the 709.Infanterie-Division. On D-Day, GR.914 was heavily involved in chasing down paratroopers as it was the element of the division closest to the landing sites. Aside from the anti-paratrooper patrols, it did not see very much combat on D-Day. One of its battalions was committed late on D-Day to smash the Ranger defenses at Pointe-du-Hoc.[2]

The division's third regiment, GR.916, was stretched from Omaha Beach to Port-en-Bessin. As a result, it was heavily committed to the fighting on D-Day. Since all three of the division's infantry regiments were committed to the D-Day fighting, reserves were lacking. Late on D-Day, Gen Kraiss committed two of his meager reserves to the Omaha Beach sector. These were the division's engineer battalion, Pioner-Bataillon.352, and the Landes-Bau-Bataillon.17, a construction battalion involved in fortification work on the Normandy coast. Pioner-Bataillon.352 was assigned to recapture the defenses in the St Laurent draw.

The LXXXIV.Armee-Korps offered its remaining reserve, Schnelle-Brigade.30, to Kraiss in the hopes of stemming the American breakout. Schnelle-Brigade.30 had spent much of the early hours of D-Day chasing down reports of Allied paratroopers. The brigade, which was bicycle-mobile and lightly equipped, did not arrive in the 352.Infanterie-Division sector until nightfall on D+1, June 7.

Early on the morning of June 7, Kraiss attempted to bottle up the western side of the Omaha Beach breakout by sending a Kampfgruppe of GR.916 against Vierville, while Pionier-Bataillon.352 was again assigned to attack down the St Laurent draw. These attacks were slow to materialize due to the heavy casualties suffered by GR.916 on D-Day and the lack of reinforcements.

As a result of these actions, a meeting engagement brewed up between the Rangers heading out of Vierville to Pointe-du-Hoc, and a Kampfgruppe of GR.916 heading to retake Vierville.

ADVANCE TO THE POINTE

Around 0600hrs on D+1, the senior American commanders in Vierville held a meeting to discuss the day's upcoming operations. Those attending included Col Canham, the 116th RCT commander, Lt Col John A. Metcalfe, commander of the 1/116th Infantry, and Col Max Schneider, the Ranger Force commander.

Since the sector to the west of Vierville had been quiet for most of the night of June 6/7, Canham agreed to make the 4-mile advance to Pointe-du-Hoc. Task Force Metcalfe would consist of the three companies of the 2nd Rangers, the 5th Rangers, the 1/116th Infantry, and eight M4 Sherman tanks of the 743rd Tank Battalion. The three companies of the 2nd Rangers were less than half-strength, with barely eighty men. The 1/116th Infantry was likewise in rocky shape after their D-Day losses, and the relief column consisted mostly of Charlie Company under Capt Bert Hawks, totaling about 130 men. The 5th Rangers were closer to strength, minus Parker's platoon and a platoon from Fox Company, and so more than 400 men. The column advanced out of Vierville between 0730 and 0800hrs.

In the meantime, an initial probe by the GR.916 Kampfgruppe struck Baker Company, 121st Engineers, in the "Chateau" (Ormel farm) early in the morning, starting at 0530hrs. The isolated engineer company held off the German attack for the time being.[3] The main Kampfgruppe then proceeded to Vierville, with their attack starting around 0900hrs after much of Task Force Metcalfe had departed westward. Under these circumstances, Canham instructed the four companies of the 5th Rangers (A, B, E, and F) at the rear of the Metcalfe column to remain in Vierville to defend the village. This reduced the size of Task Force Metcalfe to about 400 men.

Around 1000hrs, the GR.916 Kampfgruppe reported that its attack on Vierville "was making progress. It had been possible to push the enemy to the extreme northern end of Vierville."[4] This success was short-lived, however, due to the casualties inflicted on the German infantry by the defending American forces. Around 1030hrs, the German pressure on Vierville had been reduced to the point that the Rangers there were able to send a relief force, along with a few tanks from the 743rd Tank Battalion, to the besieged Baker Company, 121st Engineers, at the Ormel farm. After the morning attacks were halted, the GR.916 Kampfgruppe attempted another attack in company strength around 1400hrs. This assault was stopped by Easy Company, 5th Rangers.[5]

In spite of this threat to their rear, Task Force Metcalfe moved rapidly forward throughout the morning of June 7. German resistance consisted mainly of isolated patrols. Upon encountering any determined opposition, the tanks were brought up to clear the way. The Germans in the vicinity later dubbed it the "crazy march," since the column didn't bother to clear out German positions on the northern side of the road along the cliffs. Behind Task Force Metcalfe, elements of the 834th Engineer Aviation Battalion were moving into the area between the Vierville–Grandcamp road and the coast in order to establish an emergency landing strip east of St Pierre-du-Mont. The engineers cleared out many of the remaining German defenses from WN 73 westward. The first phase of construction of

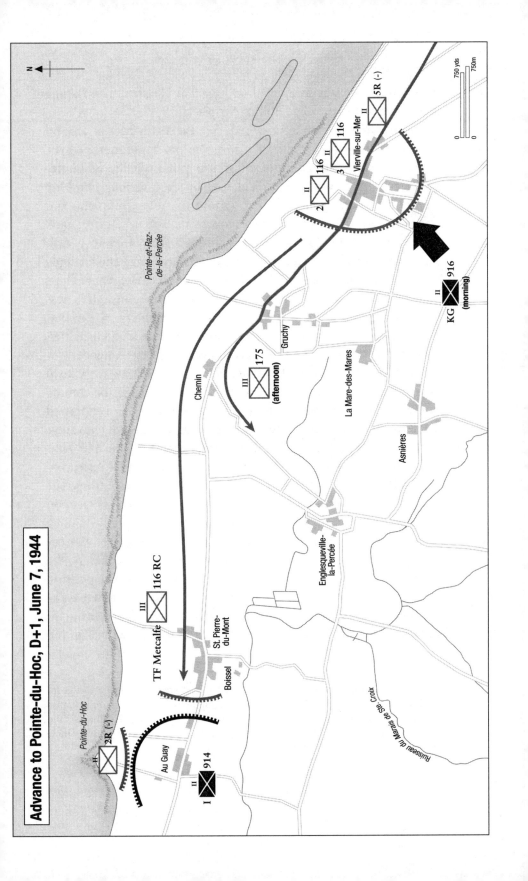

Advance to Pointe-du-Hoc, D+1, June 7, 1944

the landing strip was completed on June 8 at 1800hrs, with the site designated as Emergency Landing Strip 1 (ELS A-1).*

Task Force Metcalfe reached St Pierre-du-Mont around 1100hrs, a few thousand yards from the outer perimeter of the Pointe-du-Hoc strongpoint. About 200 yards outside St Pierre-du-Mont, the area was badly cratered by the previous bombing attacks and naval gunfire. Capt Arnold of Able Company, 2nd Rangers, sent a runner back to request that an M4 dozer tank move forward to help make a path through the craters to permit the other tanks to proceed. The first resistance was encountered from a German position in the hamlet of Au Guay, where there was a German squad with emplaced machine guns. This was followed by the first concentrated German artillery of the day, when the 1/116th Infantry suffered some thirty to forty casualties, a substantial proportion of the 130 men in the detachment.[6]

The accompanying SFCP-3 (Shore Fire Control Party-3) spoke to local French civilians who suggested that the fire might be coming from the Maisy batteries or Criqueville-en-Bessin. SFCP-3 contacted the destroyer USS *McCook* and asked that USS *Texas* deal with these batteries using its spotter aircraft to verify their location. The *Texas* at the time was farther east off Omaha Beach, and so instructed HMS *Glasgow* to engage the Maisy batteries using air spotting. The *Glasgow* fired for about half an hour, starting at 1300hrs, whereupon the artillery fire on the Rangers ceased for the time being.[7]

The column's point patrol, numbering seven Rangers, was cut off from the remainder of the column by the artillery strikes. At the outskirts of Au Guay, they ran into a prepared German position with four machine guns. T-5 Ray of Alpha Company, known as the "Standing BAR man" due to his practice of advancing and firing his automatic rifle from the hip, "performed a notable action" in the

---

*The initial emergency landing strip had a 3,400ft x 120ft grass/dirt runway suitable for small Grasshopper observation aircraft. Continued improvements led to it being upgraded to a Refuelling and Rearming Strip (RRS A-1) and then to an Advanced Landing Ground (ALG A-1), able to handle aircraft up to the size of the C-47 transport. A P-38 Lightning squadron began using the airfield on June 11.

subsequent encounter, helping to knock out one of the machine-gun positions.[8] The patrol took twelve prisoners, but the scale of the German opposition forced them to withdraw to St Pierre-du-Mont.

There was still a great deal of confusion at this time about the status of Rudder and the Rangers at Pointe-du-Hoc.[9] While operating forward of St Pierre-du-Mont, Task Force Metcalfe looked for some signal from Rudder and his men, but saw no evidence of any activity. Believing that the Rangers at Pointe-du-Hoc had been withdrawn or overrun, the column requested naval gunfire on Pointe-du-Hoc before proceeding. At this point, the Navy declined to do so, noting that Rudder and the Rangers were still occupying Pointe-du-Hoc and were in contact with warships offshore. This was the first evidence that the 5th Rangers had obtained about the fate of Rudder's Rangers.

THE "CRAZY MARCH" STALLS

A planned final push by Task Force Metcalfe to Pointe-du-Hoc in the afternoon of D+1 fizzled out owing to the chaos and confusion on Omaha Beach. The German attack against Vierville had been stopped for the moment, but there were some signs that the Germans were preparing a counterattack against the relief column. The German attacks on the morning and early afternoon of D+1 had been strong enough that Col Canham of the 116th RCT wanted the tanks back into the village by evening to reinforce the regiment's defenses. As a result, the eight tanks withdrew from St Pierre-du-Mont and headed back to Vierville.

Grenadier-Regiment.916 attempted another assault into Vierville in the late evening. By day's end, "the reinforced Grenadier-Regiment.916 had suffered considerable losses and was severely weakened physically and morally. Counterattacks could not continue on 8 June," according to a German divisional account.[10] By the end of D+1, Grenadier-Regiment.916 was a spent force and was forced to retreat from the Vierville sector.

Amidst this continuing fighting around Vierville, an officer from the 29th Division met the Rangers in St Pierre-du-Mont during the afternoon of D+1, claiming that Vierville had been retaken by the Germans and that enemy armor was coming up the road from the village against the rear of the 5th Rangers. This was completely false, and the origins of his report are unclear. Unfortunately, Task Force Metcalfe believed his report to be entirely credible, which only reinforced the decision to halt the move to Pointe-du-Hoc in favor of setting up a defensive perimeter at St Pierre-du-Mont. Lacking reliable radio communications with the 116th RCT headquarters in Vierville, Captains Raaen and Wise flipped a coin to see who would walk back to Vierville to discover what was really happening. Raaen lost the toss and began walking back to the village.

On his way to Vierville, Raaen encountered an officer of the 116th Infantry nonchalantly riding a bicycle toward St Pierre-du-Mont. He seemed unnaturally calm if indeed German tanks were heading up the road from Vierville. The officer assured Raaen that the 175th Infantry Regiment, the third regiment of the 29th Division assigned to Omaha Beach, had successfully landed earlier in the day and was already passing through Vierville with tank support. He expected that the regiment might arrive at the forward Ranger positions within a few hours. Raaen later remarked that this was the first firm evidence the Rangers received that the invasion was succeeding. Nevertheless, the column of the 175th Infantry did not reach St Pierre-du-Mont since it had been instructed to turn off the Vierville–Grandcamp road to head south toward the main Bayeux–Isigny highway. As a result, the Rangers received no further support from the 29th Division that day.

During the evening, ammunition and rations were brought up to St Pierre-du-Mont by the two surviving M3 75mm GMC half-tracks of the Rangers' Mounted Cannon Company. This unit had landed on Omaha Beach from two LCTs near the Les Moulins draw, where two of the half-tracks of Lt Frank Kennard's platoon were lost;[11] the other two of Lt Conway Epperson's platoon were trapped on the beach for most of D-Day until the draws could be opened, and finally joined the rest of Ranger Force C on D+1. This gave the Rangers a bit of firepower, but the half-tracks were also extremely useful in hauling vital supplies from Omaha Beach up to the forward positions.

Task Force Metcalfe set up defensive positions in two fields near St Pierre-du-Mont. Around 2000hrs, German artillery fire resumed. SFCP-3 again contacted USS *McCook*, which began engaging the suspected artillery battery at Criqueville, and there was further gunfire from HMS *Glasgow*. This put a temporary end to the German artillery harassment.

Chapter 17

Relief from the Sea

By dawn of D+1, Rudder's Force A at Pointe-du-Hoc had been reduced to about ninety men able to bear arms. There were some fifty seriously wounded Rangers, plus many walking wounded.

Communications with the outside world were still very erratic. Early in the morning, SFCP-1 managed to contact the neighboring VII Corps on Utah Beach about their plight. At 0724hrs, this message was forwarded to Rear Admiral John L. Hall, USN, leader of Omaha Beach's Task Force 124 aboard the command ship USS *Ancon*. Not receiving any response, half an hour later the Rangers contacted the destroyer USS *Harding*, again requesting an urgent supply of small-arms ammunition, supplies, and the evacuation of the wounded.

At 0845hrs, for a second time, USS *Ancon* ordered LCI(L) 86 to send two LCVPs to Pointe-du-Hoc to evacuate the wounded and prisoners. Once again, this failed to occur, for unknown reasons, though likely due to the sheer volume of activity in transferring troops ashore that morning. On the morning of June 7, Bradley's First US Army headquarters, now on Omaha Beach, sent another request to Gerow's V Corps headquarters for relief supplies to Pointe-du-Hoc. Gerow's staff ashore contacted other Army staff officers on the *Ancon* to deal with the issue. In response to Gerow's request, at 1125hrs, Rear Adm Hall's staff answered to V Corps that they would transfer reinforcements to Pointe-du-Hoc via LCTs and LCVPs; at 1202hrs, Hall ordered the *Ancon* to send two craft to Pointe-du-Hoc, apparently bypassing the LCI(L) 86 option. The plan was to stage the operation from the battleship USS *Texas*.[1]

Army officers on the *Ancon* had become aware that the 1st Platoon, Fox Company, 5th Rangers, had been separated from the rest of the battalion to the east near the Les Moulins draw on D-Day. This platoon, which was the most obvious source for reinforcements, was contacted by Maj Jack Street on Hall's staff to prepare to be transferred to Pointe-du-Hoc via LCVP in the afternoon.

At 1405hrs, two LCVPs under the command of Lt (jg) R. C. Hill departed USS *Ancon* with food, water, and .30cal ammunition to the beach at Pointe-du-Hoc. The two LCVPs also evacuated fifty-two wounded Rangers, a dead Coastguard man, and twenty-seven prisoners of war to the *Texas* and a neighboring LST.* Thirty-five of the most badly wounded remained on the *Texas* for medical treatment. Maj Jack Street then directed another LCVP to Omaha Beach to transfer 1st Platoon, Fox Company, 5th Rangers, to Pointe-du-Hoc. These two dozen Ranger reinforcements arrived around 1700hrs.

About the same time, Rudder's Force A finally made radio contact with Task Force Metcalfe in St Pierre-du-Mont with the message, "Try and fight thru to us." However, Col Canham, the 116th RCT commander, had ordered the relief force to sit tight for the night.[2]

After dark, Capt John Raaen of the 5th Rangers HQ company assigned a two-man patrol of Sgt Moody and T-5 McKissock to infiltrate about 3 miles across the fields between St Pierre-du-Mont and Pointe-du-Hoc and contact Rudder. They encountered no German troops, but ended up too far west along the cliffs. After doubling back, they entered the Ranger lines and were taken to see Col Rudder. After they explained the situation, Rudder indicated that the Rangers could hold out until Thursday, D+2. The pair returned to St Pierre-du-Mont and dragged a reel of field telephone line back with them, establishing a secure telephone contact between

---

* The twenty-seven PoWs comprised twenty Germans, four Italians, and three French workers. They were shipped off to Britain aboard LCT 266.

Rudder and the relief force. They were accompanied by seven men from the 1st Platoon, Fox Company, 5th Rangers, who had arrived at Pointe-du-Hoc by LCVP in the late afternoon of D+1. These Rangers were assigned to serve as guides the following morning for the relief force. The nine Rangers reached St Pierre-du-Mont around 0800hrs. Moody and McKissock were subsequently awarded the Distinguished Service Cross for their actions that night.

D+2: RUDDER'S RANGERS RELIEVED

After the confusion of D+1, the situation on the morning of D+2 was more straightforward. The German attacks on Vierville had been stopped and American reinforcements continued to pour into the Vierville area. With the arrival of the 29th Division's third regiment, the 175th Infantry, the overall plan was to push west to reach the objectives originally earmarked for D-Day. This entailed the 116th RCT advancing along the Vierville–Grandcamp road past Pointe-du-Hoc, clearing the German defenses in Grandcamp and Maisy, and pushing down to Isigny. In the meantime, the 175th RCT would advance on a parallel course towards Isigny via the Bayeux–Isigny highway, a mission originally assigned to the 115th RCT in the *Neptune* plans. However, the counterattacks by the German 352.Infanterie-Division convinced the 29th Division to use the 115th Infantry to create a defense line south of Vierville to shield the push westward.

The final advance to reach the Rangers at Pointe-du-Hoc was the first step of this larger scheme. From the broader perspective, this was the first critical stage in linking up Omaha Beach with Utah Beach to the west. The remaining elements of Schneider's Force C in Vierville, consisting of three companies of the 5th Rangers, began marching to St Pierre-du-Mont at 0630hrs, accompanied by an additional two battalions of the 116th RCT and sixteen tanks of the 743rd Tank Battalion.* This force reached

---

* This included six DD tanks of Able Company and ten conventional M4/M4A1 medium tanks of Charlie Company.

St Pierre-du-Mont around 0815hrs, having encountered very little German resistance. By this stage, most of the German defenses along the coast between Vierville and Pointe-du-Hoc had been flushed out by the engineers creating the temporary airstrip east of St Pierre-du-Mont. The 352.Infanterie-Division had ordered a general retreat to new defense lines after the defeat of their final attack on Vierville the evening before.

The movement of the relief force from St Pierre-du-Mont to Pointe-du-Hoc began around 0900hrs against no appreciable opposition. Col Metcalfe of the 1/116th Infantry and several Ranger officers reached Rudder's command post around 1000hrs. Although the relief had been accomplished without any problems, a subsidiary action created chaos. The German positions around the western Flak bunker were still actively firing on Pointe-du-Hoc, so the 3/116th Infantry decided to settle the issue by attacking it from the south with the support of five tanks from the 743rd Tank Battalion.

This assault was based on hasty planning and faulty geographic information. As a result, the attack force bumped into the 2nd Rangers' defense lines on the western side of Pointe-du-Hoc rather than the German positions. The confusion was aggravated since some of the Rangers were using German weapons due to a shortage of American ammunition. The distinctive sound of these weapons convinced the 3/116th Infantry that they were facing German troops. The German MG 34 and MG 42 light machine guns had a very distinctive sound due to their very high rate of fire.* Instead of the staccato sound of most American machine guns, the German guns made a ripping sound more like a chainsaw, earning the MG 42 the nickname "Hitler's buzz saw."

Due to the confusion, sporadic small-arms and mortar fire broke out. Lt Eikner, with Rudder near the Ranger headquarters,

---

* The rate of fire of the MG 42 – introduced into the Wehrmacht in 1942 – was around 1,200 rounds per minute, more than double the 500rpm of the US Army's .30cal M1919 Browning medium machine gun. Even the older German MG 34 had a rate of fire of about 900rpm.

was monitoring the tanks' radio traffic. He told them to cease fire and that he would set off colored smoke grenades to identify the location of the Ranger headquarters. While some of the tanks did indeed halt their fire, the ignition of the smoke grenade near the eastern Flak bunker prompted other tanks to open up. Several Rangers attempted to move their large American flag to a position visible to the tanks, but some of them were knocked off their feet when tank rounds detonated nearby.

Three of the tanks ran over German mines at the edge of the strongpoint, after which the tank fire subsided. Fox Company of the 2nd Rangers sent out a patrol to convince the 116th Infantry and the tanks to stop firing. One lieutenant from the 2nd Rangers "ran out of the cover, jumped on one of the tanks, beat on the turret until he got the attention of the crew, put his pistol to the head of the tank commander who opened the turret, and with that, the attack by the 743rd stopped in its tracks. The 5th Ranger casualties from that attack were two killed and four wounded."[3] It took some thirty to forty minutes to finally get everyone to stop shooting.

Lt Joseph Ondre, a tank platoon leader in Able Company, 743rd Tank Battalion, later recalled, "No prior reconnaissance and lack-of co-ordination marked the whole affair. I was sorry to hear that some of those Rangers whom we were rescuing got shot up as we swept in with those 75s blazing. But we didn't know exactly where they were… It was simply a 'stumble-footed' attack that hadn't been coordinated by the people in charge."[4] The belated relief of the Rangers at Pointe-du-Hoc had ended on a bitter note.

During the reorganization of the Rangers following the relief, Baker Company, 2nd Rangers, was sent to flush out remaining German positions from Pointe-du-Hoc eastward through Pointe-et-Raz-de-la-Percée. By this stage, US Army Air Forces engineer units had been clearing the area to create an emergency landing strip, and most of the German defenses had been abandoned. Once the relief of Pointe-du-Hoc was completed by late morning of June 8, D+2, the 116th RCT and associated Rangers and tanks continued their mission westward toward Utah Beach.

Chapter 18

Final Mission: The Maisy Gun Batteries

The original plans for the 116th RCT on D-Day envisioned a drive westward out of Vierville along the Vierville–Grandcamp road, clearing out the two German gun batteries in Maisy, the German garrison in Grandcamp, and associated defenses along the eastern side of the Vire estuary, and then swinging southwest to reach the town of Isigny.

The first tactical objective was a pair of small road bridges near the sluice gate where the Vierville–Grandcamp coastal road intersected the Ruisseau Fontaine-Sainte-Marie stream. The Germans had blocked the stream earlier in 1944 to flood the area to the south as part of a broader effort to discourage paratroop and glider landings in the area.

Baker and Easy Companies of the 5th Rangers were given this assignment and headed westward along the coastal road, reaching the area around 1000hrs on D+2. Baker Company reached within 25 yards of the eastern bridge when they came under a heavy concentration of mortar and machine-gun fire from the I./Grenadier-Regiment.914 that was defending the Grandcamp area. They were eventually reinforced by Dog Company, 5th Rangers.

A task force consisting of elements of the 2nd and 3rd Battalions, 116th Infantry, plus tanks of Charlie Company, 743rd Tank Battalion, arrived on the scene around 1230hrs. The tank company had lost half its tanks during the attack on Pointe-du-Hoc: three to mines and two to engine problems. The HQ Section and Able Company of the 743rd Tank Battalion was also expected to take part in the fight for Grandcamp. However, on the approach to Grandcamp, the tanks encountered so many mines that they decided to try to reach the village by heading inland via Criqueville-en-Bessin and Maisy. As will be related below, they missed the Grandcamp fighting but ended up engaged in the neighboring struggle for Maisy. The task force was accompanied by forward observers from SFCP-24 who were in touch with the cruiser HMS *Glasgow*.

The *Glasgow* began engaging targets around 1100hrs to the west of Grandcamp, and continued firing at targets around the village in support of the operation until 1825hrs. The *Glasgow* fired 271 rounds during the course of the afternoon. The destroyer USS *Harding* was also called in to provide fire support based on spotting by SFCP-3, firing 160 5in. rounds. Charlie Company, 743rd Tank Battalion, provided some fire support, but after losing yet another tank to mines, decided against proceeding any farther. After Army field artillery preparation, the 116th RCT task force assaulted Grandcamp-les-Bains around 1445hrs and captured it shortly afterward. The quaint seaside village had been turned to rubble by the continual artillery fire.

During this engagement, T/Sgt Frank Peregory, a platoon sergeant in K Company, 3/116th Infantry, eliminated a particularly strong German position, defense nest WN 78, on a hill on the outskirts of the village. He managed to reach the periphery of the position, jump into one of the trenches, and then overwhelm the German squad, killing eight Germans with grenades and bayonet and capturing three. Peregory was killed in a skirmish several days later and posthumously awarded the Medal of Honor for his heroism this day.

While the 116th RCT assaulted Grandcamp, Dog and Easy Company, 5th Rangers, were assigned to guard the sluice gate and clear out remaining German pockets along the coast back eastward to Pointe-du-Hoc.

ADVANCE ON MAISY

Following the capture of Grandcamp, another task force was formed to clear Maisy, based around the badly depleted 1st Battalion, 116th Infantry. The elements of the 5th Rangers assigned to this task force were Able, Charlie, and Fox Companies, 5th Rangers, supported by the two half-tracks of Epperson's cannon platoon.

On the afternoon of June 8, the task force moved toward Maisy, with the 1/116th Infantry advancing from the eastern side of the village via Jucoville and the Rangers advancing down the road from Grandcamp. The advance was slow because the terrain had been flooded by the Germans to discourage airborne landings. The 1/116th Infantry reached a point half a mile east of Maisy. At 1440hrs, SFCP-3 requested naval fire support, and USS *Harding* fired seventy-three 5in. rounds on the village. Around this time, Able Company of the 743rd Tank Battalion had arrived to the east of Maisy, trying to join the 116th RCT in its fight for Grandcamp. A platoon of tanks actually passed through Maisy during the naval barrage, believing it to be German fire directed at them. Exiting the south side of Maisy, Able Company brushed up against the Maisy I battery in WN 83/Les Perruques and shot up two bunkers. Failing to find a safe route to Grandcamp, the company withdrew back eastward to the bivouac area near Vierville.

At 1815hrs, the task force requested another naval fire mission, with the *Harding* firing 114 5in. rounds until 1900hrs. The fire-control party reported that the fire had been effective. The task force remained on the outskirts of Maisy for the night: Col Canham of the 116th RCT didn't want the task force to remain inside the village after dark for fear of snipers. An hour after midnight, SFCP-3 requested that HMS *Bellona* engage Target 16, the Maisy battery, based on sounds from the area. The *Bellona* subsequently fired twenty-six rounds. It is not clear if the Maisy battery was still active, but there were still batteries of AR.352 in the area which may have displaced to this sector during the day.[1]

GERMAN DEFENSES NEAR MAISY RECONFIGURED

With the defenses northeast of Isigny collapsing in the face of the 116th RCT attack, the 352.Infanterie-Division tried to reinforce the battered I./GR.914. Some of the reinforcements came from Ost-Bataillon.439 garrisoned in Isigny.[2] This was one of a number of Eastern battalions in Normandy organized from former Soviet prisoners of war. In 1943, Berlin had transferred twenty German infantry battalions from the West to the Russian Front, exchanging them for sixty of these Eastern battalions.[3] The battalion in Isigny was made up of Ukrainian troops with German officers and NCOs. It had a strength of about 405 men on D-Day, organized into three companies. Local commanders were skeptical of the combat value of these units, and they were pulled back from the coastal defenses in the spring of 1944 and put in rear areas. The German commanders had good reason for skepticism: the first element of Ost.Bataillon.439 to come in contact with US forces, its horse-mounted platoon, immediately surrendered.

It was also decided to convert the troops of the artillery batteries of III./AR.1716 at Maisy into infantry, yielding an additional 300 men. On June 8, the Maisy batteries were ordered to quietly spike their guns and begin moving westward to join with I./GR.914.[4] It is unclear how the two Maisy batteries of III./AR.1716 responded to these orders. The remaining 155mm howitzers at Maisy I were moved away sometime on June 8. A later prisoner-of-war interrogation indicated that the guns had been moved to the coast, immediately west of Grandcamp.[5] The 100mm field howitzers at Maisy II were still present on June 9, though it is not clear whether they were still operative.

ATTACK ON THE MAISY BATTERIES

On the morning of D+3, Friday, June 9, the three Ranger companies under Maj Richard Sullivan were detached from the 1/116th Infantry task force to deal with the Maisy batteries south of the village. The two companies of the 1/116th Infantry spent the day cleaning up remaining German positions around the village of Maisy until 1400hrs, and then headed west to clear German forces around Gefosse-Fontenay. The other three companies of the 5th Rangers not assigned to the Maisy mission established a bivouac east of Osmanville on June 9. Easy Company conducted mopping-up operations between Grandcamp and Pointe-du-Hoc on D+3.

Sullivan's Ranger task force was supported by the two Ranger M3 75mm GMC half-tracks, four 81mm mortars from Charlie Company, and the 4.2in. mortars of B Company, 81st Chemical Weapons Battalion. In addition, there was a forward observer officer with Sullivan's headquarters, providing fire support from the 58th Armored Field Artillery Battalion. Naval fire support for the attack was lacking: USS *Harding* had lost contact with SFCP-3 around 1920hrs the previous evening, and had been unable to reestablish contact through the morning of June 9, when it was relieved by USS *Satterlee* at 0730hrs.[6] The *Satterlee* was unable to re-establish communication with either the Rangers or the 1/116th Infantry until about 1100hrs, three hours after the start of the attack.

The farm fields north of the Maisy gun batteries were flooded and swampy. Another hazard was the presence of German anti-personnel mines, some of which were duds after having been saturated when the fields were flooded. Due to the minefields, Sullivan planned to attack both sites in a column of companies in the order: Fox, Able, Charlie. This would reduce the vulnerability of the Rangers to mines compared to a broad-front attack.

The attack started around 0800hrs with a preliminary artillery bombardment of 126 rounds from the M7 self-propelled 105mm howitzers of the 58th Armored Field Artillery Battalion, along with 81mm and 4.2in. mortar fire.

As Fox Company moved down the dirt road to the site, they came under sporadic machine-gun fire. Capt John Raaen, with the headquarters company, later recalled, "Crossing through the hedgerows and fields, we were taken under long-range machine gun fire several times. However, we were beyond tracer burn-out and the Germans were never able to adjust their fire well enough to even bother us."[7]

Prior to reaching the batteries, Able Company split off to the west to advance on WN 84/Maisy-Les Perruques. Once off the road, movement through the flooded farm fields was difficult; the ground was sodden and muddy, and footing was unpredictable. There were a number of dead American paratroopers in the fields who had been dropped far away from their intended landing zone and killed in skirmishes with the local German garrisons.

Fox Company began its attack on WN 83/Maisy-Martinière along its northern perimeter. The WN 83 defense nest had several reinforced firing positions on its perimeter, including a Tobruk. The Rangers smothered the machine-gun positions with small-arms fire to allow Lt Reville's platoon to get close enough for a grenade attack. Three positions were destroyed in this fashion, using grenades or satchel charges. In the meantime, Charlie Company, along with the two half-tracks, continued down the road and struck the position from the southeast. The 75mm guns on the half-tracks were used to good effect against targets of opportunity. During the start of the engagement, Sullivan had been riding in one of the half-tracks. He stepped out of it to direct the fighting on foot, and when a mine went off nearby, he was lightly wounded.

The attack on WN 83/Maisy-Martinière from two different sides created a certain amount of confusion and the threat of friendly-fire casualties. Sullivan therefore ordered Charlie Company and the half-tracks to disengage, skirt around the southern side of WN 83, and attack the neighboring WN 84/Maisy-Les Perruques from the rear in support of Able Company. The garrison in WN 83 was smaller than in the neighboring WN 84, presumably due to the evacuation order the previous day. The three surviving 100mm guns in the new casemates were turned to face out of the rear entrance toward the southeast. Ranger accounts do not mention them firing, and it is possible that they had already been spiked as ordered the day before.

As Fox Company attacked WN 83/Maisy-Martinière, Able Company began its assault against WN 84/Maisy-Les Perruques.

Of the original four 155mm howitzers, only one was still at the site, knocked off its platform by previous bombardments. Lt "Ace" Parker ordered "Fix bayonets" as the company began its assault. There were substantially more German troops in the WN 84/Maisy-Les Perruques strongpoint than in the neighboring Maisy-Martinière battery, but they had poor morale and began surrendering upon seeing the charging Rangers.

It's not clear what German troops remained at Maisy-Les Perruques. As mentioned previously, the battery had been ordered to evacuate the day before and may have done so. If this was the case, it is possible that the defenses were held by less reliable troops such as the Ost-Btl.439. Parker later recalled, "They gave up fairly rapidly. We were shouting at them and they were coming out real good. They were putting down their weapons, putting their hands behind their heads and coming out".[8] Some German officers began shouting at the surrendering men, and the Rangers reported that these officers shot their own men in the back as they gave themselves up. The prompt and brutal actions of the German officers put an end to the initial wave of surrendering. This adds further credence to the belief that these may have been men from an Eastern battalion rather than German troops. Some Rangers later claimed that these officers were SS, though there is no evidence of any SS units in Maisy at the time.[9]

When the wave of surrenders ceased, Able Company was obliged to fight for the remaining strongpoints. "Ace" Parker recalled the day's fighting as more intense than that of D-Day, although this is a bit of hyperbole since Parker's platoon had not engaged in any direct confrontations with defended strongpoints on D-Day.

Sullivan requested tank support to assist both attacks. Baker Company, 743rd Tank Battalion, had been sent to Maisy earlier in the day to assist the 1/116th Infantry, so it provided a few tanks to assist the Rangers. The tanks were used to reduce several bunkers and were released by the Rangers at 1800hrs once the area was secure.

The fighting for the two Maisy batteries took about five hours due to the large size of the multiple sites. It took the Rangers a

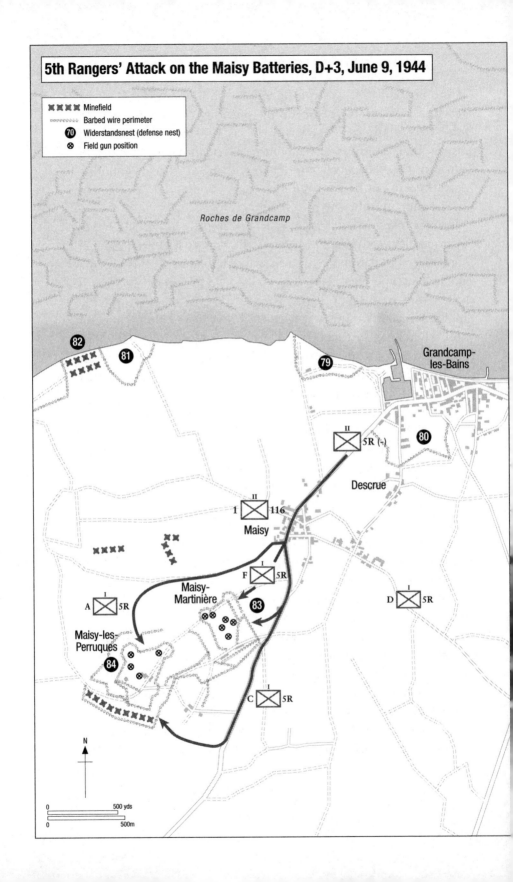

5th Rangers' Attack on the Maisy Batteries, D+3, June 9, 1944

Legend:
- ✕✕✕✕ Minefield
- Barbed wire perimeter
- **70** Widerstandsnest (defense nest)
- ⊗ Field gun position

Roches de Grandcamp

82
81
79
Grandcamp-les-Bains
80
Descrue
II 5R (-)
II 1 ☒ 116
Maisy
F I ☒ 5R
A I ☒ 5R
Maisy-Martinière
83
D I ☒ 5R
Maisy-les-Perruques
84
C I ☒ 5R

N

0 ___ 500 yds
0 ___ 500m

considerable amount of time to clear the numerous entrenchments, casemates, and small bunkers. In addition, the Rangers cleared the area of the Fouché farm where the Maisy I guns had been temporarily stored, finding it unoccupied and shattered by naval gunfire.[10] A total of about twenty Germans were killed and 130 captured. Most of the captured prisoners came from Maisy-Les Perruques, numbering about ninety men. Besides the captured German prisoners, one Ranger from Charlie Company found a German payroll suitcase containing roughly 2½ million francs, equivalent to about $50,000. Later in the day, a T2 tank recovery vehicle of Able Company, 743rd Tank Battalion, moving towards the unit's new bivouac outside Maisy, encountered about forty German soldiers near the Maisy strongpoint. The T2 was based on the old M3 Lee medium tank, but lacked the usual 37mm and 75mm guns, having dummy guns instead. The Germans, failing to realize this, surrendered without a shot being fired.[11]

The 5th Rangers suffered eighteen men wounded or missing on D+3, of whom eleven were part of the Maisy attack, the remainder having taken part in Easy Company's mopping-up operation along the coast.[12] Following the fighting, the two Ranger half-tracks were used to evacuate the wounded Rangers back to the beach, while Sullivan's task force marched west to join up with the remainder of the 5th Rangers in a bivouac 400 yards east of Osmanville.

On D+4, Saturday, June 10, half of the 5th Rangers – including Charlie, Delta, and Fox Companies – were assigned to clear out Stützpunkt Gefosse-Fontenay, the string of fortified defense nests along the Vire estuary from Grandcamp southward to Isigny. At 2000hrs on June 9, the German LXXXIV.Armee-Korps decided that the 352.Infanterie-Division would withdraw to new defense positions to the southwest. The orders were issued around 2300hrs. Any troops remaining in the coastal defenses of Stützpunkt Gefosse-Fontenay were presumably those that were out of contact with higher headquarters or trapped in the area after the 116th RCT had advanced to Isigny earlier in the day.

The Ranger operation was led by Capt Hugo Heffelfinger, the battalion's executive officer and S-3 (operations). The Rangers were supported by M8 light armored cars of the 102nd Cavalry Reconnaissance Squadron. The mission started at Gefosse-Fontenay, heading northeast, and met "little resistance."[13] For the most part, the German defenders surrendered. There was also no German artillery fire that day. Aside from the capture of the Maisy batteries on the previous day, the I./AR.1352 was no longer active in this area. This artillery battalion had lost all of its remaining horse-drawn artillery the previous day when it was cut off by the unexpectedly rapid advance of the 116th RCT on Isigny. The 400 troops of the battery had managed to escape and were assigned as infantry with the battered and understrength I./GR.914.

The Ranger patrols eventually finished mopping up the coastal defenses by 1530hrs that afternoon and returned to the bivouac area with 235 German prisoners. Casualties that day were just three men wounded, mainly to mines. This was the last combat action of the 5th Rangers in Normandy. During the five days of fighting, Schneider's 5th Rangers had suffered twenty-three men killed, eighty-nine wounded, and two missing for a total of 114 casualties, or about a quarter of their starting strength on D-Day. They had taken 850 prisoners and estimated that they had killed 350 German troops. By comparison, as of June 8, Rudder's 2nd Rangers had suffered seventy-seven killed, 152 wounded, and thirty-eight missing for a total of 267 casualties, or sixty percent of their initial strength.

Chapter 19

Battle Analysis

What were the lessons of the battle for Pointe-du-Hoc? In 1977, US Marine Corps general Donald Weller conducted a study on the future of amphibious fire support for the US Naval Sea Systems Command. Although the study did not directly address Pointe-du-Hoc, Weller made several important points about the lessons of dealing with enemy coastal gun batteries during World War II:

The coastal defense gun turned out to be a 'paper tiger,' in spite of the enormous resources that the Germans and Japanese devoted to that system [in World War II]. Coastal defense guns never succeeded in interfering significantly with transport unloadings or with landing craft and control vessels engaged in the ship-to-shore movement. Occasionally, a transport had to shift its unloading position or a 'small boy' engaged in close-in minesweeping was hit, but very few surface combatants or amphibious ships were even damaged; none were sunk. How can this failure be explained?

It was significant that at least through the first week of the operation, no battery could be considered destroyed unless captured. There were several instances of positions which were believed, on the basis of air and sea observation, to have been destroyed. Yet guns in these positions subsequently opened fire. In some of these cases, there is evidence that casements protected the guns against lethal damage although they were rendered inoperative during the bombardment and for many hours thereafter. The latter was probably the case at Crisbecq, which battery was one of the most important on the east coast of the Cherbourg Peninsula. The position contained two 210mm guns in casements, one 210mm in an open emplacement, and six 88mm dual purpose in open revetted emplacements. The casements had roofs of reinforced concrete 12½ feet thick and walls ranging from 10 to 16 feet. This position had been subjected, both before and after D-day, to especially heavy air and naval bombardment. The guns in casemates were undamaged except for minor fragmentation scars, the casemates themselves were also entirely unscratched even by close misses. On the other hand, all communication leading to them from the observation post and rangefinders were disrupted which probably rendered accurate fire extremely difficult. All the other guns in the battery which were not enclosed were destroyed or nearly so.

Thus, the success of the heavy naval guns is explained by the characteristics of the coastal defense weapons system. While very few coastal guns were literally destroyed, some component of the system, be it the range finders, fire-control stations, communications, or operating personnel, was degraded by the destructive and psychological power of the heavy-caliber naval projectiles. It was, of course, necessary to repeat suppressive fires when the damaged components of the system had been repaired. The fact remains that the coastal defense weapons system, which the Germans believed would disrupt the Allied landings, was never a factor.[1]

As I have detailed, the Pointe-du-Hoc battery was combat-ineffective before the Rangers arrived. Did this invalidate the need for the Ranger mission? As suggested by Weller's analysis, the answer most certainly is "No." One of Weller's most important points was that these coastal gun batteries needed to be captured by ground troops in order to ensure that they could not be returned to action. Allied planning anticipated that the Pointe-du-Hoc battery would be neutralized before the Ranger landing in order to shield the Transport Area from its guns at the start of the landing operations. The Ranger mission was not to eliminate the guns, but rather to make certain that they remained inoperable following the air and naval bombardment. This was accomplished by physically occupying the strongpoint and disabling the hidden guns.

What would have happened if the Rangers had not been assigned to capture Pointe-du-Hoc? Examples of other German coastal artillery batteries near Pointe-du-Hoc suggest the answer. Two batteries in particular offer some important evidence. The Saint-Marcouf/Crisbecq batteries were located northwest of Utah Beach and the Longues-sur-Mer battery between Omaha and Gold Beaches. These batteries were neutralized by the preliminary D-Day bombardment but not occupied by Allied special forces troops. In spite of very intense bombardments, they were able to fire at Allied naval forces on D-Day morning after the gun crews repaired the battery sites.

The Saint-Marcouf coastal guns consisted of a pair of batteries of HKAA.1261, the 3.Batterie near Crisbecq was armed with massive 210mm guns in enclosed casemates, and the 2.Batterie had a 105mm K331(f) gun.[2] The Crisbecq battery is the one mentioned above in Weller's post-war assessment. Both batteries were enclosed in casemates, and so very well protected. Even though both batteries were heavily bombed and subjected to naval gunfire prior to the D-Day landings, both remained functional.[3] These batteries were connected to forward observers along the coast. On D-Day morning, they began firing at the US Navy destroyers USS *Corry* and *Fitch*, starting around H-85 minutes (0505hrs). Both destroyers were supposed to be shielded by a smokescreen, but the *Corry* was not covered. The *Corry* and *Fitch* returned fire on the Saint-Marcouf batteries, but the *Corry* was soon straddled by accurate fire. The *Corry* tried to evade the fire, but in so doing, struck a mine around H+3 (0633hrs), cutting it in half. German accounts claim it was a victim of the Saint-Marcouf coastal guns, but a later US Navy enquiry concluded it was a mine.[4] The reason for the *Corry*'s loss remains controversial.

In order to silence the two batteries, various US Navy ships began an extended gun duel. The cruiser USS *Quincy* put the batteries under fire, followed by the battleship USS *Nevada*. The *Nevada* scored a direct hit on the one of four bunkers with a 5in. round, but it was a dud, passing through the bunker and out of the other side. The Crisbecq battery lost the first of three guns in the early-morning exchange, the second at 1557hrs, and the last at 1830hrs. Both batteries continued to be a major nuisance to the expansion of the Utah bridgehead northward, and they were not finally captured until June 9–11 after intense ground combat.[5] The Crisbecq commander, Oberleutnant zur See Walter Ohmsen, was awarded the Knight's Cross for his prolonged defense of the battery site.

Longues-sur-Mer was another naval coastal artillery battery with fully casemated 150mm destroyer guns.[6] It was the 4.Batterie of HKAA.1260, the same battalion as the Pointe-du-Hoc battery. However, this battery was originally constructed as a Kriegsmarine naval battery, with naval guns and naval fire controls. It was the single most sophisticated coastal artillery battery on the invasion coast, with a particularly advanced fire-control system. Fire solutions computed in the fire-control bunker could be electronically transmitted to the four gun casemates via underground communication cables. However, the battery was never fully completed and lacked the full fire-control suite on D-Day.

Longues-sur-Mer was heavily bombed and shelled in the early hours of D-Day. At 0530hrs, HMS *Ajax* bombarded the battery without inflicting fatal damage. The battery began firing on the command ship HMS *Bulolo* around 0600hrs, forcing it to move station. HMS *Ajax* returned, along with HMS *Argonaut*, and began bombarding the battery again. It ceased fire around 0845hrs after two of its guns were knocked out by direct hits through the open embrasures. The cruisers had fired a total of 179 rounds against the battery. The German battery crew cleaned up the position in the late morning, and the remaining two guns opened fire again in the afternoon towards Omaha Beach, prompting the attention of the French cruiser *Georges Leygues* which was defending the American sector. This final bombardment put the battery out of action for the last time on D-Day after it had fired 115 rounds during the course of the day's action. The battery also had a 122mm gun for illumination purposes, and it fired at both Gold and Omaha Beach during the course of the day. German infantry defending the battery were withdrawn to Bayeux on June 7, leaving it exposed to ground attack. After the battery was softened up by RAF fighter-bombers on the morning of June 7, it was assaulted by the 2nd Devons of the British 231st Brigade. Of its original 184-man garrison, 120 surrendered when the battery was captured around 1100hrs.

The examples of the Saint-Marcouf and Longues-sur-Mer batteries help explain why the Ranger mission against Pointe-du-Hoc was necessary. Allied planners were concerned that if the Rangers did not occupy the battery site, then the Pointe-du-Hoc battery might be able to recover from the preliminary air and naval bombardment and begin to fire on the transport ships off Utah and Omaha Beaches, or against the landing beaches themselves. As the Graham Report had predicted, preliminary bombardment by aircraft and warships could be expected to temporarily neutralize a coastal gun battery, but bombardment alone could not guarantee that a gun battery would remain suppressed.

POINTE-DU-HOC CONTROVERSIES

While few doubt the heroism of Rudder's Rangers, controversies have arisen over the years about whether the Pointe-du-Hoc mission was necessary. The first of these arguments arose from Cornelius Ryan's book *The Longest Day*, and more precisely, the film version of the book. In the movie, the Pointe-du-Hoc scene concludes with one of the Rangers saying, "We've come all this way for nothing." Since the guns were not in the battery positions, the presumption was that the mission was unnecessary. The film failed to point out that, in fact, the Rangers did find operational guns and did disable them.

Many of the revisionist arguments about the need for the Ranger mission revolve around the issue of whether the Allies knew that the guns at Pointe-du-Hoc had been removed. As discussed in Chapter 5, the French Resistance did inform Allied intelligence that the guns had been moved. This is based on second-hand recollections from the Ranger leaders and cryptic recollections by members of the French Resistance.

Even if the French reports were accepted by Allied intelligence, this did not mean that the guns no longer posed a threat to Operation *Neptune*. Guns that had been moved away from Pointe-du-Hoc could be moved back again. Allied intelligence knew that two of the guns had been moved in March 1944 due to the casemate construction program, then moved back again. This pattern had been repeated elsewhere in Normandy, including the Maisy II battery, where guns had been moved out of the gun pits during the spring 1944 construction program before being returned. This pattern was common in Normandy, including with the batteries at Vers-sur-Mer and Riva-Bella/Ouistreham. So even if the Allies did accept the French reports that the Pointe-du-Hoc guns had been moved, this did not mean that they had gone permanently and would not return by D-Day.

Furthermore, the Allies were unable to verify the French reports. In more recent years a retired US Air Force photo interpreter re-examined the aerial photos of the Pointe-du-Hoc area from May 1944. Even knowing the precise location that the guns were moved to, he could not identify the guns in the photos since they were well hidden under trees.[7] The last major Allied intelligence assessment of the German coastal gun batteries, completed on May 31, 1944, and released on June 1, concluded that the guns were present at Pointe-du-Hoc.[8] We now know that these "guns" were simply telephone poles in the gun pits covered by camouflage nets. The level of detail on the photos was insufficient to permit the interpreters to recognize the ruse. To Allied photo interpreters, therefore, the guns appeared to be present at Pointe-du-Hoc in light of the most recent photo-reconnaissance missions.

On the eve of D-Day, the status of the guns at Pointe-du-Hoc was clouded by the usual "fog-of-war." If the guns were still there, they could cause havoc to the invasion fleet in the Transport Area.

If they were not there, the Rangers had other D-Day missions to complete. Under these ambiguous circumstances, there was no reason to cancel the Ranger mission.

Questions over the need for the Ranger mission have been revived in recent years, mainly by Gary Sterne, owner of a new Normandy museum on the Maisy I-Les Perruques artillery battery site. Sterne has argued in several books and articles that the Maisy battery was a more significant threat on D-Day than Pointe-du-Hoc, and should have been the Rangers' primary objective. These arguments have reverberated through the press and military history magazines.[9]

Nevertheless, Allied intelligence did not regard either of the Maisy batteries to be as serious a threat as Pointe-du-Hoc. The Maisy batteries could reach the Utah Beach Transport Area, but not that of Omaha Beach. The absence of a control bunker and the type of armament of the batteries suggested to Allied intelligence that they were primarily for bombarding the beaches, not for engagement of naval targets. This was indeed the case, as described in more detail here in Appendix B. Nor were the batteries expected to pose a decisive threat to the landing areas. The Maisy batteries could reach Utah Beach, but could barely reach the western edge of Omaha Beach. There is very little evidence that the Maisy batteries had any significant impact on the D-Day fighting, as there are few records regarding how many rounds they fired or what targets they engaged. About 180 tons of ammunition were removed from the sites after the fighting, suggesting that they did not fire much of their available ammunition.[10]

Had the Ranger mission to Pointe-du-Hoc been cancelled, there were other coastal batteries that were more likely candidates than the Maisy batteries, such as the Saint-Marcouf or Longues-sur-Mer batteries.

The reason that the Rangers remained focused on Pointe-du-Hoc was that the mission of the Provisional Ranger Group was far greater than Pointe-du-Hoc alone. It should be recalled that the final Ranger plan had only a quarter of the Provisional Ranger Group, three of twelve companies, landing in the first wave at Pointe-du-Hoc. The remaining nine companies had other objectives, including the elimination of the battery at Pointe-et-Raz-de-la-Percée. As described earlier,[11] the mission of Schneider's Ranger Force C had two options: reinforcing Rudder at Pointe-du-Hoc if the mission was quickly accomplished or acting as a back-up to seize Pointe-du-Hoc from the landward side.

All the various Ranger plans presumed that the initial missions would be accomplished by the afternoon of D-Day. At this point, the Rangers were assigned to assist the 116th Regimental Combat Team in accomplishing its mission of pushing westward out of the Vierville draw as the first step in linking up with Utah Beach. Essentially, the Rangers constituted the covering force for the right flank of the Omaha Beach landings.

In the event, the Ranger plan was not executed as planned, for a variety of reasons. Rudder's Force A did secure Pointe-du-Hoc, but the delay in landing meant that Schneider's Force C landed at Vierville rather than Pointe-du-Hoc. Would the Omaha Beach landings have been more successful if Schneider's Force C had landed at Pointe-du-Hoc?

An argument can certainly be made that the Force C landing near the Vierville draw was ultimately more productive on D-Day than a landing at Pointe-du-Hoc. If Schneider's force had successfully landed at Pointe-du-Hoc, it may have combined with Rudder's Force A and pushed farther southwest towards the eventual goals of the 116th RCT in the direction Grandcamp–Maisy–Isigny. However, the combination of Ranger Force A and Force C constituted only two understrength light infantry battalions, and it is by no means clear that they could have pushed deep into the German defenses in the Grandcamp sector without further support from the 116th RCT. A stalemate most likely would have ensued until reinforcements from the 116th RCT arrived.

In the event, Schneider's Force C landed east of the Vierville draw and did not carry out their intended mission of advancing immediately on Pointe-du-Hoc from the landward side. This had nothing to do with Schneider's intentions, but was forced on the Rangers by the 116th RCT commander, Col Canham. The

1/116th Infantry suffered horrible losses on Dog Green Beach, and Schneider's Force C provided most of the momentum for getting the troops over the bluffs in the Vierville sector. This was a singularly vital accomplishment for the overall Omaha Beach mission on D-Day morning. Furthermore, Schneider's Ranger unit was relatively intact and so provided Canham with an immediate reserve that could be used to shield the right flank of Omaha Beach from German counterattacks against Vierville. As a result, Schneider's Rangers spent D-Day and the morning of D+1 defending the Vierville sector of Omaha Beach rather than marching on Pointe-du-Hoc. It can certainly be argued that this was a far more necessary mission than reinforcing Rudder's Rangers at Pointe-du-Hoc. Schneider's Rangers thus prevented the danger of the Germans overrunning the western flank of Omaha Beach on D-Day and D-Day evening.

One questionable aspect of the *Neptune* plan was the inordinate firepower aimed at Pointe-du-Hoc. This was not specific to the Ranger plan, but rather a part of the Joint Fire Plan. As detailed earlier in this book,[12] Pointe-du-Hoc was pulverized by the Operation *Flashlamp* aerial bombardment in the pre-dawn hours of D-Day. As part of this devastating effort, the only battleship assigned to bombard Omaha Beach, USS *Texas*, was directed to attack Pointe-du-Hoc. Of the 437 tons of naval gunfire available to attack Omaha Beach, 203 tons was devoted to Pointe-du-Hoc. In contrast, the Vierville draw, the site of the slaughter of the 1st Battalion, 116th Infantry, was subjected to only 24 tons of naval gunfire from the smaller guns of the destroyers. The Colleville draw, site of the costly landing of the 16th RCT, was hit by only 12 tons of naval gunfire due to the failure of the rocket ships. The 5in. destroyer guns used at Omaha Beach in the preliminary bombardments were incapable of penetrating the Atlantic Wall Standard B steel-reinforced concrete of the German gun casemates and major fortifications.

In post-invasion US Navy assessments, it was recognized that the initial mission of USS *Texas* at Pointe-du-Hoc was a waste.[13] The same amount of firepower directed against the German defenses in the Vierville draw might have made a significant difference in the battle for Dog Green Beach. The *Texas* did turn its attention to the Vierville draw later in the day, and to good effect. But by the time it intervened, the 116th Infantry Regiment had already suffered horrible casualties.

The D-Day battles certainly confirmed the old adage that "No plan survives first contact with the enemy." The original Ranger plan fell victim to the predictable complications of war. Yet the Rangers' excellent training, and the astute judgment of their combat leaders, made it possible for the Provisional Ranger Group to adapt to the circumstances and prevail in its mission. The capture of Pointe-du-Hoc remains the most vivid legacy of the Rangers on D-Day, but their other actions around Vierville had equally vital consequences on D-Day.

Afterword

The Rangers in Cinema

Popular perceptions of famous battles are often shaped by films. Paradoxically, in an age of near-universal literacy, the imagery of popular media often overwhelms the printed word. In the case of the Rangers on D-Day, two blockbuster films have most strongly influenced the popular image: *The Longest Day* (1962) and *Saving Private Ryan* (1998). These two films were separated by more than three decades and differ considerably in their approach and style. The aim of this essay is not to evaluate them as films, but to take a look at their historical depictions and the way they shape or distort our perceptions of the Rangers on D-Day.

THE LONGEST DAY

Daryl F. Zanuck's *The Longest Day* was based on Cornelius Ryan's bestseller of the same name. The movie format was a quasi-documentary epic with an international all-star cast. It was shot in black and white to give it historical verisimilitude.

The Ranger assault on Pointe-du-Hoc is only a very small part of the movie. The French government allowed the film crew to use the actual Pointe-du-Hoc setting, adding to its realism. The cliff-scaling episode cemented Pointe-du-Hoc in the popular imagination.

From a historian's perspective, *The Longest Day* suffers from the usual constraints of Hollywood filmmaking. Zanuck once said,

"There is nothing duller than being accurate but not dramatic." The film fell in the middle ground regarding realism and authenticity. Filmmaking often involves spatial compression to heighten the action and drama. This was particularly the case in 1960s epics. The scaling of the cliffs at Pointe-du-Hoc has the action compressed into a very small area, with far too many Rangers in too small an area. Likewise, the action shows far greater German resistance than the actual event.

The casting for the Rangers was in keeping with films of the time. The heroic leads were two up-and-coming young stars, George Segal and Robert Wagner, both plausible as "hard men for dirty work." The comic relief was provided by three teen idols and singers of the time: Paul Anka, Tommy Sands, and Fabian. Yet these three come across as more buffoonish than heroic, which was typical of Zanuck's style in the film, juxtaposing light, semi-comical incidents with more serious drama.

Zanuck took a cue from Ryan's book, depicting the Pointe-du-Hoc mission as ultimately futile. One of the Rangers in the final Pointe-du-Hoc scene complains that "We've come all this way for nothing" when they fail to locate the guns. There is no suggestion that the guns were ultimately found and destroyed. This was in part due to Ryan's over-reliance on a single Ranger, Sgt William "L-Rod" Petty, for much of his information on the Pointe-du-Hoc mission. Petty was regarded by the Ranger officers as an excellent soldier, but prone to misadventures and poor judgment that led to his demotion on several occasions. Petty's jaundiced view of the Rangers colored Ryan's portrayal of the Pointe-du-Hoc mission. Once again, Zanuck preferred drama over historical accuracy: a failed mission was easier to depict in a short episode than the complications of the actual mission.

Unsurprisingly, *The Longest Day* was not popular with Ranger veterans. Tom Hatfield's biography of Rudder provides a fuller picture of this controversy.

The scenes in *The Longest Day* about Omaha Beach exhibit similar problems. There are no significant attempts to depict the Rangers' role on Omaha Beach. The film shows a far greater density of troops in the Omaha Beach scenes than is authentic. The landing scenes were shot on Corsica in bright sunlight, rather than in the overcast conditions and rough seas of D-Day. The uniforms, landing craft, and ships are a hodge-podge of World War II surplus and 1950s-era equipment. Yet details of the uniforms and equipment were not embarrassingly bad, since a great deal of World War II equipment was still available at the time. However, the costume designers didn't bother to add specific D-Day details such as the use of assault vests by the initial waves of landing troops.

The defenses on Omaha Beach have too many German troops and do not bear a close resemblance to the actual strongpoints. The scene with Major Pluskat in a forward observation post of Artillerie-Regiment.352 was shot in the massive Longues-sur-Mer coastal battery command post rather than in a more modest and realistic example.

Overall, *The Longest Day* provides the casual movie viewer with a reasonably accurate depiction of D-Day, although it suffers from its outdated style and numerous compromises in detail and historical authenticity.

SAVING PRIVATE RYAN

Steven Spielberg's *Saving Private Ryan* is a fundamentally different type of movie from *The Longest Day*, and a far more successful film. Spielberg depicts a fictional Ranger company that lands on Dog Green Beach on D-Day. The first twenty-five minutes of the film are some of the most harrowing and intense combat scenes portrayed up to that time in a popular movie. I went to see the movie along with my father when it was first released. My grandfather had landed on Omaha Beach on D-Day in an engineer unit, while my dad landed on Omaha Beach a few weeks after D-Day as part of the US Army build-up. We left the cinema speechless.

American war movies were irreversibly changed by the Vietnam War. Patriotic epics of the sort that were common in the 1950s and early 1960s, such as *The Longest Day*, were viewed as jingoistic and old-fashioned. American war films of the Vietnam era and subsequent years tended to be anti-heroic, with the likes of *The Dirty Dozen* (1967), *Kelly's Heroes* (1970), *The Deer Hunter* (1978), *The Big Red One* (1980), *Hamburger Hill* (1987), and *Platoon* (1988).

Popular attitudes had gradually changed by the 1980s. US President Ronald Reagan visited Normandy in 1984 as part of the 40th anniversary commemorations, and gave his famous speech extolling the "Boys of Pointe-du-Hoc" while standing next to the Ranger memorial on top of the German command post bunker. D-Day came to symbolize the American experience in the European theater, and Pointe-du-Hoc was the most visible symbol of D-Day for Americans. Spielberg's film was released a decade later in 1998, the same year as NBC anchorman Tom Brokaw's influential best-seller, *The Greatest Generation*. Anti-war sentiment had mellowed over the two decades since the end of the Vietnam War. Books like Brokaw's viewed their parents' generation with greater admiration for having persevered through the hard times of the Depression, followed by the war.

Spielberg had grown up watching the old war films; his father was a World War II veteran. As a result, Spielberg's film was less bitter than Vietnam War films such as *Platoon* or *Hamburger Hill*. It was at once reverential towards the wartime generation but also far more hard-bitten and cynical than the classic war films of the 1940s and 1950s, such as *Battleground* (1949) and *Sands of Iwo Jima* (1949). American soldiers are shown by Spielberg as both heroic and cowardly. Many American troops are depicted as noble, but some soldiers are casually brutal, for example where they shoot surrendering Germans.

I was very impressed with the film for its gut-wrenching reality and sincere attempts at historical accuracy. There was considerable attention to small detail: the D-Day assault vests, the Ranger and 29th Division insignia, etc. I would like to avoid snotty nit-picking, as Spielberg did not intend to create a historical documentary and the characters are entirely fictional. But where does the fiction clash most with the history? The focus here is on the initial portion of the film dealing with D-Day.

What does *Saving Private Ryan* actually depict? Since it is not a documentary, it does not portray a specific unit in a specific location. It refers to C Company, 2nd Rangers, based on the advice of Gen Omar Bradley and author Stephen Ambrose. However, the film made no effort to actually depict the actions of Goranson's isolated company on D-Day. The film fits closest to the experiences of Able and Baker Companies, 2nd Rangers, who landed to the east of the Vierville draw killing zone. It is something of a pastiche of the experiences of the Rangers and A/116th Infantry on Dog Green. Tom Hanks's character, Capt Miller, may be loosely based on Col Max Schneider, commander of the 5th Rangers. He was one of the few Rangers on Omaha Beach with prior combat experience in the Mediterranean theater.

Film-making invariably involves compression, both in the terms of spatial compression and temporal compression. The initial Dog Green Beach sequence is about half an hour in length, even though the actual event, from the approach to the beach to the penetration of the German defenses, lasted from dawn until early afternoon. The time compression helps to accentuate the drama, even if not literally accurate.

The spatial compression is probably less obvious to the casual moviegoer. From the standpoint of visual content, the images have more "stuff" in each frame than would have been seen by a camera on the beach on D-Day. The Dog Green Beach scene, shot on the coast of Ireland, involved a supporting cast of 750 soldiers of the Irish army in a few acres, when in history there were only about 200 soldiers in dozens of acres. Such visual compression is also a valuable tool in enhancing the drama and visual experience of the viewer.

The cinematography in *Saving Private Ryan* is one of its most striking accomplishments, making the movie viewer feel as though they are present at the event. The desaturation of color in the opening Omaha Beach sequence provides an innovative visual link between the black-and-white imagery of World War II newsreels and the vivid color-saturation of contemporary TV news and movie imagery.

The dialog and battlefield dynamics of *Saving Private Ryan* are also impressive. Spielberg employed Captain Dale Dye and his

"Warriors Incorporated" consulting firm to train the actors for the movie. Dye's training was intended to eradicate the phoniness of the sort common in older war films such as *The Longest Day*.

One of the drawbacks of visual compression is that it creates false impressions about the distances involved on the modern battlefield. In the film, the German machine gunners on the bluff overlooking the Rangers appear to be only a few hundred feet away, when in fact the distance from the German machine guns in WN 71 on top of the bluffs to the edge of the beach at low tide was about 2,000ft. This is very apparent to anyone who has visited Omaha Beach and walked from the low tide area up to the bluffs.

The film has several minor technical stumbles. It depicts the Rangers landing in LCVP/Higgins boats rather than in LCAs. This is probably due to the fact that Higgins boats, replicas, or computer-generated imagery were easier to obtain than the more obscure LCAs. This actually undermines the horror of the disembarkation scenes, since the narrow bow ramp of the LCAs led to far worse casualties than on LCVPs as it slowed the soldiers' exit from the craft. It was also the reason that many soldiers jumped over the sides of the LCAs, actions that are depicted in the film.

If the Ranger veterans were disappointed with *The Longest Day*, tank veterans were angry at *Saving Private Ryan*. The Tom Hanks character, Capt Miller, complains over the radio that there were no tanks on the beach. The 743rd Tank Battalion was the first US unit ashore in this sector on D-Day. As I have detailed in this book, they had a number of interactions with the Rangers. This mistake is all the more surprising in view of the close attention to detail paid to the uniforms and weapons.

Although the film was remarkably accurate in regards to details of the uniforms and weapons, the depiction of the German beach defenses is probably the most problematic aspect of the sequence from a historian's perspective. I must admit I am unusually sensitive to this issue, having written several books on German defenses in Normandy. The set designers seem to have borrowed their iconography from the coastal gun fortifications at Longues-sur-Mer to the east of Omaha Beach rather than the actual

Omaha defenses. The German machine-gun bunker on the bluff overlooking the beach resembles a miniaturized German coastal artillery command post bunker. Most German machine guns on Omaha Beach, however, were in foxholes, Tobruks, or very small improvised pillboxes. This bunker makes the German positions seem far more elaborate than they actually were on D-Day. The beach scenes also omit the numerous beachside houses and hotels that were present on the Vierville coast on D-Day.

The scene most removed from the actual events is the final scene in the beach sequence when the Rangers overrun a complex of German bunkers in the Vierville draw. To begin with, the Rangers were not involved in clearing the bunkers in the Vierville draw. They went over the bluffs, avoiding the heaviest concentration of bunkers. The bunkers of WN 72 were eventually cleared by the tanks and infantry of the 116th RCT. The bunkers in the film bear no resemblance to the actual bunkers in the Vierville draw, but appear to have been inspired by the impressive and massive coastal artillery bunkers at Longues-sur-Mer.

I suspect that the fortification scenery designed for *Saving Private Ryan* was exaggerated to pictorially explain the carnage on the beach. The actual bunkers on Omaha Beach are visually underwhelming. When I first visited the Vierville draw in the early 1980s, I recall how unimpressive the German defenses appeared. The two key bunkers in WN 72 are still there, though heavily reconstructed since the war. The 88mm gun bunker now forms the base for the US Army National Guard memorial. The neighboring 50mm gun bunker is boarded up, lacks its tank turret, and has been partly truncated. The German defenses of WN 71 on the bluff on the eastern side of the Vierville draw were mostly temporary earth entrenchments and have now largely reverted to farmland or have become overgrown. In the end, the movie bunkers do resemble specific types of German fortifications, even if not appropriate for Omaha Beach. The Ranger triumph against the bunker complex offers the audience a measure of righteous revenge after the vivid scenes of carnage on the beach at the beginning of the sequence.

The later scenes in the movie veer off in a completely fictional direction. There were no large towns in the area where the Rangers saw combat, while the inclusion of Waffen-SS troops and a Tiger tank in the final scenes are even further removed from the Ranger experience.

Saving Private Ryan has had enormous visual impact on the iconography of subsequent media, especially video games. Probably the most impressive is the popular *Call of Duty 2*, where Pointe-du-Hoc is the seventeenth level, and the first American level of the game. This depicts the actual Pointe-du-Hoc mission rather than Dog Green Beach, but the visuals were strongly inspired by *Saving Private Ryan*.

In our digital age, the visual has overwhelmed the literary. The ubiquitous cell phone has encouraged the creation of trillions of "selfies" and other photographic images of the most mundane daily events. It is hard to recall that less than a century ago, visual images of cataclysmic events such as D-Day were rare and exceptional. There were no film cameras at Pointe-du-Hoc on D-Day. The surviving photos of Pointe-du-Hoc were taken days after the battle.

As a result, cinema has often intervened to offer a visual depiction of famous events to fill in the pictoral gap. Today, it is hard to recall a historical figure such as Gen George S. Patton except through his flamboyant recreation by George C. Scott in the movie *Patton*. Fortunately, in the case of the Rangers at Pointe-du-Hoc, the Hollywood recreations have not distorted our perception of the event in any fundamental way. Rather, films such as *Saving Private Ryan* have helped inspire new generations to explore the history of battles and soldiers that might otherwise have been forgotten.

Appendix A

Ranger Organization, Equipment, and Combat Awards

Ranger unit organization was an amalgam of British Commando and US infantry organization. The units were tailored to raiding operations, which had two consequences on organization. On the one hand, the basic Ranger company was kept small enough that it could be delivered on two LCA landing craft. On the other hand, the company had minimal organic logistics and support, on the presumption that raiding missions would be brief. On D-Day, the two Ranger infantry battalions were based on the February 29, 1944, Table of Organization and Equipment (T/O&E).

Starting from the bottom up, the **Ranger platoon** consisted of a platoon headquarters (lieutenant, platoon sergeant, two EM [enlisted men]), two assault sections, and one special weapons section. The term "section" for the platoon sub-formation is another reminder of the British Commando connection; section is a term more commonly used in the British Army. Each assault section had a section leader (NCO), a light machine-gun (LMG) squad, and an assault squad. The LMG squad had a squad leader (NCO) armed with an M1 rifle, a machine gunner armed with an M1918A4 .30cal air-cooled light machine gun, an assistant loader, and two ammo bearers armed with M1 rifles. The assault squad included a squad leader and four riflemen, all armed with M1 rifles. The special weapons section on paper was an unusual organization, armed with a 60mm light mortar, 2.36in. "bazooka" rocket launcher, and .55cal Boys antitank rifle, and including two NCOs and four EM. In total, a Ranger platoon had thirty-two men, including one officer, nine NCOs, and twenty-two EM. In comparison, a regular infantry rifle platoon had forty-one men.

A **Ranger company** included a headquarters platoon with a company commander (captain), a company sergeant, and two EM.[1] Company commanders and sergeants were usually armed with .45cal M1A1 Thompson sub-machine guns. Each company included two Ranger platoons as described above, with a total company strength of sixty-eight men (three officers, twenty NCOs, and forty-five EM). In comparison, a regular infantry rifle company had 193 men, or almost triple the size. The significant difference in size was due to the fact that the infantry rifle company included four platoons compared to the Rangers' two: three rifle platoons and a weapons platoon.

A **Ranger battalion** consisted of a headquarters and headquarters company and six Ranger companies lettered A–F.[2] The headquarters company had a headquarters (seven officers), an administration and personnel platoon (one officer, four NCOs, and twenty-four EM), an intelligence and operations platoon (two NCOs and five EM), a supply and transport platoon (six NCOs and twenty-five EM), and a communications squad (one NCO and twenty-one EM). The supply and transport platoon contained the battalion's only vehicles, and on paper included seven motorcycles, nine jeeps, four ¾-ton weapons carriers, and one ¾-ton command car.[3] These were somewhat similar in concept to the ground echelons in airborne divisions. On D-Day, they did not land in the initial assault, but were brought in on later waves. The battalion usually had an attached medical detachment including one officer, one NCO, ten EM, and a ¾-ton weapons carrier used as an ambulance. The headquarters company also controlled a pool of weapons that would be distributed to the companies as needed, including seven .55cal Boys antitank rifles, six 60mm mortars, and six 81mm mortars. The basic Ranger battalion included 516 men (twenty-seven officers, 128 NCOs, and 361 EM). Including its enlisted cadre and medical detachment, the battalion comprised 608 men. In contrast, a regular infantry battalion had 871 men. There was not as great a disparity in size between a Ranger battalion and an infantry battalion as there was between a Ranger company and rifle company. This was because infantry battalions were not independent formations; they were part of an infantry regiment which also included a cannon company, anti-tank company, and service company. If a "slice" of the regimental support is included, the infantry battalion plus support would total about 1,085 men.

The small arms in a Ranger battalion included 326 M1 Garand rifles, twelve M1903A4 sniper rifles, fifty-six M1A1 .45cal Thompson sub-machine guns, and 198 .45cal M1911 pistols. The sniper rifles were issued on a scale of one per Ranger platoon HQ. Ranger riflemen on D-Day generally carried between eighty and 128 rounds of ammunition and either six fragmentation grenades or two or three of the larger white phosphorus smoke grenades.

Rudder's Rangers made some substitutions of weapons compared to the official equipment allotments. In 1944, the M1 .30cal carbine was beginning to appear as a substitute for the .45cal M1911 pistol, and typically these were issued to crew-served weapons crews.

The crew-served weapons of the Ranger battalion included twenty-one .30cal light machine guns, twenty .55cal Boys antitank rifles, fourteen 2.36in. bazooka antitank rocket launchers, eighteen 60mm mortars, and six 81mm mortars. Photos of the Rangers at Pointe-du-Hoc as well as written accounts indicate that the Ranger units had four BAR .30cal automatic rifles per company, even though not formally included in the T/O&E. These were presumably substituted for the .30cal light machine guns since they were much more portable when climbing cliffs. Photos from Pointe-du-Hoc do show some .30cal light machine guns in use, so presumably the substitution was not universal. The .55cal Boys antitank rifle was regarded as useless and needlessly cumbersome. It was not used by the 2nd and 5th Rangers, and was formally discarded in the July 1944 change to the basic February 1944 T/O&E. It is possible that additional bazookas were acquired as substitutes.

2ND RANGER INFANTRY BATTALION

Commanding Officer: Lieutenant Colonel James E. Rudder
Executive Officer: Major George S. Williams
S-1: 1st Lieutenant Frank L. Kennard
S-2: Captain Harvey J. Cook
S-3: Captain Frank H. Coder
S-4: Captain James A. Malaney
Surgeon: Captain Walter E. Block
Sergeant Major: Master Sergeant Robert N. Lemin
    Headquarters Company: Captain James W. Eikner
        Executive Officer: Captain Frederick G. Wilkin
        Platoon Leader: 1st Lieutenant Conway E. Epperson
        Platoon Leader: 1st Lieutenant William G. Heaney
        Platoon Leader: 1st Lieutenant James McCullers
        Platoon Leader: 1st Lieutenant Elmer H. Vermeer
        First Sergeant: 1st Sergeant John Erdely
    A Company: Captain Joseph A. Rafferty (KIA June 6, 1944)
        Platoon Leader: 1st Lieutenant Robert T. Edlin
        Platoon Leader: 1st Lieutenant Stanley E. White
        First Sergeant: 1st Sergeant Edward L. Sowa (KIA June 6, 1944)
    B Company: Captain Edgar L. Arnold
        Platoon Leader: 1st Lieutenant Robert M. Brice (KIA June 6, 1944)
        Platoon Leader: 1st Lieutenant Robert C. Fitzsimmons
        First Sergeant: 1st Sergeant Manning L. Rubenstein
    C Company: Captain Ralph E. Goranson
        Platoon Leader: 1st Lieutenant William D. Moody
        Platoon Leader: 1st Lieutenant Sidney A. Salomon
        First Sergeant: 1st Sergeant Henry S. Golas
    D Company: Captain Harold K. Slater
        Platoon Leader: 1st Lieutenant Morton L. McBride
        Platoon Leader: 2nd Lieutenant George F. Kerchner
        First Sergeant: 1st Sergeant Leonard G. Lomell

E Company: Captain Richard P. Merrill
    Platoon Leader: 1st Lieutenant Theodore E. Lapres
    Platoon Leader: 1st Lieutenant Joseph E. Leagans
    First Sergeant: 1st Sergeant Robert W. Lang
F Company: Captain Otto Masny
    Platoon Leader: 1st Lieutenant Jacob J. Hill
    Platoon Leader: 1st Lieutenant Robert C. Arman
    First Sergeant: 1st Sergeant Charles E. Frederick

5TH RANGER INFANTRY BATTALION

Commanding Officer: Lieutenant Colonel Max F. Schneider
Executive Officer: Major Richard P. Sullivan
S-1: Captain Edmund J. Butler
S-2: Captain William P. Byrne Jr
S-3: Captain Hugo W. Heffelfinger
S-4: Captain William F. Murray
Surgeon: Captain Thomas G. Petrick
Chaplain: 1st Lieutenant Joseph Lacy
Sergeant Major: Master Sergeant Minor C. Dean
    Headquarters Company: Captain John C. Raaen Jr
        Executive Officer: 1st Lieutenant Howard E. Van Riper
        Communication Officer: 1st Lieutenant Louis J. Gombosi
        Operation Officer (Asst): 1st Lieutenant Stanley L. Askin
        Platoon Leader: 2nd Lieutenant Quentin L. Knollenberg
        Platoon Leader: 1st Lieutenant Richard J. Nee
        Platoon Leader: 1st Lieutenant Jack A. Snyder
        First Sergeant: 1st Sergeant Russell Woodhill
    A Company: 1st Lieutenant Charles H. Parker Jr
        Platoon Leader: 1st Lieutenant Aloysius Wybroski
        Platoon Leader: 1st Lieutenant Stanley D. Zlesky
        First Sergeant: 1st Sergeant Morris E. Mooberry

B Company: Captain George P. Whittington Jr
    Platoon Leader: 1st Lieutenant Bernard M. Pepper
    Platoon Leader: 2nd Lieutenant Matthew Gregory
    First Sergeant: 1st Sergeant Avery J. Thornhill
C Company: Captain Wilmer K. Wise
    Platoon Leader: 2nd Lieutenant John J. Reville
    Platoon Leader: 2nd Lieutenant Jay H. Mehaffey
    First Sergeant: 1st Sergeant Thomas T. Sloboda
D Company: Captain George R. Miller
    Platoon Leader: 1st Lieutenant Francis W. Dawson
    Platoon Leader: 2nd Lieutenant Philip V. Thomas
    First Sergeant: 1st Sergeant Raymond M. Herlihy
E Company: Captain Edward S. Luther
    Platoon Leader: 1st Lieutenant Rayford E. Dendy
    Platoon Leader: 1st Lieutenant Dee C. Anderson
    First Sergeant: 1st Sergeant Sandy Martin Jr
F Company: Captain William M. Runge
    Platoon Leader: 1st Lieutenant Frank E. Zidjuna
    Platoon Leader: 1st Lieutenant William J. Mulligan
    First Sergeant: 1st Sergeant Howard A. McDonald

RANGER DECORATIONS FOR OPERATION *NEPTUNE*

Presidential Unit Citation
2nd Ranger Battalion
5th Ranger Battalion

Distinguished Service Cross

Col J. Earl Rudder	CO/2nd Rangers
Col Max F. Schneider	CO/5th Rangers
Maj Richard P. Sullivan	S-3/5th Rangers
Capt Otto Masny	F/2nd Rangers
Capt George P. Whittington	B/5th Rangers
Capt Edgar L. Arnold	B/2nd Rangers
Capt Ralph E. Goranson	C/2nd Rangers
1st Lt Francis W. Dawson	D/2nd Rangers

1st Lt. Charles H. Parker	A/5th Rangers
1st Lt. Joseph R. Lacy	Chaplain/5th Rangers
1st Lt William D. Moody*	C/2nd Rangers
2nd Lt George F. Kerchner	D/2nd Rangers
1Sgt Leonard G. Lomell	D/2nd Rangers
SSgt Gail H. Belmont*	A/2nd Rangers
TSgt John W. White	A/2nd Rangers
Sgt Joseph W. Urish*	A/5th Rangers
Sgt Julius W. Belcher	C/2nd Rangers
Sgt William J. Courtney*	D/2nd Rangers
Sgt Theodore A. James*	A/2nd Rangers
Sgt Willie W. Moody	C/5th Rangers
Sgt Denzil O. Johnson*	A/5th Rangers
T-5 Howard D. McKissick*	5th Rangers
T-5 William J. Fox	5th Rangers
Pfc William E. Dreher Jr*	A/2nd Rangers
Pfc Alexander W. Barber	HQ/2nd Rangers
Pfc Otto K. Stephens	C/2nd Rangers

*decorations for actions June 7–10

Appendix B

The Pointe-du-Hoc Guns: Doctrine and Technology

The combat effectiveness of the guns of Pointe-du-Hoc depended upon multiple factors, including their ballistic performance and the precision of their fire controls.

THE POINTE-DU-HOC FIRE-CONTROL POST

The accuracy of the Pointe-du-Hoc battery when engaging naval targets at sea was heavily dependent on its fire-control system. The fire controls for the Pointe-du-Hoc battery were concentrated in the Regelbau H636a command post bunker located at the tip of the promontory. To understand how it functioned, a detailed examination is useful.

The H636a command bunker was multi-layered, with an open observation position on the roof for the battery's optical rangefinder and a heavily protected observation post below and at the front of the structure looking out toward the sea. Inside was the main plotting room, accommodations for the staff, and rooms for the various telephone and radio communications systems. This bunker will be familiar to most tourists who have visited Pointe-du-Hoc because the famous Ranger memorial is located on the roof above the observation chamber.

The main interior of the bunker was entered through an armored door at the rear of the bunker on its south side. The door was defended by two "murder holes": protected machine-gun embrasures. Upon entering the bunker, there was an anti-gas atrium. Most Atlantic Wall bunkers had this feature, based on the lessons of World War I. Although gas was not used in World War II, Atlantic Wall bunkers usually had some form of gas defense in the expectation that gas warfare might eventually take place. These atriums provided an enclosed shelter where troops could scrub themselves clean of chemical agents before entering the bunker interior. The interior itself was sealed from chemical agents. There was a gas-filtration system to scrub chemical agents from air being drawn through the ventilation system into the interior.

Access from the anti-gas atrium into the bunker interior was through two armored doors. The door to the left entered the living quarters for the bunker, which were located on the western side of the bunker. This area had bunks for nine men, stowage lockers, tables, the ventilation system, and a small room containing a furnace to heat the bunker in winter. There was also an emergency exit chamber located in the furnace room that led up to the roof.

Access through the right door in the atrium led to the main interior room, which was designated as the plotting room. This served as the main battery command post, with tables and chairs for the battery officers and their aides. On the far right side of the interior were three small alcoves. The alcove in front was used by the battery officers as temporary sleeping quarters. The officers usually slept in the farmhouses south of the strongpoint, but could use the bunks in the fire-control bunker while on duty or during combat. The other two rooms consisted of the radio room and the main telephone switchboard. Data from the rangefinder on the roof and the observation room in the front was passed to this room, as well as any other information from forward observers of other units.

Field telephones were the primary means of communication between the command post and the individual gun pits.

Communications outside the strongpoint were conducted via a communication trunk line running from Pointe-du-Hoc to a regional communication hub in St Pierre-du-Mont that connected to other German gun batteries and observation posts. The fire-control bunker had radios for communicating with more distant posts. There was also a special team assigned to the bunker to serve as an electronic listening post to monitor British radio networks.

On the exterior of the fire-control bunker were two small additions that deviated from the standard Regelbau H636a plan. A Tobruk was attached on the southeastern corner of the bunker for defense. "Tobruk" was the nickname given to small fortifications with a circular opening in the roof that were used for crew-served weapons. The other addition to the fire-control bunker was a small room attached to the right of the main entrance. This was used as a mess area for the bunker crew, but had no direct access into the bunker except through the nearby main armored door.

AIMING AT LAND TARGETS

German coastal artillery batteries were primarily intended to fight against amphibious landing operations. The role of the German Army coastal artillery batteries was described in a 1943 document on the defense of the Normandy coast:

> The aim of the artillery defense is to smash enemy landing operations before they reach the zone of our own infantry weapons, at the latest in front of the infantry's main combat line (waterline at high tide). The main tasks are: 1.) fighting naval targets, 2.) breaking up landing attempts, 3.) supporting the infantry in defense and fighting against the landed enemy.[1]

Engaging naval targets, particularly moving ships, was the greatest technical challenge for these Army batteries since they were armed with field guns, not dedicated naval guns. These guns generally lacked dedicated armor-piercing ammunition, and so were useless against better-armored warships such as cruisers and battleships.

The challenges of engaging naval targets are described in more detail below.

The standard method for coastal batteries to aim at targets was by means of observation survey posts (*Peilstanden*). Pointe-du-Hoc had two dedicated survey posts located a few miles on either side of the battery. The western survey post was in defense nest WN 76 near Moulin-de-Criqueville, the ruins of an old windmill. The eastern survey post was in Stützpunkt Le Guay. Both of these survey posts were better suited to observing naval targets than the beaches to the east and west due to the local geography.

In the case of the more remote beaches, the artillery regiment of the 352.Infanterie-Division had observation posts overlooking Omaha Beach and the eastern side of the Vire estuary. Correspondingly, the artillery regiment of the 709.Infanterie-Division had observation posts overlooking Utah Beach and the western side of the Vire estuary. The observation posts on the east side of the river Vire reported to central artillery command posts in Isigny for the western divisional sector and in Maison, south of Port-en-Bessin, for the eastern sector. These command posts could forward data from the forward observers to the Pointe-du-Hoc battery, though the process was more time-consuming than from the battery's own survey posts.

To simplify the hand-off of land targets, German coastal artillery relied on the pre-registration of targets. A gun battery would fire one or more registration rounds on a target, recording the elevation and azimuth data. As part of the process, specific sectors of the beaches on either side of Pointe-du-Hoc were given codenames. For example, the beach immediately east of the Vierville draw where the 5th Ranger Battalion landed on D-Day was codenamed Ascherleben.[2] Similarly, areas of likely approach by naval landing forces were calculated in advance as barrage-fire targets (*Sperrfeuer*). This accelerated the fire-control process during combat since forward observers could contact the battery and specify the target by a codename rather than a geographic coordinate. Should the first rounds not hit where intended due to wind or other conditions, corrections could then be given.

This type of pre-registration of targets was suitable for stationary targets, but inefficient for moving targets.

LONG-BASE FIRE-CONTROL SYSTEM

The German Army coastal artillery batteries used a system called the "Long-Base" technique for targeting moving naval targets.[3] This name stemmed from the fact that the two survey posts that provided target data were located a long distance away from the command post, as this permitted more accurate triangulation of the target. The Long-Base system provided the battery with a means to quickly engage naval targets, to follow moving naval targets and progressively alter the direction and range of the guns, and to compensate for the movement of the naval target both laterally and in range. The system relied on basic trigonometry to aim the guns. It was based on a precise survey of the battery command post and associated survey posts in order to accurately calculate ballistic solutions for the guns.

The calculating devices of the Long-Base system should have been located in the plotting room of the H636a command post bunker. However, there is some evidence that this system had not been fitted by D-Day.[4] Due to the uncertainties of whether Pointe-du-Hoc had a Long-Base plotting table, the description below examines a "best case" scenario about how the system would have worked if it was in fact in place on D-Day. This type of system was present at other German coastal gun batteries, notably those on the Cotentin peninsula facing Utah Beach.

Pointe-du-Hoc's two survey posts were connected to the command bunker via field telephones using a special armored cable buried 6½ft underground. Each survey post had a three-man team. The survey post commander was an NCO, equipped with binoculars. An enlisted man served as the observer and was equipped with a plotting device such as the Peilsäule S.3 C.41. This type of device is called a pelorus in English and is more familiar in naval gunnery than army field artillery. It was used primarily to provide a precise bearing from the survey post to the target. It also contained a second telescope that could be used to measure the bearing of the fall-of-shot once the engagement started. A second enlisted man, called the "reader," took notes of the tracking data from the plotting device and was responsible for sending this data back to Pointe-du-Hoc via a field telephone.

At the Pointe-du-Hoc H636a command bunker, there were two additional observation posts. At the front of the bunker was an enclosed observation post with a narrow slit that provided 220-degree coverage toward the sea. This observation post could be used if the battery was under fire, or could be employed for routine observation. It was too small to contain the main measuring instrument of the battery, a stereoscopic rangefinder that was mounted on the roof of the bunker in an enclosed pit. It could use a smaller but less-precise stereoscopic rangefinder from within the observation room, but there is no evidence that one was ever fitted. Unlike Kriegsmarine command posts, the rooftop observation post did not have an overhead concrete cover, so the Pointe-du-Hoc observation team was vulnerable to counter-battery fire.

The observation post on top of the bunker roof had a five-man crew. The battery commander operated the stereoscopic rangefinder. He wore a head-set with an attached throat-microphone for communicating to the plotting room inside the bunker. An NCO stood near the battery commander with binoculars since the stereoscopic rangefinder had a very narrow field of view and so required coarse direction cues. An enlisted man, called the "Fall-of-shot calculator," was equipped with a stopwatch to measure the time from when the guns first fired to when the rounds impacted near the target. Another officer, the Inclination Officer, stood nearby with a measuring device to observe the target. He was supported by an enlisted man with another stopwatch who also passed along the Inclination Officer's data to the plotting room via a field telephone connection.

The plotting room inside the bunker was the brains of the battery, receiving data from the two distant survey posts as well as from the observation post on the bunker roof overhead. There were eleven men in the plotting room itself, plus additional enlisted men in the adjacent communication rooms operating the switchboard for the numerous field telephone communications. The principal figure in the room was the Plotting Officer, usually the battery's executive officer. He stood over a plotting table with a map of the area, fitted with a Long-Base Device.[5] The Long-Base Device was essentially a mechanical calculator built into a plotting device. It can be compared to an elaborate, multi-function slide rule, with the Plotting Officer inputting data from the various observation points that in turn provided direction and elevation data for aiming the guns. Next to him was an NCO called the Plotting Officer's Assistant who also had a stopwatch to monitor the time-of-flight of the gun salvoes. The Plotting Officer's Assistant had a chart that translated the time of projectile flight into range. One enlisted man, designated as the Plotting Room Exchange, stood between the plotting table and the neighboring communication room to coordinate data coming in from the various observation posts. Two other enlisted men moved the indicators on the Long-Base Device, based on data coming from the two remote survey posts. Two other enlisted men read off the bearing and range output data from the Long-Base Device, and this was used by two other enlisted men to calculate the future bearing and range of the target. Finally, two other enlisted men took all of this data, plus meteorological data such as cross-wind speed, to calculate the ballistic corrections. This information was then passed on to the guns by means of the field telephone switchboard inside the bunker to a telephone near the gun.

In the kettle gun pits, each gun chief listened to the information coming from the plotting room over a head-set. Two other gun crewmen were responsible for inputting the ballistic corrections, one operating the elevation wheel of the gun and the other the bearing/azimuth wheel of the gun, based on instructions from the plotting room. These were located on the left side of the gun trunnion along with the gun sight.

Not all Normandy batteries had a plotting room with the Long-Base Device. For example, the two Maisy batteries were both divisional field gun batteries and so were not intended to engage moving naval targets.

ENGAGEMENT OF NAVAL TARGETS: AN EXAMPLE

To get some idea of the complexity of this process, let's listen in on a notional engagement between the battery and an approaching British cruiser.[6]

The battery commander on the observation platform began the sequence by announcing via the telephone, "Enemy cruiser approaching from the left. Lay on – right funnel, left edge. Observe!" This was the command that would prompt the survey posts to begin feeding data to the plotting room, with the left edge of the ship's funnel as the aiming point. The inclination officer then reported, "Bow right. Inclination minus 3. Speed 18 knots." The two remote survey posts have been alerted and began passing on their data: "Black [right survey post] 6380," "Red [left survey post] 0775." The survey posts continued to pass along the data because it changed as the ship moved. So the right survey post reports in a monotonous sequence, "6382; 6384; 6385." As this data is received in the plotting room, the data is inputted into the Long-Base Device. The range-reader follows the calculations of the device and reports to the plotting officer, "Range 12,300." The bearing-reader likewise reports, "Bearing 0370 mils." The plotting officer passes this on to the battery commander and meteorological team, "First bearing 0370, first range 12,300." The meteorological team then calculates for wind-drift and reports, "Meteor for wind bearing 02, range 13,000."

This process is continuous since the ship continues to move, possibly in an evasive fashion. So the range- and bearing-readers continue to report new data based on the output from the Long-Base Device, which is periodically corrected by the plotting officer based on input from the survey posts. Once the battery commander is confident that they have established the basic trajectory data, it is passed to the gun crew from the plotting room.

The firing sequence begins when the battery commander gives the gun crew final ammunition instructions, "Charge – normal. Fuze – instantaneous. Shell – High Explosive. All guns ranging. Fire by order of the plotting officer. From the right – fire!" These instructions told the gun crew the amount of propellant, type of ammunition, and the fuze to use. The first salvo was generally considered a "ranging" salvo since it was presumed it would miss. The various plotting crews began their stopwatches on the sound of the guns firing, and halted them based on reports of impacts. At a range of 15,000 meters, it could take forty to fifty seconds for the rounds to fly out to the target. The process began again with necessary corrections based on the location of the miss, as well as continual reporting on the movement of the target ship. Once the impacts began to straddle the target ship, the battery commander would order, "Five rounds. From the right. Rapid fire!" Corrections would have continued to be put into the Long-Base Device until the target was hit.

DEBATE WITH THE KRIEGSMARINE

The Kriegsmarine felt that the Long-Base system was outdated and poorly suited to engaging moving targets at sea. Allied intelligence did not appreciate the difference between German Army and Navy tactical doctrine for the deployment of coastal batteries. These doctrinal differences help to explain some of the weak points of the Pointe-du-Hoc battery.

Throughout World War I, coastal artillery had been the responsibility of the Kriegsmarine. It was the German Navy that was responsible for protecting the Belgian coast from Allied amphibious operations between 1915 and 1918. In 1940, the German Army began bringing railroad guns and long-range artillery to the Channel coast in anticipation of the Operation *Sealion* invasion of Britain. Eventually, the Army began deploying coastal artillery as an expedient means of defense along the coastline of occupied Europe, contesting the Kriegsmarine's traditional dominance of this mission.

The Kriegsmarine had traditionally viewed coastal batteries as being an extension of the fleet, and so deployed the batteries along the edge of the coast where they could most easily take part in naval engagements. One of the Allies' main advantages during amphibious landings in World War II was heavy naval gunfire. This was very evident during the fighting in the Mediterranean from 1942–44. As a result, the Kriegsmarine became determined to deploy enough coastal artillery to force the Allied warships away from the coast and thereby undercut this advantage.

Kriegsmarine coastal batteries were patterned on warship organization. The four to six guns in a battery were deployed with a direct line of sight to the sea. However, the guns were not independently aimed at targets, but were directed by an elaborate fire-control bunker which possessed optical rangefinders and plotting systems similar to those on warships to permit engagements against moving targets. The Army derided these batteries as "battleships of the dunes" and argued that their placement so close to the shore made them immediately visible to enemy warships, and therefore vulnerable to naval gunfire. In addition, the proximity to the shore made the batteries especially vulnerable to raiding parties or to infantry attack in the event of an amphibious assault.

The Kriegsmarine thought that the Army coastal artillery batteries were ineffective in engaging targets at sea. The Long-Base system relied on continual data collection and manual data inputs from multiple sources. Errors in this chain could badly affect accuracy. The system was also cumbersome and slow. On top of this, the Army's field guns did not have the precision aiming features of naval guns.

Hitting moving targets at sea was the Kriegsmarine's specialty. Indeed, warship fire controls face an additional hurdle because the ship itself is moving. So ship fire controls have to predict not only the movement of the target ship, but the movement of their own ship during the engagement. As a result, naval director systems were a level of magnitude more sophisticated than the Army system and relied on a much higher level of automation. The naval director received data automatically from the ship's sensors, such as the stereoscopic rangefinder and radar. The director automatically calculated the fire solution. In older ships, this could be passed along via a telephone. In newer designs, the data was fed to a display located at the guns, and the crews matched the gun elevation and azimuth to the data on the display. In the most sophisticated naval systems, the director could control the gun automatically using a Selsyn network of electric relays and servos.

The Kriegsmarine planned to use these types of directors in their coastal artillery emplacements, such as the Longues-sur-Mer battery east of Omaha Beach.[7] The Kriegsmarine command post bunkers were laid out like the bridge of a destroyer, with the same type of devices but within a concrete structure. These bunkers were fitted with sophisticated naval directors such as the Zielsäule C.38. The data was fed to the guns via a buried armored cable and appeared on an electro-mechanical display located on the gun.

The German Army was aware of the limitations of the Long-Base system. Fire-control systems similar to the Kriegsmarine directors were used by Luftwaffe and Army Flak units. These Flak directors automatically fed data to the Flak guns. There were a variety of barriers to adapting these systems to Army coastal artillery. The basic problem was cost and availability: these electro-mechanical directors were precision instruments and available in limited supply. The Luftwaffe Flak units involved in the defense of the Reich from Allied heavy bomber attack had priority for this production.

In addition, the Army coastal batteries could not take full advantage of this technology since their guns in most cases were simple field guns that were not designed to track and engage moving targets. The worst were the batteries that were using the standard field carriage, such as the Pointe-du-Hoc 155mm GPF guns. Their effectiveness in engaging naval targets was especially dubious when they were first deployed in 1942 in open field entrenchments. The field carriage offered a traverse of 60 degrees: 30 degrees to either side. The traverse was entirely manual and mechanical, and was neither fast nor smooth. In the event that the target moved sufficiently fast, the crew would have to move the entire 9-ton gun by digging out the entrenching spades at the rear of the trail and then manhandling the gun to a new position. This took precious time and was completely impractical.

The expedient solution was the use of kettle-gun pits, as employed at Pointe-du-Hoc in 1943 and 1944. The main advantage of this mounting was that the gun was attached to a *Drehsockel* (swivel socket) platform. As in the case of the basic gun, the crew could still take advantage of the 60 degrees of traverse of the gun trunnion on the carriage. However, in the case of a fast-moving, crossing target that exceeded this traverse, the gun could be moved more quickly than an entrenched gun. The gun trails fitted into a set of grooves along the perimeter of the kettle position, so the bulky entrenching spades were not needed. In combination with the swivel socket platform, the crew could much more quickly move the entire gun.

The third and final evolution to adapt field guns to coastal artillery missions was the *Drehbettung* (swivel mounting). The type planned for the 155mm guns such as those at Pointe-du-Hoc was the *schwere Drehbettung 32. To* (32-ton heavy swivel mounting). When using this system, the gun and trunnion were removed from a wheeled carriage and attached directly to a swivel mounting. This mounting was somewhat similar to the earlier swivel socket, but offered a much smoother mechanical traverse system. In principle, it offered full 360-degree traverse, though in reality, its traverse was usually less since this system was nearly always used inside fully enclosed gun casemates. Another advantage of this system was that it could employ an automated data feed from the command post bunker to an electro-mechanical display on the gun, which increased the speed and accuracy of the fire-control process.

The Pointe-du-Hoc battery was scheduled to receive this third-generation system as part of the enhanced fortification program in April 1944 with the H694 gun casemate bunkers. However, the *schwere Drehbettung 32. To* never arrived at Pointe-du-Hoc and the guns were not mounted in the unfinished casemates. Furthermore, once the guns were moved from their kettle pits to the tree-lined road south of the strongpoint, this severed the connections with the Long-Base fire-control system in the bunker. There is little evidence that the battery ever managed to reconnect the guns and the fire-control system after the guns were moved.

In conclusion, it is worth noting that the combat-effectiveness of the Pointe-du-Hoc battery was significantly diminished by its outdated mounting in the open kettle pits and its probable lack of a

Long-Base fire-control system. Had the battery been fully upgraded as planned with the new enclosed casemates, enhanced swivel mounting, and Long-Base fire-control, it would have had improved combat capabilities against naval targets. However, the Allied air bombardment campaign halted work on the improvements.

Instead, the guns were removed to field positions away from the strongpoint. Only three of the original six guns were functional, and their crude field positions made them unsuitable for engaging naval targets. While they could have engaged land targets such as Utah Beach or Omaha Beach, their rate of fire would have been poor due to a lack of available ammunition, and their targeting would have been poor due to their limited communication with the battery fire-control bunker. In the event, the battery was completely ineffective on D-Day due to the abandonment of the guns by their drunken crews.

Appendix C

Naval Fire Support for the Rangers

The *Neptune* plans devoted considerable attention to providing naval fire support for the amphibious operation. Naval fire support was essential to the Pointe-du-Hoc mission, not only for the preliminary bombardment, but also for subsequent fire support after the initial landings.

The traditional US Navy organization consisted of fleets, flotillas, squadrons, and divisions. For Operation *Neptune*, they were given temporary task designations as Task Forces, Task Groups, and Task Units. These were sometimes used in conjunction with alternative designations, so it is worthwhile to briefly survey the order of battle of the naval forces off Omaha Beach. It should be noted that the naval operation was unified and multinational, with British landing craft flotillas serving under US commands for Operation *Neptune*, and likewise, US navy flotillas serving under British command.

The US amphibious force for Operation *Neptune* was Task Force 122, commanded by Rear Admiral Alan G. Kirk, with overall responsibility for Operation *Neptune* off Utah and Omaha Beaches.[1] The Omaha sector was the responsibility of Task Force 124, commanded by Rear Adm J. L. Hall, also known as Assault Force O ("O" for Omaha). Its flagship was USS *Ancon* (ACG-4). Each Task Group of Assault Force O received a designation, so for example the heavy naval bombardment element was Task Group 124.9, also called Bombarding Force C, led by Rear Adm

Carleton F. Bryant.* Task Group 124.7, the Western Assault Convoy Escort Group under Capt Harry Sanders, became the Destroyer Gunfire Support Group once its initial tasks were completed on D-Day morning.†

The US Navy elements supporting the neighboring Utah landings were Assault Force U/Task Force 125 under Rear Adm Don P. Moon, with fire support coming from Task Group 125.8 under Rear Adm Morton L. Deyo.

The *Neptune* plan included an extensive program of preliminary bombardment of the coastal batteries prior to H-Hour to minimize the threat they posed to the landing force. Each major target received a "Target Number," so for example, Pointe-du-Hoc was Target 1 (T1) and Maisy I was Target 5. The target lists were keyed to Lambert Grid references, based on the standard British Army GSGS (General Staff Geographical Section) 1:25,000 maps. These were the standard references for fire support during Operation *Neptune*, and were used both by the Navy ships providing fire support as well as by fire-control parties and Army units requesting fire support. The warships assigned to Bombarding Force C were assigned to attack their targets prior to H-Hour with a specified number of rounds of ammunition.

OMAHA BEACH PRE-LANDING NAVAL BOMBARDMENT[2]

Warship	Target designation	Target (German designation)	Assigned Ammunition
USS *Texas*	T1, T85	Pointe-du-Hoc	250 × 14"
USS *Texas*	T88, T89	WN 76, WN 77	12 × 14" + 100 × 5"
HMS *Glasgow*	T59, T61	WN 66	400 × 6"
USS *Satterlee*	T75, T76	WN 74	300 × 5"
USS *McCook*	T71	WN 71	300 × 5"
USS *Carmick*	T66, T67, T68	WN 70	250 × 5"

---

*Bryant was the commander of Battleship Division 5, US Atlantic Fleet.
† Sanders was the commander of US Navy Destroyer Squadron 18 that provided the bulk of the destroyers used in this group.

HMS *Talybont*	T77, T76, T82, T83	Stp Le Guay	600 × 4"
USS *Arkansas*	T60, T63, T65	WN 66, WN 68	385 × 12"
USS *Arkansas*	T166	Trévières	50 × 12"
USS *Arkansas*	T43	WN 62	250 × 5"
Montcalm	T22–T29	WN 59, Port-en-Bessin	300 × 6"
LCG(L) 424	64829187	WN 73	120 × 4¾"
LCG(L) 426	64589190	WN 73	120 × 4¾"
LCG(L) 449	64479200	WN 73	120 × 4¾"
LCG(L) 487	T43	WN 62	120 × 4¾"
LCG(L) 811	T54	WN 65	120 × 4¾"
LCT(R) 366	T40	WN 60	5" rockets
LCT(R) 450	T43	WN 62	5" rockets
LCT(R) 482	T47	WN 62	5" rockets
LCT(R) 447	T53	WN 65	5" rockets
LCT(R) 473	T59	WN 66	5" rockets
LCT(R) 483	T65	WN 70	5" rockets
LCT(R) 423	T66–67	WN 70	5" rockets
LCT(R) 464	T72	Vierville-sur-Mer	5" rockets
LCT(R) 452	T74–75	WN 74	5" rockets

Once the pre-bombardment phase was completed, Bombarding Force C was assigned to provide continuing fire support during the landing phase. To prevent intermixing of the warships and landing craft, there were segregated corridors in the bay of the Seine off Omaha Beach. These included Fire Support Area 3 immediately north of Pointe-et-Raz-de-la-Percée and Fire Support Area 4 immediately north of Port-en-Bessin to the east of Omaha Beach. The Boat Lane for the landing craft was the corridor in between the two Fire Support Areas. Pointe-du-Hoc was within Fire Support Area 3, as was the western side of Omaha Beach, such as the Vierville draw where the 5th Ranger Battalion landed.

Much of the fire support in the early hours of D-Day was provided by destroyers as they could maneuver closer to shore than the battleships and cruisers. A total of eleven destroyers were assigned to the Destroyer Gunfire Support Group of Bombarding Group C at Omaha Beach, as detailed below.

DESTROYER GUNFIRE SUPPORT GROUP, OMAHA SECTOR

Fire Support Area #3	Fire Support Area #4
USS Satterlee	HMS Tanatside
HMS Talybont	USS Emmons
USS Thompson	USS Baldwin
USS McCook	USS Harding
USS Carmick	USS Doyle
	HMS Melbreak

Although some larger US warships such as battleships and cruisers had OS2U Kingfisher and SOC Seagull catapult floatplanes that could be used for air spotting of targets, the *Neptune* plan decided against using them due to their vulnerability to Luftwaffe fighters. This was a lesson from the Operation *Husky* landings on Sicily in July 1943. There was also concern over their vulnerability to Flak. As an alternative, Britain provided 104 land-based fighters for spotting, mainly Spitfires.[3] In the case of the US warships assigned to Omaha Beach, the pilots from various spotter aircraft of the battleships and cruisers were consolidated under VCS-7 and retrained on the Spitfire Mk Vb for D-Day.[4]

The use of single-seat fighters based in England was an effective but inefficient method of targeting, as the commander of Task Group 125.8 later wrote:

The greatest handicap was the short range of the Spitfires. Basing at Lee-on-the-Solent, roughly 100 miles from the Normandy coast, each flight would be able to remain with us a bare 45 minutes in good weather before returning to base for fuel. They would, in fact, be at their maximum operating limit. They worked in pairs, each spotting plane having its 'weaves' to watch for enemy planes. There would be another pair en-route to and from base and still two more fueling at base. That made a total of six planes for each spotting mission; a costly business and a makeshift. But lacking longer-range planes or aircraft carriers, it had to do.[5]

After the preliminary bombardment concluded at H-Hour (0630hrs), the warships could engage targets of opportunity until Shore Fire Control Parties (SFCP) reached shore around H+30 minutes.

SHORE FIRE CONTROL PARTIES

There were 44 SFCPs assigned to Army units for *Neptune*, plus nine Parachute Naval Gunfire Support teams for the 101st Airborne Division.[6] Army units often called these groups a "FOO Party," for Forward Observer Officers. The SFCP were deployed on a scale of one in each of the infantry battalions in the infantry regiments of the three assaulting divisions (1st, 4th, and 29th). Additional parties were assigned to headquarters and field artillery units of the divisions. SFCP-1 was assigned to the 2nd Rangers at Pointe-du-Hoc, SFCP-2 to the 5th Rangers, and SFCP-3 to the 1/116th Infantry.

Each SFCP consisted of one Army and one Navy officer along with twelve enlisted men. It comprised two sections, an Army forward observer section led by an Army officer and a naval liaison section led by an NGLO (naval gunnery liaison officer).

On paper, each SFCP received two of the new SCR-609 FM radios.[7] This was the standard US Army field artillery radio, weighing 28lb and operating in the FM bands. The ships were fitted with the corresponding SCR-608. Many units, including the Rangers' SCFP-1, also had the older SCR-284 AM radio. The reason for the two types of radios was that some ships did not have the SCR-608 FM radio, but could communicate with the SCR-284 on the AM bands. The SCR-284 was large and heavy, weighing over 100lb when fully assembled. Its combat debut was during the 1942 Operation *Torch* landings, and it became the standard radio for communicating between Army amphibious landing units and supporting US Navy warships. It was disassembled for transport, with the main component, the 45lb BC-654 transmitter, roughly the weight, size, and shape of a modern window air-conditioning unit. These radios were supposed to be mounted on jeeps once the vehicles arrived, but in the meantime, they were broken down into multiple loads and laboriously carried ashore.

SFCP-1 with Ranger Force A at Pointe-du-Hoc was led by a US Army officer, Capt Jonathan H. Harwood of the 293rd Signal Company, while the NGLO was Lt (jg) Kenneth S. Norton from the US Navy. It is worth noting that SFCP-1 with the Rangers was the only Shore Fire Control Party on Omaha Beach that established working communications with their assigned warship early on D-Day morning. As was noted earlier in this book,[8] this was due to the fact that they had brought along a signal lamp to supplement their radios. Nearly all of the other SFCPs had problems with waterlogged, damaged, or lost radios. Two other warships, USS *Carmick* and USS *Doyle*, established radio links with their SFCP after H+100.[9] HMS *Glasgow* attempted to connect with the 5th Ranger team, SFCP-2, around 0830hrs on D-Day, but without success. As a result, the Rangers at Pointe-du-Hoc enjoyed the most effective naval fire support of any Army unit in the Omaha sector on D-Day. Some ships finally established links with their SFCP late on D-Day.

Besides the SFCP, the air spotting aircraft remained on patrol during D-Day to provide targets for the warships. These were used primarily to find targets of opportunity, and especially to hunt out German field artillery batteries. It was quickly realized that Allied intelligence had failed to identify the various batteries of Artillery-Regiment.352 that were constantly bombarding Omaha Beach. This became a major focus of the air spotters over Omaha Beach on D-Day.

The accompanying chart below details the fire support provided to the Provisional Ranger Group for Operation *Neptune*.[10] It primarily focuses on targets assigned by SFCP-1 with Ranger Force A and the subsequent missions once the Provisional Ranger Group became consolidated on June 8. It does not cover fire support for Ranger Forces B and C on D-Day, since neither group received any direct fire support due to communication problems with SFCP-2 and SFCP-3. The ships in these sectors engaged targets of opportunity during D-Day, as has been detailed in previous chapters, sometimes experiencing episodes of "blue-on-blue" fratricide, as was the case with Ranger Force B and USS *McCook*.[11]

As can be seen, the most important connection was between Ranger Force A and USS *Satterlee* on D-Day. The exceptional performance on D-Day was based on joint pre-invasion exercises, as related in the *Satterlee's* war diary:

Our Shore Fire Control Party came aboard before the Fabius exercise. We worked with them in a later shore bombardment exercise. We had several communication drills. They came aboard again in Portland just before D-Day. There was a complete and intimate understanding between the ship and the Ranger Shore Fire Control Party. As a result, during the close support firing, communications were uniformly excellent. It was as if the Shore Fire Control Party was in our CIC [Combat Information Center]. Incidentally, these fine young men were a great source of inspiration to the *Satterlee*. Everyone who had contact with them was greatly impressed by their enthusiasm, determination, and courage. They knew they had a tough assignment and were ready for it. And they had the ship ready to back them. To this one factor can be attributed the success of the mission. There could be no better method of authentication than to send "Hello Rocky!" and then hear the familiar voice come back "Hello Joe, this is Rocky." This should provide a valuable lesson for future operations.[12]

The *Satterlee* was relieved by USS *Thompson* (DD627) at 1910hrs on D-Day after firing 919 rounds of 5in. AA Common,* 246

* The US Navy definition states: "These projectiles differ from Armor-Piercing and Special Common projectiles in that they have no cap or hood; the windshield threads directly on to the body. Also, the explosive cavity is slightly larger."

rounds of 5in. Common, 144 rounds of 40mm, and 215 rounds of 20mm in support of the Rangers at Pointe-du-Hoc. The Satterlee was obliged to withdraw and head back to Portland in the early morning hours of D+1 since it was US Navy practice to do so after 70 percent of ammunition had been expended.

It will be noticed that on D+1 and D+2, some of the naval fire support for the Provisional Ranger Group west of Pointe-du-Hoc near Grandcamp came from warships of Bombarding Force A/ Assault Group U. This was because the objectives of the 116th RCT such as Maisy and Isigny were outside Omaha Beach's Fire Support Area 3 and inside Utah Beach's Fire Support Area 4. During this fighting on D+1 and D+2, SFCP-1 was supplemented by SFCP-2 from the 5th Rangers and SFCP-3 from the 1/116th RCT. Where detailed in the ship logs, the SFCP or air spotting used for targeting are identified in the chart below.

June 6, D-Day	Time	Grid	Target notes
USS *Texas*	0550–0624	586939	Pointe-du-Hoc, 255 × 14" (155 AP, 100 HC), air spot
HMS *Talybont*	0550–0615	586939	Pointe-du-Hoc, direct fire
USS *Texas*	0626–0630	575939	Strongpoint (WN 76), 11 × 14" AP, air spot
HMS *Talybont*	0640–0700		Cliffs east of Pointe-du-Hoc, direct fire
USS *Satterlee*	0731–0744	576939	T88 (WN 76), SFCP-1, "successful"
USS *Texas*	0742–0747	586932	fortified positions of Pointe-du-Hoc, 17 × 14" HC, air spot
USS *Satterlee*	0745–0755	574939	T89 (WN 79), SFCP-1
"	0758–0803	602938	T83, Chateau Le Févre, SFCP-1
"	0814–0836	586931	T85, Au Guay, SFCP-1
"	0914–0916	558934	T86, Au Guay, SFCP-1
"	0926–0932	581925	Infantry E. of PdH, SFCP-1

"	0941–1004	586931	T85, Au Guay, SFCP-1, "successful"
"	1004–1012	596936	German MGs, SFCP-1, "successful"
"	1016–1025	586931	T85, Au Guay, SFCP-1, "target destroyed"
"	1029–1040	599929	Ardenne, bivouac area, SFCP-1
"	1042–1059	585931	Au Guay, observation post, SFCP-1, "target destroyed"
"	1157–1203	550932	Grandcamp, German infantry, SFCP-1
"	1228–1240	601915	Road junction nr Beaumont, SFCP-1
"	1243–1247	581925	Infantry E of PdH, SFCP-1, "successful"
"	1319–1324	552931	S of Grandcamp, SFCP-1
"	1351–1405	564936	SE of Grandcamp, German MGs, SFCP-1, "successful"
"	1424–1516	581935	Pillbox, fire adjustments in area by SFCP-1
"	1516–1526	579936	Pillbox near western Flak bunker, SFCP-1
USS *Barton*	1522–1625	599939	MG position E of PdH, 130 × 5"
USS *Thompson*	1536–1632	579937	Pillboxes near western Flak bunker, fire adjusted by SFCP-1
USS *Barton*	1645–1700		Road E of Grandcamp, 43 × 5"
USS *Thompson*	1757–1847	574939	Area near WN 76, SFCP-1
USS *Barton*	1902–1925	556912–24	German troops SE of Grandcamp, 44 × 5"
USS *Thompson*	1954–1956	578928	Chateau de M le Baron, 8 × 5", "target destroyed"

	Time	Grid	Target notes
"	2015–2029		Fortified house E of Chateau de M le Baron, 24 × 5", "fire ineffective"
"	2030–2033	593928	Pillbox nr St Pierre-du-Mont, 12 × 5", "fire effective"
"	2043–2054	583932	Railroad, 21 × 5", "fire effective"
"	2222–2225	565936–558933	T91, T93, E of Grandcamp, 26 × 5" "fire effective"
June 7, D+1	*Time*	*Grid*	*Target notes*
USS *Thompson*	0440–0450	574932-35	Road, fields W of PdH, 66 × 5"n
"	0457–0505	590920-26	Fields S of Au Guay, 84 × 5"
"	0508–0510	581932	6 Flak guns near Chateau de M le Baron, 40 × 5"
"	0525–0547	565935	Flak battery E of Grandcamp, 30 × 5", "target destroyed"
"	0600–0603	575938	Flak battery S of WN 76, 20 × 5", "fire effective"
USS *Harding*	0641	587938	MG W of Pointe-du-Hoc, 35 × 5", SFCP, "successful"
USS *Barton*	0745–0900		Targets from SFCP-1, 185 × 5"
USS *McCook*	0724–0738	624935	T76, Pillbox, radar in Stp Guay, mortars
USS *Harding*	0746	547931	Ranger SFCP request, 16 × 5"
"	0806–0821	586931	T85, Ranger SFCP, 28 × 5"
USS *Glennon*	0900	533918	T5, SFCP-34, target "demolished"
USS *Harding*	0949	594929	Fortified house near T84, 16 × 5", "mission successful"

	Time	Grid	Target notes
"	1011		Neutralization fire S of Pointe-du-Hoc, 28 × 5", "successful"
"	1131–1132		40mm fire S of Pointe-du-Hoc, SFCP
"	1249–1310	565936	T91, 100 × 5", SFCP, "target destroyed"
"	1420	573933	Road behind T90, 44 × 5", SFCP, "successful"
USS *O'Brien*	1013–1014	585964	Chateau de M le Baron, one salvo (6 × 5"), SFCP
"	2026–2033	586931	Chateau de M le Baron, 54 × 5", SFCP, "target destroyed"
"	2035–2048	586931	German roadblock, 86 × 5", SFCP, "mission successful"
"	2128–2133	579937	MG nest on cliff, 60 × 5", SFCP, "mission successful – nice job"
HMS *Glasgow*	1303–1327	533918-528916	T5, T16 at Maisy, 63 × 7½", air spot, "several direct hits"
USS *Harding*	2200	573933-36	Targets near T90/T91, 48 × 5", SFCP, "successful"
HMS *Glasgow*	1527–1600	533918-528916	Targets T5 and T16 Maisy batteries, 48 × 7½", air spot, "fire effective"
"	2110	578918	Gun battery near Cricqueville, 18 × 7½", air spot, "results not known"
USS *McCook*	2148–2158		Targets from SFCP (Criqueville, Maisy)
June 8, D+2	*Time*	*Grid*	*Target notes*
USS *Ellyson*	0929–0952	579938	German light gun, 100 × 5", "mission successful"
"	0959–1022		German guns in Grandcamp firing to sea; 124 × 5"

USS *Texas*	0955–1000	579938	German tanks firing at Rangers E of Grandcamp, 9 × 14" HC, SFCP
USS *Harding*	1432		Grandcamp waterfront, 160 × 5", SFCP-3
"	1440	537925	Maisy, 73 × 5", SFCP-3
HMS *Glasgow*	1455	555932	Troops in Grandcamp, 68 × 7½", SFCP-2
	1600	553930	Water tower OP point in Grandcamp, 45 × 7½", direct spotting
USS *Harding*	1815–1900	537925	Intermittent fire on Maisy, SFCP-3, "highly effective"
June 9, D+3	*Time*	*Grid*	*Target notes*
HMS *Bellona*	0100	528916	T16 Maisy, 26 × 5¼", SFCP-3
HMS *Bellona*	0130		Isigny, 20 × 5¼", SFCP-3

Appendix D

The Guns of Maisy

The final objective of the 5th Rangers was the elimination of the two fortified gun batteries near Maisy. This appendix is intended to provide a thumbnail sketch of their creation and their role in the D-Day operations. The story of these guns is both obscure and controversial. The controversy has been stirred up by British military historian Gary Sterne, who purchased the Maisy-Les Perruques site and opened it as a museum in June 2006. Over the past decade, he has promoted the museum with provocative claims.

Both batteries were located in farm fields immediately south of the small town of Maisy.* The battery at Maisy-Martinière was originally designated as Batterie-Brasilia, while the neighboring battery at Maisy-Les Perruques was originally designated as Stellung-Batterie-Küste.315. In the autumn of 1943, these two batteries were absorbed into the divisional artillery of the 716. Infanterie-Division, with Batterie-Brasilia becoming the 8.Batterie, Artillerie-Regiment.1716, and St.B.K.315 becoming the 9.Batterie. The battery fortified areas were designated as WN 83 for Maisy-Les Perruques and WN 84 for Maisy-Martinière. Allied intelligence

---

* The towns of Grandcamp-les-Bains and Maisy were merged in the 1970s into what is now Grandcamp-Maisy.

referred to WN 84/Maisy-Martinière as Maisy I and WN 83/Maisy-Les Perruques as Maisy II.

In 1943, Batterie-Brasilia was armed with three 75mm FK 16 (n.A.) guns, a standard German divisional field gun from World War I.[1] In the spring of 1944, after being attached to the 716.Infanterie-Division as the 8.Batterie, this unit was re-equipped with six of the more powerful Czechoslovak 100mm lFH 14/19 (t) guns. This type was already in service with eight other batteries of Artillerie-Regiment.1716, making it the most common field howitzer in the 716.Infanterie-Division on D-Day.

This Czech light field howitzer had been manufactured by the Škoda arsenal in Plzeň for the Austro-Hungarian Army in World War I, and modernized by the Czechoslovak Army in 1919 as the 100mm Houfnice vz. 14/19. Additional guns of this type were captured from the Polish and Yugoslav armies between 1939 and 1941. There were 273 of these guns in Wehrmacht service in 1944, with 233 of them in the Atlantic Wall defenses of Heeresgruppe B, making it one of the most common types in this category.[2] Ammunition for the type was ample, with 4.4 units of fire available.[*] Although there have been claims that these weapons were re-bored to fire the 105mm ammunition of the standard German 105mm lFH.18 gun, there is no evidence of this in German records. The whole point of using war-booty artillery and ammunition was to expend the large ammunition stockpiles captured from 1938–41. The 7.Armee in Normandy had a stockpile of 1.65 million rounds for the 100mm lFH 14/19(t).[3]

The 9.Batterie was armed with four war-booty French Schneider 155mm howitzers. This was the standard World War I French divisional howitzer, known at the time as the Canon de 155C mle 1917 Schneider.[†] These were designated by the Wehrmacht as

---

[*] Ammunition units of fire (Mun.Ausstattung) was a standardized figure for the amount of ammunition needed for three average days of fighting. A daily unit of fire (1.Munitions Ausstattung) for a single light field howitzer was 225 rounds, and the Ausstattung for a battery (three days of combat) was 2,700 rounds.

[†] The "C" indicated "Court" (short), an alternative method of distinguishing a howitzer from a gun.

15.5cm s.FH.414(f). There was also a 7.65cm FK 17(t) for firing illumination rounds. The Schneider 155mm was the single most common medium field howitzer in the Atlantic Wall arsenal, with 271 in service in 1944 and 3.8 units of fire per gun.[4]

The gun positions at the two Maisy batteries were originally simple concrete platforms with a central metal pivot for a traversable Leichte Drehbettung (Light swivel mounting) attached to the gun carriage. The Maisy platforms were simpler than the kettle positions used at Pointe-du-Hoc, lacking the walls of the kettle pan.

As part of the autumn 1943 Schartenstand Programm, the 8.Batterie was improved with enclosed casemates. Construction of four Regelbau 612 gun casemates began in 1944, of which two were ready on D-Day.[*] During the construction program in March 1944, the guns were moved out of WN 84 to the Fouché farm to the southeast.[†]

As part of the upgrade effort, the crews were provided with Regelbau 622 shelters. In order to provide better observation of targets on the Vire estuary, the 8.Batterie in WN 84 had a wooden observation tower erected within the battery site. Additional site improvements included Tobruks and other reinforced positions.

There have been suggestions that the 9.Batterie/Maisy I was to eventually be enclosed in Regelbau 669 casemates, but this had not started at the time of D-Day. However, the battery position was improved in 1943/44 with two Regelbau 622 personnel bunkers, a Regelbau 502 personnel bunker, and a heavily reinforced Vf.7b ammunition bunker. Site defense included Tobruk machine-gun positions.

As part of Stützpunkt Vire (Vire Strongpoint), the Maisy batteries were primarily oriented to defend westward toward the Vire estuary and Utah Beach. The Beobachtungsraum (control zone) for 8.Batterie extended from the right at WN 81 in Grandcamp to the left at WN 93 near St Clement. The 9.Batterie covered from

---

[*] These were designated as Bauwerk 731–734.
[†] This farm is variously identified as Fouché or Foucher, which sound very similar in French.

WN 77, immediately west of Pointe-du-Hoc, to the divisional border near WN 106 on the other side of the river Vire, overlapping the coverage of 8.Batterie due to the greater range of their 155mm howitzers.[5] The 8.Batterie had two forward observation posts on the coast, on the left in WN 90 Gefosse-Fontenay-La Dune and on the right in WN 88 Gefosse-Fontenay-La Dune.[6] The forward observation post in WN 88 was shared with 9.Batterie. Besides the shared post in WN 88, the 9.Batterie had a second forward observation post in WN 82 Maisy-le-Casino. These forward observation posts were hard-wired to the batteries using protected cable, buried 2 meters underground. In the D-Day context, the Maisy batteries were primarily intended to fire at targets in the vicinity of Utah Beach, not Omaha Beach.

Unlike Pointe-du-Hoc, neither Maisy battery had a fire-control bunker with plotting room because neither battery was intended for engaging naval targets. Targeting was done in the traditional field artillery manner. Prior to D-Day, selected targets located in the batteries' control zones were pre-registered and given codenames. These pre-registered targets were located along the eastern coast of the Vire estuary. When fire was required, the forward observers would use the codewords for the various target areas. The batteries would aim their guns based on the pre-registration data and the forward observers would then provide corrections based on the initial fall of shot.

Although claims have been made that 9.Batterie could bombard Omaha Beach, the 155mm howitzer could actually barely reach the western side of the Vierville draw. German artillery maps, such as the fire plan of the 716.Infanterie-Division, show the 155mm howitzers reaching 12,000 meters to the western fringe of Dog Green Beach in the Omaha sector.[7] In contrast, the 352.Infanterie-Division had batteries of two of its artillery battalions within range of Omaha Beach on D-Day.[8] Three 105mm lFH 18/40 howitzer batteries of I./AR.352 had their forward observers immediately on Omaha Beach in WN 59, WN 62, and WN 73. Additional AR.352 batteries were also within range of Omaha Beach, including some of those from IV./AR.352 with the 150mm sFH 18.

Both Maisy complexes were well protected from infantry attack with the MF.95 minefield. This was a complex patchwork of smaller minefields, mainly oriented northwest toward the coast which was the anticipated avenue of any attack. The minefields were primarily anti-personnel mines.

In addition to the field artillery batteries in this sector, the Luftwaffe's 3.Flak Korps deployed Oberst Werner von Kistowski's Flak-Regiment.32 to the Grandcamp–Maisy area between June 3 and June 5, 1944.[9] The gem.Flak-Abt. (mot).497 defended the Isigny–Grandcamp sector.* The battalion had five batteries, three heavy Flak batteries each with four 88mm guns, a medium battery with nine 37mm guns, and a light battery with twelve 20mm guns. The three 88mm Flak batteries were along the coast, with a battery east and west of Grandcamp and one north of Gefosse. The 20mm battery was near Fontenay and the 37mm battery appears to have been on the Isigny–Vierville road near La Cambe.[10] On D-Day, Kistowski's Flak regiment claimed two B-26 Marauder bombers, two P-38 Lightnings, two P-47 Thunderbolts, and a single P-51 Mustang shot down. Late on D-Day, he was ordered to move his regiment away from the coast, but was unable to do so since his prime movers were still in St Germain. In the days afterwards, his 88mm Flak gun batteries were subordinated to the 352.Infanterie-Division and may have been used to attack ground targets such as Pointe-du-Hoc. However, records for operations after D-Day are lacking.

ALLIED AIR ATTACKS ON MAISY

The two Maisy batteries were not subjected to any major air attacks in April 1944 at the start of the *Neptune* bombing campaign.[11] Neither battery was included in the *Neptune* German Coastal Batteries

---

*The designation gem.Flak-Abt. (mot) indicates a mixed, motorized Flak battalion. The other two battalions in the regiment were the gem.Flak-Abt. (mot).226 and the le.Flak-Abt. (mot).90 light Flak battalion. Flak-Regiment.32 was renamed Flak-Sturm-Regiment.1 in mid-June 1944, and is sometimes referred to by that name in D-Day reports.

scheme of April 14, presumably because they were considered divisional artillery, not oriented toward the naval mission.[12] Once the Germans began to build casemates for the guns, both Maisy batteries were added to subsequent bombardment plans, including the ultimate May 27, 1944, plan.[13]

The first significant raid was made on the afternoon of May 23 when IX Bomber Command dispatched 58 B-26 Marauders to bomb coastal batteries at Étretat/Sainte-Marie-Au-Bosc, Maisy I, and Mont Fleury. The attack on Maisy I was conducted using blind-bombing tactics and little or no damage was inflicted. These missions were carried out to give the crews experience in new blind-bombing tactics in the event of cloud cover on D-Day, and the training function was viewed as more important than the actual results.[14] A reconnaissance mission on May 24 concluded that at Maisy I, "No damage was caused to the emplacements, all four of which are occupied. The road in front of the battery is cratered and one bomb hit in the wire perimeter."[15] The assessment of the damage to Maisy II concluded, "Recent raids on this battery were without effect on the four gun casemates u/c [under construction]. Some damage may have been caused to the light anti-aircraft guns in the vicinity, and at least 175 mines have been detonated between the two bolts of perimeter wire at the rear of the battery. At least three guns of this battery are still in their temporary position at 531194."

The May 29 assessment of coastal batteries indicated that 8.Batterie had not suffered any damage to the new casemates or the guns; the guns at this point were still away from WN 84 to the southwest. Maisy I had not been damaged and all emplacements were occupied.[16]

A major raid by RAF Bomber Command was planned for the night of May 31/June 1. However, the mission was aborted due to dense cloud cover over the target area. The first major Bomber Command raid of Operation *Flashlamp* was staged against Maisy on the night of June 4/5. Due to Eisenhower's rule that multiple diversionary targets had to be attacked for every *Neptune* target, only fifty-two Lancasters of 5 Group took part in the mission of the 118 heavy bomber sorties.[17] The other groups bombed gun batteries in the Pas-de-Calais area. Maisy was covered with clouds again, so the target was marked by Mosquito Pathfinders of the No 8 Pathfinder Group using the Oboe navigation system. The bomber crews could see nothing below the clouds, only the eerie glow of the red and green Target Indicator flares descending through the thick cloud cover.

On D-Day eve, RAF Bomber Command launched its largest massed raid on German coastal batteries. The missions started at 2330hrs on June 6 and lasted through to 0515hrs on June 6. A total of 5,268 tons of bombs were dropped during 1,136 sorties. From west to east, the batteries targeted were La Pernelle, Crisbecq, St Martin de Varreville, Maisy, Pointe-du-Hoc, Longues-sur-Mer, Mont Fleury, Ouistreham, Merville/Franceville, and Houlgate. The attack on Maisy included 111 heavy bombers, consisting of 106 Halifaxes from No 4 Group supported by five Lancasters, and five Mosquitoes from No 8 Pathfinder Group. This mission delivered 592 tons of ordnance from around 0320hrs, amounting to about two-thirds of all the bombs dropped on the Maisy batteries in 1944.[18] Due to cloud cover, it was again conducted with the assistance of Pathfinder Mosquitos using Oboe navigation aids and marking the target with Target Indicators. Due to the weather conditions, the attack largely missed the Maisy batteries and instead struck the neighboring town of Maisy, killing a number of French civilians. Some bombs hit as far away as Isigny.[19]

The pre-dawn RAF Bomber Command raids on D-Day were followed by daylight missions by the US 9th Air Force. The first attack at 0638hrs by eighteen P-47 Thunderbolts of the 366th Fighter Group dropped 54 500lb bombs, with the results judged to be "excellent." This was followed at 0759hrs by seventeen B-26 Marauders of the 391st Squadron dropping thirty-three 2,000lb bombs on Maisy II, with the results reported as "good."[20] A single German Fw 190 fighter was claimed during this raid. A repeat attack was staged by twenty P-47 Thunderbolt fighter-bombers of the 366th Fighter Group at 1114hrs, with thirty-six 1,000lb bombs; the results were judged as "excellent."[21] Until D+1, June 7,

73 USAAF sorties were conducted against the Maisy sites, totaling 98.5 tons of bombs.[22]

In total, the Maisy batteries were attacked with 942 tons of bombs, of which 293 were delivered prior to D-Day, mainly during the June 5/6 night mission. The bulk of the tonnage, 649 tons, was delivered on D-Day. On paper, the site was hit with about 3.1 tons per acre, though in reality, the density was considerably less due to the poor accuracy of the main June 5/6 night attack. A US Army engineer officer who visited the site as part of the War Department Observers Board remarked that the fields around Maisy reminded him of the devastation around Verdun that he had witnessed in 1918.[23] At least one gun at each site was knocked out, though it is not clear whether this was due to aerial attack or the subsequent naval bombardment. Overall, the pre-invasion bombardment of the Maisy batteries was poor.

NAVAL BOMBARDMENT OF THE MAISY BATTERIES

Both Maisy batteries were eventually added to the pre-invasion naval bombardment plan. The 8.Batterie in Maisy-Martinière was identified as Target 16; the guns located away from the battery were Target 16A. The 9.Batterie in Maisy-Les Perruques was identified as Target 5. Due to their location near Utah Beach, these targets were initially assigned to Bombarding Force A of Force U that was assigned to provide fire support for Utah Beach. The boundary between Force U/Utah Beach and Force O/Omaha Beach was the eastern edge of the Roches des Grandcamp shoal, immediately west of Pointe-du-Hoc.

Target #	Target Name	Interservice Target No.	Grid	Defense nest	Battery	Gun type	Location
5	Maisy I	9/J/7	533918	WN 83	9.Batterie/ AR.1716	155mm sFH.414(f)	Maisy-Les Perruques
16	Maisy II	9/J/8	528916	WN 84	8.Batterie/ AR.1716	100mm FH 14/19	Maisy-Martinière
16A	Maisy IIa	9/J/8	531914	-	8.Batterie temporary		SE Maisy-Martinière

Pre-landing bombardment of the Maisy batteries on D-Day was assigned to the cruiser HMS *Hawkins* using its 7.5in. guns. German accounts indicate that Maisy first came under heavy warship fire from 0652–0656hrs.[24] The *Hawkins* fired 110 rounds at WN 83/Maisy-Les Perruques, of which eighteen were considered hits. The *Hawkins* then turned its attention to WN 84/Maisy-Martinière, with twenty-four hits of fifty-seven rounds based on their spotting aircraft's report.[25]

The naval Bombarding Force C assigned to Force O at Omaha Beach reported the Maisy batteries to still be active around 0824hrs.[26] By this time, Bombarding Force A covering Utah Beach was preoccupied with suppressing heavy German coastal batteries near Saint-Marcouf on the northwestern side of Utah. This had been prompted in part by the sinking of the destroyer USS *Corry*, hit by a coastal battery at 0710hrs. There is still some dispute about whether the *Corry* was sunk after hitting a naval mine or solely by the Marcouf battery of 3./HKAA.1261, armed with 210mm guns. When Bombarding Force A shifted its focus to dealing with the German coastal batteries northwest of Utah Beach, the targeting of Maisy was turned over to Bombarding Force C.

The battleship USS *Texas*, while operating near Pointe-du-Hoc, turned its guns on Target 5/Maisy-Les Perruques, hitting it with twenty-six High Capacity rounds from its 14in. guns from 0810–0824hrs. Its spotter aircraft reported the strike to be "effective… Several Direct hits on emplacement." At 0945hrs, the *Texas* forwarded a report from its spotting aircraft that "Batteries at Maisy were completely destroyed." As will become evident below, these assessments were overly optimistic.

On D-Day, a number of warships operating off Grandcamp were fired on by German artillery, some of which may have come from Maisy, directed by their forward observers. It is difficult to be certain what batteries were firing on the ships since there were several batteries in the area besides the Maisy batteries. Three batteries of gem.Flak-Abt. (mot).497 armed with a dozen 88mm Flak guns were located around Grandcamp, and some may have had fields-of-fire out to sea. In addition, batteries of Artillerie-Regiment.352

were in the vicinity of Osmanville–Fontenay on D-Day, to the southwest of the Maisy batteries. In the one instance when a ship was able to identify the source of the fire from its spotter planes, USS *Shubrick* at 0740hrs on D-Day, this was identified as near the church in Fontenay, coordinates 507899, which was one of the 105mm batteries of AR.352.[27]

A message late on D-Day at 2040hrs from V Corps to the 1st Infantry Division headquarters on the command ship USS *Ancon* requested that Force U engage Targets 5, 16, and 16A near Maisy since they were believed to be still firing on Utah Beach. As a result, the following morning, June 7, USS *Glennon* (DD620) began shelling Target 5/Maisy-Les Perruques and several other artillery targets around 0900hrs, based on spotting by SFCP-34. This SFCP was attached to the 2/22nd Infantry on Utah Beach, and so presumably, Maisy I still was believed to be firing against Utah. The fire-control party later reported "all targets were demolished."

In the early afternoon, the Ranger relief column near St Pierre-du-Mont came under heavy artillery fire. SFCP-3, accompanying the column, learned from French civilians that the fire might be coming from the Maisy batteries or a battery located near Criqueville-en-Bessin, presumably from Artillerie-Regiment.352. SFCP-3 contacted USS *McCook* and also requested that USS *Texas* engage the targets using air spotting. The *Texas* at the time was farther east off Omaha Beach, and so forwarded the target request to the cruiser HMS *Glasgow*. The *Glasgow* engaged Target 5/Maisy-Les Perruques again with sixty-three rounds at 1315hrs, with its spotting aircraft noting "fire effective, several direct hits, many within 50 yards."[28] One of the Shore Fire Control Parties nearby reported seeing several large explosions, possibly mines.[29] Nevertheless, the *Glasgow* was obliged to return to the target again at 1527hrs with forty-eight more rounds, with the results reported as "Hits obtained, fire effective."

In the early morning of D+2, June 8, SFCP-3 again tried to contact USS *Texas* to engage the Maisy batteries, but the *Texas* forwarded the request to HMS *Bellona*, which fired on Maisy around 0100hrs. This was the last known engagement of the Maisy batteries by Allied naval gunfire.

In the late morning of D+2, after Rudder's force had been relieved at Pointe-du-Hoc, the 116th RCT continued to advance toward Grandcamp and Maisy.[30] The Ranger/116th RCT task force heading toward Maisy came under accurate artillery fire, believed to be coming from Isigny or Osmanville. USS *Harding* provided fire support against the village of Maisy on two occasions that afternoon, while the *Texas* and *Bellona* engaged suspected artillery targets in Isigny and Osmanville.

The actual effectiveness of the Allied bombardment of the Maisy batteries is not clear as there are no German records of the batteries on D-Day. A US Navy assessment indicated that 9.Batterie in Maisy-Les Perruques had one of its Schneider 155mm howitzers knocked off its emplacement by naval gunfire or aerial bombardment, and postwar photos show this gun. The other three guns "were withdrawn when the enemy retreated," according to post-invasion Navy survey teams.[31] The 9.Batterie in Maisy-Martinière still had one of its 100mm guns away from the site due to the incomplete construction of the four casemates. This gun was destroyed. Three other guns were located in the casemates, but when found by US survey teams, the guns had been mounted to fire out of the rear doors rather than the usual embrasure.[32] US engineers later removed about 180 tons of ammunition from the Maisy batteries, suggesting they did not use up very much of their munitions on D-Day.[33]

Endnotes

1 From Lord Mountbatten's Foreword in: James Ladd, *Commandos and Rangers of World War II*, op cit., p.7.

CHAPTER 1: THE GUNS OF POINTE-DU-HOC

1 Operation *Overlord* planning was based on the British GSGS maps (Geographical Section, General Staff MI-4). Regarding the use of "Pointe-du-Hoe," see the 1:25,000 GSGS map: St. Pierre-du-Mont, Sheet No. 34/18 NE, 2nd Edition, April 1944.

2 It is also the origin of a variety of other common French geographical terms such as Hague, Hogue, Hougue, and Hoguette; Raoul de Félice, *La Basse-Normandie: étude de géographie régionale*, Hachette, Paris (1907), p.288.

3 Carte géologique de la France: Grandcamp-Maisy à 1/50,000. Bureau de recherches géologiques et minières, Service Géologique National, Orléans (1989).

4 Pointe-du-Hoc has been extensively studied over the past few decades as part of an effort by the American Battle Monuments Commission to mitigate the effects of coastal erosion. See for example, Suwimon Udphuay *et. al.*, "Three-dimensional resistivity tomography in extreme coastal terrain amidst dense cultural signals: Applications to cliff stability assessment at the historic D-Day site" in *Geophysical Journal international*, No. 185 (2011), pp.201–220.

5 Alain Chazette, "La Heeres-Küstenartillerie-Abteilung 832: Des côtes du Pas-de-Calais à la Normandie" in *Guerre 39-45 Magazine*, No. 247 (Jul–Aug 2007), pp.70–75.

6 GPF: Grande Puissance Filloux/Filloux High Power, referring to its designer, Col Louis Filloux.

7 The "f" suffix indicating "französische" or French. "Le Canon de 155 GPF sur l'Atlantikwall" in *Guerre 39–45*, No. 161 (Nov 1999), pp.36–49.

8 Steven Zaloga, *US Field Artillery of World War II*, Osprey New Vanguard 131 (2007).

9 Coast Artillery Field Manual FM 4-25, *Seacoast Artillery, Service of the Piece, 155mm Gun*, US War Department, Washington DC (1940).

10 GenLt Ernst Goettke, *Coast Artillery-Atlantic Wall*, FMS B-663 (1947), p.2.

11 *Ibid.*, p.4.

12 The origins and missions of the Commandos are discussed in more detail in Chapter 3, "Hard Men for Dirty Work."

13 Oberbefehlhaber West: Supreme Command West. GenLt Bodo Zimmermann, *OB West: Atlantic Wall to the Siegfried Line, Chapter 2: Preparation of Coastal Defenses against Invasion*, FMS B-308 (1948), p.22.

14 Helmut Konrad von Keusgen, *Pointe-du-Hoc: Énigme autour d'un point d'appui allemande*, Heimdal, Bayeux (2006), pp.34–35.

15 The 2./HKAA.770 equipped with three 170mm K18 Mrs.Laf and one 155mm sFH 414 (f) howitzer was located near Berneval-sur-Mer northeast of Dieppe, while a reinforced battery of the HKAA.813 equipped with four 220mm K532 (f), four 105mm K35 (t) guns, and one 155mm sFH 414 (f) howitzer was located to the southwest. After the war, the Canadian Army conducted a historical study of the Dieppe defenses that was published as *The Development of the German Defence in the Dieppe Sector 1940–1942*, Report No. 36, Historical Section (GS), Army Headquarters (March 31, 1950).

16 Instructions for this program were released by the General of Engineers, OB West, on August 25, 1942, as "OB West Basic Order No. 14: development of the Channel and Atlantic Coasts" and reprinted in Canadian Dieppe Report No. 36 op cit., pp.86–88.

17 Directive for the defense of the Coast in the Sector of the 716.Infanterie-Division, in the divisional Kriegstagebuch (War Diary) Vol VI, Appendix on Küstenverteidigung/Coast Defense.

18 The strategic disagreements over coastal defense in Lower Normandy were detailed by the OB West Inspector of Fortifications, GenLt Rudolf Schmetzer, in *Atlantic Wall: Invasion Sector June 1942–January 1944*, FMS B-668 (1947), pp.5–6.

19 This was the battery's "Beobachtungsraum" (Control zone), not necessarily its engagement zone. These details were contained in the Kriegstagebuch (War Diary) of the 716.Infanterie-Division found in NARA RG 242, T315, Roll 2260, Frame 890.

20 The history of the Organization Todt in France is detailed in two of the studies by German officials for the US Army-Europe's Historical Division under the Foreign Military Studies Program: Xaver Dorsch, *Organization Todt – France*, FMS B-670 (1946), and Xaver Dorsch, *Organization Todt – Operations in the West*, FMS B-671, US Army Historical Division.

21 STO: Service du travail obligatoire.

22 For a critical survey of the French role in the construction of the Atlantic Wall, see Jérôme Prieur, *Le Mur de l'Atlantique: Monument de la Collaboration*, Denoël, Paris (2010).

23 This is discussed in more detail in Chapter 5, "Spying on Pointe du-Hoc: The Intelligence Battle."

24 Keusgen, *op cit.*, p.54.

25 The complex functioning of these fire controls is described in detail in Appendix B.

26 As explained in the Appendix on German fire control, the battery needed input from two forward observer posts. The British ships were not visible to the western forward observation post, and so insufficient data was available for a fire solution.

27 The probable reason for his disappearance is discussed in Chapter 7, "Obliteration."

28 9. Flugmelde-Leit-Kompanie, Luftnachrichtenregiment.53: 9th Air Identification Company, Air Surveillance Regiment.53.

29 This is described in detail in Appendix B.

30 The OKW instructions were issued on January 2, 1943. Herbert Jäger, "Leichte und mittlere Geschütze des Atlantikwalls" in *Fortifikation*, Ausgabe 20 (2006), p.86.

31 Goettke, *op cit.*, pp.6–8.

32 This was verified after the D-Day landings by the examination of coastal gun batteries in Normandy by German engineers. GenLt Rudolf Schmetzer, *Atlantic Wall-The Effect of Bombing and Naval Artillery*, FMS B-669 (1947), pp.15–17.

33 Adm Theodor Krancke, *Marine Gruppenkommando West: 1943–14 June 1944*, FMS B-169 (1946), p.12.

34 The smaller Mittlere Drehbettung (16 ton) (Medium Dry Platform 16 ton) had entered production in February 1943 for 105mm field guns and 155mm howitzers. The 155mm GPF required the use of the heavy 32-ton platform due to its substantial recoil. When these platforms were used, the gun barrel and trunnion assembly was removed from the usual wheeled carriage, and directly attached to the platform. Jäger, *op cit.*, p.89.

35 Reproductions of the actual plans for the Regelbau Nr 694 Schartenstand für 15.5cm K418(f) auf Drehsockel can be found in: Alain Chazette, *Mur de l'Atlantique: Batteries de côte série 600*, Histoire et fortification, Vertou (2014), pp.107–08.

36 RAF Medmenham Interpretation Reports B80 (March 9, 1944) and B811 (March 11, 1944). AIR 34/109, TNA.

37 Georges Bernage, "Wilhelm Kirchhoff: j'étai aussi à la Pointe du Hoc" in *Guerre 39–45 Magazine*, No. 322 (May 2014), p.70.

ENDNOTES

CHAPTER 2: THE COASTAL GUN THREAT

1 Mesut Uyar, *The Ottoman Defence against the ANZAC Landing 25 April 1915*, Australian Army History Unit, Canberra (2011). Michael Forrest, *The Defence of the Dardanelles: From Bombards to Battleships*, Pen & Sword, Barnsley (2012).

2 Mark Karau, *Wielding the Dagger: The Marinekorps Flandern and the German War Effort 1914–1918*, Prager, Westport (2003). Franck Vernier, *Le premier "Mur de l'Atlantique": Les batteries allemandes au littoral belge 1914–1918*, Patrimonie Militaire, Liège (2012).

3 *The Development of the German Defence in the Dieppe Sector 1940–1942*, Report No. 36, Historical Section (GS), Army Headquarters (March 31, 1950).

4 Numerous accounts of the Dieppe raid have been published, and one of the official histories has recently appeared in print: *The Dieppe Raid: The Combined Operations Assault on Hitler's European Fortress August 1942*, Pen & Sword, Barnsley (2019).

5 The Raid on Dieppe: Lessons Learnt, C.B. 04244(1). Combined Operations Headquarters, September 1942. Digital History Archives, "Raid on Dieppe Lessons Learnt."

6 Frédéric Saffroy, *Le Bouclier de Neptune: La politique de défense des bases françaises en Méditerranée, 1912–1931*, Presses universitaires de Rennes (2015), p.331.

7 For more details, see Chapter XI in: George Howe, *Northwest Africa: Seizing the Initiative in the West*, US Army Center of Military History, Washington DC (1991).

8 John Grehan & Martin Mace, *Operations in North Africa and the Middle East 1942–1944: El Alamein, Tunisia, Algeria and Operation Torch*, Pen & Sword, Barnsley (2015), pp.125–26.

9 Edith Rodgers, *The Reduction of Pantelleria and Adjacent Islands, 8 May–14 June 1943*, Army Air Forces Historical Study No. 52 (May 1947), p.11.

10 Rodgers, *op cit.*, p.63.

11 *Ibid.*, pp.63–64.

12 Zuckerman's original report, "Report on Plan and Execution of Operations at Pantelleria", was first released on June 2, 1943, followed by a more complete version on July 20.

13 Steven Zaloga, *Sicily 1943: The debut of Allied joint operations*, Osprey Campaign 251 (2013), pp.17–18.

14 A temporary placeholder organization existed for a short time before this, called the "Combined Commanders." *History of COSSAC, 1943 – 1944*, SHAEF Historical Sub-Section (May 1944).

15 "Digest of Operation Overlord", COSSAC (July 23, 1943), in: Quadrant Conference August 1943, Papers and Minutes of Meetings, Office of the Combined Chiefs of Staff, Washington DC (1943), p.103.

16 The assignment of two Ranger battalions was contained in a COSSAC Plan published on July 30, 1943, under the label COS (43) 416 (O), and the subsequent iteration CCS 304 of August 10, 1943.

17 Graham Report: Fire Support of Seaborne Landing against a Heavily Defended Coast, Report by the Fire Support of Seaborne Landings Sub-committee, COS (43) 770 (O), Joint Technical Warfare Committee, UK War Cabinet (January 7, 1944). TNA, CAB 80/77, pp.14–15.

18 *United States Naval Administration in World War II, The Invasion of Normandy, Vol. 5*, Chapter 8: Bombardment and Other Defensive Operations Against Enemy Land Forces, United States Naval Forces, Europe (1945), p.458.

19 Graham Report, *op cit.*, p.5.

CHAPTER 3: "HARD MEN FOR DIRTY WORK"

1 The US Army did institute a "Commando Division" at its Amphibious Training center on Cape Cod, Massachusetts, to provide physical enhanced training to infantry units during amphibious assault training, but this did not result in actual Commando-type raiding units. Charles H. Briscoe, "Commando & Ranger Training: Preparing America's Soldiers for War, Part 1" in *Veritas*, Vol 10, No 1 (2014), pp.64–79.

2 H. Paul Jeffers, *Command of Honor: General Lucian Truscott's Path to victory in World War II*, New American Library, New York (2008), p.60.

3 Jeffers, *op cit.*, p.63.

4 Lucian Truscott, *Command Missions*, Presido, Novato (1990), p.40.

5 "Rangers (US) Adm. Nr. 279," Administrative History Collection, Historical Section, ETOUSA (September 22, 1943).

6 Metacomet's English name was King Philip, hence the name for the conflict. Gabriele Esposito, *King Philip's War 1675–76*, Osprey Campaign 354 (2020), pp.34–35.

7 A former *New York Times* reporter, Capt Ted Conway, attributed the name to Truscott in an August 20, 1942, article in the paper.

8 The debate over the role of the Rangers is detailed in: David Hogan Jr., *Raiders or Elite Infantry? The Changing Role of the US Army Rangers from Dieppe to Grenada*, Greenwood, Westport (1992).

9 Jim DeFelice, *Rangers at Dieppe: The first Combat Action of the US Army Rangers in World War II*, Penguin, New York (2008).

10 Robert Black, *The Ranger Force: Darby's Rangers in World War II*, Stackpole, Mechanicsburg (2009).

11 Joseph Ewing, *29 Let's Go! A History of the 29th Infantry Division in World War II*, Infantry Journal Press, Washington DC (1948), p.18.

12 Hogan, *op cit.*, pp.35–36.

13 John R. Slaughter, *Omaha Beach and Beyond: The Long March of Sgt. Bob Slaughter*, Zenith, St Paul (2007), p.71.

14 Rangers (US) Administrative History, *op cit.*, p.2.

15 Mark Moyar, *Oppose Any Foe: The Rise of America's Special Operations Forces*, Basic Books, New York (2017), p.13.

16 David Rowland & John Curry (ed.), *The Stress of Battle: Quantifying Human Performance in Battle for Historical Analysis and Wargaming*, History of Wargaming Project, Middletown (2019), p.174.

17 The Army Troop Basis was a formal process undertaken at least once a year to establish the overall authorized strength and composition of the US Army as approved by the War Department. Maurice Matloff & Edwin M. Snell, *Strategic Planning for Coalition Warfare 1941–42*, US Army Center of Military History, Washington DC (1990), pp.350–53.

18 Charles H. Briscoe, "Commando & Ranger Training: Preparing America's Soldiers for War, Part 2" in *Veritas*, Vol 12, No 1 (2016), p.3.

19 Hogan, *op cit.*, p.37.

20 Edwin Sorvisto, *Roughing it with Charlie: 2nd Ranger Battalion*, Planograpfia, Plzeň (1945), p.7.

21 Thomas Hatfield, *Rudder: From Leader to Legend*, Texas A&M University Press, College Station (2011).

22 James Schneider, *My Father's War: The Story of Max Ferguson Schneider – A Ranger Commander*, Lulu (2012), pp.75–76.

23 Sorvisto, *op cit.*, p.13.

24 This meeting is described in more detail in Chapter 4, "Refining the Ranger Plan."

25 Hatfield, *op cit.*, p.97.

26 Hogan, *op cit.*, p.68.

27 Richard Hathaway, *Training for Bloody Omaha: Activation, Training, and Combat of the 5th Ranger Infantry Battalion through 8 June 1944*, Vantage, New York (2002), pp.3–6.

28 The three captains involved were John T. Eichnor, George P. Whittington Jr., and Hugo W. Heffelfinger. Noel Mehlo, *The Lost Ranger: A Soldier's Story*, CreateSpace, Middletown DE (2014), p.174.

29 Robert W. Jones, Jr, "From Omaha Beach to the Rhine: The 5th Ranger Battalion in the European Theater" in *Veritas*, Vol 5, No 2 (2009), p.4.

30 Robert Ross, *The Supercommandos: First Special Service Force 1942–1944*, Schiffer, Atglen (2000), p.237.

31 For an overview of the Slapton Sands exercises, see: Mark Khan, *D-Day Assault: The Second World War Assault Training Exercises at Slapton Sands*, Pen & Sword, Barnsley (2014).

32 Lt Clifford L. Jones, *The Administrative and Logistical History of the ETO – Neptune: Training, Mounting, The Artificial Ports*, Historical Division, USAFET (1946), pp.267–68.

33 John Raaen Jr correspondence, DGI/KE.

CHAPTER 4: REFINING THE RANGER PLAN

1 Lt Col Edgar Wilkerson, *et al.*, *V Corps Operations in the ETO 6 Jan 1942–9 May 1945*, V Corps G-3 Historical Sub-Section (1945), p.20.

2 The first wave of Bigot clearances were January 15, 1944, for corps and division commanders, February 1 for divisional staffs including their G-2 (intelligence), G-3 (operations), and G-4 (logistics), April 1 for regimental commanders and staff, and May 1 for battalion commanders and staff as well as separate organization commanders. This schedule was connected to the planning cycle since the corps, division, regiment, and battalion plans were prepared in sequence. *Report on Observations of Normandy Operation, 8 May–23 July 1944*, Memorandum for Assistant Chief of Staff, G-2, Army Ground Forces.

3 "Agenda for Headquarters V Corps, Conference, 1030 hours, 4 February 1944, on Planning for Operation Overlord," NARA RG407 Pre-Invasion Planning, Entry NM-3 427-D, Box 19244.

4 G-3 Section V Corps to Chief of Staff V Corps, February 27, 1944, "Visit to Headquarters First Army re: Employment of Rangers in Overlord," NARA RG 407 Pre-Invasion Planning, NM-3 427-D, Box 19244.

5 Lt Col T. H. Trevor, After-Action Report – Assault on Pointe du Hoe Battery, July 12, 1944.

6 This was accomplished by damming up the Ruisseau de la Fontaine Ste Marie and the river Véret, and an area already prone to flooding. V Corps G-2 Estimate of the Situation, Map No 5, April 1, 1944.

7 Trevor, After-Action-Report, *op cit.*

8 The issue of bombarding Pointe-du-Hoc is detailed in subsequent chapters.

9 *Mechanical Aids for Scaling Cliffs*, COHQ Bulletin X/40, September 1944, p.1.

10 Hatfield, *op cit.*, p.104.

11 Ranger Plan, Annex 19 to V Corps Operations Plan Neptune, April 20, 1944, pp.2.

12 This was the 1:25,000 GSGS map: St. Pierre-du-Mont, Sheet No. 34/18 NE, 2nd Edition, April 1944.

CHAPTER 5: SPYING ON POINTE-DU-HOC:
THE INTELLIGENCE BATTLE

1 RAF Medmenham Interpretation Report B 297, August 24, 1942, TNA AIR 34/102.

2 A survey of Resistance actions in Normandy can be found in: Raymond Ruffin, *La résistance normande face à la Gestapo*, Presses de la Cité, Paris (1977).

3 The escapade at the Organization Todt office in Caen is told in detail in: Richard Collier, *Ten Thousand Eyes: The Amazing Story of the Spy Network that Cracked Hitler's Atlantic Wall before D-Day*, E. P. Dutton, New York (1958), pp.78–88.

4 Raymond Ruffin, *La Résistance dans l'Opération Overlord*, France-Empire, Paris (2004).

5 Maj Gen Donald Weller, *Naval Gunfire Support of Amphibious Operations: Past, Present, and Future*, Naval Sea Systems Command, Dahlgren (1977), pp.12-13.

6 US Fleet Task Force One-Two-Two, Operation Overlord-Report of Naval Commander Western Task Force (CTF 122), Annex B1-Intelligence, July 25, 1944, pp.15–16.

7 Gunfire Support Plan, Appendix I to Annex C, Operation Order No. 3-44, Western Naval Task Force, Task Group 124.8, May 25, 1944. NARA II, RG 38 Records of the Office of Chef of Naval Operations: Plans, Orders and Related Documents, Box 112.

8 *Technical Manual TM 9-2005, Vol. 3, Ordnance Materiel-General*, Ordnance School, Aberdeen Proving Ground (1942), p.63.

9 *Technical Manual TM 9-345 155mm Gun Materiel M1917, 1918 and Modifications*, War Department, Washington DC (1942), p.10.

10 Pierre Touzin & F. Vauvillier, *Les Canon de la Victoire, Tome 1: L'artillerie de campagne*, Histoire & Collections, Paris (2006), p.55.

11 Minutes of Meeting Held at TIS at 1430, Tuesday, January 18, 1944, German Coastal Artillery in the West February 1944, COSSAC/2GX/ INT, German Coastal Artillery Batteries 1944, DHA.

12 *Technical Manual TM 9-1907 Ballistic Data, Performance of Ammunition*, War Department, Washington DC (1944), p.196.

13 Cornelius Ryan conducted interviews with Mercader and Marion for his book *The Longest Day*, and these reside in the Ryan collection in the library at Ohio University. There is very little detail in these interviews about the Pointe-du-Hoc discovery.

14 A detailed description of the wartime actions of the Resistance in Vierville was found on the town's website in 2012: http://vierville.free.fr/811 -ResistanceVierville.htm. This site has apparently disappeared since then.

15 Wilhelm Krichbaum, *The Secret Field Police*, Foreign Military Studies C-029 (1947).

16 Jean-Louis Perquin, *Resistance: The Clandestine Radio Operators*, Histoire et Collections, Paris (2011), p.56.

17 Gordon Corera, *Operation Columba, The Secret Pigeon Service: The Untold Story of World War II Resistance in Europe*, Wm Morrow, New York (2018).

18 Div. Tagesbefehl Nr. 375, 716.Infanterie-Division, March 3, 1944, NARA II RG 242, T-315, R2261, F.158.

19 *Special Questions for 352.Infanterie Division Chief-of-Staff Fritz Ziegelmann*, Foreign Military Studies B-021, p.2.

20 Cassel Bryan-Low, "UK Code-Crackers Stumped" in *Wall Street Journal*, November 24/25, 2012, p.A9; Reuters, "Enigmatic code found on WWII pigeon" in *Washington Post*, November 24, 2012.

21 F. H. Hinsley, *et. al.*, *British Intelligence in the Second World War*, Vol 3, Part 2, HMSO, London (1988), pp.59, 793–98.

22 Giskes wrote an account of German counterintelligence activities after the war, but it focuses mainly on the Netherlands: H. J. Giskes, *London Calling North Pole*, Bantam (1982).

23 "Summary of present situation of Batteries which might affect the Neptune beaches or their approaches – 31 May 1944," TNA, WO 205/172, p.3.

CHAPTER 6: SOFTENING POINTE-DU-HOC

1   Steven Zaloga, *Operation Pointblank 1944: Defeating the Luftwaffe*, Osprey Campaign 236, Oxford (2011).

2   Admiral, Allied Naval Commander, Expeditionary Force, April 8, 1944, *Joint Fire Plan*, p.1.

3   Oboe is described in detail in the following chapter on p.122.

4   Minutes of the AEAF C-in-C Conferences, TNA, AIR 37/536.

5   For a detailed study of the Wehrmacht's appreciation of Allied invasion planning, see: Hans Wegmüller, *Die Abwehr der Invasion: Die Konzeption des Oberbefehlhabers West 1940–1944*, Rombach, Freiburg (1986).

6   Steven Zaloga, *Operation Crossbow 1944: Hunting Hitler's V-weapons*, Osprey Air Campaign 4, Oxford (2018).

7   William Wolf, *US Aerial Armament in World War II, Vol. 2: Bombs, Bombsights and Bombing*, Schiffer, Atglen (2010), p.257.

8   Recollections of Unteroffizier Emil Kaufmann in: Keusgen, *op cit.*, p.69.

9   Interpretation Report No SA 1517, Attack on Coastal Gun Positions at Pointe du Hoe on 25.4.44, TNA AIR 34/371.

10 Pre D-Day Batteries, Joint Fire Plan, TNA WO 205/172.

11 From war diary of Admiral Kanalküste (Admiral of the Channel Coast), Vizeadmiral Friedrich Rieve. This headquarters contained four subordinate commands: Seekommandant Pas-de-Calais (HQ at Wimille), Seekommandant Seine-Somme (HQ at Le Havre), Seekommandant Normandie (HQ at Cherbourg), and Seekommandant Kanalinseln (Channel Islands – HQ at Jersey). These subordinate commands reported on Allied air attacks along the coast on a daily basis. These war diary entries are reprinted in Hans Sakkers (ed.), *Normandie 6 Juni 1944 im Spiegel der deutschen Kriegstagebücher: Der Großangriff auf den Atlantikwall*, Biblio Verlag, Osnabrück (1998), p.138.

12 RAF Medenham Intepretation Report B859, April 28, 1944. TNA AIR/109.

13 This study was originally published in Swedish in 1953 as "Alarm I Atlantvallen." The author used the French edition: Bertil Stjernfelt, *Alerte sur le mur de l'Atlantique*, Presses de la Cité, Paris (1961), pp.129–30.

14 Keusgen, *op cit.*, p.71.

15 https://www.infoclimat.fr/cartes/observations-meteo/archives.

16 Sakkers, *op. cit.*, p.150.

17 The Center for Heritage Conservation of Texas A&M University has conducted extensive studies of Pointe-du-Hoc as part of their efforts on behalf of the American Battle Monument Commission. Their bomb damage assessments can be found in their presentation to the 5th International Fields of Conflict Conference, held at Ghent, Belgium, from October 17–20, 2008. Richard Burt, *et al.*, Crater Analysis at Pointe du Hoc, Historic Site, Normandy, France. PowerPoint presentation, Slide 20.

18 RAF Medenham Intepretation Report B884, May 23, 1944, based on a May 20 photo sortie. TNA AIR/109.

19 Kriegstagebuch 7.Armee (AOK.7), NARA RG 242, T313, Roll 1565, Frame F679.

20 Sakkers, *op cit.*, p.154.

21 AEAF Daily Int/Ops Summary No. 103 Sunrise to 2100 hrs May 22, 1944, TNA AIR 37/394.

22 Special Interpretation Report No. 33, 21st Army Group, May 22, 1944, TNA WO 205/172.

23 Special Interpretation Report No. 37, 21st Army Group, TNA WO 205/172.

24 Sakkers, *op cit.*, p.155.

25 Sakkers, *op cit.*, p.163.

26 Sakkers, *op cit.*, p.167.

27 Konteradmiral Walter Henneke, based in Cherbourg, was Seekommandant Normandie, responsible for the naval defense of the Normandy coast. This excerpt came from: US Fleet Task Force One Two Two, Operation Overlord-Report of Naval Commander Western Task Force (CTF 122), Annex B1-Intelligence, July 25, 1944, p.16.

CHAPTER 7: OBLITERATION

1 Interpretation Report SA 1963: Attack on Tactical Targets in the Caen Area on 5.6.44. TNA, AIR 40/645.

2 Sakkers, *op cit.*, p.169.

3 Details of the use of Oboe and Target Indicators can be found in: John MacBean & Arthur Hogben, *Bombs Gone: The development and use of British air-dropped weapons from 1912 to the present day*, Patrick Stephens, Wellingborough (1990), pp.104–13.

4 RAF Pathfinders website, accessed January 2021: https://raf-pathfinders .com/d-day-the-loss-of-the-carter-crew/.

5 AIR 27/1921, TNA.

6 Chris Goss, *Luftwaffe Hit-and-Run Raiders: Nocturnal Fighter-Bomber Operations over the Western Front 1943–45*, Ian Allen, London (2009).

7 For an overview of RAF efforts to suppress Luftwaffe radars prior to D-Day, see Alfred Price's presentation about D-Day at the Electronic Warfare conference at RAF Museum-Hendon on April 10, 2002, reprinted in *Royal Air Force Historical Journal,* No 28 (2002), pp.43–50.

8 Jean-Bernard Frappé, *La Luftwaffe face au débarquement: Normandie 6 juin–31 août 1944*, Heimdal, Bayeux (2018), pp.332–33.

9 This was the first recorded aerial combat of D-Day over France, but it is unclear whether the Me 410 was on a mission connected to D-Day activities such as reconnaissance of the fleet, or whether it was returning from an intruder sortie over England. Chris Goss, "Over the Beaches: D-Day Luftwaffe Air Operations" in *Iron Cross*, No 1 (2019), p.12.

10 Helmut Eberspächer, "Flugtag Juni 1944" in *Luftwaffen-Revue*, I/95, p.20.

11 Eberspächer, *op cit.*, p.20.

12 Kill claims can be found on the Ciel de Gloire website: http://www .cieldegloire.com/skg_010.php.

13 Stephen Darlow, *D-Day Bombers: The Veterans' Story*, Grub Street, London (2004), p.155.

14 "For the love of Vera: D-Day Lancaster bomber crew identified 68 years on by poignant inscription on dead airman's ring" in the *Daily Mail* (October 1, 2012).

15 Jean-Bernard Frappé, *op cit.*, pp.332–33.

16 Goettke, *op cit.*, FMS B-663, p.3.

17 Marion was also active in the French Resistance. Jean Marion interview, Cornelius Ryan Collection, "The Longest Day," Mahn Center for Archives and Special Collections, Ohio University Libraries.

18 This account is based on an interview by historian David Bedford with the Guérin family in 2002. The explosive device was described as

a "mine," but it may have been some other type of explosive. E-mail correspondence, DGI/KE.

19 This seems to be confirmed by an account of a Swedish naval artillery specialist who visited Pointe-du-Hoc immediately after the war and spoke to some of the local residents. He reported that a new commander was assigned to Pointe-du-Hoc a week after the explosion, but had no name. Bertil Stjernfelt, *Alerte sur le mur de l'Atlantique*, Presses de la Cité, Paris (1961), pp.129–30.

20 See Chapter 11: "Force A Strikes Pointe-du-Hoc."

21 Keusgen, *op cit.*, p.110.

22 Bernage, *op cit.*, pp.74–75.

23 Keusgen, *op cit.*, p.86.

24 Logbook of USS *Texas*, June 6, 1944, NARA RG 24 Logbooks of US Ships.

25 Some of the sites were to be attacked by large tonnages on D-Day which did not hit the sites; hence the "0" in D-Day density. Solly Zuckerman, "Observations on Air Attacks on Coastal Defenses based on experience gained in Overlord," RAF Bombing Analysis Unit, February 6, 1945, p.6, TNA DEFE 2/487.

CHAPTER 8: ASSAULT GROUP O-4

1 Early in the war, this craft was called an ALC (Armoured Landing Craft), but the name was changed to LCA as part of a process to standardize Royal Navy and US Navy terminology. Brian Lavery, *Assault Landing Craft: Design, Construction & Operations*, Seaforth, Barnsley (2009).

2 Lavery, *op cit.*, p.39.

3 Lavery, *op cit.*, pp.78–80.

4 Lytle subsequently was decorated with the Distinguished Service Cross for heroism while serving as Commanding Officer, 1st Battalion, 358th Infantry Regiment, 90th Infantry Division, in action against enemy forces on 20 September 1944, along the Moselle River in France.

5 Omar Bradley, *A Soldier's Story*, Henry Holt, New York, 1951, p. 269.

6 Hatfield, op cit., pp.114-115.

CHAPTER 9: CARNAGE ON CHARLIE BEACH

1 Robert Rowe interview with Lt James Eikner, July 25, 1989, transcript page 52, in Rowe Papers, MHI/AHEC.

2 Sorvisto, *op cit.*, p.25.

3 USS *Thompson* (DD627) Operations June 5–17, 1944, NARA II, RG 38.

4   1st Battalion, 116th Infantry Regiment Command Group After Action Report, June 6, 1944, NARA II RG 407.

5   USS *McCook* (DD496) war diary, June 6, 1944, NARA II, RG 38.

6   This after-action report was prepared from seven survivors of the company. A Company, 1st Battalion, 116th Infantry Regiment After Action Report, June 6, 1944, NARA II, RG 407.

7   Sorvisto, *op cit.*, p.26.

8   Ralph Goranson correspondence, February 19, 2000, DGI/KE.

9   Sydney Salomon correspondence, February 21, 2000, DGI/KE.

10 Ralph Goranson reminiscences, transcribed June 1993 in Gurnee, Illinois.

11 Technician Fifth Grade, equivalent to corporal in the US Army.

12 Ralph Goranson reminiscences, *op cit.*

13 War Diary, USS *Harding*, June 9, 1944, NARA II, RG 38.

14 Robert Rowe interview with Lt James Eikner, July 25, 1989, *op cit.*, p.52.

15 Action Report USS *Thompson* June 5–17, 1944, p.2. NARA II, RG 38.

16 USS *McCook* (DD496) Log, June 6, 1944, Part II, Enclosure B. NARA II, RG 38.

17 Command Group, 1st Battalion, 116th Infantry Regiment, After-action report, June 6, 1944, NARA II, RG 407.

18 Maj John W. Nicholson Jr, "Omaha Beach, 6 June 1944: Lessons from Company C, 2nd Ranger Battalion" in *Infantry* (May–June 1994), p.10.

19 USS *Carmick* (DD493) Narrative Report – June 5 to June 17, 1944, June 23, 1944, NARA II, RG 38, p.4.

20 Sorvisto, *op cit.*, p.30. During the fighting until June 10, C Company lost twenty-three men killed and about twenty-five wounded.

CHAPTER 10: THE STORMY VOYAGE TO POINTE-DU-HOC

1   HMS *Prince Charles* – Operation Neptune: Chronological Report, NARA II, Record Group 38.

2   John C. Raaen Jr correspondence, July 8, 2002, DGI/KE.

3   Combat Interviews, Omaha Beach 2nd and 5th Rangers, NARA II, RG 407, pp.4–5.

4   Report by T/Lt Colin Beever to Commander, HMS *Prince Charles*, June 12, 1944, NARA II Record Group 38.

5   "Report on Assault Bombardment HMS Talybont", from CO, HMS *Talybont* to CO, Assault Force O, USS *Ancon*, June 24, 1944, NARA II Record Group 38.

6   LCS(M) 91 drifted eastward toward Dog Green Beach and the crew was rescued by ML 304 around 0940hrs. Report of LCS(M) 91 in Operation *Neptune*, to HMS *Prince Baudouin*, June 8, 1944, NARA II, RG 38.

7   Report of LCS(M) 102 Operation *Neptune*, to HMS *Prince Leopold*, June
    7, 1944, NARA II, RG 38.
8   USS *Satterlee* (DD626) War Diary, Part I, NARA II, Record Group 38, p.2.

CHAPTER 11: FORCE A STRIKES POINTE-DU-HOC

1   Curiously enough, the 501st Flotilla "Report on Operation Neptune"
    states that it received the "Crowbar" signal at 0645. This does not agree
    with several other sources and was probably a mistake.
2   USS Satterlee (DD626) Narrative and Chronological Order of Events,
    21 June 1944, NARA II, RG 38, p. 2, part 1.
3   Bernage, "Wilhelm Kichhoff", op cit., p. 76.
4   Report by T/Lt Colin Beever to Commander, HMS *Prince Charles*, June
    12, 1944, NARA II Record Group 38.
5   Helmut Konrad von Keusgen, *Pointe du Hoc: Rätsel um einen deutschen
    Stützpunkt*, HEK-Creativ, Garbsen (2011), p.97.
6   Combat Interviews, 2nd Ranger Battalion. NARA II, RG 407 Entry
    427A (unpaginated manuscript).
7   Louis Lisko Testimony, Rowe Collection, *op cit.*, p.137. Lisko was one of
    the two radio men assigned to the SCR-284, and after the war he became
    the unofficial historian of the 2nd Rangers.
8   Log of Fire Control Communication with US 2nd Ranger Battalion, USS
    Satterlee (DD626) War Diary, Enclosure A, NARA II, RG 38.
9   Details on the Shore Fire Control Parties can be found in Appendix C.
10 For a complete listing of the naval fire missions in support of the Rangers,
    see Appendix C.
11 Missing Air Crew Report 1757. This report includes short testimonies
    from Johnston, Crouch, and Goodgal about the incident. NARA II/Fold3.
12 This incident was mentioned in the war diary of the 352.Infanterie-
    Division. Sakkers, *op cit.*, p.66.
13 Army Recommendation forms, TNA Kew, WO 373/50.

CHAPTER 12: SPIKING THE GUNS

1   *Combat Interviews, op cit.*, p.39, *Small Unit Actions, op cit.*, p.31.
2   This account is based on the interviews conducted by US Army historians
    in the weeks immediately after D-Day and located in the *Combat
    Interviews* files at NARA, as cited above.
3   See for example his interview in the 2019 PBS documentary "D-Day at
    Pointe-du-Hoc," or his interview in the book by Chris Ketcherside &
    George Despostis, *Rangers Led the Way: WWII Rangers in their own Words*,
    Schiffer, Atglen (2020).

4 Alain Chazette, *et al.*, *Atlantikwall: Omaha Beach de Port-en-Bessin à Grandcamp–Maisy*, Histoire & Fortifications, Vertou (2014), p.83.

5 The machine-gun nest was identified at 596 936. USS *Satterlee* (DD626) Log of Fire Control Communications with US 2nd Ranger Battalion Shore Fire Control Party No 1, June 6, 1944, p.2. NARA II, RG 38.

6 Combat Interviews, 2nd Ranger Battalion, *op cit.* NARA II, RG 407 Entry 427A, p.50.

7 The origin of the projectile is not clear. 1st Lt James "Ike" Eikner later recalled that it came from HMS *Glasgow*. Eikner correspondence, March 1, 2000, DGI/KE.

8 Raaen E-mail correspondence with the author, February 2021.

9 Commander Assault Force O, Chronological Order of Events, June 6, 1944, NARA II, RG 38.

CHAPTER 13: THE GERMANS STRIKE BACK

1 Details of these batteries can be found in Appendix D.

2 The telephone log of the 352.Infanterie-Division indicates that the divisional Ia (Operations) reported to LXXXIV.Armee-Korps at 1225hrs that Pointe-du-Hoc had been taken by two companies of enemy troops and that a counterattack had been launched by III./GR.726. The telephone log was reprinted in: Oberstleutnant Fritz Ziegelmann, *352nd Infantry Division 6 June 1944*, FMS B-388, p.17.

3 Oberstleutnant Fritz Ziegelmann, *The 352nd Infantry Division (5 Dec. 1943–6 Jun. 1944)*, FMS B-432, 1946, p.28.

4 Some Ranger accounts suggest the artillery fire came from Maisy, but this is probably because they were aware of the two artillery batteries at Maisy from pre-invasion intelligence reports, but were not aware of the artillery batteries of the 352.Infanterie-Division in the area. The Rangers had no technical means to determine the source of the artillery fire.

5 Combat Interviews, 2nd Ranger Battalion, *op cit.*, NARA II, RG 407 Entry 427A, p.51.

6 There are no detailed German accounts of this attack. The US Army accounts are contradictory about the origins of the attack. The original Combat Interviews manuscript indicates the attack emanated directly from Au Guay, which meant that it could have been from the 9./GR.726 in St Pierre-du-Mont. The published version in "Small Unit Actions" indicates it came from the west, emanating out of the area of the western Flak bunker, which suggests the 12./GR.726.

7 See Chapter 15: "Ranger Force C on Dog Green Beach."

8 Marcia Moen & Margo Heinen, *Reflections of Courage on D-Day: A Personal Account of Ranger "Ace" Parker*, DeForest Press, Elk River (1999), p.95.

9 Hathaway, *op cit.*, p.44.
10 German Quartermaster records from Normandy in the spring of 1944 noted that many forms of ammunition had been stored under improper conditions in 1942 and 1943 and had become faulty. There was a program in May 1944 to recall a significant amount of munitions for quality control.
11 Small Unit Actions, War Department Historical Division, Washington DC, 1946, p.51.
12 As described in Chapter 16: "The Crazy March on D+1."

CHAPTER 14: NIGHT ATTACK

1 Ziegelmann, FMS B-432, *op cit.*, p.32.
2 Ziegelmann, FMS B-388, *op. cit.*, p.21.
3 Ziegelmann, FMS B-388, *op cit.*, p.21.
4 Lt G. K. Hodenfield, "I Climbed the Cliffs with the Rangers" in *Saturday Evening Post*, August 19, 1944, pp.18, 93.
5 Hodenfield, *op cit.*

CHAPTER 15: RANGER FORCE C ON DOG GREEN BEACH

1 See Chapter 4: "Refining the Ranger Plan."
2 Report of Proceedings HMS *Prince Leopold* Group O-4, Force O, D-Day. NARA II, RG 38.
3 The Combat Interview manuscript of the 2nd Rangers on D-Day indicates that the 5th Ranger Battalion was informed of the touchdown of Ranger Force A "by 0709" but it is not clear if this message was forwarded from the Royal Navy based on the "Crowbar" message from ML 304 or a direct radio message from Rudder, presumably via an SCR-300. T-5 Theodore Wells of the HQ Company, 5th Rangers, had been attached to the HQ, Provisional Ranger Group, specifically to conduct radio transmissions from Rudder to the 5th Ranger Battalion, and he was in LCA 888 with Rudder on D-Day with an SCR-300 radio. His later account does not mention any such radio communications: John Raaen Jr, *Intact: A First Hand Account of the D-Day Invasion from a 5th Rangers Company Commander*, Reedy Press, St Louis (2012), pp.25–29.
4 The Narrative History of the Second Ranger Battalion 1944, p.11.
5 *Small Unit Actions*, War Department Historical Division, Washington DC, 1946, p.7.
6 Henry Glassman, *Lead the Way Rangers: History of the 5th Ranger Battalion*, Hausser, Markt Grafing (1945), p.20.

7 Lt R. D. Turnbull, Report on Operation Neptune, 501st Flotilla, NARA II, RG 38.

8 Lt J. M. Cassidy, RNVR, Report of the movements of 504 LCA Flotilla during Operation Neptune, NARA II, RG 38.

9 Pfc Morris Prince, *Company A, 2nd Ranger Battalion: Overseas and then-Over the Top*, 2nd Ranger Battalion, 1945.

10 5th Rangers, Combat Interviews, NARA II, RG 407 Entry 427A (unpaginated manuscript).

11 Other Rangers, including Morris Prince, reported that Rafferty was killed by an artillery blast.

12 Robert Edlin Correspondence, November 19, 1998, DGI/KE.

13 2nd Ranger Battalion After-Battle Report June 1944 (July 22, 1944), NARA II, RG 407, Entry 427.

14 Roderick Bailey, *Forgotten Voices of D-Day*, Ebury Press, London (2009), pp.283–84.

15 The decision to land farther left in the Dog White sector was apparently mutually agreed with Col Schneider. Most Ranger records credit Schneider with the decision; the Royal Navy accounts credit Cassidy.

16 Lt J. M. F. Cassidy RNVR, Report on movements of 504 LCA Flotilla during Operation *Neptune* from time of lowering. NARA II, RG 38.

17 Lt E. H. West, Report on Operation *Neptune*, LCA Flotilla 507, NARA II, RG 38.

18 USCG Lt (jg) Arend Vyn, Participation in Operation *Neptune* by USS LCI(L) 91. Other accounts suggest that the fire erupted when a soldier carrying a flamethrower was hit, igniting the pressurized fuel tanks on his back.

19 Combat Interviews, 5th Ranger Battalion. NARA II, RG 407 Entry 427A (unpaginated manuscript).

20 See Chapter 17: "Relief from the Sea."

21 Cota interview with Cornelius Ryan, May 8, 1958, in Cornelius Ryan Collection, "The Longest Day," Box 006, Folder 15. Mahn Center for Archives and Special Collections, Ohio University Libraries.

22 John C. Raaen Jr correspondence, January 17, 2001, DGL/KE.

23 Report by Lt Jack Shea, Cota's aide on D-Day, in Cota file in Cornelius Ryan collection, *op cit.*, Folder 15, p.4.

24 Fifth Ranger Infantry Battalion, Action against the Enemy. D-Day 6 June 1944, NARA II, RG 407, Entry 427.

25 See Chapter 13: "The Germans Strike Back."

26 The battalion commander's name was reported in the postwar recollections of Lt Hans Heinze as "Grimme," but as "Griesel" in a PoW interrogation of Lt Berthy.

27 Berthy was captured by the 2nd Rangers west of Vierville on June 7. He indicated that his company reached within 100 yards of WN 68, where it was overwhelmed on June 7 after running out of ammunition. However, he was captured west of Vierville, which suggests that the company in fact was engaged in the fighting around Vierville, not St Laurent, and had become lost in the featureless farm country south of Omaha Beach. Two versions of his interrogation survive: a printed version in CSDIC (UK) SIR 363 and a hand-written version in V Corps G-2 records.

28 Charlie Company, 116th Infantry, 29th Infantry Division, After Action Report, June 1944, NARA II RG 407.

29 Avery Thornhill Questionnaire, Cornelius Ryan Longest Day Collection, *op cit.*, Box 10, Folder 55. Other accounts such as the 1944 "Combat Interviews" paint a somewhat different picture, indicating that the encounter was between Cota and Lt Pepper, not Capt Whittington.

30 See Chapter 9: "Carnage on Charlie Beach."

31 Ziegelmann, in his Foreign Military Studies, lists the officer as being in WN 76 at Pointe-et-Raz-de-la-Percée, which is obviously incorrect since WN 76 was west of Pointe-du-Hoc and could not see Dog Green Beach due to the promontory. He presumably mistook WN 76 for the correct WN 74 designation.

CHAPTER 16: THE CRAZY MARCH ON D+1

1 From March to early June 1944, GR.915 was not subordinate to its division headquarters, but had been assigned as the reserve of LXXXIV. Armee-Korps.

2 See Chapter 14: "Night Attack."

3 121st Engineer Combat Battalion After Action Report, 7 June 1944, RG 407, NARA II.

4 Oberstleutnant Fritz Ziegelmann, *352nd Infantry Division, 7 June 1944*, FMS B-433, p. 1.

5 5th Ranger Battalion After Action Report, D+1, 7 June 1944, NARA II, RG 407.

6 Joseph Ewing, *29 Let's Go!: A History of the 29th Infantry Division in World War II*, Infantry Journal Press, Washington DC (1948), p.61.

7 Lt (jg) Coit Coker, Preliminary Report, NSFCP-3, Operation *Neptune*, D-Day Onward, First US Army Artillery Information, Service Memo July 1944, Eisenhower Presidential Library, Courtney Hodges Papers, Box 25, Folder 1.

8 The Narrative History of the Second Ranger Battalion, *op cit.*, p.14.

9 US Army historians who interviewed the participants after the battle remarked in their manuscript that "After getting evidence from Capt.

Raaen, D Company (5th Rangers), A Company (2nd Rangers) and some of the other officers present, the conflict of details became worse. Capt. Raaen's story is the clearest, but is flatly contradicted at several points by other interviews."

10 Ziegelmann, B-433, *op cit.*, p.7.

11 John Kennard, *D-Day Journal: The Untold Story of a US Ranger on Omaha Beach*, Koehler Books, Virginia Beach (2018), pp.56–57.

CHAPTER 17: RELIEF FROM THE SEA

1 *Action Report: Assault on Colleville-Vierville Sector, Coast of Normandy*, Commander Assault Force O Western Naval Task Force (July 27, 1944), NARA II, RG 38, p.26.

2 2nd Ranger Battalion After Action Report, June 7, 1944. NARA II, RG407.

3 John Raaen Jr, *Intact: A First-hand Account of the D-Day Invasion from a 5th Rangers Company Commander*, Reedy Press, St Louis (2012), pp.100–01.

4 29th Division, Combat Interviews, NARA II, RG 407, Entry 427A, p.57.

CHAPTER 18: FINAL MISSION: THE MAISY GUN BATTERIES

1 The V Corps G-2 placed 4.Batterie, II./AR.352, south of Maisy on June 9, based on a captured map. Message, G-2 V Corps, 091251B June 1944, V-Corps G-2, NARA II, RG 407. Other units may have been operating in the area, but the location of two of four battalions of Artillerie-Regiment.352 were not identified between June 7 and 9.

2 This unit had been renamed as IV.(Ost)/Festung-Grenadier-Regiment.726 in the spring of 1944, but is better known by its original name. See for example the divisional organization chart for the 716. Infanterie-Division on May 1, 1944, in the divisional Kriegstagebuch annex, NARA II, RG 242, T-312, R156, F215. Ziegelmann in his account of 352.Infanterie-Division identifies the reinforcing unit as Ost. Btl.621, but this appears to be a mistake.

3 GenLt Bodo zV.Zimmermann, OB West: Atlantic Wall to the Siegfried Line – A Study in Command, FMS B-308 (1948), p.30.

4 Oberstleutnant Fritz Ziegelmann, FMS B-434, *op. cit.*, p.8.

5 A PoW interrogation indicated that two of the 155mm howitzers were at grid reference 536933. G-2 Report, HQ, 29th Division, June 10, 1944.

6 War Diary, USS *Harding*, June 9, 1944, NARA II, RG 38.

7 John Raaen Jr, *Intact: A First-Hand Account of the D-Day Invasion from a 5th Rangers Company Commander*, Reedy Press, St Louis (2012), p.105.

8 Marcia Moen & Margo Heinen, *Reflections of Courage on D-Day: A Personal Account of Ranger "Ace" Parker*, DeForest Press, Elk River (1999), p.121.

9 The only Waffen-SS unit in this area of Normandy was the 17.SS-Panzergrenadier-Division "Götz von Berlichingen." The division started moving from Thouars in western France to the Carentan area on D-Day. A few vehicles of the division's reconnaissance battalion, SS-Aufklärungs-Abt.17, serving as the division's forward security screen during the movement, reached as far as the town of Les Veys on June 9, about 8 miles southwest of the Maisy batteries. There is no evidence that any elements of the division took part in any fighting on June 9. Jean-Claude Perrigault & Rolf Meister, *Götz von Berlichingen–Normandie*, Heimdal, Bayeux (2004), pp.202–03.

10 This was the site called Target 16A on Allied intelligence maps.

11 Wayne Robinson, *Move Out and Verify: The Combat Story of the 743rd Tank Battalion*, self-published, Germany (1945), p.36.

12 Journal, 5th Ranger Battalion, June 9, 1944, NARA II, RG 407.

13 After Action Report, 5th Ranger Battalion, June 10, 1944, NARA II, RG 407.

CHAPTER 19: BATTLE ANALYSIS

1 Maj Gen Donald Weller, *Naval Gunfire Support of Amphibious Operations: Past, Present, and Future*, Naval Sea Systems Command, Dahlgren (1977), pp.12–13.

2 Helmut Konrad von Keusgen, *Les canons de Saint-Marcouf*, Heimdal, Bayeux (2005).

3 Yannick Rose, *L'Artillerie côtière de l'est Cotentin HKAR 1261*, Editions ACREDIC, Alençon (1995).

4 Action Report and Report of Loss of Ship, USS *Corry* (DD463), June 19, 1944, NARA, RG 38.

5 Grégory Pique, *Une garnison en Normandie: La batterie allemande d'Azeville 1942–1944*, Editions OREP, Bayeux (2014).

6 Rémy Desquesnes, *The German Battery at Longues-sur-Mer*, Editions OREP, Bayeux (2006).

7 Col Roy M. Stanley, *Looking Down on War: The Normandy Invasion June 1944*, Pen & Sword, Barnsley (2012), p.215.

8 "Summary of present situation of Batteries which might affect the *Neptune* beaches or their approaches – 31 May 1944," TNA, WO 205/172, p.3.

9 For some typical stories based on Sterne's promotion of the Maisy museum, see for example: David Lesjak, "Does Pointe du Hoc Still

Matter?" in *World War II* (October 2006), pp.26–33. Scott Higham, "One of D-Day's most famous, heroic assaults may have been unnecessary" in *Washington Post* (June 2, 2019).

10 John Raaen Jr, *Intact: A First-Hand Account of the D-Day Invasion from a 5th Rangers Company Commander*, Reedy Press, St Louis (2012), p.108.

11 See Chapter 15: "Ranger Force C on Dog Green Beach."

12 See Chapter 7: "Obliteration."

13 Adm E. C. Kalbfus, *US Naval Administration in World War II: Commander-in-Chief, Atlantic Fleet, Vol. 1, Part 1*, Office of Naval History, Washington DC (1946), p.722.

APPENDIX A

1 T/O&E No. 7-87, Ranger Infantry Company, War Department, February 29, 1944.

2 T/O&E No. 7-85 Ranger Infantry Battalion, War Department, February 29, 1944.

3 T/O&E No. 7-86 Ranger Headquarters and Headquarters Company, War Department, February 29, 1944.

APPENDIX B

1 Kreigstagebuch, 716.Infanterie-Division, NARA RG 242 T315, Roll 2260, Frame 890.

2 The *Zielpunkte* (aim-points) for Omaha Beach can be found on a map captured by the 26th Infantry Regiment, 1st Division, in Normandy and currently preserved in the Cartographic collection at NARA II. Additional *Zielpunkte* to the west of Pointe-du-Hoc can be found in captured German records at NARA such as the Kriegstagebuch (War Diary) of 716.Infanterie Division, in RG 242 T315, Roll 2260.

3 *Preliminary Report on German Coast Artillery Fire Control Equipment*, Military College of Science, Bury, February 1945, p.2.

4 A report by the UK Joint Technical Warfare Committee to the War Cabinet reported that "No fire control table was installed (at Pointe du Hoc)." Joint Technical Warfare Committee, *Fire Support of Seaborne Landings*, Report TWC (45) 10, Office of the War Cabinet, May 10, 1945, p.17. In Digital History Archives, "Fire Support of Seaborne Landings May 1945."

5 Langbasis Gerät 42 H. *German Plotting Board Long Basis Gerät, ETO Ordnance Technical Intelligence Report No. 100*, December 27, 1944. NARA, Record Group 165, Military Intelligence Division, Entry 79.

This was based on the German Army technical manual Druckvorschriften
D 2050 Langbasis Gerät 42 H.
6 This is a very simplified summary of the process. For more detail, see:
"German Coast defenses: Coast Artillery, Fire-Control and Observation,"
21st Army Group Intelligence Report INT/1162(A). Digital History
Archives, *German Coastal Artillery Batteries 1944*.
7 As in the case of Pointe-du-Hoc, there is some evidence that the Longues-
sur-Mer battery never received its full fire-control system prior to D-Day.
"Fire Support of Seaborne Landings," *op cit.*, p.17.

APPENDIX C

1 This command, part of the US Navy Twelfth Fleet, was created on
November 10, 1943, to carry out Operation *Neptune*. Its flagship was the
cruiser USS *Augusta*. Greg Williams, *The US Navy at Normandy: Fleet
Organization and Operations in the D-Day Invasion*, McFarland, Jefferson
(2020), p.70.
2 The target list can be found in Operation Order No. 3-44, May 25, 1944,
and the assignment of targets in the Annexes of Operation Plan No. 2-44,
April 21, 1944, and in Appendix 3 to Annex E of Operation Order BB-
44: Schedule of Fires, May 20, 1944 (NARA RG38 Records of the Office
of the Chief of Naval Operations, Box 112, Plans, Orders & Related
Documents, TF 122, May 1944).
3 "Provisions for Air Spotting," Appendix 4 to Annex D, Gunfire Support
Plan, Operation Plan No. 2-44, April 21, 1944.
4 VCS-7 (Cruiser Scouting Squadron 7) was also sometimes called
VOS-7 (Cruiser Observation Squadron 7). The reorganized VCS-7
became operational on May 28, 1944, and moved to Royal Naval Air
Station (RNAS) Lee-on-Solent on the south coast of England. This base
consolidated the ten squadrons of Operation *Neptune*'s Air Spotting
Pool, 34th Tactical Reconnaissance Wing, 2nd Tactical Air Force. This
force included five RAF, four Royal Navy, and one US Navy spotter
squadrons.
5 Vice Admiral Morton L. Deyo, *Naval Guns at Normandy*, US Navy
Historical Center (1956), p.18.
6 Naval Fire Support Plan, Annex D to Operation Plan 2-44 of the
Western Naval Task Force, ANEF, April 21, 1944.
7 Coit Coker, "Fire Control on Omaha Beach" in *Field Artillery Journal*,
Vol 36, No 9 (September 1946), pp.530–33.
8 See Chapter 11: "Force A Strikes Pointe-du-Hoc."
9 Maj Gen Donald Weller, *Naval Gunfire Support of Amphibious Operations:
Past, Present, and Future*, Naval Sea Systems Command, Dahlgren (1977).

10 This chart is based on the war diaries of various ships of Assault Group O and Assault Group U located at NARA II in RG 38. The level of detail in these diaries varies from ship to ship, with some providing very detailed accounts of fire missions and others only limited details. Some of the ships prepared an additional war diary report for D-Day with more detail than usual entries.

11 See Chapter 9: "Carnage on Charlie Beach."

12 USS *Satterlee* (DD626) Report of Action, June 6, 1944, Part II, p.2, NARA II, RG 38.

APPENDIX D

1 Kriegstagebuch 716.Infanterie-Division, NARA II, RG 242, T-315, R2260, F883.

2 The 233 consisted of 199 of the basic Czechoslovak version plus thirty-four of the war-booty Yugoslav guns, called the 100mm le.FH.316 (j). Kriegstagebuch Herresgruppe B ab 29.I.1944 bis 22.IV.1944, NARA RG242, T311, R01, F0458. Of the 273 in German hands in April 1944, 245 were with the Field Army (Feldheer), twenty-one in the Replacement Army (Ersatzheer), and seven in supply/repair (Nachschub). "Waffen in Stück, 1.4.1944," Records of the Waffenamt, OKH, NARA II RG 242, T-78, R146, F77240.

3 These were in three of the main ammunition dumps, Gneisenau (850k); Moltke (300k), and Martha (500k). Kriegstagebuch Heeresgruppe B, *op cit.* F0496.

4 Kriegstagebuch Heeresgruppe B, NARA II, T-311 R01, F0460.

5 Kriegstagebuch, 716.Infanterie-Division, NARA RG 242 T-315, R2260, Frame 890.

6 Leitungsnetz-Fernsprechanschluß map, Anlagen, Kriegstagebuch, 716. Infanterie-Division, NARA RG 242 T-315, R2260.

7 There are several of these fire plans (Feuerplan) in the Kriegstagebuch 716. Infanterie-Division, NARA II, RG 242, T-315, R2260, F000734 *et passim*.

8 Map Annex, Fritz Ziegelmann, FMS-432, *op cit.*

9 Werner von Kistowski interview, Box 27, Folder 18 in Cornelius Ryan Collection, "The Longest Day," Mahn Center for Archives and Special Collections, Ohio University Libraries.

10 German map of artillery dispositions around Omaha Beach, Robert A. Rowe papers, Series 3: Maps, Diagrams & Photographs, Boxes 12–13, US Army Heritage and Education Center, Carlisle, PA.

11 AEAF: Targets Attacked Month of April 1944, AIR 37/60, TNA.

12 For example, see *Neptune* Plan 1A: German Coastal Batteries April 14, 1944, contained in map case "Operation Neptune Plans 1–14" in *Invasion Europe: D-Day Landings*, HMSO, London (1994).

13 Both Maisy I and Maisy II were included in the second revision of the Annex 12 *Neptune* Bombardment plan from May 27, 1944. They can also be seen on maps of planned targets such as: Invasion Europe, *op cit.*, *Neptune* Plan 1B, Pre-Arranged Bombardment.

14 Charles McArthur, *Operations Analysis in the US Army Eighth Air Force in World War II*, American Mathematical Society, Providence (1990), pp.156–57.

15 "Artillery in the Neptune Area," Appendix A to *Neptune–Argus* Reports, May 27, 1944. G-2 Intelligence Division, SHAEF, NARA II, RG 331, Entry 13.

16 Pre D-Day Bombing of Batteries – *Neptune* Area, May 29, 1944, WO 205/172, TNA.

17 Martin Middlebrooke & Chris Everitt, *The Bomber Command Diaries: An Operational Reference Book*, Pen & Sword, Barnsley (2014), p.519.

18 Other accounts suggest that 105 bombers of an initial 111 attacked the target with 588.2 tons of bombs; the discrepancy is probably due to the fact that five Halifax bombers aborted before reaching the target. Another tally counted 525.2 tons of bombs and 6.4 tons of incendiaries. *A Review of Air Operations Preparatory to and In Support of Operation Neptune*, Air Staff, HQ AEAF (1944), p.33.

19 Stephan Bourque, *Beyond the Beach: The Allied War against France*, Naval Institute, Annapolis (2018), pp.213–15.

20 AEAF Daily Int Ops Summary No 133 for June 6, Para 7 – Effort on Overlord Targets and Preliminary Estimate of Damage. AIR 37/59, TNA.

21 Ken Delve, *D-Day: The Air Battle*, Crowood, Ramsbury (2004), p.182.

22 Details of Attacks on Overlord Targets: Coastal Defense and Gun Positions, AIR 37/60, TNA.

23 Col E. G. Paules, *Observations on Invasion of France and Fall of Cherbourg, 3 June – 6 July 1944*, War Department Observers Board Report No 23, July 25, 1944, p.65.

24 Sakkers, *op cit.*, pp.255–46.

25 Bombardment Group Force U, War Diary for Operation Neptune, NARA II, RG 38, p.15.

26 Commander Assault Force O (11th Amphibious Force), Action Report, Assault on Vierville–Colleville Sector, Coast Of Normandy (July 27, 1944), NARA II, RG 38, p.19.

27 War Diary, USS *Shubrick* (DD639), NARA II, RG 38.

28 HMS *Glasgow* Operation *Neptune* Chronological Narrative Report, NARA II, RG 38.

29 USS *McCook* (DD496) War Diary, NARA II, RG 38.

30 The fighting for the Maisy batteries is described in detail in Chapter 19: "Battle Analysis."

31 US Fleet Task Force One-Two-Two, Operation *Overlord* – Report of Naval Commander Western Task Force (CTF 122), Annex B1-Intelligence, July 25, 1944, p.18.

32 *Ibid.*, p.20.

33 John Raaen Jr, *Intact: A First-Hand Account of the D-Day Invasion from a 5th Rangers Company Commander*, Reedy Press, St Louis (2012), p.108.

Further Reading

The essential account of the Rangers at Pointe-du-Hoc is the chapter in the US Army monograph *Small Unit Actions*, first published in 1946. The Pointe-du-Hoc chapter was based on interviews of the Rangers conducted by the ETO Historical Section in the summer of 1944, including the well-known historian Forrest Pogue. The Pointe-du-Hoc chapter was written by a young medieval historian from Harvard, Charles Holt Taylor. Taylor, a newly minted professor in 1942, received his commission into the US Army as a military intelligence officer, and transferred to Historical Division of the War Department shortly after its creation in 1943.

While the *Small Unit Actions* account of Pointe-du-Hoc is well known, its source material in the Combat Interviews collection of Record Group 407 at the National Archives and Records Administration II in College Park, Maryland, is not widely known nor widely used. The source material is more detailed than the printed version, and also contains intriguing notes and marginalia by the Army historians regarding controversies about certain incidents and requests for the clarification of some important points in the accounts.

The US Army's principal World War II records collection from the office of the Adjutant General was first transferred to the NARA depository at Suitland, Maryland, in 1976, but was subsequently moved to the new NARA II facility in College Park, MD, when it opened in 1994. The after-action reports (AAR) of the 2nd and 5th Rangers for D-Day are sparse, barely a page or two in length. Some other records such as the daily journals contain more detail. This is also true of the units most closely associated with the Rangers, such as the 116th Infantry Regiment, 29th Division, and 743rd Tank Battalion. The after-action reports provide a basic factual skeleton, but a far more detailed narrative can be found in the combat interviews collection at NARA II.

Pre-invasion planning records are ample. The numerous iterations of the *Neptune* plans can be found at NARA II, but in some cases, digital versions are at the Ike Skelton Combined Arms Research Digital Library of the US Army Command and General Staff College in Fort Leavenworth, Kansas. Some of these records are also available on the Fold3 archival website. Background information on the formulation of the Ranger mission is scattered through a variety of record groups at NARA II, as can be seen from the notes in this book.

The "Martian Reports" and related Allied intelligence documents on the Atlantic Wall can be found at NARA II in Record Group 331 SHAEF G-2 documents. Marc Romanych's research firm, Digital History Archives, offers DVD collections of some intelligence collections, notably a collection entitled "German Coastal Artillery Batteries" which includes several of the key COSSAC reports.

Naval records, and especially the warship deck logs/war diaries, can be found in Record Group 38 at NARA II. Many of these have been digitized by Fold3 and many are available on the NARA digital website.

For the aviation side of the story, I have relied heavily on documents from various record groups at The National Archives in Kew, London. These are mainly reports from the Allied Expeditionary Air Force relating to RAF and USAAF bombing attacks on the German coastal batteries.

One of the most useful collections of D-Day documents is the Robert A. Rowe Papers at the US Army Military History Institute, US Army Heritage and Education Center (AHEC), in Carlisle, Pennsylvania. Rowe was a US Navy officer in World War II and Korea and was working on a D-Day history entitled "Neptune's First Wave." It was not published prior to his death in 1991. His research material totals 38 archive boxes and contains an excellent collection of basic source documents, primarily about the US Army and US Navy on D-Day. Rowe also conducted numerous interviews with veterans over the years, including several with Ranger veterans. In addition, the unofficial Ranger historian, Louis Lisko, contributed further Ranger material to Rowe. Most of the Ranger material is in Box 28.

During the preparation of his bestseller *The Longest Day*, Cornelius Ryan amassed a substantial collection of questionnaires and interviews. These are currently preserved at the Mahn Center for Archives and Special

Collections at the Ohio University library. The Ranger material is thin, lending credence to the idea that he may have lost some of the interviews he is known to have collected. But there are intriguing accounts from Gen Norman Cota and at least two members of the French Resistance in Lower Normandy.

German D-Day documents are very scarce due to the widespread destruction of records during the August 1944 retreat from France. Immediately after the war, the United States, Britain, and Canada cooperated in the creation of a master collection of captured German military documents. The US Army collection was microfilmed in the 1950s and the original paper documents returned to the Bundesarchiv in Germany, where they currently reside. The US microfilm collection resides in Record Group 242 at NARA II. The German records are best at the higher command levels, such as OB West and Heeresgruppe B. There is extensive documentation on the construction of the Atlantic Wall, mainly from these higher command levels. The German records become progressively more sparse at lower command levels, such as 7.Armee, LXXXIV.Armee-Korps, and the various infantry divisions. The surviving records for the 716.Infanterie-Division are better than those rare remaining documents from 352.Infanterie-Division. At the higher command levels, the compilation of German documents by Hans Sakker, mentioned in the bibliography below, is enormously useful. Sadly, there are virtually no German divisional records for D-Day, although some details can be pieced together using Allied prisoner of war accounts and the small number of veterans' reminiscences.

Another major source on the Wehrmacht in Normandy is the Foreign Military Studies series prepared for the US Army in the late 1940s and early 1950s. The Historical Division of the US Army-Europe organized a program to collect reports of German military actions by senior German commanders. These reports vary enormously in quality. Some German officers had access to unit records, maps, or other data; many did not. Fortunately, Oberstleutnant Fritz Ziegelmann, the operations officer of the 352.Infanterie-Division, had some important records in the preparation of his reports, including the divisional telephone log for D-Day. His reports are the best single source on the division during the D-Day fighting. Even in this case, some care has to be taken, as mentioned elsewhere in this book, as there are numerous errors and omissions in these reports. The Fold3 site has them in both English and German language versions; paper copies are available at AHEC and NARA II. The most readily accessible versions are in David Isby's compilations cited below. The German versions are helpful, since the English translations often have dodgy translations of German military terms. The 352.Infanterie-Division veterans' organization (Kameradenschaft) published a divisional history, but it is very hard to find and is mainly based on the Ziegelmann reports.

One of the best sources from the German perspective on Pointe-du-Hoc is the work of Helmut Konrad von Keusgen. He has conducted tours of the Normandy beaches for German veterans, and in the process has collected several unique accounts by German survivors of the Pointe-du-Hoc fighting. There are several editions of his book; the most recent German edition has some additional material added.

There are ample and detailed accounts of the Atlantikwall in Normandy. "Bunkerology" has become a popular hobby in Europe, and French bunker enthusiasts have done a particularly good job in cataloging and identifying the many surviving structures. The work of Alain Chazette is particularly noteworthy. On the web, the sub-forum "Fortifications, Artillery, & Rockets" of the Axis History Forum has had some particularly informative discussions of the Atlantikwall in Lower Normandy.

ARCHIVAL RECORDS

National Archives and Records Administration II, College Park, MD
Record Group 24
 Records of the US Navy, Logbooks of US Ships
Record Group 38
 Records of the Office of Chief of Naval Operations, Plans, Orders and Related Documents
 Records of the Office of Chief of Naval Operations, Ship War Diaries
Record Group 165
 Military Intelligence Division
Record Group 331
 G-2 Intelligence Division, SHAEF
Record Group 242 Captured German Records
 Kriegstagebuch OB West, T311
 Kriegstagebuch Heeresgruppe B, T311

Kriegstagebuch 7.Armee (AOK.7), T313
Kriegstagebuch 352.Infanterie-Division, T315
Kriegstagebuch 716.Infanterie-Division, T315
Records of the Waffenamt, OKH, T-78
Record Group 407, Entry NM-3 427-D
    Pre-Invasion Planning
Record Group 407, Entry 427
    After-Action reports, Unit Journals
        2nd Ranger Battalion
        5th Ranger Battalion
        743rd Tank Battalion
        116th Infantry Regiment
        1st Infantry Division
        29th Infantry Division
        V Corps
Record Group 407, Entry 427A
    Combat Interviews
        2nd Ranger Battalion
        5th Ranger Battalion
        116th Infantry Regiment
        29th Infantry Division

DIGITAL HISTORY ARCHIVE DVD
COLLECTIONS FROM NARA II

Fire Support of Seaborne Landings May 1945
German Coastal Artillery Batteries 1944
Report on Beach & Coastal Defenses in the Cherbourg Area 1944
WWII Allied Technical Intelligence Reports 1944–45: German Artillery & Fortifications
WWII British Combined Operations Headquarters Amphibious Operations Bulletins 1942–44

The National Archives, Kew
AIR 27/1921
    RAF Operations records
AIR 34/102, AIR 34/109
    RAF Medmenham Interpretation Reports

AIR 37/59, 37/60
   Allied Expeditionary Air Force, later Supreme Headquarters Allied
      Expeditionary Force (Air)
AIR 37/536
   Minutes of the AEAF C-in-C Conferences
DEFE 2/487
   RAF Bombing Analysis Unit
WO 205/172
   Pre D-Day Bombing of Batteries – Neptune Area

Eisenhower Presidential Library
Courtney Hodges Papers

Ohio University Libraries, Mahn Center for Archives and Special Collections
Cornelius Ryan Collection, "The Longest Day"

US Army Heritage and Education Center, Carlisle, PA
Robert A. Rowe papers

US Army Historical Division: Foreign Military Studies
Dorsch, Xaver, *Organization Todt – France*, B-670 (1946).
Dorsch, Xaver, *Organization Todt — Operations in the West*, B-671 (1947).
von Gersdorff, GenMaj, *A Critique of the Defense against the Invasion*,
   A-895 (1945).
Goettke, GenLt Ernst, *Preparations for the Defense of the Coast*, B-663
   (1947).
Krancke, Adm Theodor, *Defensive Measures Against Invasion taken by
   Naval and Army Group OB-West*, B-169 (1946).
Pemsel, GenLt Max, *Construction of the Atlantic Wall Part III: The prepa-
   rations in the Invasion Area 'til the end of January 1944*, B-668 (1947).
Pickert, Gen d Flak Wolfgang, *III Flak Corps: Orders for the Initial
   Commitment in Normandy*, B-597 (1947).
Schmetzer, GenLt Rudolf, *Atlantic Wall: Invasion Sector June 1942–
   January 1944*, B-668 (1947).
Schmetzer, GenLt Rudolf , *Construction of the Atlantic Wall Part IV: The
   Effect of Bombs and Heavy Naval Guns on the Fortified Defense System
   of the Atlantic Wall*, B-669 (1947).

Speidel, GenLt Hans, *Ideas and Views of Genfldm Rommel on Defense and Operations in the West in 1944*, B-720 (1947).
Triepel, GenMaj, *Coastal Artillery Sector 1 – Cotentin from 6 June until 18 June 1944*, B-260 (1946).
Weissmann, Gen Eugene, *Flak in Coastal and Air Defense: the Atlantic Wall*, D-179 (1947).
Ziegelmann, Oberstleutnant Fritz, *352nd Infantry Division 6 June 1944*, B-388, 1947.
Ziegelmann, Oberstleutnant Fritz, *352nd Infantry Division – 5 Dec 1943–6 Jun 1944*, B-432 (1946).
Ziegelmann, Oberstleutnant Fritz, *352nd Infantry Division, 7 June 1944*, B-433 (1946).
Ziegelmann, Oberstleutnant Fritz, *Special Questions for 352.Infanterie Division Chief-of-Staff Fritz Ziegelmann*, B-021 (1946).
Zimmerman, GenLt Bodo, *OB West: Atlantic Wall to Siegfried Line, Chapter 2: Preparation of Coastal Defenses Against Invasion*, B-308 (1948).

US Army Technical Manuals and Orders
Field Manual FM 4-25, *Seacoast Artillery, Service of the Piece, 155mm Gun*, US War Department, Washington DC (1940).
T/O&E No. 7-87, *Ranger Infantry Company*, War Department (February 29, 1944).
T/O&E No. 7-85 *Ranger Infantry Battalion*, War Department (February 29, 1944).
T/O&E No. 7-86 *Ranger Headquarters and Headquarters Company*, War Department (February 29, 1944).
Technical Manual TM 9-1907 *Ballistic Data, Performance of Ammunition*, War Department, Washington DC (1944).
Technical Manual TM 9-345, *155mm Gun Materiel M1917, 1918 and Modifications*, War Department, Washington DC (1942).
Technical Manual TM 9-2005, Vol 3, *Ordnance Materiel-General*, Ordnance School, Aberdeen Proving Ground (1942).

Government Reports, Studies, and Document Collections
The Development of the German Defence in the Dieppe Sector 1940–1942, Report No 36, Historical Section (GS), Canadian Army Headquarters (March 31, 1950).

V Corps Operations in the ETO 6 Jan 1942–9 May 1945, V Corps G-3
    Historical Sub-Section (1945).
History of COSSAC, 1943–1944, SHAEF Historical Sub-Section (May
    1944).
The Narrative History of the Second Ranger Battalion, 2nd Ranger
    Infantry Battalion (1945).
Quadrant Conference August 1943, Papers and Minutes of Meetings, Office
    of the Combined Chiefs of Staff, Washington DC (1943).
Weller, Maj Gen Donald, *Naval Gunfire Support of Amphibious
    Operations: Past, Present, and Future*, Naval Sea Systems Command,
    Dahlgren (1977).

BOOKS

Bailey, Roderick, *Forgotten Voices of D-Day*, Ebury Press, London
    (2009).
Balkoski, Joseph, *Beyond the Beachhead: The 29th Infantry Division in
    Normandy*, Stackpole, Mechanicsburg (1989).
Balkoski, Joseph, *Omaha Beach: D-Day June 6, 1944*, Stackpole,
    Mechanicsburg (2004).
Black, Robert, *Rangers in World War II*, Presidio Press, Novato (1992).
Black, Robert, *The Battalion: The Dramatic Story of the 2nd Ranger
    Battalion in World War II*, Stackpole, Mechanicsburg (2006).
Black, Robert, *The Ranger Force: Darby's Rangers in World War II*,
    Stackpole, Mechanicsburg (2009).
Bourque, Stephan, *Beyond the Beach: The Allied War against France*,
    Naval Institute, Annapolis (2018).
Bradley, Omar, *A Soldier's Story*, Henry Holt, New York (1951).
Brinkley, Douglas, *The Boys of Pointe du Hoc: Ronald Reagan, D-Day,
    and the US Army 2nd Ranger Battalion*, Harper, New York (2006).
Chazette, Alain, *Artillerie côtière: Atlantikwall et Südwall en France*,
    Fortifications et Patrimonie, Paris (1999).
Chazette, Alain, *Mur de l'Atlantique: Batteries de côte série 600*, Histoire
    et Fortifications, Vertou (2014).
Chazette, Alain, *et al.*, *Atlantikwall: Omaha Beach de Port-en-Bessin à
    Grandcamp-Maisy*, Histoire et Fortifications, Vertou (2014).
Chazette, Alain, *et al.*, *Stations radar et radio-navigation sur le Mur de
    l'Atlantique*, Histoire et Fortifications, Vertou (2015).

Collier, Richard, *Ten Thousand Eyes: The Amazing Story of the Spy Network that Cracked Hitler's Atlantic Wall before D-Day*, E. P. Dutton, New York (1958).

Corera, Gordon, *Operation Columba, The Secret Pigeon Service: The Untold Story of World War II Resistance in Europe*, Wm Morrow, New York (2018).

DeFelice, Jim, *Rangers at Dieppe: The first Combat Action of the US Army Rangers in World War II*, Penguin, New York (2008).

De Félice, Raoul, *La Basse-Normandie: étude de géographie régionale*, Hachette, Paris (1907).

Delve, Ken, *D-Day: The Air Battle*, Crowood, Ramsbury (2004).

Desquesnes, Rémy, *The German Battery at Longues-sur-Mer*, Editions OREP, Cully (2006).

Ewing, Joseph, *29 Let's Go! A History of the 29th Infantry Division in World War II*, Infantry Journal Press, Washington DC (1948).

Forrest, Michael, *The Defence of the Dardanelles: From Bombards to Battleships*, Pen & Sword, Barnsley (2012).

Frappé, Jean-Bernard, *La Luftwaffe face au débarquement: Normandie 6 juin–31 août 1944*, Heimdal, Bayeux (1999).

Giskes, H. J., *London Calling North Pole*, Bantam, New York (1982).

Glassman, Henry, *Lead the Way Rangers: History of the 5th Ranger Battalion*, Hausser, Markt Grafing (1945).

Grehan, John & Mace, Martin, *Operations in North Africa and the Middle East 1942—1944: El Alamein, Tunisia, Algeria and Operation Torch*, Pen & Sword, Barnsley (2015).

Groult, Hubert, *Bataille pour la Pointe du Hoc*, Heimdal, Bayeux (2020).

Hatfield, Thomas M., *Rudder: From Leader to Legend*, Texas A&M University Press, College Station (2011).

Hathaway, Richard, *Training for Bloody Omaha: Activation, Training, and Combat of the 5th Ranger Infantry Battalion through 8 June 1944*, Vantage, New York (2002).

Hinsley, F. H., *et al.*, *British Intelligence in the Second World War, Vol 3, Part 2*, HMSO, London (1988).

Hogan, David, *Raiders or Elite Infantry? The Changing Role of the US Army Rangers from Dieppe to Grenada*, Greenwood, Westport (1992).

Howard, Peter, *Pointe du Hoc*, Ian Allen, London (2006).

Howe, George, *Northwest Africa: Seizing the Initiative in the West*, US Army Center of Military History, Washington DC (1991).

Isby, David (ed.), *Fighting in Normandy: The German Army from D-Day to Villers-Bocage*, Greenhill, London (2001).

Isby, David (ed.), *Fighting the Invasion: The German Army at D-Day*, Greenhill, London (2000).

Jeffers, H. Paul, *Command of Honor: General Lucian Truscott's Path to victory in World War II*, New American Library, New York (2008).

Jones, Clifford L., *The Administrative and Logistical History of the ETO – Neptune: Training, Mounting, The Artificial Ports*, Historical Division, USAFET (1946).

Karau, Mark, *Wielding the Dagger: The Marinekorps Flandern and the German War Effort 1914–1918*, Prager, Westport (2003).

Kennard, John, *D-Day Journal: The Untold Story of a US Ranger on Omaha Beach*, Koehler Books, Virginia Beach (2018).

Kepher, Stephen, *COSSAC: Lt Gen Sir Frederick Morgan and the Genesis of Operation Overlord*, Naval Institute, Annapolis (2020).

Ketcherside, Chris & Despostis, George, *Rangers Led the Way: WWII Rangers in their own Words*, Schiffer, Atglen (2020).

von Keusgen, Helmut Konrad, *Les canons de Saint-Marcouf*, Heimdal, Bayeux (2005).

von Keusgen, Helmut Konrad, *Pointe-du-Hoc: Énigme autour d'un point d'appui allemande*, Heimdal, Bayeux (2006).

von Keusgen, Helmut Konrad, *Pointe du Hoc: Rätsel um einen deutschen Stützpunkt*, HEK-Creativ, Garbsen (2011).

Khan, Mark, *D-Day Assault: The Second World War Assault Training Exercises at Slapton Sands*, Pen & Sword, Barnsley (2014).

Kirkland, William, *Destroyers at Normandy: Naval Gunfire Support at Omaha Beach*, Naval Historical Foundation, Washington DC (1994).

Ladd, James, *Commandos and Rangers of World War II*, St Martin's, New York (1978).

Lane, Ronald, *Rudder's Rangers: The True Story of the 2nd US Ranger Battalion's D-Day Combat Action*, Ranger Associates Inc, Longwood (2004).

Lavery, Brian, *Assault Landing Craft: Design, Construction & Operations*, Seaforth, Barnsley (2009).

Lewis, Adrian, *Omaha Beach: A Flawed Victory*, University of North Carolina Press, Chapel Hill (2001).

MacBean, John & Hogben, Arthur, *Bombs Gone: The development and use of British air-dropped weapons from 1912 to the present day*, Patrick Stephens, Wellingborough (1990).

McArthur, Charles, *Operations Analysis in the US Army Eighth Air Force in World War II*, American Mathematical Society, Providence (1990).

McDonald, JoAnna, *The Liberation of Pointe du Hoc: The 2nd Rangers at Normandy: June 6–8, 1944*, Rank and File, Redondo Beach (2000).

Matloff, Maurice & Snell, Edwin M., *Strategic Planning for Coalition Warfare 1941–42*, US Army Center of Military History, Washington DC (1990).

Middlebrooke, Martin & Everitt, Chris, *The Bomber Command Diaries: An Operational Reference Book*, Pen & Sword, Barnsley (2014).

Milano, Vince & Conner, Bruce, *Normandiefront: D-Day to Saint-Lô through German Eyes*, Spellmount, Stroud (2012).

Moen, Marcia & Heinen, Margo, *Reflections of Courage on D-Day: A Personal Account of Ranger "Ace" Parker*, DeForest Press, Elk River (1999).

Morison, Samuel Eliot, *The Invasion of France and Germany 1944–45*, Little, Brown, New York (1957).

Moyar, Mark, *Oppose Any Foe: The Rise of America's Special Operations Forces*, Basic Books, New York (2017).

O'Donnell, Patrick, *Dog Company, The Boys of Pointe de Hoc*, De Capo, New York (2012).

Perquin, Jean-Louis, *Resistance: The Clandestine Radio Operators*, Histoire et Collections, Paris (2011).

Perrigault, Jean-Claude & Meister, Rolf, *Götz von Berlichingen – Normandie*, Heimdal, Bayeux (2004).

Pique, Grégory, *Une garnison en Normandie: La batterie allemande d'Azeville 1942–1944*, Editions OREP, Bayeux (2014).

Prieur, Jérôme, *Le Mur de l'Atlantique: Monument de la Collaboration*, Denoël, Paris (2010).

Prince, Morris, *Company A, 2nd Ranger Battalion: Overseas and then – Over the Top*, 2nd Ranger Battalion (1945).

Raaen, John Jr, *Intact: A First Hand Account of the D-Day Invasion from a 5th Rangers Company Commander*, Reedy Press, St Louis (2012).

Robinson, Wayne, *Move Out and Verify: The Combat Story of the 743rd Tank Battalion*, self-published, Germany (1945).

Rose, Yannick, *L'Artillerie côtière de l'est Cotentin HKAR 1261*, Editions ACREDIC, Alençon (1995).

Rowland, David & Curry, John Curry (eds), *The Stress of Battle: Quantifying Human Performance in Battle for Historical Analysis and Wargaming*, History of Wargaming Project, Middletown (2019).

Ruffin, Raymond, *La Résistance dans l'Opération Overlord*, France-Empire, Paris (2004).

Ruffin, Raymond, *La résistance normande face à la Gestapo*, Presses de la Cité, Paris (1977).

Ryan, Cornelius, *The Longest Day*, Simon & Schuster, New York (1959).

Saffroy, Frédéric, *Le Bouclier de Neptune: La politique de défense des bases françaises en Méditerranée, 1912–1931*, Presses universitaires de Rennes (2015).

Sakkers, Hans (ed.), *Normandie 6 Juni 1944 im Spiegel der deutschen Kriegstagebücher: Der Großangriff auf den Atlantikwall*, Biblio Verlag, Osnabrück (1998).

Saunders, Tim, *Pointe du Hoc*, Pen & Sword, Barnsley (2018).

Schneider, James, *My Father's War: The Story of Max Ferguson Schneider – A Ranger Commander*, Lulu (2012).

Slaughter, John R., *Omaha Beach and Beyond: The Long March of Sgt Bob Slaughter*, Zenith, St Paul (2007).

Sorvisto, Edwin, *Roughing it with Charlie: 2nd Ranger Battalion*, Planograpfia, Plzeň (1945).

Stanley, Roy M., *Looking Down on War: The Normandy Invasion June 1944*, Pen & Sword, Barnsley (2012).

Sterne, Gary, *Allied Intelligence and the Cover Up at Pointe Du Hoc: The History of the 2nd & 5th US Army Rangers, 1943–30th April 1944*, Pen & Sword, Barnsley (2018).

Sterne, Gary, *D-Day Cover Up at Pointe du Hoc: The History of the 2nd & 5th US Army Rangers, 1st May–10th June 1944*, Pen & Sword, Barnsley (2018).

Sterne, Gary, *The Cover Up at Omaha Beach: Maisy Battery and the US Rangers*, Pen & Sword, Barnsley (2013).

Stjernfelt, Bertil, *Alerte sur le mur de l'Atlantique*, Presses de la Cité, Paris (1961).

Taylor, Thomas, *Rangers – Lead the Way!*, Turner, Paducah (1996).

Touzin, Pierre & Vauvillier, F., *Les Canons de la Victoire, Tome 1: L'artillerie de campagne*, Histoire et Collections, Paris (2006).

Truscott, Lucian, *Command Missions*, Presido, Novato (1990).

Vernier, Franck, *Le premier "Mur de l'Atlantique": Les batteries allemandes au littoral belge 1914–1918*, Patrimonie Militaire, Liège (2012).

Wegmüller, Hans, *Die Abwehr der Invasion: Die Konzeption des Oberbefehlshabers West 1940–1944*, Rombach, Freiburg (1986).

Williams, Greg, *The US Navy at Normandy: Fleet Organization and Operations in the D-Day Invasion*, McFarland, Jefferson (2020).

Wolf, William, *US Aerial Armament in World War II, Vol 2: Bombs, Bombsights and Bombing*, Schiffer, Atglen (2010).

Yung, Christopher, *Gators of Neptune: Naval Amphibious Planning for the Normandy Invasion*, Naval Institute, Annapolis (2006).

Zaloga, Steven, *D-Day 1944 1: Omaha Beach*, Osprey Campaign 100, Osprey, Oxford (2003).

Zaloga, Steven, *D-Day Fortifications in Normandy*, Osprey Fortress 37, Osprey, Oxford (2005).

Zaloga, Steven, *Rangers Lead the Way: Pointe-du-Hoc D-Day 1944*, Osprey Raid No 1, Osprey, Oxford (2009)

Zaloga, Steven, *Sicily 1943: The debut of Allied joint operations*, Osprey Campaign 251, Osprey, Oxford (2013).

Zaloga, Steven, *The Atlantic Wall 1: France*, Osprey Fortress 63, Osprey, Oxford (2007).

Zaloga, Steven, *The Devil's Garden: Rommel's Desperate Defense of Omaha Beach, D-Day 1944*, Stackpole, Mechanicsburg (2014).

Zetterling, Niklas, *Normandy 1944: German Military Organization, Combat Power and Organizational Effectiveness*, Casemate, Havertown (2019).

n.a., *Carte géologique de la France: Grandcamp-Maisy à 1/50,000*. Bureau de recherches géologiques et minières, Service Géologique National, Orléans (1989).

n.a., *Die Geschichte der 352.Infanterie-Division*, Kameradschaft: n.d.

n.a., *The Dieppe Raid: The Combined Operations Assault on Hitler's European Fortress August 1942*, Pen & Sword, Barnsley (2019).

n.a., *Invasion Europe: D-Day Landings*, HMSO, London (1994).

n.a., *Omaha Beachhead 6 June–13 June 1944*, Historical Division, War Department (1945)

n.a., *Small Unit Actions*, War Department Historical Division, Washington DC (1946).

ARTICLES

Bernage, Georges, "Wilhelm Kirchhoff: j'étai aussi à la Pointe du Hoc" in *Guerre 39–45 Magazine*, No 322 (May 2014), p.70.

Briscoe, Charles H., "Commando & Ranger Training: Preparing America's Soldiers for War, Part 1" in *Veritas*, Vol 10, No 1 (2014); "Part 2" in *Veritas*, Vol 12, No 1 (2016).

Bryan-Low, Cassel, "UK Code-Crackers Stumped" in *Wall Street Journal* (November 24/25, 2012).

Burt, Richard, *et al.*, "Crater Analysis at Pointe du Hoc, Historic Site, Normandy, France", *5th International Fields of Conflict Conference*, Ghent, Belgium (October 17–20, 2008).

Chazette, Alain, "La Heeres-Küstenartillerie-Abteilung 832: Des côtes du Pas-de-Calais à la Normandie" in *Guerre 39–45 Magazine*, No 247 (Jul–Aug 2007), pp.70–75.

Chazette, Alain, "Le Canon de 155 GPF sur l'Atlantikwall" in *Guerre 39–45 Magazine*, No 161 (Nov 1999), pp.36–49.

Coker, Coit, "Fire Control on Omaha Beach" in *Field Artillery Journal*, Vol 36, No 9 (September 1946), pp.530–33.

Hodenfield, Lt G. K., "I Climbed the Cliffs with the Rangers" in *Saturday Evening Post* (August 19, 1944), pp.18, 93.

Jager, Herbert, "Leichte und mittlere Geschütze des Atlantikwalls" in *Fortifikation*, Ausgabe 20 (2006), p.89.

Jones, Robert W., Jr, "From Omaha Beach to the Rhine: The 5th Ranger Battalion in the European Theater" in *Veritas*, Vol 5, No 2 (2009), p.4.

Udphuay, Suwimon, *et al.*, "Three-dimensional resistivity tomography in extreme coastal terrain amidst dense cultural signals: Applications to cliff stability assessment at the historic D-Day site" in *Geophysical Journal International*, No 185 (2011), pp.201–20.

Glossary

AHEC	US Army Heritage and Education Center, Carlisle Barracks, Pennsylvania
AOK	Armeeoberkommando: field army high command, used as shorthand for Army (eg AOK.7)
Bauform	construction plan
Calvados	French department in Lower Normandy stretching from Grandcamp-les-Bains to Honfleur
DHA	Digital History Archives
EM	Enlisted man
Festung	Fortress
FH	Feldhaubitze: Field howitzer
FK	Feldkanone: Field gun
GR	Grenadier Regiment
GrW	Granatwerfer: Mortar
Heer	German Army
HKAA	Heeres-küsten-artillerie-abteilung: Army coastal artillery battalion
HMG	heavy machine gun
Kompanie	Company: in 352.ID, usually about 180 men, in 716. ID, usually about 160 men
Kriegsmarine	Germany Navy
KWK	Kampfwagen Kanone: Tank gun
LCA	Landing Craft Assault
LCI	Landing Craft Infantry

LCT	Landing Craft Tank
LCVP	Landing Craft Vehicles and Personnel
LMG	light machine gun
LSI	Landing Ship Infantry
LST	Landing Ship Tank
MAA	Marine-artillerie-abteilung: Navy Artillery Battalion
MF	Minenfeld: Minefield
MG	Maschinengewehr, machine gun
MHI	Military History Institute, AHEC, Carlisle Barracks, PA
NARA II	National Archives and Records Administration, College Park, Maryland
NCO	non-commissioned officer, typically a sergeant
OB-West	Oberbefehlshaber-West: Supreme Command-West; Rundstedt's HQ
OKH	Oberkommando des Heeres: Army High Command
OKW	Oberkommando der Wehrmacht: Armed Forces High Command
PaK	Panzerabwehr Kanone: Antitank gun
Regelbau	construction standard for German bunkers
SMG	sub-machine gun
StP	Stützpunkt: Strongpoint (company-sized defense position)
TNA	The National Archives, Kew, UK
Tobruk	A class of small bunkers with circular openings for a crew-served weapon
Vf	Verstarkfeldmässig: Reinforced field position such as a Tobruk
Wehrmacht	German armed forces
Westwall	German fortifications created in the late 1930s on the French–German border, also known as Siegfried Line
WN	Widerstandsnest: Defense nest (platoon-sized defense position)

Index

References to images are in **bold**.